D0284300

# Advance Praise for
## *Integrated Enterprise Excellence,*
## *Volume II—Business Deployment*

**"A unique and innovative approach to applying Lean Six Sigma."**
—René Kapik, ASQ Certified BB; MBB; Senior Continuous Improvement Engineer, Precision Fabrics Group, Inc.

**"Finally a systematic way to actually make things better. Most companies focus on their issues the wrong ways, resulting in issue after issue without real improvement. Forrest Breyfogle shows how to apply the IEE approach so that with the same effort, just about every business problem can be improved. This well written, concise, clear and accessible book should the basis for every business improvement plan."**
—Bob Ashenbrenner, Senior Computer Architect, Motion Computing Previously Director of Engineering for Dell's Notebook PCs

**"[Forrest] takes us to the next level of skill development using Six Sigma to improve customer service and bottom line growth."**
—Janet L. Hammill, Business Process Excellence Lead, MBB, Rohm and Haas Company

**"Other books are light years behind Forrest's 4-book suite, which not only provides senior management with Lean Six Sigma performance scorecards, but also a how-to roadmap for Enron-effect avoidance."**
—Frank Shines, Black Belt, TDLeanSigma, Director, Tech Data Corporation; Author, *The New Science of Success*

**"The book is the most comprehensive one I've found on the tools and specific pathways to achieving excellence. By using a balanced IEE approach a company can leverage their resources to rapidly improve and compete successfully in our 21st century environment."**
—Bill Baker, Retired Knowledge Management & Benchmarking Champion, Raytheon Company; Principal and Founder, Speed To Excellence

Integrated Enterprise Excellence
Volume II—Business Deployment

# Integrated Enterprise Excellence Volume II—Business Deployment

## A Leaders' Guide for Going Beyond Lean Six Sigma and the Balanced Scorecard

Forrest W. Breyfogle III
Founder and CEO
Smarter Solutions, Inc.

Forrest@SmarterSolutions.com
www.SmarterSolutions.com
Austin, Texas

Integrated Enterprise Excellence, Volume II—Business Deployment: A Leaders' Guide for Going Beyond Lean Six Sigma and the Balanced Scorecard

Published by Bridgeway Books in cooperation with Citius Publishing, Inc.
P.O. Box 80107
Austin, TX 78758

For more information about our books, please write to us, call 512.478.2028, or visit our website at www.bridgewaybooks.net.

Library of Congress Control Number: 2007940065

ISBN-13: 978-1-934454-15-2
ISBN-10: 1-934454-15-X

10  9  8  7  6  5  4  3  2  1

*To my beloved wife, Becki, who has made so many sacrifices in support of my work.*

# Contents

# Foreword

I was there when the phenomenon of Six Sigma took off in corporate America. I had the rare privilege of witnessing my father, Bob Galvin, say "yes," in the 1980s to Dr. Bill Smith, when Bill asked for Motorola's investment in and endorsement of Six Sigma as a crucial measurement of corporate performance, employee empowerment, and customer satisfaction. My father joins me in saluting Mr. Forrest Breyfogle III for providing this excellent roadmap for taking Six Sigma and accountability to the next level.

## Motorola, Quality and, The Baldrige Award

Embracing the creation of Six Sigma Quality enthusiastically at its very origin was energizing for Motorola Inc.'s change management efforts. The pursuit of Six Sigma Quality, which recast the problem to *defect elimination and variation control,* rather than *getting it right,* granted all Motorola employees permission—even obligation—to challenge and change existing management practices and metrics in the pursuit of high quality. Six Sigma initiatives revolutionized Motorola's product design and manufacturing capabilities, and, they led to worldwide recognition when Motorola was the first corporation to win the national Malcolm Baldrige award for quality in 1988.

Over time, Six Sigma Quality's importance to corporate performance became profound in its global reach. The unique quality process, named after the $6^{th}$ standard deviation defined in statistics, grew to positively influence the quality processes of hundreds of profit and not-for-profit organizations around the world. The Six Sigma Quality change initiative led to decades of successful work by business leaders passionate about designing management processes to systematically improve quality in everything we do.

Renewal in quality process marched on. Lean system concepts, which began in the 1950s, coupled with Six Sigma Quality efforts to emerge as Lean Six Sigma. I was privileged to lead Motorola Inc's superb management team during massive corporate restructuring from 2000-2003. During those turbulent years, we augmented our traditional Six Sigma Quality and reformulated it as Digital Six Sigma. Motorola and other multinationals learned to successfully integrate Digital 6 Sigma with new product innovation.

## Outcomes

This book speaks of outcomes. The Motorola RAZR cellular phone, which captured the hearts and minds of the world's consumers, was an outcome of two things: first, an enormous injection of creativity into the new product innovation process from 2000-2003; and secondly, the aggressive harnessing, balancing and alignment of Motorola's creative talent with the rigors of solid engineering and Six Sigma Quality process thinking.

*Achieving Enterprise Excellence – Volume II* chronicles a significant renewal in the methodologies applied to achieve total quality at the enterprise level. Here, we see companies seeking to achieve the optimum highest potential for enterprise results with a thoughtfully integrated approach.

The processes invented in pursuit of quality and lean systems have evolved and emerged over time. Each quality or lean program created over the last 50 years was a tool originally designed to solve a specific set of problems affecting product design and manufacturing. Early on, Six Sigma Quality initiatives focused on factory output, while subsequent Six Sigma efforts addressed a much broader spectrum of quality problems.

This volume insightfully points out the pros and cons, i.e., the trade-offs, associated with choosing one quality program tool over another. The author delineates the insight of *the things to think deeply about* both prior to and during implementation of enterprise wide quality efforts. He very effectively frames and describes the leader's considerations in the enterprise's quality strategies, judgments and tactics of deploying the re-mix of the best quality and lean techniques.

Perhaps the most important *next new thing* in this work is Integrated Enterprise Excellence (IEE), the blend of analytics and innovation at both the enterprise and project execution levels. The emphasis here is on the importance of personal commitment to change that redefines Six Sigma. Mr. Breyfogle has learned, as have I, that even the best of tools cannot effect change in a vacuum. People must embrace change and score cards must be aligned and integrated in an organization to ensure the continuous improvement and innovation demanded by the marketplace.

I learned the power of Six Sigma at Motorola, and watched it redefine that company's products and technology for more than two decades. Now, as I focus my efforts in the areas of modern portfolio theory investing, real estate private equity investing, global change, and leading operating businesses, *A Leaders' Guide for Taking Lean Six Sigma and the Balanced Scorecard to the Next Level* will be at my side. This timely and important work provides the glue and the playbook that will help organizations everywhere to minimize errors, save time in re-invigorating performance initiatives and significantly enhance innovation. It is a stimulating, disciplined guide and a lessons-learned architecture very much worth the read. It would be an excellent addition to the bookshelves of corporate and government leaders, and to global MBA curricula. I endorse this book and encourage you to join me in putting its wisdom to work.

*Christopher B. Galvin*
*Chairman Harrison Street Capital LLC*
*Former Chairman and CEO, Motorola Inc.*

# Preface

Volume II of this three-volume series helps managers and leaders *understand and develop* an Integrated Enterprise Excellence (IEE) system that resolves the following frequently encountered challenges:

- Business goals are not being met
- Scorecards often lead to the wrong activities
- Day-to-day firefighting of problems that don't seem to go away
- Business strategies that are very generic and/or difficult to translate to organizational work environments
- The need to create and develop innovative ideas that can be very beneficial to customers and the business as a whole
- Lean events and other improvement projects consume a lot of resources but often do not have much, if any, quantifiable benefit to the business as a whole
- Lean Six Sigma:
  - Existing deployment that has projects, which are either not timely completed or reporting large financial claims that often cannot be translated into true benefits for the business as a whole
  - Existing deployment that has stalled out and needs rejuvenation
  - New deployment desires to create a system where improvement and design projects are in true alignment with business needs and where projects are executed using an effective roadmap that truly integrates Six Sigma with Lean tools

Volume II of this series is divided into the following three parts:

1. Management Solutions and Their Evolution
2. Enterprise Process Define-Measure-Analyze-Improve-Control (E-DMAIC) roadmap
3. Appendix

This volume provides the high-level E-DMAIC thought process, while Volume III describes tool usage for the described chart creations and data analyses.

## Part 1

In part one, the stage is set by describing IEE at a high level and then summarizing the highlights of Dr. Edwards Deming's management philosophy. Many of the current popular management performance measures, strategic plans, and scorecards (both red-yellow-green scorecards and the balanced scorecard) are discussed.

It further describes how current management and measurement systems have led to problems such as the collapse of Enron and organizations doing the wrong things—actions that can be detrimental to the system as a whole; e.g., Krispy Kreme managers shipping donuts that they knew would be returned so they would meet short-term financial goals.

Finally, this volume shows execution of a system that helps businesses avoid these types of problems. The demonstrated unique measurement system is consistent with the philosophy of Dr. Deming and can get organizations out of the firefighting mode.

## Part 2

Part two describes the execution of the E-DMAIC system. Included in this system are goal setting, a unique/powerful scorecard system, strategic analysis, and strategy building. Included also is how to use Theory of Constraints (TOC) to identify enterprise constraints that need to be the focus for process improvements. Integrated also are Lean tools and their assessments, along with the identification of project improvement opportunities.

## Part 3

The appendix includes many fundamental concepts that are used in the enterprise process or project execution roadmap steps.

These methodologies were placed in the appendix to avoid disruption with the roadmap methodology flow. Included are Six Sigma metrics, basic Six Sigma/Lean tools, and distributions characteristics.

# SERIES DESCRIPTION: AN INTEGRATED SET OF REFERENCES

This is the second volume of a three-volume series that documents the Integrated Enterprise Excellence (IEE) system—a set of management techniques that, when effectively implemented, improve an organization's measurement and improvement system so that there is an increase in predictable and sustainable bottom-line benefits. The IEE system embeds a set of best practices derived from the strengths of past systems—applying structured metrics and a no-nonsense roadmap to initiate process improvement and achieve substantial benefits. IEE takes Lean Six Sigma and the balanced scorecard to the next level in the pursuit of enterprise excellence.

The book, *The Integrated Enterprise Excellence System: An Enhanced, Unified Approach to Balanced Scorecards, Strategic Planning, and Business Improvement* (Breyfogle 2008d), introduced new perspectives on what to measure and report; when and how to report it; how to interpret the results; and how to use the results to establish goals, prioritize work efforts, and continuously enhance organizational focus and success.

In this three-volume series, *Integrated Enterprise Excellence: Going Beyond Lean Six Sigma and the Balanced Scorecard* (Breyfogle 2008a, 2008b, 2008c), there is both further elaboration on the shortcomings of traditional systems and the details of an IEE implementation.

A content summary of this volume series is:

- *Integrated Enterprise Excellence Volume I—The Basics: Golfing Buddies Go Beyond Lean Six Sigma and the Balanced Scorecard*—An IEE onset story about four friends who share their experiences while playing golf. They see how they can improve their games in both business and golf using this system, which goes beyond Lean Six Sigma and the balanced scorecard. The story compares IEE to other improvement systems.

- *Integrated Enterprise Excellence Volume II—Business Deployment: A Leaders' Guide for Going Beyond Lean Six Sigma and the Balanced Scorecard*—Discusses problems encountered with traditional scorecard, business management, and enterprise improvement systems. Describes how IEE helps organizations overcome these issues utilizing an enterprise process define-measure-analyze-improve-control (E-DMAIC) system. Volume II systematically walks through the execution of this E-DMAIC system.

- *Integrated Enterprise Excellence Volume III—Improvement Project Execution: A Management and Black Belt Guide for Going Beyond Lean Six Sigma and the Balanced Scorecard*—Describes IEE benefits and its measurement techniques. Provides a detailed step-by-step project define-measure-analyze-improve-control (P-DMAIC) roadmap, which has a true integration of Six Sigma and Lean tools.

Volumes of this series build upon each other so that readers develop an appreciation and understanding of IEE benefits and its implementation. These volumes and the previous described book were written to stand alone. Because of this, several concepts and examples are described in more than one book or volume. I felt it was important to repeat key concepts in multiple publications because each book or volume is more than a presentation of tools and examples—that is, focus was given in each book and volume to present IEE so that the reader gains insight to the interconnection of the concepts and determination of how they can benefit from the techniques.

## OVERVIEW

Businesses that have adopted the Lean Six Sigma methodology have a built-in foundation for implementing this enhanced system. Others will learn how to establish the foundation for this system. For both groups, this series describes an enterprise process roadmap and a project execution roadmap, together with all the tools needed for enterprise excellence.

This series of three volumes describes how to orchestrate activities, which can provide the highest yields at points where these efforts will have the greatest bottom-line impact. In addition, focus will also be given in this orchestration so that activities will occur at the most opportune times throughout the entire organization.

Simply put, the described system helps an organization move toward the three Rs of business: everyone doing the Right things and doing them Right at the Right time throughout the organization. Rather than seeking out product or service flaws, this system determines whether the process itself is flawed. Rather than force projects where benefits could be questionable, designs and improvements are made that impact the overall systems for doing business. This system elevates every business unit to a new, more productive "business way of life."®

The ultimate goal for an enterprise management system is to achieve maximum, measurable, predictable, and sustainable bottom-line results for the entire corporation. The volumes in this series describe an Integrated Enterprise Excellence (IEE) business management system, which presents the structure and tools you can use to accomplish these objectives. This IEE methodology provides a power-enhancing performance measurement scorecard/dashboard system that serves as an enterprise-wide route to increase corporate profitability continually.

This series describes how IEE takes Lean Six Sigma and the balanced scorecard to the next level. This system helps organizations overcome some difficulties encountered with previous systems. In IEE, a value-chain performance measurement system provides organizations with a no-nonsense metric system that leads to the orchestration of day-to-day value-added activities so that there is true business–needs alignment. Improvement or design projects are created whenever business or operational metrics need betterment. This is in contrast to the search, selection, and creation of Six Sigma/Lean projects that often are not in true alignment with business goals. Organizations can gain a competitive advantage when this system becomes a business way of life.

This volume and other volumes of this series describe the IEE system, which addresses the following example needs:

- Executives want a structured system that can assist them with meeting their financial goals.
- An organizational executive or a change manager is looking for an enterprise management structure that will coordinate, track, enhance, control, and help predict corporate results.

- Leadership wants to become more of a data-driven/data-decision based company so that the right questions are asked before decisions are made.
- Executives want a system that helps them create a strategy that is more specifically targeted so that everyone has consistent focus toward meeting the organizational goals that they would like to achieve.
- Company leadership wants to reduce the amount of waste that they routinely experience when fighting the problems of the day, which never seem to go away.
- Management wants a no-nonsense measurement and improvement system.
- Leadership wants a streamlined enhancement to their Sarbanes-Oxley (SOX) system so that the company benefits more from its implementation with less effort.
- Lean Six Sigma deployment leaders want to integrate Lean and Six Sigma concepts and tools so that they are using the right tool at the right time.
- Management wants to improve its performance measurement and improvement systems.
- Managers and practitioners want an easy-to-follow roadmap that addresses not only project execution but also enterprise issues as well.
- Organization leaders want a system that can help them orchestrate people's activities so that everyone is doing the right things and doing them right at the right time.
- Lean Six Sigma deployment leaders want a system that consistently leads to projects that are most beneficial to the overall enterprise.

CEOs benefits from this series include:

- CEOs want to avoid the problem: "Chiefs (CEOs) are being pushed out the door as directors abandon their laissez-faire approach to governance following the prosecutions at Enron Corp., WorldCom Inc., and other companies." (Kelly 2006)
- CEOs want to create a legacy system of organizational efficiency and effectiveness that outlives their tenure as company heads.
- CEOs want to create more customers and cash.

Table 0.1 describes how the volumes of this series can address differing readers' needs and interests. Note, the syntax for figure

**Table 0.1** Where to Start?

| Where to start? | | |
|---|---|---|
| **Role** | **I want to:** | **Source** |
| Executives, Champions, Managers, MBBs, BBs, GBs, and YBs | Assess the benefits of an IEE measurement and improvement system over other systems (novel format). | Volume 1 |
| Executives, Champions, Managers, and MBBs | Understand the benefits of IEE when compared to other business systems and utilize a roadmap for IEE implemention at the enterprise level. | Volume 2 |
| MBBs, BBs, GBs, and other practitioners | Execute effective process improvement projects, benefit from the project execution roadmap, and effectively utilize tools at both the project and enterprise level. | Volume 3 |

*See Glossary for descriptions.*

MBB = Master black belt          BB = Black belt          GB = Green belt          YB = Yellow belt

*E-DMAIC (Roadmap):* An IEE enterprise define-measure-analyze-improve-control roadmap, which contains among other things a value chain measurement and analysis system where metric improvement needs can pull

*P-DMAIC (Roadmap):* An IEE project define-measure-analyze-improve-control roadmap for improvement project execution, which contains a true integration of Six Sigma and Lean tools.

or table references in this volume series is that the first number is the chapter number. A zero was the first number in this table reference since the table is in the preface.

# NOMENCLATURE AND SERVICE MARKS

The glossary and list of acronyms and symbols near the back of this volume are a useful reference for the understanding of unfamiliar statistical terms or acronyms/symbols. Book and publication references are also located near the back of this volume and will be referenced using the syntax (Author Name, Publication Date).

To maximize the clarification of illustrations that span several years, some examples include specific month-year entries. I did this at the risk of making the volume appear to be dated in the years to come. Hopefully the reader will understand my reasoning for making this selection and this decision will not deter the reader from benefiting from the volume's concepts for many years to come.

Integrated Enterprise Excellence, IEE, Satellite-level, 30,000-foot-level, and 50-foot-level are registered service marks of

Smarter Solutions, Inc. In implementing the programs or methods identified in this text, you are authorized to refer to these marks in a manner that is consistent with the standards set forth herein by Smarter Solutions, Inc., but any and all use of the marks shall inure to the sole benefit of Smarter Solutions, Inc. Business way of Life and Smarter Solutions are registered service marks of Smarter Solutions, Inc.

# ACKNOWLEDGMENTS

I want to thank those who helped contribute specific sections of this volume: Bob Ashenbrenner contributed to Section 3.12, Gary Ekstrom contributed to Section 6.7; Rick Haynes helped refine content of several sections; Keith Moe contributed to Sections 5.5 and Example 9.1; John Watson contributed to portions of Section 1.2 and Chapter 5 introduction. Dorothy Stewart helped through her editing. Bob Ashenbrenner, John Hannon, Joe Knecht, Cheryl Ray, and John Watson gave great detailed and very helpful manuscript feedback. Fred Bothwell provided great manuscript and marketing inputs, along with superb publishing and printing coordination.

Thanks also need to go to those who gave other helpful improvement suggestions or helped in some other way in the overall process: Bill Baker, David Behrendsen, Becki Breyfogle, Wes Breyfogle, Alvin Brown, Bob Cheshire, Sonja Cline, Larry Dalton, Donn Fisher, Joe Flagherty, Kiran Gurumurthy, Jesse Hamilton, Bob Jones, Arch Holder, Lally Marwah, Todd Minnick, Mallary Musgrove, George Nicholas, Andy Paquest, Tanya Roberts, Jerri Saunders, Janet Shade, Frank Shines, Jeannine Siviy, Gary Wietharn, Bill Wiggenhorn, Brian Winterowd, Johnny Yu, and Brian Zievis.

Statistical analyses were conducted using Minitab. Flowcharts were created using Igrafx.

# WORKSHOP MATERIAL AND ITS AVAILABILITY

We at Smarter Solutions, Inc. take pride in creating an excellent learning environment for the wise application of tools that will improve organizational business systems. Our IEE approach and workshop handout materials are continually being enhanced and expanded. Our training includes executive, champion, black belt, green belt, yellow belt, master black belt, Lean, design for Six Sigma (DFSS) or design for integrated enterprise excellence (DFIEE), and other specialty courses. Workshops follow the E-DMAIC and P-DMAIC roadmaps, and often contain roadmap drill-downs not included in published books. Many who have already been trained as a black belt or master black belt have found our graduate workshop to be an excellent resource for their continuing education. This one-week graduate workshop walks through the IEE roadmaps, describing the unique measurements and tool applications described in this volume, with benefits. Public or on-site IEE workshops describe the overall system and its benefits.

Licensing inquiries for training material can be directed through www.SmarterSolutions.com. Articles, newsletters, and the latest information on how Smarter Solutions, Inc. is working with various organizations and universities are also described at this website.

## ABOUT SMARTER SOLUTIONS, INC., CONTACTING THE AUTHOR

Your comments and improvement suggestions for this book-volume series are greatly appreciated. For more information about business measurements and improvement strategies, sign up for our newsletter, webinars, or e-mail us for a free initial business consultation.

FORREST W. BREYFOGLE III
*Smarter Solutions, Inc.*
*11044 Research Blvd., Suite B-400*
*Austin, TX 78759, USA*
*Forrest@SmarterSolutions.com*
*www.SmarterSolutions.com*
*512-918-0280*

# PART I
## Management Systems and their Evolution

# 1

# Background

## 1.1  Messages in this Volume

Major topics discussed in this volume are:

- **Integrated Enterprise Excellence (IEE) = a system to achieve the three Rs of business:** People can be busy and an organization can be pushing for the creation of improvement projects, but it's still possible to lose sight of the big picture. This can lead to much wasted effort and enterprise system suboptimization. IEE provides a system (See Figure 4.2) for transitioning from firefighting daily or weekly problems to achieving the three Rs of business: everyone doing the Right things and doing them Right at the Right time. In IEE, metrics and goals are created so that there is a pull for project creation (See Figures 4.9 and 4.10) where project completion positively impacts the business as a whole.
- **E-DMAIC = a long-lasting enterprise framework for measurements and improvement that is refined over time:** Organizations can be very successful through the directives and insight of a few key individuals. However, things can quickly degrade if these individuals are no longer with

the company. The E-DMAIC system process (See Figure 4.7) provides a foundation for an enhanced enterprise performance measurement, analysis, and improvement system that is systematically refined over time and remains stable with leadership and organizational changes.

- **Improved analytics and innovation = better strategy building:** IEE is a business system which includes the use of analytics and innovation for more effective focused strategies building. This leads to targeted improvement and design projects which benefit the business as a whole, and avoid sub-optimization. Often organizations build their year-to-year efforts around a strategy that was developed in an executive retreat (See Figure 3.4). With this approach, functions in the organization create plans to execute these strategies, which can change from year-to-year or with leadership transitions. In addition, opinion-based strategy statements that rely solely on intuition and insight by the leadership may not lead to the best efforts throughout the organization. If the strategies are set after a thorough understanding of the enterprise performance and constraints, they are more effective in driving change and improving the business as a whole. The ability to support a strategic plan with performance data improves the buy in and acceptance across the organization. In the E-DMAIC process, strategies are formulated (See step 5 in Figure 4.7) around the use of analytics and innovation to create an enterprise improvement plan (See Figure 12.1).

- **Building from the Define and Measure steps of E-DMAIC = a consistent over-time enterprise foundation:** Instead of building from a retreat-developed strategy, IEE leads through the E-DMAIC define and measure phase (See Chapters 6 and 7), which include the creation of an enterprise value chain (See Figure 7.1) that has 30,000-foot-level and satellite-level metric reporting. This 30,000-foot-level and satellite level metric view provides an enterprise-wide measurement system offering predictive statements (See Figure 7.7, Figure 7.8, Figure 7.9, and Figure 7.10). This is unlike common tabular and graphic metric reporting (See Figures 3.1, Figure 3.2, and Figure 3.3) that provide stories of what happened in the past and provide little, if any, insight to what can be expected in the future unless something changes.

- **The right business metrics and presentation method = the right behavior and better business performance:** The selection of the right enterprise business metrics can lead to improved performance, while some business metrics will not lead to the right behavior. Even with the right enterprise business metrics, the method to display or present such dashboards and scorecards may not lead to the right behavior (See Figure 3.14 and Figure 3.15). The IEE system for metric creation and posting improves organizational resource utilization since common-cause variability will not be treated as though it were a special-cause condition; i.e., IEE is a means of implementing a fire-prevention system, as opposed to firefighting the problems of the day.
- **Analyzing the enterprise as a whole in E-DMAIC = business constraint removal and true enterprise improvement:** Resolving business problems and issues that are not constraining throughput, profit, or other satellite-level business metrics does not generally return the savings that are expected. In E-DMAIC, analyses identify enterprise-wide business performance constraints for exploitation. This effort in IEE results in improved resource utilization and true overall enterprise benefits, which is accompanied by a system for maintaining the gains (See Chapters 8 – 14).

## 1.2   Volume Layout

The purpose of this section is to provide the reader insight to this volume's layout. This understanding can help readers determine where they should start their reading.

Another book, *Integrated Enterprise Excellence: Going Beyond Lean Six Sigma and the Balanced Scorecard* (Breyfogle 2008d) provides a high-level view of the IEE system and its benefits. *Integrated Enterprise Excellence Volume I - The Basics: Golfing Buddies Go Beyond Lean Six Sigma and the Balanced Scorecard* (Breyfogle 2008a) contrasts several measurement and improvement systems in a novel format, illustrating the benefit of IEE.

This volume is not a quick-read book that has no future usefulness. My intent is that this how-to volume will be frequently referenced by practitioners and management to gain insight to what could be done to improve their existing enterprise management system. Since I am not sure about the reader's background relative to their understanding of key points in the two previously described books (Breyfogle 2008a and 2008d), in Part I of this Volume I reiterate important fundamental concepts that were described in these books.

Part II of this volume provides a step-by-step execution sequencing of the E-DMAIC process steps. For readers who want to immediately proceed to a description of the framework and execution of the overall E-DMAIC system, Part II is the place to start.

Since readers have various needs and backgrounds, I thought it was important to provide a foundation so everyone would begin reading the E-DMAIC Part II portion of this book with a similar understanding about management systems and the shortcomings of commonly used metrics and improvement strategies. In addition, I thought it was also important to provide a high-level view of IEE and leadership needs.

I addressed these needs in the following Part I chapters. Readers can choose to read the chapters that best address their specific needs:

- Chapter 1: Background
- Chapter 2: What is Six Sigma and Lean Six Sigma?
- Chapter 3: Scorecards, dashboards, performance metrics, and strategic planning
- Chapter 4: Improving management governance and innovation through IEE
- Chapter 5: Leadership and building successful teams

The appendix Part III tool listings were positioned in this volume so that the overall E-DMAIC description flow was not disrupted. Readers who are unfamiliar with a particular described tool can reference that part of the volume as needed.

## 1.3   Integrated Enterprise Excellence (IEE)

Learning disabilities are tragic in children, but fatal in organizations. Because of these disabilities, few corporations live half as long as a person; most die before they reach the age of forty (Senge 1990). This series of volumes describes an Integrated Enterprise Process Excellence (IEE) system, which allows a company to transition to a learning organization that defies the odds and overcome learning disabilities to achieve enterprise excellence.

In this system, an organization builds upon what it has done right and wrong in the past so that in the future, it becomes more profitable and better meets customer needs. Through this approach, an organization evolves into a learning organization, which has aligned organizational activities leading to improved effectiveness and efficiencies that positively impact the bottom line. IEE takes Lean Six Sigma and scorecards to the next level.

Everyone within a business should be focusing his/her efforts toward creating **M**ore **C**ustomers and **C**ash. The **E**xistence and **E**xcellence of organizations depend on it; i.e., $E=MC^2$, the same formula as Albert Einstein's famous equation. However, in reality, people can often be very busy and are far from achieving the three *R*s of business: everyone doing the Right things and doing them Right at the Right time throughout the organization, from an enterprise process point of view. Organizations can have a very difficult time orchestrating activities so that all personnel are in step to the rhythm that is necessary to obtain their business objectives and goals.

When we think about accomplishing activities in the workplace, we might immediately think of the phrase "What you measure is what you get" as being the corner stone for this organizational orchestration. However, we must be careful. Data collection procedures and report-out formats can stimulate the wrong activities. I prefer to paraphrase this statement as "What and how you measure can stimulate what you get."

> Data collection procedures and report-out formats can stimulate the wrong activities.

Traditional management metrics often include tabular reporting and perhaps classic trend and bar charts. Management can also use a scorecard system to monitor and track both financial and nonfinancial areas of the business against measurement goals established for each of these metrics. With this scorecard approach, metric owners are tracked against and are responsible for achieving established goals for their metrics. These goals might be part of the balanced scorecard (Kaplan and Norton 1992) system, where the four perspectives of financial, customer, internal business process, and learning & growth are to be addressed throughout the organization.

Scorecard balance is important because if there is not balance, one metric could be getting more focus than another, which can lead to problems. However, the natural balance described later in this volume is much more powerful than forcing a structure throughout the business via an organizational chart, which can change over time. In addition, the balanced scorecard system can lead to the suboptimization of processes, which can be detrimental to the enterprise as a whole.

Volumes in this series reference the system for enhancing scorecards and more as Integrated Enterprise Excellence or IEE. IEE goes beyond Lean Six Sigma and the balanced scorecard. In these volumes, tools and the overall thought process are presented in a step-by-step format that begins with the enterprise process and leads to the specifics of selecting and executing process improvement projects that are in true alignment with business goals.

IEE provides an enhanced scorecard and improvement project execution roadmap system. Included roadmaps provide a true integration of Lean and Six Sigma tools within the traditional define-measure-analyze-improve-control (DMAIC) roadmap. These roadmap steps are not only followed at the project execution level but also at the enterprise level as well. This volume focuses on applying the DMAIC roadmap at the enterprise level. Volume III focuses on applying the roadmap at the project execution level. In this volume, the reader is referred to Volume III, when appropriate, for more details on a project execution topic or tool instructional details.

Figure 4.2 illustrates the overall IEE system roadmap, which is introduced in this series of volumes. In this system, an **En**terprise (process) E-DMAIC roadmap (center figure five-step sequence) has linkage in the improve phase to the improvement **P**roject P-DMAIC roadmap (bottom five-step sequence) or design project define-measure-analyze-design-verify (DMADV) roadmap (top five-step sequence).

In IEE, the value chain (see Figure 7.1) describes in flowchart fashion both primary and support organizational activities and their accompanying 30,000-foot-level or satellite-level metrics. Example primary activity flow is develop product—market product—sell product—produce product—invoice/collect payments—report satellite-level metrics. Example support activities include IT, finance, HR, labor relations, safety & environment, and legal.

In this system, organizational value-chain metrics improvement needs *pull for project creation* for either process improvement or design projects that are in true alignment with business needs (see Glossary "pull for project creation", plus Figures 4.9 and 4.10). This volume describes the advantage of this enterprise process measurement pull system for project selection over traditional Lean Six Sigma implementations where there is a *push for project creation*; i.e., "let's list potential projects and decide which project to work on first" (see Glossary "push for project creation").

The flow of this series volume will follow the overall thought process of evaluating the enterprise process (E-DMAIC) to the mechanics of executing a specific improvement project (P-DMAIC), as illustrated in Figure 4.2. I will highlight the benefits of Six Sigma and Lean tools that are most applicable and challenge some of the traditional Six Sigma/Lean Six Sigma techniques that can lead to questionable results. I will also expand on other techniques that are beyond the boundaries of these methodologies.

This volume describes how to select and track the right measures within a company so that Lean/Six Sigma efforts best meet the strategic needs of the business and reduce day-to-day firefighting activities of the organization. This volume describes the infrastructure for selecting and managing projects within an organization. Volume III describes the P-DMAIC project execution roadmap for executing Lean/Six Sigma projects so that the most appropriate Lean or Six Sigma tool is used when executing both manufacturing and transactional projects. All size organizations can reap very large benefits from this pragmatic approach to implementing Six Sigma/Lean Six Sigma, no matter if the organization is in the manufacturing, service, or development area.

The strategies and techniques described in this volume are consistent and aligned with the philosophies of such quality authorities as W. Edwards Deming, J. M. Juran, Walter Shewhart, Genichi Taguchi, Kaoru Ishikawa, and others. *Implementing Six Sigma* (Breyfogle 2003a) described the integration of these methods with initiatives such as ISO-9000, Malcolm Baldrige Award, Shingo prize, and GE Work-Out.

In my opinion, the Malcolm Baldrige award and Shingo prize are the result of high score achievement tests. IEE is an enabling business system that can not only dramatically help achieve business goals but also help create an infrastructure for achieving the Malcolm Baldrige Award and Shingo prize.

## 1.4   History

Imagine a product or service provided by a company that is mired in cumbersome processes and administered by complicated, bureaucratic controls intended to reduce errors and improve the quality of output (Watson 2006). Customers are the primary source of error detection. Improvements are initiated only to address known defects, which have, in most cases, been identified due to a customer complaint.

Resources and timelines for delivery and rework are seldom deemed adequate. Suppliers are left guessing at schedules, priorities, and specifications. Decision making is inconsistent. Standard operating procedures and training are available, but are so outdated and time-consuming that they are generally regarded as worthless. Knowledge of how processes really work exists only in the minds and experience of workers who have long been conditioned by the mantra "whatever it takes, get it done." Rework and waste are extensive. Rules and requirements contribute to, rather than clarify, the noise of the process.

In this setting, it is impossible to know with certainty the causes of defects, partly because there is no systematic method in place to identify, report, analyze, and address the problems. Over time, goals are set to improve quality, but little happens in that direction. Each year brings a new round of budget cuts, or worse, targeted efforts to reach financial goals through the manipulation of costs and accounting.

Finally, out of luck or desperation, the company identifies an opportunity to put an end to the waste and confusion. True customer requirements are incorporated into the design and delivery of every product and service. Processes are simplified and standardized, and defects are reliably identified and measured before escaping to the next step or to the customer, without the use of extensive inspection and quality controls. Excursions from expected results are predictable and are addressed, often in advance, in a methodical, statistically measured way.

While this might sound like a set of circumstances facing any contemporary company, it exactly reflects business conditions faced by our predecessors since the start of the industrial revolution, and it is to those conditions that we can trace the origins of the quality and lean movement (Berger et al. 2002, Strategosinc 2006, Vitalentusa 2006):

- About 1799: Eli Whitney perfected interchangeable parts in fulfilling a U.S. Army contract for 10,000 muskets.
- Early 1900s: Frederick Taylor developed work specialization. During this time specialized inspectors were created.
- Beginning about 1910: Henry Ford and his engineers created a continuous system for manufacturing the Model T automobile. This system is considered by many to be the first practical application of just-in-time (JIT) and Lean manufacturing.

- Late 1920s: Walter Shewhart developed the control chart and statistical process control.
- 1940s: During World War II the United States required quality charting, which brought operators back to looking at their quality. However, many organizations continued to rely on inspectors.
- Beginning about 1949: Taichii Ohno and Shigeo Shingo at Toyota Motor Company began to incorporate Ford production and other techniques into an approach called Toyota production system. This just-in-time system recognized the central role of inventory and product variety flexibility, which addressed setup and changeover problems.
- In 1951: Armand Feigenbaum first published the book *Total Quality Control*, which initiated the total quality management (TQM) movement.
- In the 1950s: W. Edwards Deming visited Japan and initiated wide-scale statistical training with an emphasis on monitoring work process variation and systematic investigation/analyses for improvement.
- In 1954: Joseph Juran introduced formalized quality planning methods that addressed a systematic, business-level total quality control approach for quality implementation.
- 1960s and 1970s: Quality circles and employee involvement were utilized.
- In 1979: Phil Crosby wrote the book *Quality is Free*, which touted the "do it right the first time" philosophy.
- 1980s: Statistical process control had resurgence.
- Mid 1980s: Motorola initiated Six Sigma as a quality improvement methodology (Breyfogle 1992).
- 1990s: Focus was given to the International Organization for Standardization's (ISO) quality management system (QMS), ISO 9000, and Malcolm Baldrige National Quality Award assessments.
- Mid 1990s: Jack Welch at GE embraced Six Sigma as a quality improvement system in which trained practitioners worked on projects that had finance-validated costs savings.
- 1980s and 1990s: Additional methodologies utilized included value analysis/value engineering, kaizen events, poka-yoke, Theory of Constraints (TOC).
- Early 2000s: Six Sigma and Lean had a popular integration called Lean Six Sigma.
- 2005: Introduction of the IEE business system that takes Lean Six Sigma and traditional scorecards to their next level.

# 1.5   Deming's Seven Deadly Diseases and Fourteen Points for Management

Dr. Deming's concepts provided the foundation for IEE. It was he who emphasized that the key to quality improvement was in the hands of management. Dr. Deming demonstrated that most problems are the result of the system and not of employees. He used statistical quality control techniques to identify special and common cause conditions, in which common cause was the result of systematic variability, while special cause was erratic and unpredictable. He described the seven deadly diseases of the workplace and fourteen points for management.

Based on many years of experience, I have found Dr. Deming's philosophy to be a powerful guiding light to build a long-lasting system that can make companies more competitive. Below is a listing of Dr. Deming's seven deadly diseases and his original fourteen points for management. These two listings summarize Dr. Deming's basic philosophy. This series of volumes provides a how-to guide for implementing his methodologies.

The following are Dr. Deming's seven deadly diseases:

1.   Lack of constancy of purpose in planning product and service that will have a market, keep the company in business, and provide jobs
2.   Emphasis on short-term profits: short-term thinking (just the opposite of constancy of purpose to stay in business) fed by fear of unfriendly takeover and by push from bankers and owners for dividends
3.   Evaluation of performance, merit rating, or annual review
4.   Mobility of management: job hopping
5.   Management by use of visible figures only, with little or no consideration of figures that are unknown or unknowable
6.   Excessive medical costs
7.   Excessive cost of liability, swollen by lawyers who work on contingency fees

The following are Dr. Deming's original fourteen points for management with discussion (Deming 1982):

1.   "Create constancy of purpose toward improvement of product and service, with the aim to become competitive and to stay in business and to provide jobs."

For the company that wants to stay in business, the two general types of problems that exist are the problems of today and the problems of tomorrow. It is easy to become wrapped up with the problems of today, but the problems of the future demand, first and foremost, constancy of purpose and dedication to keep the company alive. Decisions need to be made to cultivate innovation, fund research and education, and improve the product design and service, remembering that the customer is the most important part of the production line.

2. "Adopt the new philosophy. We are in a new economic age. Western management must awaken to the challenge, must learn their responsibilities, and take on leadership for change."

   Government regulations and antitrust activities need to be changed to support the well-being of people. Commonly accepted levels of mistakes and defects can no longer be tolerated. People must receive effective training so that they understand their job and also understand that they should not be afraid to ask for assistance when it is needed. Supervision must be adequate and effective. Management must be rooted in the company and must not job-hop between positions within a company.

3. "Cease dependence on inspection to achieve quality. Eliminate the need for inspection on a mass basis by building quality into the product in the first place."

   Inspection is too late, ineffective, and costly. It is too late to react to the quality of a product when the product leaves the door. Quality comes not from inspection but from improving the production process. Corrective actions are not inspection, scrap, downgrading, and rework on the process.

4. "End the practice of awarding business on the basis of price tag. Instead, minimize total cost. Move toward a single supplier for any one item, on a long-term relationship of loyalty and trust."

   Price and quality go hand in hand. Trying to drive down the price of anything purchased without regard to quality and service can drive good suppliers and good service out of business. Single-source suppliers are desirable for many reasons. For example, a single-source supplier can become innovative and develop an economy in the production process that can only result from a long-term relationship with the purchaser. Lot-to-lot variability within a one-supplier process is often enough to disrupt the purchaser's process. Only additional variation can be expected with two suppliers. To qualify a supplier as a source for parts in a manufacturing process, perhaps it is better first to discard manuals that may have been used as guidelines by unqualified examiners to rate suppliers. Instead, suppliers could be asked to present evidence of active involvement of management, encouraging the application of many of the IEE concepts discussed in this volume. Special note should be given to the methodology used for continual process improvement.

5. "Improve constantly and forever the system of production and service, to improve quality and productivity, and thus constantly decrease costs."

    There is a need for constant improvement in test methods and for a better understanding of how the customer uses and misuses a product. In the past, American companies have often worried about meeting specifications, while the Japanese have worried about uniformity, i.e., reducing variation about the nominal value. Continual process improvement can take many forms. For example, never-ending improvement in the manufacturing process means that work must be done continually with suppliers to improve their processes. It is important to note that, like depending on inspection, putting out fires is not a process improvement.

6. "Institute training on the job."

    Management needs training to learn about all aspects of the company from incoming materials to customer needs, including the impact that process variation has on what is done within the company. Management must understand the problems the worker has in performing his or her tasks satisfactorily. A large obstacle exists in training and leadership when there are flexible standards for acceptable work. The standard may often be most dependent on whether a foreperson is having difficulty in meeting a daily production quota. It should be noted that money and time spent would be ineffective unless the inhibitors to good work are removed.

7. "Institute leadership. The aim of supervision should be to help people and machines and gadgets to do a better job."

    Supervision by management is in need of overhaul, as well as supervision of production workers. Management should lead, not supervise. Leaders must know the work that they supervise. They must be empowered and directed to communicate and to act on conditions that need correction. They must learn to fix the process and not react to every fault as if it were a special cause, which can lead to a higher defect rate.

8. "Drive out fear, so that everyone may work effectively for the company."

No one can give his best performance unless he feels secure. Employees should not be afraid to express their ideas or ask questions. Fear can take many forms, resulting in impaired performance and padded figures. Industries should embrace new knowledge because it can yield better job performance and should not be fearful of this knowledge because it could disclose some of their failings.

9. "Break down barriers between departments. People in research, design, sales, and production must work as a team to foresee problems of production and use that may be encountered with the product or service."

Teamwork is needed throughout the company. Everyone in design, sales, manufacturing, etc., can be doing superb work, and yet the company can be failing. Why? Functional areas are suboptimizing their own work and not working as a team for the company. Many types of problems can occur when communication is poor. For example, service personnel working with customers know a great deal about their products, but there is often no routine procedure for disseminating this information.

10. "Eliminate slogans, exhortations, and targets for the work force asking for zero defects and new levels of productivity."

Such exhortations only create adversary relationships, as the bulk of the causes of low quality and low productivity belongs to the system and thus lies beyond the power of the work force. Exhortations, posters, targets, and slogans are directed at the wrong people, causing general frustration and resentment. Posters and charts do not consider the fact that most trouble comes from the basic process. Management needs to learn that its main responsibility should be to improve the process and remove any special causes for defects found by statistical methods. Goals need to be set by an individual for the individual, but numerical goals set for other people without a road map to reach the objective have an opposite effect.

11a. "Eliminate work standards (quotas) on the factory floor. Substitute leadership."

Never-ending improvement is incompatible with a quota. Work standards, incentive pay, rates, and piecework are manifestations of management's lack of understanding, which leads to inappropriate supervision. Pride of workmanship needs to be encouraged, while the quota system needs to be eliminated. Whenever work standards are replaced with leadership, quality and productivity increase substantially, and people are happier on their jobs.

11b. "Eliminate management by objective. Eliminate management by numbers, numerical goals. Substitute leadership."

Goals such as "improve productivity by 4 percent next year" without a method are a burlesque. The data tracking these targets are often questionable. Moreover, a natural fluctuation in the right direction is often interpreted as success, while small fluctuation in the opposite direction causes a scurry for explanations. If there is a stable process, a goal is not necessary because the output level will be what the process produces. A goal beyond the capability/performance of the process will not be achieved. A manager must understand the work that is to be done in order to lead and manage the sources for improvement. New managers often short-circuit this process and focus instead on outcome (e.g., getting reports on quality, proportion defective, inventory, sales, and people).

12a. "Remove barriers that rob the hourly worker(s) of their right to pride of workmanship."

The responsibility of supervisors must be changed from sheer numbers to quality. In many organizations, the hourly worker becomes a commodity. He may not even know whether he will be working next week. Management can face declining sales and increased costs of almost everything, but it is often helpless in facing the problems of personnel. The establishment of employee involvement and of participation plans has been a smoke screen. Management needs to listen and to correct process problems that are robbing the worker of pride of workmanship.

12b. "Remove barriers that rob people in management and in engineering of their right to pride of workmanship."

This means, inter alia, abolishment of the annual or merit rating and of managing by objective. Merit rating rewards people who are doing well in the system; however, it does not reward attempts to improve the system. The performance appraisal erroneously focuses on the end product rather than on leadership to help people. People who are measured by counting are deprived of pride of workmanship. The indexes for these measurements can be ridiculous. For example, an individual is rated on the number of meetings he or she attends; hence, in negotiating a contract, the worker increases the number of meetings needed to reach a compromise. One can get a good rating for firefighting because the results are visible and quantifiable, while another person only satisfied minimum requirements because he or she did the job right the first time; in other words, mess up your job, and correct it later to become a hero. A common fallacy is the supposition that it is possible to rate people by putting them in rank order from last year's performance. There are too many combinations of forces involved: the worker, coworkers, noise, and confusion. Apparent differences in the ranking of personnel will arise almost entirely from these factors in the system. A leader needs to be not a judge but a colleague and counselor who leads and learns with his or her people on a day-to-day basis. In absence of numerical data, a leader must make subjective judgment when discovering who, if any, of his or her people are outside the system, either on the good or the bad side, or within the system.

13. "Institute a vigorous program of education and self-improvement."
An organization needs good people who are improving with education. Management should be encouraging everyone to get additional education and engage in self-improvement.

14. "Put everybody in the company to work to accomplish the transformation. The transformation is everybody's job."
Management needs to take action to accomplish the transformation. To do this, first consider that every job and activity is part of a process. A flow diagram breaks a process into stages. Questions then need to be asked about what changes could be made at each stage to improve the effectiveness of other upstream or downstream stages. Everyone can be a part of the team effort to improve the input

and output of the stages. Everyone on a team has a chance to contribute ideas and plans. A team has an aim and goal toward meeting the needs of the customer.

## 1.6   Organization Management and Quality Leadership

Management structure can discourage effective decision-making (Scholtes 1988). American managers have often conducted much of their business through an approach that is sometimes called *management by results*. This type of management tends to focus only on the end result: process yield, gross margin, sales dollars, and return on investment. In most organizations, emphasis is placed on a chain of command with a hierarchy of standards, objectives, controls, and accountability. Objectives are translated into work standards or quotas that guide the performance of employees. Use of these numerical goals can cause short-term thinking, misdirected focus on fear (e.g., of a poor job performance rating), fudging the numbers, internal conflict, and blindness to customer concerns. This type of management is said to be like trying to keep a dog happy by forcibly wagging its tail.

Enron and WorldCom epitomized this type of management focus at the beginning of the 21st century, where focus was given to achieving a single point calendar-based goal, even if it led to questionable accounting practices and ethics issues. The reason for the failure of these two companies and others that have been involved in similar situations is no doubt complex and controversial. Table 1.1 is a simplistic attempt to provide readers who are not familiar with these high profile corporate failures a generalization of some of the things that went wrong in these companies.

Because of these corporate problems Sarbanes-Oxley (SOX) legislation act was created in 2002 (see Appendix Section C.1) partly in response to high profile corporate financial scandals. SOX is now costing companies a huge percentage of their total revenue to manage and can often lead to the creation of less efficient processes so that no issues later surface.

The Enron/WorldCom form of management is in contrast to focusing on managing and improving the day-to-day activities, which later lead to an improved response. The Enron and World-Com management style can lead to the downfall of companies, where executives spend time behind bars. One conjecture for this happening is that Enron groupthink created an environment where otherwise unacceptable ethics were rewarded.

Ask yourself whether you think that all the unethical MBAs migrated to Enron or whether Enron created the unethical behavior. I believe the management system in Enron created the unethical behavior. In Enron, executive management had to do whatever it took to meet the numbers. Enron lacked metrics that gave a true picture of what was happening. This resulted in a smoke and mirror system which had integrity issues relative to the handling of business challenges. In addition, this system encouraged executive management to have no respect for either the financial or the general well being of others inside and outside the company. In this series of volumes, I make reference to the result of this management style as the Enron effect.

Not all management by results behavior is as severe as that of Enron; however, this generic behavior has occurred to lesser extremes in other company; i.e., things occur which are not consistent with the long-term health of the company. For example, Krispy Kreme shipped donuts that they knew would be returned so that their quarterly financial objectives would be met (Lloyd 2005). The Enron problem and other similar management-style problems would not occur if a no-nonsense governance system were in place with a metric system that discouraged playing games with the numbers.

This series of volumes describe the IEE system, which can help organizations move toward an orchestration so that everyone is doing the right things and doing them right at the right time. The IEE system provides the framework for this to occur using, among other things, an integration of a no-nonsense 30,000-foot-level metric system with the business' value chain. IEE integrates the standardization of processes with a system to face waste reduction and business improvement issues head-on.

Quality leadership is an alternative that emphasizes results by working on methods. In this type of management, work process are studied and constantly improved so that the final product or service not only meets but also exceeds customer expectations. The principles of quality leadership are: customer focus; obsession with quality; effective work structure; a balance of control and freedom, i.e., management in control of employees yet freedom given to employees; unity of purpose; process defect identification; teamwork; and education and training. These principles

**Table 1.1** Simplistic High-Level Generalizations of Potential Failure Points for Five Business Cases (Source: Various Internet Sites)

Potential failure points for five business cases

| Company | Enron | WorldCom | KrispyKreme | Tyco | Adelphia |
|---|---|---|---|---|---|
| Business | Energy | Communications | Donuts | Electronic components, Health care, Fire safety, Security, and Fluid control | Cable |
| Symptom of issue | --Failed hedges.<br><br>--Question company partnerships to increase profits and decrease debts of Enron.<br><br>--Company stock sell off at crucial points of partnerships being started/defunct. | --Instances of hiding bad debt, understating costs, and backdating contracts spoken about by ex-employees.<br><br>--Suffered multiple downgrades of its credit rating.<br><br>--Wall Street analysts recommended its shares be sold. | --Grew too big, too fast; went against the strength of its hot doughnut sales and saturated its markets with cold grocery- and convenience-store pastries.<br><br>--Grew faster than they were being efficient.<br><br>--Allegations in a stockholder lawsuit of padded sales figures.<br><br>--Restated its earnings.<br><br>--Warned investors of being in danger of defaulting on a $150 million credit line. | --Tyco director received a $10 million fee on the CIT Group/Tyco deal, and another $10 million went to a charity where he was a director.<br><br>--The New York Times reports that Tyco CEO and CFO sold more than $100 million of their Tyco stock the previous fiscal year despite public statements that they rarely sold their stock.<br><br>--Shareholders were not informed of the $170 million in loans and $430 million obtained by fraud in the sale of company shares taken by Tyco's CEO, CFO, and chief legal officer. The loans, many of which were taken interest free and later written off as benefits, were not approved by Tyco's compensation committee. | --Extravagant owner/top level executive lifestyle:<br>--Several vacation homes and luxury apartments in Manhattan<br>--Several private jets<br>--Construction of a world-class 18-hole golf course<br>--Majority ownership of the Buffalo Sabres<br>--$700,000 membership in an exclusive golf club |
| Failure mode | Inadequate adherence to standard financial and accounting practices | Inadequate adherence to standard financial and accounting practices | Inadequate adherence to standard financial and accounting practices | Inadequate adherence to standard financial and accounting practices | Inadequate adherence to standard financial and accounting practices |
| Contributing Inputs | --Management arrogance<br><br>--Personal/Corporate greed<br><br>--Behavior | --Management arrogance/ignorance<br><br>--Personal/Corporate greed<br><br>--Behavior | --Improper mangement practices | --Management arrogance<br><br>--Personal/Corporate Greed<br><br>--Behavior | --Owner was characterized as exhibiting:<br>--Egocentrism<br>--Omniscience<br>--Omnipotence<br>--Invulnerability<br><br>--Other contributers:<br>--Violation of RICO act<br>--Breach of fiduciary duties<br>--Waste of corporate assets<br>--Abuse of control by family-managed practice/board of directors<br>--Breach of contract<br>--Unjust enrichment<br>--Fraudulent conveyance<br>--Conversion of corporate assets |
| Outcome | --Time in prison/payment of fines<br><br>--Community service | Time in prison/payment of fines | Time in prison/payment of fines | Time in prison/payment of fines | Time in prison/payment of fines |

are more conducive to long-term thinking, correctly directed efforts, and a keen regard for the customer's interest.

Quality leadership has a positive return on investment. In 1950, Dr. Deming described the chain reaction of getting a greater return on investment as: improve quality→decrease costs→improve productivity→decrease prices→increase market share in business→provide jobs→increase return on investment. Quality is not something that can be delegated to others. Management must lead the transformation process.

To give quality leadership, the historical hierarchical management structure needs to be changed to a team structure that has a more unified purpose. A single person can make some difference in an organization. However, one person rarely has enough knowledge or experience to understand everything within a process. Major gains in both quality and productivity can often result when a team of people pools their skills, talents, and knowledge using an IEE strategy.

Teams need to have a systematic plan to improve the process that creates mistakes/defects, breakdowns/delays, inefficiencies, and variation. For a given work environment, management needs to create an atmosphere that supports team effort in all aspects of business. In some organizations, management may need to create a process that describes hierarchical relationships between teams, the flow of directives, the transformation of directives into actions and improvements, and the degree of autonomy and responsibility of the teams. The change to quality leadership can be very difficult. Transforming an entire organization requires dedication and patience.

Realities dictate that management still needs to meet its numbers in both for-profit and non-profit organizations. In the past, it seems that the quality leadership movement within an organization has taken on the spirit of a quality improvement program orchestrated by the quality department. When there is lack of alignment of quality leadership to the bottom line and other metrics of an organization, these efforts often are short-lived.

What is needed is a *results orchestration* (RO) approach that leads to *knowledge-centered activity* (KCA). Organizations need a system in which their organizational measurements are aligned with the metric needs of the business.

The IEE approach differs from a traditional *management by results* approach in that, with the IEE approach, management uses satellite-level and 30,000-foot-level metrics to help identify and manage important business activities. Satellite-level and 30,000-foot-level metrics provide a high-level time-series scorecard/dashboard of business and operational metrics (see Figures 7.1–7.10), which is not bounded by calendar quarters or years. In addition, for stable processes these metrics provide a predictive statement.

> Satellite-level and 30,000-foot-level metrics provide a high-level time-series scorecard/dashboard of business and operational metrics, which is not bounded by calendar quarters or years.

Satellite-level metrics are not to replace existing financial metrics but provide a time-series financial view of the enterprise as a whole over time. This view can provide insight that is needed to make process improvements that have a long-lasting positive impact on the business as a whole.

Metrics at the 30,000-foot-level can be used to orchestrate operational activities. These measures, in conjunction with an enterprise value-chain analysis, can provide insight that leads to the formulation of a strategic plan, which leads to the creation of projects that are directly aligned to the business goals (see Figure 12.1).

When 30,000-foot-level metrics indicate that a common cause problem is prevalent which needs resolution, management can orchestrate improvement by initiating an IEE project. This can lead to a different set of management activities. Instead of criticizing someone about not meeting a numbers goal, management can inquire about the status of the project, perhaps offering helpful suggestions to overcome organizational barriers to achieve a timelier project completion.

With this RO approach we create a pull for the project creation system, rather than push for project creation (see Glossary). This implementation approach provides a continuing stimulus for the sustaining of IEE within an organization, overcoming a problem many companies have experienced with a traditional rollout of Six Sigma or Lean Six Sigma.

The overall IEE structure still allows for immediate problem containment using methodologies that current exist in an organization; e.g., the 8 Disciplines or 8D (Breyfogle 2003b). The advantage of using the overall IEE structure is that this approach encourages the creation of system changes that yield long-lasting improvements. This activity can be viewed as fire preventive action, which leads to a reduction in firefighting.

The RO approach helps reduce the problems often associated with traditional *management by results*. With RO, management focuses not only on creating activities that are in alignment with the needs of this business but also on actively considering the capability/performance of the system before actions are created. This re-focus can help organizations avoid the problems often associated with *management by results*: short-term thinking, misguided focus, internal conflict, fudging the figures, greater fear, and blindness to customer concerns.

# 1.7   Quality Management and Planning

Quality management achieves, monitors, controls, and improves the functional, financial, and human relationship performance of the enterprise process. Procedures include mechanisms for allocating, organizing, and improving resources. Quality management procedures should incorporate quantitative metrics and other report card criteria that monitor and evaluate the performance of the units and personnel of the organization (Juran and Godfrey 1999).

The purpose of traditional quality planning is the prevention of defects and validation of designs (Berger et al. 2002). Broad groupings for quality planning are strategic plans, tactical plans, and operational plans. For business needs, these groupings can have time lines of:

- Strategic quality plan: 3–5 year plan or 2–3 year plan.
- Tactical quality plan: product and service development that aligns with strategic goals.
- Operational quality plan: short-term day-to-day needs which include internal audits, inspection, equipment calibration, testing, and training courses.

In strategic quality planning, organizational strengths, weaknesses, opportunities, and threats (SWOT) should be assessed. With this strategic risk analysis, organizations can leverage the strength of the organization, improve any weaknesses, exploit opportunities, and minimize the potential impact of threats. Strategic planning should then create the vision, broad goals, and objectives for an organization. Through this risk assessment, organizations can then optimize their systems as a whole. Organizations should avoid the optimization of sub-processes, which can be detrimental to the system as a whole. Within the IEE overall roadmap, strategic planning is addressed in the E-DMAIC analyze phase, where data analyses are an integral part of the overall process. A strategic plan then leads to a tactical quality plan.

In tactical quality planning, organizations create specific tasks that have a schedule, along with methods and responsibilities. These plans are sometimes called advanced quality planning (AQP) or advanced product quality planning (APQP). AQP ensures that a new product or service will meet customer expectations.

Tactical quality planning is part of the E-DMAIC improve phase. The Process DFSS and Product DFSS chapters of *Implementing Six Sigma* (Breyfogle 2003a) describe a roadmap to accomplish this.

In operational quality planning, we need a system that describes the tasks and procedures for accomplishing these tasks. In IEE, the value chain can be used to drill down not only the quality operations noted above (internal audits, inspection, etc.) but also other operating procedures. These value-chain tasks are documented in the E-DMAIC define phase, where improvements to these operations are identified and developed through the E-DMAIC analyze and improve phases.

With an IEE implementation, strategic planning leads to doing the right things, and tactical and operational planning leads to doing those things right. In addition, this approach leads to a closed-loop assessment, resulting in effective knowledge management of the overall system document objectives achieved and lessons learned for the identification and creation of additional opportunities. Results from strategic planning can be tracked at the financial-level using a satellite-level metric, while tactical and operational results can have a scorecard/dashboard tracking at the 30,000-foot-level. This strategy is useful not only to implement the plan through projects but also to help create a strategic and tactical plan that is aligned with these metrics.

## 1.8   IEE Values

The IEE system described in this series of volumes can become an enabling tool to adopt Dr. Deming's ideals in business.

- It provides guidance on the development or identification of the best measurements to run a business. This helps organizations avoid three of Dr. Deming deadly diseases: (2) an emphasis on short-term thinking, (3) evaluations of performance, and (5) management by only visible figures.
- It recognizes the different uses of business measures, from process management to business management. A value chain is introduced that connects the business functions to their performance measures, which allows a business to avoid the fifth deadly disease through the creation of measures for all aspects of performance.

- It reinforces that all aspects of business improvement should support the system goals, not just be beneficial to a single area. This addresses the first deadly disease related to an inconsistency of purpose through avoiding local improvements that are not beneficial to the entire system.
- It provides a methodology to identify the business-process functional values with a linkage to business measures. This implementation addresses the first deadly disease, which is related to an inconsistency of purpose through linking improvements to the business goals.
- It describes issues with commonly used performance measures that can drive the wrong type of activities throughout the organization, which are not consistent with true customer needs. IEE offers improvements to the balanced scorecard (Kaplan and Norton 1992) and traditional dashboard metrics. Red-Yellow-Green scorecards often lead to short-term thinking that drives the wrong activities. IEE helps organizations focus on long-term objectives that are healthy to the enterprise as a whole, thus avoiding the second deadly disease.
- It supports the creation and utilization of business metrics that not only monitor the system but also provide information to the entire workforce so that they can effectively utilize the information to learn and improve performance on their own. This methodology creates opportunities to address performance issues—Dr. Deming's third deadly disease.
- One important aspect of IEE is to determine the best reporting system for these metrics. The IEE measurement system is based on Dr. Deming's definitions of common and special cause variation. This system enhances traditional control charting techniques so that results are in better alignment with Dr. Deming's common and special cause definition. In this business metric system, sources of common cause process variability include the typical variability exhibited by process input variables which in traditional control charting might have been signaled as assignable causes. With this approach, special cause conditions are in direct alignment with Dr. Deming's definition description of "fleeting events."

As past Intel CEO and chairman of the board, Grove (1999) states, "only the paranoid survive." IEE is a systematic methodology that can facilitate this corporate survival without creating the bad stress that often accompanies paranoia.

## 1.9  Exercises

1.  For a company, government office, or social organization, list five of Dr. Deming's fourteen points where there are opportunities for improvement. Describe your reason for each listed point.
2.  List some compensation issues that need to be addressed in teamwork environments.
3.  Dr. Deming's fourth point suggests working with a small number of suppliers. Describe criteria for evaluating suppliers.
4.  Describe the positive and negative aspects of ranking employees.

# 2

# What are Six Sigma and Lean Six Sigma?

The last chapter described business systems. This chapter provides a high-level view of Six Sigma and Lean Six Sigma. Unlike IEE, Six Sigma and Lean Six Sigma are not an enterprise business management system.

Six Sigma and Lean Six Sigma are statistical quality performance measurement and management systems that focus on creating/completing projects which reduce the frequency of errors. These projects utilize both statistical and non-statistical tools to improve processes, where emphasis is given to creating projects that have validated financial benefits.

Six Sigma also addresses process improvement relative to voice of the customer (VOC) needs. The success of Six Sigma deployments is typically touted as a financial project savings total; however, as discussed later, claims from these finance-validated projects can often be challenged as to whether they truly impacted the bottom-line organizational benefits positively.

The term *sigma* (σ), in the name *Six Sigma*, is a letter in the Greek alphabet used to describe variability; i.e., standard deviation. The classical Six Sigma unit of measure is defects per opportunity. Sigma quality level offers an indicator of how often defects are likely to occur, where a higher sigma quality level indicates a process that is less likely to create defects. A Six Sigma quality level is said to equate to 3.4 defects per million opportunities (DPMO). Appendix Section B.1 describes the determination of this number and other sigma quality level performance level numbers; e.g., 4 sigma quality level equates to 6210 DPMO. A 3.4 ppm process defect rate is often considered near perfection; hence, a Six Sigma quality level is often considered a goal.

Lean has typically been associated with manufacturing, but the techniques apply to all business areas. In Lean, focus is given to process speed and efficiency. Lean focus has been given to the reduction of waste. The seven types of waste frequently referenced with Lean are overproduction, waiting, transportation, inventory, over-processing, motion, and defects. More recently some have added people utilization to this list; however, we can expand the list even further to include wasted space, wasted effort, wasted energy, and so forth.

Lean Six Sigma basically combines the tools, methods, and infrastructure of Six Sigma and Lean. Companies have reported billions in financial benefits from executing Six Sigma and Lean Six Sigma projects.

## 2.1   Six Sigma Background

When Bill Wiggenhorn was senior vice president of Motorola, he contributed a foreword to the first edition of *Implementing Six Sigma* (Breyfogle 1999). The following is a condensed version of his historical perspective about the origination of Six Sigma at Motorola:

> The father of Six Sigma was the late Bill Smith, a senior engineer and scientist. It was Bill who crafted the original statistics and formulas that were the beginning of the Six Sigma culture. He took his idea and passion for it to our CEO at the time, Bob Galvin. Bob urged Bill to go forth and do whatever was needed to make Six Sigma the number one component in Motorola's culture. Not long afterwards, Senior Vice President Jack Germaine was named as quality director and charged with implementing Six Sigma throughout the corporation. He turned to Motorola University to spread the Six Sigma word throughout the company and around the world. The result was a culture of quality that permeated Motorola and led to a period of unprecedented growth and sales. The crown-

ing achievement was being recognized with the Malcolm Baldrige National Quality Award (1988).

In the mid 1990s, Jack Welch, the CEO of General Electric (GE), initiated the implementation of Six Sigma in the company so that the quality improvement projects were aligned to the needs of the business. This approach to implementing Six Sigma involves the use of statistical and non-statistical tools within a structured environment for the purpose of creating knowledge that leads to higher quality products in less time than the competition. The selection and execution of project after project that follow a disciplined execution approach led to significant bottom-line benefits to the company. Many large and small companies have followed GE's stimulus by implementing various versions for Six Sigma. Section A.2 of *Implementing Six Sigma* (Breyfogle 2003a) provides a summary of a Six Sigma benchmarking study that describes some of these deployments.

## 2.2   Lean Overview

The principles of Lean are (1) define customer value, (2) focus on the value stream, (3) make value flow, (4) let the customer pull product, and (5) pursue perfection relentlessly. Lean is an answer to a customer need or desire. The product or service is provided in a timely manner and at an appropriate price. You or I don't determine value; value is in the eyes of the customer.

Within Lean, we identify the value stream. This might be a process or series of process steps from concept to launch to production, order to delivery to disposition, or raw materials to customer receipt to disposal. It consists of steps that add value to a product. Within Lean, we eliminate steps that do not add value, where a product can be tangible or intangible.

Lean methods assess the operation of the factory and supply chain with an emphasis on the reduction of wasteful activities. Lean emphasizes the reduction of inconsistencies associated with manufacturing routings, material handling, storage, lack of communication, batch production, and so forth. The Toyota production system (TPS), as discussed later, is usually considered the benchmark for Lean implementation.

Lean waste-elimination efforts give focus to pull scheduling, takt time, and flow production. With pull scheduling, production builds address what the customer is currently buying, as opposed to long-range forecasts. Takt is customer demand rate. Processes should be changed so that they run at the customer-demand rate. Flow production involves the elimination of operational movement and waiting with an emphasis on eliminating batch products/transactions processing.

Lean can reduce inventory value by reducing work in progress (WIP). This can be accomplished by focusing on smaller job sizes and quicker processing times. By decreasing WIP on the floor, inventory is turned over more rapidly; i.e., inventory turns are increased.

## 2.3   Lean and Six Sigma Overview

Both Lean and Six Sigma have very powerful tools; however, deployments that don't equally consider Lean and Six Sigma methodologies are missing out on the benefits of having a complete tool set. This situation is analogous to someone using a wrench instead of a hammer to drive a nail into a board. Yes, one could complete the nailing task; however, the job would more difficult than if a hammer were used. Similarly, a Lean improvement effort to reduce machine defects might not consider the power of design of experiments (DOE) techniques as a viable tool for defect reduction if this tool is not part of the practitioner's tool set.

The IEE strategy does not suggest that Six Sigma be implemented before Lean or Lean be implemented before Six Sigma in an organization. In this strategy, the preference is to implement Lean and Six Sigma methodologies at the same time.

Lean tool execution is described in Chapters 14 and 36 of Volume III. Appendix D of this volume also describes many Lean tools in lesser detail.

## 2.4   Lean Six Sigma Infrastructure

At the beginning of the 21st century, Six Sigma and Lean evolved into Lean Six Sigma. Lean Six Sigma integrates the concepts of Lean and Six Sigma; however, organizations often still have both Lean and Six Sigma camps, where each camp describes its preference or priority of one of the techniques over the other. Later in this volume I describe the E-DMAIC system where measurements pull for the right tool, whether the tool is Lean or Six Sigma.

Companies who are implementing Lean Six Sigma create an infrastructure that supports the completion of projects and delivers significant reported financial benefits. This cannot be accomplished effectively if there is not a mixture of both core people who are 100% time-dedicated to the effort and others who receive these responsibilities as part of their current assignments.

In a company-wide deployment, the CEO and other executives decide whether the company will adopt Lean Six Sigma. They are responsible for shaping the deployment, regularly monitoring its success, and guiding the use of resources.

Champions are executive-level managers who are responsible for managing and guiding the Lean Six Sigma deployment and its projects. Business unit managers such as presidents or vice presidents need to work closely with the champion in the selection of projects that are consistent with their goals. They are accountable for meeting the CEO's Lean Six Sigma goals.

Process owners (e.g., manufacturing line managers and service-personnel supervisors) own the processes that are to be improved through Lean Six Sigma projects. They authorize changes and must be a part of a project improvement hand-off process. They are the project sponsors who are responsible for getting the right people involved in training and team meetings.

Executives and business unit managers typically have at least one-day executive overview training, while champions and process owners typically have three days of training.

Practitioner role titles are typically based upon a martial arts belting structure, where the color of an individual's belt is dependent upon his/her skill mastery.

Black belts are process improvement practitioners who typically receive four weeks of training over four months. It is most desirable that black belts are dedicated resources; however, many organizations utilize part-time resources. During training, black belt trainees lead the execution of a project that has in-class report-outs and critiques. Between training sessions, black belt trainees should receive project coaching, which is very important for their success. They are expected to deliver high quality report-outs to peers, champions, and executives. Upon course completion, black belts are expected to continue delivering financial beneficial projects; e.g., 4–6 projects per year with financial benefits of $500,000–$1,000,000. Black belts can mentor green belts, as described later.

Master black belts are black belts who have undertaken two weeks of advanced training and have a proven track record of delivering results through various projects and project teams. They should be a dedicated resource to the deployment. Before they train, master black belts need to be certified in the material that they are to deliver. Their responsibilities include coaching black belts, monitoring team progress, and assisting teams when needed.

Green belts are part-time practitioners who typically receive two weeks of training over two months. Their primary focus is on projects that are in their functional area. The inference that someone becomes a green belt before a black belt should not be made. Business and personal needs/requirements should influence the decision whether someone becomes a black belt or green belt. If someone's job requires a more in-depth skill set, such as the use of design of experiments (DOE), then the person should be trained as a black belt. Also, at deployment initiation, black belt training should be conducted first so that this additional skill set can be used when coaching others.

Yellow belts are team members who typically receive three days of training, which helps them in the effectiveness of their participation in project execution such as data collection, identifying voice of the customer, and team meetings.

Comptrollers, in my opinion, are typically not involved as much as they should be in the direction of traditional Six Sigma and Lean Six Sigma deployments and project selection. This shortcoming is addressed in E-DMAIC.

Other recommended team resources include:

- Information management support aids with hardware/software procurement and installation for black belts and teams. In addition, the organization needs to establish data collection systems that are easily reproducible and reliable.
- Finance support that helps identify and approves monetary calculations. Including a finance representative as a team member from the project start can yield the following benefits: additional savings opportunities, more timely and effective savings review/approval, and higher probability of sustained and auditable savings.
- Human resources that address employee career path job descriptions and labor relations.
- Communications systems that address internal and external communications.

- Legal to address changes that could have legal implications.
- Environmental to address changes that could have an environmental impact.
- Training that coordinates organizational training, black belt/green belt, and other training.

Some of these roles (see Appendix Section A.1) and possible technical and organizational interrelationships are shown in Figures 2.1 and 2.2.

The overall quality leader may deploy and monitor the Lean Six Sigma strategy. Some larger companies have both deployment and project champion roles. In this series of volumes, I will make reference to black belt as the practitioner; however, many of the tasks could similarly be executed by green belts. Appendix Section A.2 describes some of the characteristics for each of these roles.

This series of volumes describes an IEE system that takes Lean Six Sigma and the balanced scorecard (Kaplan and Norton 1992) to their next level.

## 2.5   Common Lean Six Sigma Deployment Problems and What To Do About Them

The following is taken from the *Six Sigma Forum Magazine* (Breyfogle 2005a), with some updates. When I wrote the article, I used the term "Six Sigma;" however, what I have found is that the issues and resolutions to these issues described in this article are still prevalent with Lean Six Sigma deployments. The IEE system described later addresses all these issues head-on.

### Common Problems (and What to Do about Them)
### Forrest W. Breyfogle III

Six Sigma deployments don't always run smoothly, so I compiled a list of twenty-one frequently encountered situations. You've likely come across at least one but may not have known how best to handle it—until now.

1. **My organization started its Six Sigma deployment five years ago, and now we're having difficulty finding projects, especially projects of value.** It appears as if projects in this Six Sigma deployment are being sought

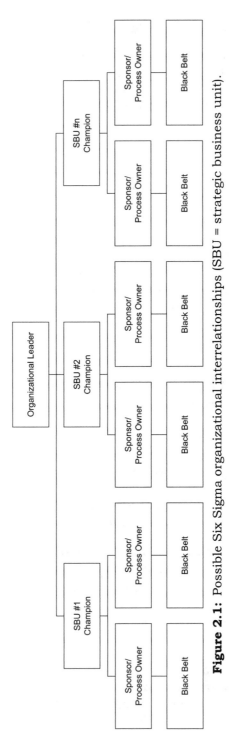

**Figure 2.1:** Possible Six Sigma organizational interrelationships (SBU = strategic business unit).

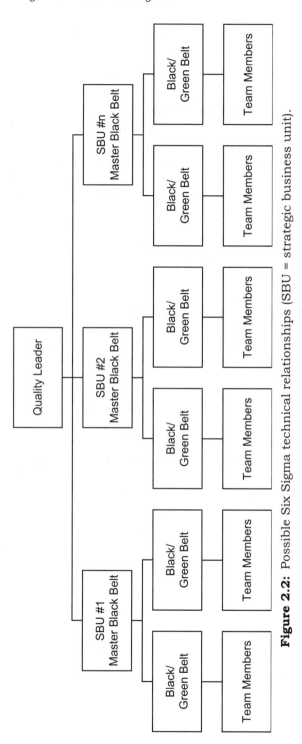

**Figure 2.2:** Possible Six Sigma technical relationships (SBU = strategic business unit).

out by the Six Sigma steering committee, even though the process owners have no true urgency for project initiation and completion. It would be better to have a deployment system where process owners solicit help that leads to the execution of Six Sigma projects, which help their business-aligned performance metrics.

2. **Our program stalled after our Six Sigma deployment executive left.** A dictatorship can be great if the dictator truly understands what is needed and addresses those needs without bureaucracy. Even if this utopia were to exist, major chaos would probably result after the dictator's departure.

   Organizations need a Six Sigma deployment that is not solely dependent on one executive's drive. They need to create a system where the process owner asks for the creation of Six Sigma projects to improve their performance metrics, which are aligned with business needs. This should happen no matter which executive is in place.

3. **A Black belt (BB) or master black belt (MBB) certification would look good on my résumé. What's the easiest way to get one?** Organizations should focus on having the best people learn how to wisely apply Six Sigma and Lean techniques to improve performance measures and better meet customer needs. A deployment that focuses on belt titles for the masses rather than results does not accomplish this.

4. **In our Six Sigma deployment, managers are measured by the number of employees trained and their validated financial savings.** With this strategy, people in all functions seek out the least painful training and the easiest projects that will provide them Six Sigma project credit. Minimal, if any, attention is given to targeting improvement efforts that impact the primary business success constraints.

5. **Our organization will be doing Lean, then Six Sigma.** Lean and Six Sigma tool usage should depend on the business and its associated metric improvement needs. A deployment rollout should address both tool sets simultaneously with a high-level operational metric system that pulls for the right tool at the right time.

6. **Our organization will have Six Sigma trainees complete an easy classroom project in which they can use the tools.** Later they can apply the methods to projects that are more important to the business. This type of statement

says training is the primary focus of the Six Sigma deployment. Instead, the organization should focus on executing projects that improve the overall enterprise metrics.

7. **Jack Welch did it wrong at General Electric (GE). He should have leaned out all business units instead of selling the business units he did not want to deal with.** Lean is a very powerful tool; however, not all businesses are profitable or aligned with the organization's mission. In a Six Sigma deployment, data should help a business decide where it can best focus its efforts and resources, even if that means it has to sell certain business units. Therefore, I believe Jack Welch did the right thing by selling the businesses that were not aligned with their overall business needs.

8. **Our organization is going to do 5S (sort, straighten, shine, standardize, and sustain) first and then move on to Six Sigma.** An organization could have a clean and efficient process to make something no one buys. Instead, it needs to create a system in which the best Lean or Six Sigma tools are used to improve business metrics and synthesize voice of the customer inputs to targeted actions. Tools such as 5S need to be applied within a Six Sigma deployment, when they are most applicable.

9. **Our company is going to conduct a pilot project to see whether Six Sigma works before considering a deployment.** This sounds like a great starting point; however, a pilot project can fail for a number of reasons, including non-dedicated resource people who don't have the time to work on a project that is not important to the process owner.

    The success or failure of a specific project is not a good test of whether Six Sigma works. Wisely applied Six Sigma with Lean works if activities are aligned to business operational metrics needs. The real question is, what can be done to ensure an organization maximizes its benefits from the concepts of Six Sigma?

10. **Our team was told a successful Six Sigma deployment must have the CEO's buy-in.** Not all CEOs have the personality and drive Jack Welch did when he kicked off Six Sigma at GE. Also, some CEOs may have had a poor introduction to Six Sigma and need to be shown how the wise application of Six Sigma and Lean tools can directly address their business needs. Executive buy-in is no excuse for not advocating a wise deployment of Six Sigma

with Lean and effective performance measures. Advocacy selling may be the first step toward jump-starting a deployment.

11. **Our Six Sigma project benefits are measured in hard savings, and we're having a difficult time determining the cost benefits for design for Six Sigma projects and those that address voice of the customer needs.** Six Sigma deployments that focus only on hard savings can lead to the wrong activities. This organization needs metrics and a deployment system that pulls for the creation of the right activity at the right time.

12. **Our organization is trying to follow a define, measure, analyze, improve, control (DMAIC) roadmap for just-do-it situations.** An organization's culture and metrics should lead to the right tool selection at the right time to improve overall enterprise metrics needs. Not all improvements need be in the form of a formalized DMAIC project. A wisely created Six Sigma deployment system addresses this systematic business improvement need.

13. **Everyone knows which easy to implement change needs to be made, but our Six Sigma coach says we still need to apply regression analysis and design of experiments to the project.** In a wisely created Six Sigma deployment system, it is okay to immediately implement agree-to, low-hanging fruit changes that are thought beneficial to the overall system. High-level control charts can assess whether implemented changes have altered key process output variable levels, while statistical tests can address significance levels. When a significant change is demonstrated, overall comparisons can then be made to the project's overall expectations.

    It is important to avoid analysis paralysis. There is nothing wrong with implementing just-do-it projects and monitoring the success of the implementation.

14. **Our organization is going to hire new BBs and MBBs rather than train people who are already part of the organization.** This is a compelling strategy; however, finding someone who has the right skill set and can fit into a company's culture is easier said than done. It is more preferable to develop those within an organization who have the right BB or MBB personality profile, have already established internal relationships for getting things done and possess the wisdom of organizational understanding.

15. **We are in the process of selecting a Six Sigma provider.** Selecting the best Six Sigma provider for an organization can be confusing. Sales pitches that sound good may not always lead to the best selection. It is important to understand the provider's basic strategy and project execution roadmap before deciding who to go with. Also, organizations need to ensure the Six Sigma organization practices what it preaches.

16. **I want to earn my green belt, BB or MBB certification by taking an e-learning class.** Building a skill set to answer predefined questions is not difficult. The hard part is defining the right problems to solve. These techniques are learned through classroom and coaching sessions where much of the dialogue centers on specific, real-life issues.

17. **I am going to attend a local Six Sigma class to save money.** It is more important to pick the Six Sigma deployment strategy and training that best fulfills an organization's needs.

18. **Our team is going to start deployment in manufacturing and then move to transactional processes.** This strategy can lead to the suboptimization of processes. The first thing an organization should do is assess the big picture and identify any constraints. The initial projects should focus on these constraints, no matter where they come from. For example, if an organization's main constraint is sales, then the first projects should focus on that.

19. **Our organization is going to save money by developing its own Six Sigma course material, where all examples will be tailored to our company. We will also save money by using newly trained BBs and MBBs to conduct these sessions.** Organizations can easily be penny wise and pound foolish when it comes to Six Sigma training material development. It takes years of continual improvements to develop effective Six Sigma material and an associated roadmap.

    Internal BB and MBB resources should initially focus on the creation of an infrastructure that pulls for the creation and completion of projects. Having internal BBs and MBBs conduct initial training detracts from this focus. In course material, it is important for students to learn how to bridge examples to their situations. With this knowledge, they will later be able to understand how to apply articles written about other industries to their situations.

20. **Our team is having difficulty determining which tool to use when.** Tool selection is important but can be confusing to novices. It is important to have and use Six Sigma project execution roadmaps combined with effective coaching. This will help a team choose the right tool for the situation at hand.

21. **In our Six Sigma training, our team was instructed to describe the process capability for all projects using metrics such as sigma quality level, $C_p$, $C_{pk}$, $P_p$ and $P_{pk}$. These metrics are not used in our day-to-day process work.** The terminology used in the execution of projects should use day-to-day metric descriptions that everyone, from the line operators to the CEO, understands. Any confusing and misleading Six Sigma metrics should be avoided (Breyfogle 2003).

Senge (1990) writes that learning disabilities are tragic in children but fatal in organizations. Because of them, few corporations live even half as long as a person—most die before they reach the age of 40. "Learning organizations" defy these odds and overcome learning disabilities to understand threats and recognize new opportunities. If we choose to break a complex system into many elements, the optimization of each element does not typically lead to total system optimization; e.g., optimizing purchasing costs by choosing cheaper parts can impact manufacturing costs through an increase in defect rates.

Organizations need to create a Six Sigma system that avoids optimizing subsystems at the expense of the overall system. With systems thinking we do not lose sight of the big picture. Wise Six Sigma deployments offer a roadmap for changing data into knowledge that leads to new opportunities. Through a wise Six Sigma deployment, organizations can become a learning organization!

## 2.6 Starting a Lean Six Sigma Initiative

The following was reproduced from ISixSigma "Ask the Expert." (Breyfogle 2004a). The IEE system described in this series of volumes addresses all these issues head-on. When I wrote the article, I used the term "Six Sigma;" however, I have found that the same issues described in this article are still prevalent with Lean Six Sigma deployments.

## Starting a Six Sigma Initiative
## Forrest W. Breyfogle III

**Q: What can an organization establishing an Office of Six Sigma/Quality learn from the companies which have been most successful at setting up such offices? How did those companies go about it and with how many people typically?**

Successful implementations of Six Sigma simply view purpose as $E = MC^2$; i.e., organization's **E**xistence/**E**xcellence equates to **M**ore customers and **C**ash. The office title and all efforts need to be directed toward this goal.

Full deployment is often suggested as the best way to initiate Six Sigma; however, it is typically better to grow into an overall system. In the real world, most companies don't have the bandwidth to create an infrastructure that can support a very large instantaneous Six Sigma deployment.

A small but committed force of the right people given the proper authority can do wonders to get things started. Companies which are successfully implement a system that builds upon the lessons learned and successes of others. Approaching initial implementation of Six Sigma through a pilot program has advantages; however, it is essential at the onset that the right people are involved, doing the right things.

Companies that have successfully implemented Six Sigma share some basic characteristics—committed leadership, use of top talent, and a supporting infrastructure. This supporting infrastructure involved creating a formal project selection process, a formal project review process, dedicated resources, and financial system integration.

However, the Six Sigma implementation team can encounter significant resource restrictions. Frequently, a major limitation is that only part-time resources are to be used. This can lead to the training of green belts or black belts, who will have little, if any, infrastructure support. Teaching Six Sigma and Lean tools without the suggested infrastructure will not provide a satisfactory evaluation of Six Sigma. Successful Six Sigma deployments also are a function of infrastructure. Hence, a pilot assessment not only needs one or more Six Sigma projects, but also must include dedicated resources and a formal project review process. To assure this, top-level management should agree at the outset that the pilot program will include a Six Sigma infrastructure modeled after other successful deployments, and will include well-defined measures to judge the pilot project's success.

As part of this pilot program, a Six Sigma steering committee needs to be created to manage the overall Six Sigma process. A Six Sigma director, who is a well-respected change agent within the company, should be chosen. He/she needs to believe in the concept of Six Sigma and have the drive to make Six Sigma successful. The Six Sigma director needs to be a dedicated resource. Exceptions to this rule are justified only for small organizations.

The steering committee should carefully select two to ten employees who will be trained in a public black belt workshop, where each trainee is a dedicated resource for the completion of assigned projects. Regularly scheduled on-site and/or remote coaching sessions also are conducted between four separate weeks of training. A project coaching session also should include the project's champion, team members and process owner.

The sessions could be conducted remotely but the frequency of coaching should emulate a full-scale deployment; e.g., weekly report-outs. Scheduled monthly executive presentation times should be established where the steering committee, sometimes with the aid of teams, presents the Six Sigma pilot status with quantifiable results.

Upon completion of a successful Six Sigma pilot, the scale of the deployment is simply expanded to other areas of the business, incorporating any lessons learned from the pilot session.

**Q: What magnitude of resources/dollars should be committed for the first three years of a Six Sigma initiative? Is there a rule of thumb?**

If Six Sigma costs anything, something is wrong. Six Sigma is an investment upon which organization and personal existence/excellence depends. When Six Sigma is implemented correctly, it should yield a return of at least twenty times the investment in three years.

When setting up an infrastructure, companies can easily become penny-wise and pound-foolish. For example, companies might insist on saving money by using black belts who are part-time. With this approach, projects can fall off the black belt's plate, resulting in project completion difficulties. Companies can achieve a much larger return on investment with dedicated resources. It is important to get the right people involved doing the right things.

In addition, organizations need to view Six Sigma as an implementation methodology that does more than just pick and complete projects. The implementation of Six Sigma must impact how people think and perform their day-to-day work. Wisely applied Six Sigma metrics and improvement strategies can get organizations out of the firefighting mode and into the fire prevention mode. For this to happen, organizations need to measure the right thing and then report it in a fashion that leads to the right activity.

**Q: Does a Six Sigma organization need to be run by a master black belt or a black belt to be effective?**

Making it a requirement that the leader of a Six Sigma organization be or become a master black belt or black belt can lead to the selection of the wrong person.

The leader of a Six Sigma organization needs to be familiar with the tools and methodologies of Six Sigma and Lean. He/she needs:

- To be able to look at the big picture and orchestrate activities that get the right people involved doing the right things.
- To be able to ask the right questions.
- To be able to motivate people so that projects are completed in a timely fashion.
- To understand the overall Six Sigma project execution, step-by-step roadmap and check sheets for project completion. (This understanding is necessary so that he/she can lead practitioners into doing and completing the right tasks in a timely manner.)
- To practice and demonstrate Six Sigma methodologies in his/her day-to-day activities.
- To be able to understand and convey the methodologies and benefits of Six Sigma to others.

A high mark in all the above skill-set categories is hard to find in any one individual. Real-time coaching of a Six Sigma leader who has all the right interpersonal relationship skills can be an effective compromise. With this approach, a Six Sigma coach works with the leader on the improvement of his skills so that he/she asks the right question; e.g., directing a practitioner to the correct Six Sigma or Lean application tool. This approach can be more effective than hiring or reassigning a black belt or master black belt to run the operation.

**Q: Should a new Six Sigma initiative be promoted by upper management? If so, how would you recommend it be communicated?**

Advocacy selling of Six Sigma can originate at any organizational level; however, the effectiveness of such promotion increases when originated at the executive level.

It has been said that the only reason people change is either to seek pleasure or avoid pain, where stimulus from avoiding pain is larger than seeking pleasure. GE employed both of these methods in their rollout of Six Sigma. People had to change or they would be terminated—the painful stick. In addition, a system was set up so that people who accomplished tangible results with Six Sigma were rewarded—the carrot. Similarly, in the $E=MC^2$ model, the letter $E$ represented Existence (i.e., the stick) and/or Excellence (i.e., the carrot).

The creation of a burning platform—a visible crisis—is an effective approach to convey the importance of instituting systematic improvements to the enterprise. The necessity of change should be presented in such a way that it is not only easy to understand but also readily internalized. The presentation should show that when there is an alignment of Six Sigma work with business needs and/or operational metrics both existence and bottom-line excellence could be achieved.

## 2.7 Exercises

1. From the article in Section 2.5, "Common Six Sigma Problems (and What To Do About Them)," comment on five points that you think could have the biggest impact in a Six Sigma deployment. (Note: These issues are directly addressed with an IEE deployment, as described later in this volume.)

2. From the article in Section 2.6, "Starting a Six Sigma Initiative," comment on the following (Note: These issues are directly addressed with an IEE deployment, as described later in this volume):
   a. Describe what companies should focus on when implementing Six Sigma.
   b. Describe an alternative to a full Six Sigma deployment and why this strategy should be considered.
   c. Describe the basic characteristics of companies that have successfully implemented Six Sigma.
   d. State how much Six Sigma should cost.
   e. Give an example of how companies can become penny wise and pound foolish.
   f. Describe the characteristics of a leader of Six Sigma in an organization.
   g. Describe an effective approach to convey the importance of implementing Six Sigma.

# 3

# Scorecards, Dashboards, Performance Metrics, and Strategic Plans

In the previous chapter, the traditional scope description for Six Sigma and Lean Six Sigma deployments made no mention of defining/reporting enterprise performance measurements, describing enterprise value-chain activities, and creating strategic plans. IEE addresses these issues in addition to aligning improvement projects to the true overall business and metric improvement needs.

This chapter describes traditional performance metrics and the alignment of metrics to strategic objectives. We'll highlight problems with these traditional techniques and describe improved methodology. Future chapters provide the details for creating the described enhanced performance measurement and improvement system.

It is said that what we measure is what we get. However, we need to be careful of what we ask for. Some questions for thought:

1. Do your metrics promote the right kind of behavior?
2. Does your presentation and reward plan that surrounds your metrics lead to the right kind of behavior?

I will now address these issues.

First, let's address creating metrics that lead to the right kind of behavior. To illustrate this, let's consider a call center's duration-of-hold-time metric. This metric makes good sense relative to assessing customer satisfaction; i.e., long hold times would probably correlate to customer dissatisfaction. However, this metric, in isolation, can drive the wrong behaviors unless safeguards are implemented to prevent abuse.

To illustrate this point, consider how operators can strive to achieve this targeted metric objective during understaffed peak call periods. For this situation, operators might simply answer the phone within the allotted time period, ask the question, "Can you hold, please?", and then quickly place the caller back on hold for a much longer period of time.

It is not bad that the operator answered the phone and responded, asking that the caller wait longer; however, this type of action should not simply be the result of wanting to make the overall duration-of-hold-time metric look good. Relative to recording the actual hold time for future customer-satisfaction analyses, it would seem better to capture the total hold time from initial connection until the incoming caller is connected to the appropriate person. In addition, management should monitor hold time as a staffing requirement, but this should not be a metric that operators are held accountable for maintaining, since this can lead to the wrong activities.

Secondly, we need data presentation and assessment formats that lead to the right kind of behavior with appropriate rewards systems in place that encourage this behavior. If an organization is measured solely on the meeting of goals, which might be arbitrary, bad things can occur. For example, as mentioned before, Krispy Kreme shipped donuts that executives knew would be returned so that they would meet quarterly targeted objectives (Lloyd 2005). Additionally Enron and, more recently, Dell made some decisions that enabled them to meet quarterly objectives but were poor in the long run. According to press reports, the senior management of Dell regularly falsified quarterly returns from 2003 through 2006 to create the appearance that the company had met sales goals (Richtel 2007).

In my opinion, data presentation and interpretation are not given adequate consideration. This chapter will present some traditional presentation formats. We will then collectively discuss these formats and offer an alternative reporting format that can lead to significantly improved actions from these metrics.

# 3.1   Performance Metrics Can Stimulate the Wrong Behavior

The book *Lean Thinking* (Womack and Jones 1996) describes companies that successfully implemented the Toyota Production System. Two companies featured in this book were Wiremold Company and Lantech, Inc. Two executives from these companies, Cunningham and Fiume (2003), later wrote *Real Numbers: Management Accounting in a Lean Organization.*

When *Real Numbers* was published, Jean Cunningham was chief financial officer and vice president of Company Services for Lantech, Inc., and was a leader in the company's transformation to Lean. Orest Fiume had retired as vice president of Finance and Administration and director of Wiremold Company.

These financial executives from two highly regarded companies make many insightful statements regarding existing accounting departments and systems. I highly recommend this book and periodically will reference statements from it. Readers need to keep in mind that these statements are from financial executives in their fields of expertise.

Cunningham and Fiume (2003) make the following points:

* Information must ... be easily understood and actionable. Over the years, however, managers have been forced to understand their own departments, not in terms of income and cost, but as variances and percentages that bear little relationship to reality; i.e., where variances mean the differences between what is expected and what actually occurs.
* Those same managers learned that variances could be nudged up or down to present a better picture of the operation—for instance, by using labor hours to make a million pieces of plastic that were not actually needed, even if that meant damaging the real business interests.
* Complex accounting created a kind of funhouse mirror, where a skinny man could look fat by simply shifting his position.

> Complex accounting created a kind of funhouse mirror, where a skinny man could look fat by simply shifting his position.

It is not uncommon for newspaper articles to make statements similar to the following (Petruno 2006):

There is a sinking feeling among technology stock investors this summer—a feeling of history repeating.

At the start of 2002, the bear market of that era had been raging for nearly two years. Then came a wave of corporate scandals that showed the Enron Corp. debacle of late 2001 was no one-off affair.

As shares of Tyco International Ltd., Adelphia Communications Corp. and WorldCom Inc. collapsed in the first half of 2002 amid allegations of massive financial fraud by executives, demoralized investors began wondering whether they could trust any number on balance sheets and income statements.

The scandals helped fuel a last burst of panicked selling, driving down the Standard & Poor's 500 index nearly 30 percent in the first nine months of 2002 and the Nasdaq composite index by 40 percent.

Now, investors' faith in corporate accounting again is under siege. Over the past few months more than sixty-five companies, most of them technology companies, have disclosed that they were under scrutiny or investigation by federal authorities for possibly manipulating executives' stock option grants to boost the potential payoffs.

In an another article, "CEO firings at a record pace so far this year" (Kelly 2006), it is stated that "chiefs are being pushed out the door as directors abandon their laissez-faire approach to governance following the prosecutions at Enron Corp., WorldCom, Inc. and other companies."

These high-profile illustrations highlight only the tip of the iceberg relative to how organizational metric reporting can lead to the wrong behaviors. Organizations need a leadership system to overcome a "laissez-faire approach to governance." I will later describe how the no-nonsense IEE approach addresses these issues.

The next section will describe characteristics of a good metric. Sections 3.3, 3.6, and 3.7 will then illustrate how commonly used organizational internal functional metric tracking and reporting can stimulate the wrong behavior throughout the organization.

## 3.2   Characteristics of a Good Metric

We have all heard the clichés:

- You get what you measure.
- What you measure is what you get.
- If you don't measure it, you can't manage it.

- Tell me how I'm going to be measured and I'll tell you how I'll perform.
- You cannot improve what you can't measure.
- Garbage in, garbage out.
- If you don't measure it, it's just a hobby.

These clichés are true! Measurements need to convey the voice of the process, which stimulate the most appropriate behavior. Measurements need to provide an unbiased process performance assessment. When process output performance is not accurately seen and reported relative to a desired result, there is not much hope for making improvements. Generic measures for any process are quality, cost, and delivery. Most processes need a balance measurement set to prevent optimizing one metric at the expense of overall process health. Metrics can also drive the wrong behavior if conducted in isolation from the overall enterprise needs. When appropriate, the addition of a people measure assures balance between task and people management.

As an illustration, consider the last customer-satisfaction survey form that you received. Do you think that a summary of responses from this survey truly provides an accurate assessment of what you experienced in your purchase process? My guess is that your response is no. It seems that often surveys are conducted so that the responses will be satisfactory but don't truly provide insight into what actually happens in a process.

Writing an effective survey and then evaluating the responses is not easy. What we would like to receive from a survey is an honest picture of what is currently happening in the process, along with providing improvement direction. A comment section in a hotel guest survey might provide insight to a specific actionable issue or improvement possibility.

> COMMON CAUSE: natural or random variation that is inherent in a process or its inputs.

Good metrics provide decision-making insight that leads into the most appropriate conclusion and action or nonaction. The objective is the creation of an entity that is measurable, auditable, sustainable, and consistent. Effective and reliable metrics require the following characteristics:

- Business alignment: Metrics consume resources for both data collection and analyses. Metrics need to provide insight to business performance, its issues, and its needs. Metrics surrounding your business alignment can be found by looking at your value chain.

- Honest assessment: Creating metrics so that the performance of someone or an organization will appear good has no value and can be detrimental to the organization. Metrics need to be able to provide an honest assessment, whether good, bad, or ugly.
- Consistency: Identified components in any metric need to be defined at the outset and remain constant. Criteria and calculations need to be consistent with respect to time.
- Repeatability and reproducibility: Measurements should have little or no subjectivity. We would like for a recorded measurement response to have little or no dependence on who and when someone recorded the response.

> SPECIAL CAUSE: Variation in a process from a cause that is not an inherent part of the current process or its inputs.

- Actionability: Often measures are created for the sake of measuring, without any thought as to what would be done if the metric were lower or higher. Include only those metrics that you will act on; that is, either remove a degradation problem or hold the gain. When the metrics response is unsatisfactory, organizations need to be prepared to conduct root-cause analysis and corrective or preventive actions.
- Time-series tracking: Metrics should be captured in time-series format, not as a snapshot of a point-in-time activity. Time-series tracking can describe trends and separate special-cause from common-cause variability in predictable processes.

> PREDICTABLE PROCESS: A stable, controlled process where variation in outputs is only caused by natural or random variation in the inputs or in the process itself.

- Predictability: A predictability statement should be made when time-series tracking indicates that a process is predictable.
- Peer comparability: In addition to internal performance measurements, benefits are achieved when comparisons can be made between peer groups in another business or company.

A good peer comparison provides additional analysis opportunities, which can identify improvement possibilities.

Metric utilization requires commitment and resource allotments; hence, it is important to do it right. When organizations strive to become more metric-driven, it is important to avoid metric-design and metric-usage errors. Common mistakes include the following:

- Creating metrics for the sake of metrics. Lloyd S. Nelson, director of Statistical Methods for the Nashua Corporation, stated: "The most important figures needed for management of any organization are unknown or unknowable;" Deming 1986).
- Formulating too many metrics, resulting in no actions.
- Lacking metric follow-up.
- Describing metrics that do not result in the intended action.
- Creating metrics that can have subjective manipulation.

If not exercised effectively, metrics can become a dark force where good energy is absorbed by bad stuff—a black hole where good resources are lost.

## 3.3   Traditional Scorecards, Dashboards, and Performance Metrics Reporting

A scorecard helps manage an organization's performance through the optimization and alignment of organizational units, business processes, and individuals. A scorecard can also provide goals and targets, helping individuals understand their organizational contribution. Scorecards can span the operational, tactical, and strategic business aspects and decisions of any business. A dashboard displays information so that an enterprise can be run effectively. A dashboard organizes and presents information in a format that is easy to read and interpret.

A performance metric is a performance-related measurement of activity or resource utilization. Year-to-date metric statements are one form of performance metric reporting, while other formats involve tables or charts.

Performance-measure report-out formats can have a dramatic influence on behaviors. Many situations can have numerous report-out options. Much unproductive work can be generated if the best scorecard/dashboard metric is not chosen.

> Performance-measure report-out formats can have a dramatic influence on behaviors. Many situations can have numerous report-out options.

This section describes some frequently used performance metrics and scorecard/dashboard reporting formats, which can create detrimental organizational behavior. Later sections of this chapter will introduce an alternative IEE scorecard/dashboard performance-measurement system that allows organizational enterprise management systems to react more quickly to favorable or unfavorable circumstances.

Table 3.1 exemplifies a commonly used performance measure report-out. This report format has calendar boundaries that reflect only quarterly and annual results. This type of chart does not present response data as though it were a result of internal processes that inherently have variability. In addition, this chart cannot identify trends, detect unusual events in a timely fashion, or provide a prediction statement.

Is there a consistent message presented in Table 3.1? Invariably you will get stories that cannot be verified in the chart.

> Look at the third line. You might hear something like "We staffed up in 2002 to prepare for annexations, but they did not happen as quickly as expected. This drove our cost per call up. As we annexed in 2003, you can see it coming down. We are on track."

It may be a true story, but is it the whole cause as it is represented? It is a good bet that the presenter will describe many of the ups and downs in the table in a story format, where in reality much of this motion is the result of common-cause variability. Have you seen tables like this before?

This form of performance reporting and of other year-to-date metric statements typically leads to *stories*. This means that someone presenting this scorecard/dashboard will typically give an explanation for the up-and-down movements of the previous quarter or year. This is not dissimilar to a nightly stock market

**Table 3.1** Traditional Performance Measures: Tabular Reporting (Austin 2004).

| Performance Measure | FY 2001 Actual | FY 2002 Actual | FY 2003 Actual | FY 2003 Amended | FY 2004 Amended |
|---|---|---|---|---|---|
| Percentage of customers satisfied with dispatch staff | 99.99% | 100% | 99.99% | 98% | 98% |
| Percentage of priority one calls dispatched to field crews within 80 minutes of receipt | 99.99% | 99% | 99.99% | 95% | 95% |
| Labor cost per customer call taken in Dispatch Operations | $4.20 | $5.31 | $5.09 | $4.88 | $5.09 |
| Number of calls taken through Dispatch Operations | 62,054 | 59,828 | 63,046 | 60,000 | 60,000 |
| Number of priority one calls dispatched to field crews | 5,797 | 4,828 | 6,686 | 5,000 | 6,500 |
| Number of work orders and component parts (segments) created in database | 8,226 | 4,724 | 7,742 | 5,500 | 6,700 |

report of the previous day's activity, where the television or radio reporter gives a specific reason for even small market movements. This form of reporting provides little, if any, value when it comes to making business decisions.

> This form of performance reporting and of other year-to-date metric statements typically leads to *stories.*

Whether in a business performance measure or a stock market report, these reported causal events may or may not have affected the output. The individual measurement value may cause an alarm that triggers some corrective action, or the numbers may be viewed only as a simple report. In either case, most measurement variability is typically the result of the system's common-cause variations.

An alternative to table presentations for a data-driven company is chart presentations. For example, user guidelines from QuickBase (2006) state: "What information do you want to show? This is always the first question you must ask yourself when creating a chart. For example, if you want to show what percentage each salesperson contributes to the bottom line, try a pie chart, which is great for showing how parts relate to a whole. Or maybe you'd prefer to show how each salesperson has been doing over the course of the year. In that case, a line chart might work best. That way you could plot each person's sales numbers through time and see who is improving."

This frequently followed charting advice could lead to a Figure 3.1 report-out. Other frequent report-out formats for this type of data are shown in Figures 3.2 and 3.3.

Similar to summarizing data through a table, the chart report formats in Figures 3.1–3.3 typically lead to *stories* about the past. The chart presentation format will dictate the presented

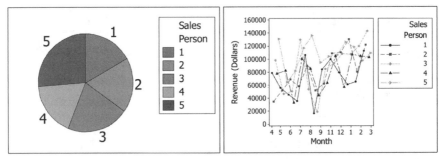

**Figure 3.1:** Salesperson monthly revenue for the last twelve months presented as a pie chart and line chart.

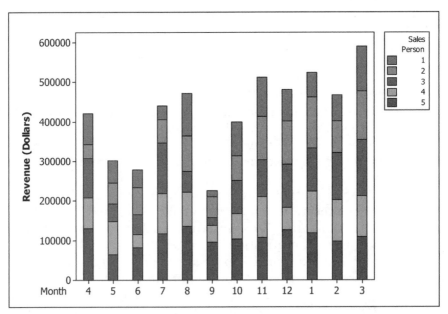

**Figure 3.2:** Salesperson monthly revenue for last twelve months presented as a stacked bar chart.

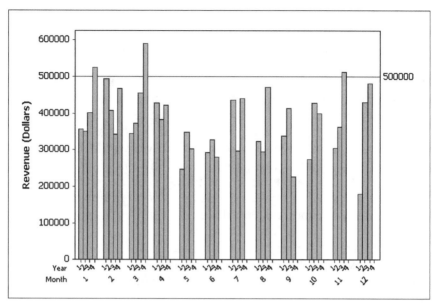

**Figure 3.3:** Year-to-year monthly revenue chart tracking against a mean monthly goal of $500,000. Years are designated as 0, 1, 2, and 3; eg., 0 = 2000 and 1 = 2001. The figure indicates that the data were compiled at the end of March, since there are four bars for months of: 1 = Jan., 2 = Feb., and 3 = Mar.

*story* type. For example, the calendar boundaries in the bar-chart reporting format in Figure 3.3 will surely lead to adjacent-month and previous year-month comparisons. This type of chart, like the other charts, can be difficult to interpret. This interpretation difficulty often leads to inconsistencies and erroneous conclusions in the stories generated by different presenters.

Consider which interests us the most, the past or the future? Most often the response to this question is "the future." Reporting individual up-and-down historical movement or arbitrary time-based comparisons does not provide insight to future process-output expectations, assuming that the process experiences no dramatic positive or negative change. However, if we could somehow estimate the future and didn't like the resulting prediction, we gain insight to improvement focus opportunities; that is, the metric improvement needs pull for creating a process-improvement project.

Reporting individual up-and-down historical movement or arbitrary time-based comparisons does not provide insight to future process-output expectations.

Report charts need to lead to activities that are beneficial to the organization. Traditional tabular and chart reporting leads to *stories* about the past without any formal system that describes what might be expected in the future. Later I will discuss an IEE alternative data-reporting system that provides increased insight as to where improvement efforts would be most beneficial.

Consider how accurate is this year-based reporting if something changed during the year? For example, if there was a fundamental sales process change in August, then we would be including old information with the latest information when examining annualized data in a pie chart. Wouldn't it be better to first identify if and when a change occurred and then either compare new to old process responses, or describe what is happening most recently?

Later in this chapter, I will discuss an IEE alternative data-reporting system that provides increased insight to where improvement efforts would be most beneficial. Example 9.3 revisits this data using an IEE analysis approach.

## 3.4   Strategic Planning

Business leaders must have a strategy to meet their objectives. Without a strategy, time and resources can be wasted on piecemeal, disparate activities. Without a strategy, mid-level managers will fill the void with their interpretation of what the business should be doing, typically resulting in a disjointed set of activities. However, "strategy has become a catchall term used to mean whatever one wants it to mean. Executives now talk about their "service strategy," their "branding strategy," their "acquisition strategy," or whatever kind of strategy that is on their mind at a particular moment" (Hambrick and Fredrickson 2001).

Consider the company strategy in Figure 3.4, which typifies other companies' strategies. An organization can spend much time creating such a strategic listing; however, it can often have difficulty interpreting what it should do relative to addressing the passed-down strategy.

In addition, what data analyses were conducted ahead of time that influenced the creation of the corporate strategy? Even if there were good pre-strategy-build data analyses, can the direction of the entire company rest on a few statements, which can change when there is leadership change?

Foxconn's objective is to maintain its position as one of the leading manufacturers of connectors, PC enclosures, and other precision components, and to successfully develop products and market its products for use in network communication and consumer electronic products. A number of strategies have been developed to attain this objective:

**Develop strategic relationship with industry leaders** — By working closely with top-tier PC and IC companies, Foxconn is able to predict market trends accurately and introduce new products ahead of its competitors.

**Focus on the development of global logistic capabilities** — This enables Foxconn to respond quickly and efficiently to the customer's requirements around the world.

**Expansion of production capacity** — Foxconn currently has production facilities in Asia, Europe, and the United States. Expanding its existing production capacity increases economics of scale.

**Achieve further vertical integration** — Further integration of the production process allows Foxconn to exercise better control over the quality of its products.

**Maintain technologically advanced and flexible production capabilities** — This increases Foxconn's competitiveness relative to its peers and allows it to stay one step ahead of the opposition.

**New products** — Foxconn will leverage off its manufacturing expertise and continue to move tirelessly into new areas of related business.

**Figure 3.4:** Corporate strategy example (Foxconn 2006).

Figure 4.7 will describe an E-DMAIC alternative that leads to specific actionable items with goals. In this process, create strategies is step 5, not step 1 or 2. An E-DMAIC process for strategy development is described in Sections 8.7 and 12.3. Figure 12.1 illustrates a drill-down from organization goals through strategies to specific actionable projects.

## 3.5   Hoshin Kanri

This section will introduce hoshin kanri concepts. Other sections of this volume will integrate some of the methodologies into the E-DMAIC roadmap.

In Japanese hoshin mean direction and shining needle (i.e., compass), while kanri means management. *Hoshin kanri* means management and control of the organization's direction needle, or focus. Hoshin kanri is a blending of the elements of management by objectives (MBO; Drucker 1954) and the Deming cycle of plan-do-check-act (PDCA). A crucial job of the entire hoshin kanri decision-making theory is consistency and compatibility across all levels of management.

Many companies that are implementing Lean or Lean Six Sigma are also using hoshin kanri; however, implementations can vary considerably. This section provides hoshin kanri highlights, as described by Babich (2005) and Jackson (2006). *An IEE alternative will be discussed later.*

Babich (2005) describes how hoshin kanri is a system of forms and rules that provide structure for the planning process. Hoshin kanri separates the organizational plan into two parts: business fundamentals and breakthroughs. The five elements of a complete hoshin kanri plan are business fundamentals plan, long-range plan, annual plan, review tables, and abnormality tables.

In hoshin kanri, the organization's mission should be deployed in every operational unit. Missions are generally deployed along organizational lines. A mission deployment divides the statements into lower-level essential activities to achieve the mission. When deploying an activity down one level, the activity becomes that level's mission, which can then have further segmented activities. Back and forth mission-development discussions, called catchball, involve give-and-take until consensus is reached. Each mission statement leads to the creation of a business-fundamental planning table that contains the mission, key activities, owners, and performance measures with action limits. Table 3.2 is an example of a corporate business-fundamentals planning table.

Each activity in a business-fundamentals planning table typically has two to four performance measures (PMs) with action limits, where multiple measures are used to prevent optimizing one measure at the expense of the overall process health. The essence of the business-fundamentals planning table is the maintenance of performance. Tactical decisions are to be captured in the business-fundamentals planning table.

The essence of breakthrough planning is significant improvement. Strategic decision making involves formulating the right question for the development of the long-range plan (strategic plan). Long-range planning is documented in the hoshin kanri planning table. Hoshin kanri is not to be used to figure out what to do. Hoshin kanri is a plan-implementation process that picks up where other planning processes stop. Hoshin kanri is used to help organizations deploy and execute what they want to do.

Deliverables are the tangible results of job or task completion. Gantt charts contain plots of the expected start date and completion date for each deliverable. In hoshin kanri, deliverables are associated with breakthrough plans. Breakthrough plans are formulated from the organization's vision of the future. Organizational vision translation into a long-range plan encompasses five, ten, or even twenty years, has few year-to-year changes, and has limited deployment with wide communication. The hoshin kanri annual plan table has specific long-range plan steps that are to

**Table 3.2** Hoshin Kanri Business-Fundamentals Planning Table, Example (Babich 2005). Reprinted With Permission From Total Quality Engineering, Inc.

| Location: Rockford International | Time Period: FY2005 |
|---|---|
| **Prepared By:** Ira M. Cool | **Date:** 12/10/2004 |

| **Situation:** Rockford International (RI) is a small organization supplying hardware for the building industry. Rockford specializes in designing, manufacturing, and selling hinges for cabinet doors. RI employs 130 people and has revenues of $10M. Its primary customers are Southern California custom cabinetmakers. RI's business is very volatile; it is difficult to predict when its next contract will be. When it does get a contract, however, the company wants to move very fast and can't wait for parts. Therefore, RI builds and stocks a wide variety of hinges and associated fasteners and is capable of delivering product within one day of the order. In the rare event when product is defective, RI commits to replacing the product the same day. By virtue of excellent delivery, RI charges premium prices for its products. |
|---|

| **Mission, based on situation:** | |
|---|---|
| **Mission (Owner)** | **PMs (Action Limits)** |
| Improve the responsiveness of Southern California custom cabinetmakers by providing hinges and fasteners with one day turnaround time. (Ira) | 1. % orders filled same day (<95%)<br>2. Revenue (<$500K/mo)<br>3. Profit (<6%)<br>4. Cust Sat (<95%) |

| **Key Activities necessary to achieve Mission:** | |
|---|---|
| **Activity (Owner)** | **PMs (Action Limits)** |
| **1.** Maintain Rockford International customer satisfaction by consistently shipping quality products within one day of receiving an order. (Chris) | 1. Line item fill rate (< 95%)<br>2. Inventory (>2 mo. supply)<br>3. Product returns (>0.5%)<br>4. Units/assembler (<150K) |
| **2.** Manage Rockford International's revenue stream by supporting current customers and attracting new customers. (Bob) | 1. Orders (<80% of forecast)<br>2. Order growth (<10%/yr)<br>3. Customer calls (>20/mo)<br>4. Sales cost (>10% of rev$) |
| **3.** Fuel Rockford International's growth by developing new products, and assure customer satisfaction by providing technical support for current products. (Jim) | 1. # stop ship (>0)<br>2. # new products introduced per year (>10)<br>3. R&D cost (>10% rev$) |
| **4.** Assure Rockford International's profitability by providing information so that sound business decisions can be made. (Janet) | 1. Profit (<target/mo)<br>2. acct receivable (>45 days)<br>3. Acct payable (>45 days)<br>4. Audit score (<95%) |
| **5.** Assure Rockford International's productivity by attracting, retaining, and training exceptional people, and assure employee satisfaction by providing a safe, comfortable, equitable, and professional working environment. (Sandy) | 1. # voluntary terminations (>2/mo)<br>2. # complaints (>5/mo)<br>3. Lost work hours (>5%) |

be accomplished the current year, keep in mind that critical-area deployment can significantly change from year to year.

The hoshin kanri form for the development and deployment of both long-range and annual plans (Table 3.3) is similar to the business-fundamentals plan table. Primary differences are the renaming of the form as Hoshin Kanri (long-range or annual) Planning Table and the replacement of the words "Mission" with "Objective," "Activities" with "Strategies," and "Action Limits" with "Goals."

**Table 3.3** Hoshin Kanri Annual Planning Table, Example (Babich 2005). Reprinted With Permission From Total Quality Engineering, Inc.

| Location: Rockford International | Time Period: FY2005 |
|---|---|
| Prepared By: Ira M. Cool | Date: 12/10/2004 |

**Situation:** For Rockford International to achieve its long-range vision, it must expand its customer base beyond Southern California. Market research has shown that new home starts are growing faster in Spain than anywhere else in the world. Spanish contractors buy almost all of their supplies from one distributor, El Partes. El Partes only distributes material, which is at least 30% Spanish labor. The company has a reputation for distributing only high quality parts at reasonable prices. It does, however, expect large discounts from its suppliers. The Spanish government wants to encourage business and will provide tax breaks and other special incentives. If RI could distribute its parts through El Partes, RI revenue could triple in 2006 with double-digit profit. To win the El Partes contract, RI will need to establish an assembly operation in Spain, with some locally sourced material. It will also need to improve product quality and reduce operating cost.

**Key Objective, based on situation:**

| Objective (Owner) | PMs (Goals) |
|---|---|
| Establish a production facility in Barcelona Spain and have RI products distributed by El Partes. | 1. Assembly plan operational (Q3, 05) <br> 2. El Partes contract signed (Q4, 05) <br> 3. Ship first hinge (1/1/06) <br> 4. Overall project cost (<$750K) |

**Key Strategies necessary to achieve Objective:**

| Strategy (Owner) | PMs (Goals) |
|---|---|
| **1.** Work with Spanish government to secure all necessary licenses and agreements. (Bob) | 1. License obtained (Q1, 05) <br> 2. Apply for Spanish grant (Q2, 05) |
| **2.** Begin assembly operation in Spain. (Chris) | 1. Building leased (Q2, 05) <br> 2. Employees hired and trained (Q3, 05) <br> 3. Local supplier selected (Q3, 05) |
| **3.** Improve the quality and reliability of the 15009 hinge family. (Jim) | 1. Quality (0.1% returns) <br> 2. Mean Time Between Failures - MTBF (1 M hrs) <br> 3. Cost (% current cost) <br> 4. New prod Intro (Q4,05) |
| **4.** Improve the cost structure of the RI business operations. (Ira-Staff) | 1. R&D Costs (<9% rev$) <br> 2. Sales Cost (<8% rev$) <br> 3. Mfg Cost (<30% rev$) <br> 4. Overhead Cost (<3% rev$) |

In both long-range and annual hoshin kanri breakthrough plans, performance improvement is achieved through successful deliverables or tasks. Hoshin kanri annual plans should have only three or four strategies for each objective.

Similar to the business-fundamentals planning table, there is a cascading of strategies throughout the organization; that is, top-level to mid-level to project level. Each objective leads to the creation of a strategy that becomes the objective for the strategy creation for the next level down. This continues until specific tasks are identified and laid out in a Gantt chart.

Up to this point, discussion has focused on the planning portion of Deming's PDCA process. The Do step of PDCA can involve steps of the P-DMAIC, or design for Six Sigma *project*-execution roadmap. The Check and Act steps are hoshin kanri periodic reviews. Monthly and annual reviews can be documented in a periodic review table summary or annual plan summary review.

Hoshin kanri can become a paperwork jungle if care is not exercised. A department's hoshin kanri plan should typically consist of fewer than twelve pages: one page for business fundamentals, one page for the organization's long-range plan, one to five pages for the department's portion of the annual plan, and four quarterly review summaries.

As noted earlier, hoshin kanri has a form-based structure. Jackson (2006) includes thirty-six files, most of which are hoshin kanri forms. Table 3.4 describes the four teams and seven PDCA cycles of hoshin kanri experiments, which are nested inside each other. Experiments in this context are different from experiments described later in this volume. In this context, plans become experiments, where all managers and employees conduct tests of hypothesized strategies, under standardized work control conditions.

A unique suite of documents is sometimes used to support strategic planning and problems. These documents are called A3s because in Japan they are printed on one side of European A3 paper, which is equivalent to American tabloid paper (11 × 17 in.).

Typically, nine good-project critical elements are included in these forms. These nine elements are theme (problem or challenge), problem statement, target statement (project scope), scientific process of investigation (e.g., PDCA), systematic analysis (why-why diagram or 5 whys, cost benefit, cause-and-effect diagram, design of experiments, etc.), proposed solution, implementation timeline, graphical illustrations, and date and reporting unit or owner at the bottom of the form. Example A3s are intelligent report, X-matrix, team charter, status report, and problem report, where an X-matrix is used in the plan phase of the hoshin kanri process. An X-matrix can be used to bundle several A3s together for the exploration of interdependencies. Hoshin kanri tools are useful for checking market conditions as part of the *enterprise process* DMAIC, or E-DMAIC, process.

As with most things, hoshin kanri implementation has pluses and minuses. Consider the following issues that should be addressed in an implementation:

**Table 3.4** Hoshin Kanri Four Teams and Seven Experiments (Jackson 2006). Reproduced with permission. Originally published as *Hoshin Kanri for the Lean Enterprise: Developing Competitive Capabilities and Managing* by Thomas L. Jackson. Copyright © 2006 Productivity Press, an imprint of Taylor and Francis Group, an Informa Business, www.ProductivityPress.com

| 4 Teams | | 7 Experiments | | |
|---|---|---|---|---|
| **1** | Hoshin Team | **1** | Long-term strategy | A general plan to action that aims over a very long period of time -- 5 to 100 years -- to make major changes or adjustments in the mission and/or vision of the business. |
| | | **2** | Mid-term strategy | A partially-complete plan of action including financial targets and measures of process improvement that aims over 3 to 5 years to develop capabilities and align the trajectory of business operations with the long-term strategy. |
| | | **3** | Annual hoshin | A highly concrete plan of action that aims over the next 6 to 18 months to develop competitive capabilities and align the trajectory of business operations in accordance with the midterm strategy. |
| **2** | Tactical Teams | **4** | Tactics | Concrete initatives of 6 to 18 months, defined by the annual hoshin, undertaken to develop specific new capabilities by applying new technologies and methodologies to general business processes. |
| **3** | Operational Teams | **5** | Operations | Concrete projects of 3 to 6 months, defined by the annual hoshin, undertaken to apply new technologies and methodologies to standardized processes of specific business functions. |
| **4** | Action Team | **6** | Kaikaku | Concrete projects of 1 week to 3 months, usually defined after the deployment of the annual hoshin, undertaken to apply new tools and techniques in standardized daily work. |
| | | **7** | Kaizen | Problem-solving in more or less real time to address defects, errors, and abnormalities that arise in the course of standardized daily work, as well as improvements resulting from employee suggestions. |

- Execution possibilities for strategies such as those shown in Table 3.4 are very team dependent and can lead to detrimental activities for the enterprise as a whole. Sections 4.1 and 4.4 provide alternative thoughts.
- The driver and infrastructure of hoshin kanri center on the cascading of executive management's strategies throughout the organization. The direction of work activity could significantly change when there is a significant change in executive leadership or leadership direction. The time could be lengthy and resource needs could be large to incorporate executive direction change into an enterprise hoshin kanri system.
- Missions and strategies are to cascade throughout the organization chart. An organizational change, company purchase, or company spin-off that redirects focus could lead to much confusion and frustration.
- For a given situation, there can be many ways to analyze data. A roadmap is needed for these analyses; for example, analyze phase of P-DMAIC.
- Table listings for performance-measure action limits can lead to the wrong activity. This format for action-limit establishment does not systematically address process shift and other situations that can be addressed only through charting. Performance-measure action limits set without examining a 30,000-foot-level control chart can lead to firefighting.

These issues are overcome when the concepts of hoshin kanri are blended within an IEE infrastructure. Hoshin kanri techniques can be integrated into the E-DMAIC roadmap to systematically address not only the creation of projects but also day-to-day business activities.

## 3.6   The Balanced Scorecard

The balanced scorecard, as presented by Kaplan and Norton (1992), tracks the business in the areas of financial, customer, internal processes, and learning and growth. In this model, each area is to address one of the following questions:

- Financial: To succeed financially, how should we appear to our shareholders?
- Customer: To achieve our vision, how should we appear to our customers?

- Internal business process: To satisfy our shareholders and customers, what business processes must we excel at?
- Learning and growth: To achieve our vision, how will we sustain our ability to change and improve?

Figure 3.5 illustrates how these metrics are to align with the business vision and strategy. Each category is to have objectives, measures, targets, and initiatives.

Scorecard balance is important because if you don't have balance you could be giving one metric more focus than another, which can lead to problems. For example, when focus is given to only on-time delivery, product quality could suffer dramatically to meet ship dates. However care needs to be given in how this balanced is achieved. A natural balance is much more powerful than forcing balance through the organizational chart using a scorecard structure of financial, customer, internal business process, and learning and growth that may not be directly appropriate to all business areas. In addition, a scorecard structure that is closely tied to the organization chart has an additional disadvantage in that it will need to be changed whenever significant reorganizations occur.

In IEE, natural scorecard balance is achieved throughout the business via the enterprise value chain (see Figure 7.1), noting that overall learning and growth would typically be assigned to HR but, when appropriate, can also be assigned to other functional performance. Metrics are assigned an owner who is accountable for the metric's performance. These metrics can be cascaded downward to lower organization functions, where these

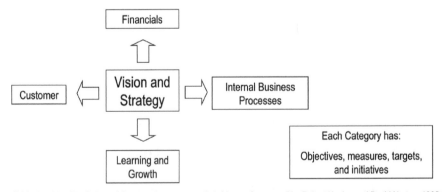

Original article: "The Balanced Scorecard – measures that drive performance," by Robert Kaplan and David Norton, 1992

**Figure 3.5:** Traditional performance measures: the balanced scorecard.

metrics also are assigned owners who have performance accountability. With this IEE system whenever there is an organizational change the basic value-chain metrics will not change, only the ownership.

When creating these metrics it is not only important to determine *what to measure* but it is also very important to focus on the *how to report* so that this metric performance tracking leads to the most appropriate action, which maybe to do nothing. Figure 3.5 illustrates how the balanced scorecard (Kaplan and Norton 1992) system is to have a created vision and strategy from which functional objectives, measures, targets, and initiatives are to be cascaded throughout the organization chart. I will describe this system and then note some methodology shortcomings which are overcome by an IEE implementation.

Collins (2001) describes in *Good to Great* a level five leader as someone who is great while leading an organization and whose affect remains after the person is no longer affiliated with the organization. I describe the level-five-leader-created legacy as being a *Level Five System.*

In my workshops, I often ask, Do you think your organization's strategy would change if there were different leadership? A vast majority give a positive response to this question. Because of this, it seems to me that it would be very difficult for an organization to create a Level Five System when the primary guiding light for the organization is its strategy, which can change with new leadership.

> It seems to me that it would be very difficult for an organization to create a level five system when the primary guiding light for the organization is its strategy, which can change with new leadership.

I don't mean to imply that organizational strategies are bad, but I do believe that strategies created without structurally evaluating the overall organizational value chain and its metrics can lead to unhealthy behavior. To illustrate this, consider the following example.

Parameters for a global service corporation dashboard were defined by the following underlying strategic executive goals for the year:

Grow revenue 25 percent per year, earn minimum of 20 percent net profit, achieve 60 percent of revenue with repeat customers, balance regional growth, fill open positions corresponding with growth, ensure that all employees are competent and high performers, realize projects within time and cost targets, limit ratio of overhead to productive time to 20 percent, and satisfy customers 100 percent.

These objectives, measures, targets, and initiatives were then set up to be monitored, as shown in Figure 3.6, where each metric is to have an owner. Color-coding is used to help clearly identify actual performance versus targets and forecasts. The exclamation marks indicate red flags, where objectives are not being met and attention is needed.

These executive dashboard metrics can then be drilled down further, as shown in Figure 3.7. Would you like to sign up to own this metric and its achievement? The strategic objectives described previously set a customer-satisfaction metric goal of 100 percent. Not a bad target; however, meeting this number is not easy. Simply setting this goal will not make it happen, at least not as the team setting the goal would like it to happen. One might wonder how this goal was determined. Do you think this goal is

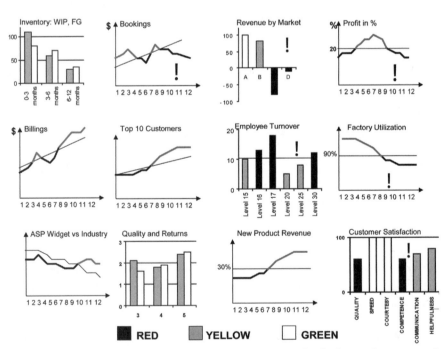

**Figure 3.6:** Traditional performance measures: the balanced scorecard executive dashboard. WIP = Work in progress, FG = finished goods.

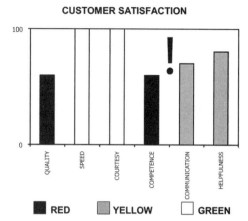

**EXECUTIVE DASHBOARD
CUSTOMER SATISFACTION EXAMPLE**

**What do you measure?**
Customer satisfaction summarizes your customer's rating of your products and services along industry specific parameters. General criteria are quality, delivery, service, and price.

**How do you measure?**
Customer ratings are standardized and quantified

**Where do you find the data?**
You always have to ask the customer. There is no "internal" customer satisfaction measurement that objectively reflects the customer's voice. Gathering data can reach from calling your customers with a prepared questionnaire, or collecting scorecards from customers, to engaging customer survey experts.

**Figure 3.7:** Traditional performance measures: the balanced scorecard/dashboard customer satisfaction drill-down.

SMART; that is, specific, measurable, actionable, relevant, time-based?

For this metric type, an unachieved goal earns an exclamation mark, indicating that the metric's owner may need reminding that his or her job-performance rating depends on achievement of this goal. What kind of activity might this type of pressure create, especially when improvement detection is immediately needed? We might initially think that the owner would, as soon as possible, start an investigation into where quality improvements need to be made. But we need to be realistic. Immediate improvements are needed to make this scorecard look better. Might there be other ways to make this happen?

Before we react, let's step back to see the bigger picture. A customer-satisfaction goal is not being met; however, is this level of customer satisfaction really a problem? What were the scores from previous reporting periods? If the scores are better now, this would be good since improvements are being demonstrated—even though the strategic goal is not being met. Without a historical time-dependent reference, could there be disagreements for what is good or bad?

Keeping in mind the type of metric described in Figure 3.7, consider the following situation:

A few years ago, when my wife and I were buying a new car, negotiating the price of the car with the sales associate got to be a game with me. After we closed the deal, the sales associate pointed to a survey that was facing us under his Plexiglas desktop. This survey had all 5s checked. He told us that we would be getting a survey in the mail. Then he said that he always gets 5s on his survey. He pointed to my wife and said that he wanted her, not me, to fill out the survey.

Consider the following points:

- The salesman said we would receive a survey in the mail.
- He pointed out that he always gets 5s, as noted on the survey form on his desk.
- He wanted my wife, not me, to fill out the survey.

Do you think he might be trying to bias the survey in his favor—perhaps a bonus is riding on these results? Do you think this type of behavior is what the metric should be creating? This is one form of trying to manage the output of the metric process, rather than systematically working to change the process, or the inputs to the process, so that an improved response occurs. Simply setting high-level goals and then managing to those goals, can lead to the wrong behavior. Making true long-lasting gains in customer satisfaction is more involved than working to get satisfactory scores on evaluation sheets. Attaining long-lasting customer satisfaction involves improving the process and the inputs to the process.

Let's next examine the profit scorecard in Figure 3.8. Notice that the x-axis units are 1 to 12. What do you think this indicates? Months is a good bet since the metric starts with 1, which is probably the first month after the company's fiscal year. Notice, also, how this tracking is made only against the goal with no indication of what kind of performance has been experienced in the past. Since the goals are annualized, the target line is drawn beginning the first month of the year, but there is no record of performance the previous year, nor whether the goal is reasonable or simply a pie-in-the-sky objective.

If people are really held accountable for achieving this metric objective, very undesirable behavior can result. Since there is an exclamation point, the owner of this metric would need to take immediate action to drive these numbers in the right direction. A high-level metric such as this could lead to the Enron effect, where money could be simply shifted from one area to the next to make things look better. Or the metric could lead to immediate cost-cutting measures that might significantly dam-

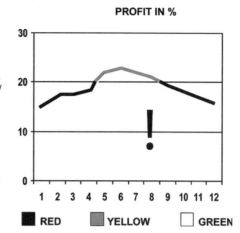

**EXECUTIVE DASHBOARD
PROFIT EXAMPLE**

**What do you measure?**
Profit is the sum of your sales revenue minus your cost. Profit indicates the efficiency of your operation. Comparing actual profit against plan will identify early on potential problems due to declining revenues or increasing cost.

**How do you measure?**
Profit is measured at period end in $ value and % of revenue

**Where do you find the data?**
Profits are part of the financial system and are easily extracted.

**Figure 3.8:** Traditional performance measures: the balanced scorecard/dashboard profit drill-down.

age the company's future outlook. You can cost cut your into profitability for only so long. At some point in time you will see diminishing returns and possible increase in fixed costs due to inefficiencies created by a lack of resources. This form of metric reporting can also lead to the previously described behavior, where Krispy Kreme shipped donuts that they knew would be returned so that quarterly expectations would be met.

Metric reporting, where focus is given only to whether output-type goals are met, can cause behavioral problems lower in the organization as well. Consider the following:

A prison representative purchased a commodity item only at the end of the supplier's quarterly financial reporting period. Near the end of every quarter, the salesperson for the supplier called, offering the prison a price incentive for immediate purchase. Because of the type of product sold, there was no reason for this cyclic behavior. Since manufacturing personnel were on overtime and were under pressure to increase production volume, quality problems were more prevalent during this period than others.

This odd behavior was eventually noticed and an investigation conducted. Asked why the prison waited until the end of the quarter to purchase the product, the representative responded that the salesperson called at the end of the quarter with a discounted price.

Additional company investigation revealed that the salesperson typically had difficulty meeting his quarterly target objective. Near the end of every quarter, the salesperson would ask his manager for approval to give customer discounts, which would help their department meet its targeted goals. If these goals were not met, there would be no personal or departmental bonuses. The manager routinely complied.

What makes this situation even worse is that the salesperson was getting paid off the top line (total products sold), while the company was taking a significant impact at the bottom line. That is, the salesperson was getting rewarded for total products sold, while the company's true profit from the transaction was reduced by the sales commission as well as additional overtime costs due to demand spike.

All these negative corporate-profitability behaviors originated with the company's salesperson commission policy. Rather than someone noticing and investigating, this type of situation could be readily identified in an E-DMAIC structure during the analyze phase. In this structure, a project could have been created that later resolved the undesirable behavior of the sales department through changing either the reward policy or discounting policy so that these demand spikes would no longer occur.

The shortcomings of many traditional performance metrics are that they often reflect only fiscal year metrics, make comparisons to a point estimate from a previous month or year, and don't have a procedure for improving the process so that gains occur and are maintained. These traditional methods don't view the enterprise process as a system of processes, where the performance metric is the result of these processes along with the variability that occurs within them. Long-lasting change is a result of systematic improvement to these processes.

> The shortcomings of many traditional performance metrics are that these metrics often reflect only fiscal year metrics, make comparisons to a point estimate from a previous month or a previous year, and don't have a procedure for improving the process so that gains occur and are maintained.

This form of metric reporting is always after-the-fact reporting and not predictive. Imagine if a customer said, "Based on past experience, our products will have a consumer half-life of only _____ years. If innovations and improvements are not sustained, our revenues will decline by _____ percent over the next _____ years." This type of data-driven statement leads to long-term thinking that can have long-lasting results.

## 3.7 Red-Yellow-Green Scorecards

The previously described balance scorecards and other scorecards that are not balanced often use red, yellow, and green to show whether actions are needed relative to meeting established objectives. The Office of Planning and Performance Management of the U.S. Department of Interior uses these metrics in the following way (U.S. Dept. of Interior 2003):

> Office of Management and Budget (OMB) has established an Executive Branch Management Scorecard to track how well departments and agencies are executing the five President's Management Agenda (PMA) components. The Scorecard also strengthens the sense of accountability on the part of these agencies. The Scorecard presents an updated assessment of the status and progress being made to address each of the President's Management Agenda (PMA) goals.
>
> Status is assessed against the standards for success that have been developed for each initiative and are published in the 2003 Budget. They are defined as follows:
>
> - Green: Meets all of the standards for success.
> - Yellow: Achieved some, but not all, of the criteria.
> - Red: Has any one of a number of serious flaws.
>
> Progress is assessed on a case-by-case basis against the deliverables and timelines that each agency has established for the five PMA components. They are defined as:
>
> - Green: Implementation is proceeding according to plans.
> - Yellow: Some slippage or other issues requiring adjustment by the agency in order to achieve the initiative objectives in a timely manner.
> - Red: Initiative [is] in serious jeopardy and is unlikely to realize objectives absent significant management intervention.

The President reviews each agency scorecard with the respective cabinet member.

Interior is using the Scorecard approach to assist in monitoring progress toward achieving the PMA goals at a departmental level. Criteria specific to Interior and its bureaus were developed through a collaborative, cross-departmental effort. The criteria were combined with rating scales from 0 to 10 using color-rating bars that visually indicate progress and status scores. Interior bureaus and offices are asked to conduct a self-assessment of their status and progress in realizing PMA goals every six months, with the first of these self-assessments conducted in May 2002. Based on the self-assessment, the Department identifies the next actions that need to be taken by specific bureaus and offices to "get to green." Actions are entered into the Department's PMA tracking system so that they can be monitored along with the Citizen-Centered Governance Plan activities to assess the Department's progress as a whole in meeting the PMA goals.

When it is conducted throughout an organization, do you think that this form of goal setting and managing to these goals will lead to the right behavior? Goals are important; however, metric targets need to be SMART. Arbitrary goal setting and management to these goals can lead to the wrong behavior!

SMART goals are specific, measurable, actionable; relevant, time-based.

Let's now discuss the presentation of red-yellow-green scorecards, which can have different presentation formats. Figure 3.9 and Table 3.5 illustrate two possible formats.

Let's further examine a scorecard like Table 3.5. When creating this type of scorecard, metrics are established throughout the organization, along with goals for the metrics. When a metric goal is being met, all is well and the color is green. When measurements are close to not being met, the color is yellow. The metric is colored red when the goal is not being met and corrective action needs to be taken.

What do you see in this scorecard? There are a lot of metrics grouped by business area. Also, many measurements are colored red and metrics even transition from red to green and back. Finally, there are a lot of metrics for one scorecard. One rule of thumb is that most scorecards should include 7–10 metrics. Any more than that and a person will struggle monitoring and acting on them.

How can you have a metric that is red for the entire reporting period? Is no one monitoring it? Is it based on an arbitrary target and just ignored? Who knows, but all are possible.

Since red-yellow-green scorecard reporting is now readily available on many ERP systems, cascading this type of scorecard throughout the organization can initially seem very appealing. However, with this form of reporting, some companies might be experiencing many, if not all, green metrics. While in other companies red-triggered events can be creating much work; however, when the metrics are examined collectively over time there does not seem to be much, if any, individual metric improvement.

When assessing these two types of company scorecard situations, one might think that there would be a big difference in how well the organizations are performing. However, this is not necessarily true.

Perhaps the first company is a supplier to a company or government agency that requires red-yellow-green scorecard reporting and includes in their agreement a penalty if the color is not green. What kind of goal-setting activity would result from this type of policy, especially if the customer is not actively involved in all goal-setting metrics?

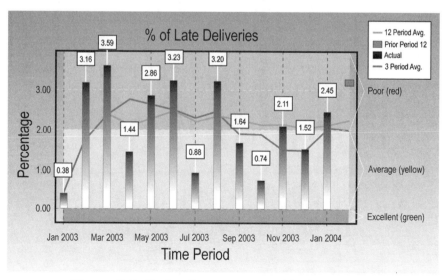

**Figure 3.9:** Red–yellow–green graphical reporting.

**Table 3.5** Red–yellow–green tabular scorecard example.

RED

YELLOW

GREEN

**Monthly SCORECARD**
**Business Unit Name**

| Measurement | Targets | Aug'04 | Sep'04 | Oct'04 | Nov'04 | Dec'04 |
|---|---|---|---|---|---|---|
| **FINANCE** | | | | | | |
| *Finance Metric A* | | 3.387525 | 2.965966 | 3.042505 | 2.891057 | 3.485847 |
| Yellow if equal to or higher than | 3.05 | 3.05 | 3.05 | 3.05 | 3.05 | 3.05 |
| Green if equal to or higher than | 3.1 | 3.1 | 3.1 | 3.1 | 3.1 | 3.1 |
| *Finance Metric B* | | 2.09819 | 2.254758 | 2.345674 | 2.207099 | 2.316309 |
| Yellow if equal to or higher than | 2.2 | 2.2 | 2.2 | 2.2 | 2.2 | 2.2 |
| Green if equal to or higher than | 2.25 | 2.25 | 2.25 | 2.25 | 2.25 | 2.25 |
| *Finance Metric C* | | 0.762611 | 0.958071 | 1.051227 | 0.867969 | 1.158351 |
| Yellow if equal to or higher than | 0.9 | 0.9 | 0.9 | 0.9 | 0.9 | 0.9 |
| Green if equal to or higher than | 0.95 | 0.95 | 0.95 | 0.95 | 0.95 | 0.95 |

CUSTOMER

FINANCE

INTERNAL BUSINESS OPS

LEARNING & GROWTH

People in the second organization are expending a lot of effort trying to improve their many metrics when they are red. It would seem like these organizations might start lobbying for lower goals when they are set for the next fiscal year.

How well red-yellow-green scorecards are performing depend upon established goals, which may not be realistic and/or lead process suboptimization effort throughout the organization chart. Metric tracking against this type of goals can lead to ineffective firefighting activities or playing games with the numbers.

Game playing to meet calendar goals can also impact bonuses. This form of activity can occur not only at the executive level or in the sales department. The following example illustrates how the wrong activity can be stimulated at an employee level by a goal-driven metric.

This company's business service involved managing large amounts of customer money. Large checks could flow to the company from its customer even though the company kept only a small portion of the money. All employees in a company were given  bonus if they met the calendar-based revenue. A company goal had been set at one level for many years, so employees became accustomed to receiving this periodic bonus compensation.

A major customer was to make an unusually large payment. The payment size required signature approval by the customer's CEO. The customer asked if they could pay in smaller amounts spread over a longer period so they could avoid the hassle of having CEO approval. The service company agreed since it wanted to be customer-driven but later determined that this agreement negated the periodic bonus.

In an attempt to resolve this employee-bonus unfairness, an administrator took it upon himself to adjust the compensation internally so it appeared that the company was paid in the period the service was performed. However, this accounting adjustment negatively impacted the customer and caused havoc.

Have you experienced any organization that has had similar issues with a goal-driven metric? A final example follows:

A salesperson calls customers who have committed to purchasing products in the next quarter, asking them if they would move up their order to the current quarter. He then offers a discount for this order shift. The salesperson's motivation for doing this was that he was having trouble meeting his quarterly numbers, which would negatively impact his pay for this quarter. The consequence of this practice is similar to the previous illustration.

Employee incentive plans are not bad; however, care needs to be exercised or the wrong activities can prevail. An alternative scorecard style to red-yellow-green metrics is described in Examples 7.1–7.4.

## 3.8  Example 3.1: Culture Firefighting or Fire Prevention?

In this example, a traditional approach will be used initially to address nonconformance issues. A high-level IEE alternative approach will then be presented, along with its benefits. Volume III describes for continuous and attribute data the mechanics of creating this alternative metric reporting format.

An organization collects data and reacts whenever an out-of-specification condition occurs or a goal is not met. The following example dialog is what could happen when attempts are made to fix all out-of-specification problems whenever they occur in a manufacturing or service environment. This scenario could apply equally to a business service process whenever the goals of an organization are not being met.

Consider a product that has specification limits of 72–78. An organization might react to collected data in the following manner:

- First datum: 76.2
  - Everything is OK.
- Second datum: 78.2
  - Joe, go fix the problem.
- Data: 74.1, 74.1, 75.0, 74.5, 75.0, 75.0
  - Everything OK; Joe must have done a good job!
- Next datum: 71.8
  - Mary, fix the problem.
- Data: 76.7, 77.8, 77.1, 75.9, 76.3, 75.9, 77.5, 77.0, 77.6, 77.1, 75.2, 76.9
  - Everything OK; Mary must have done a good job!
- Next datum: 78.3
  - Harry, fix the problem.

- Next data: 72.7, 76.3
  - Everything OK; Harry must have fixed the problem.
- Next datum: 78.5
  - Harry, seems like there still is a problem.
- Next data: 76.0, 76.8, 73.2
  - Everything OK; the problem must be fixed now.
- Next datum: 78.8
  - Sue, please fix the problem that Harry could not fix.
- Next data: 77.6, 75.2, 76.8, 73.8, 75.6, 77.7, 76.9, 76.2, 75.1, 76.6, 76.6, 75.1, 75.4, 73.0, 74.6, 76.1
  - Everything is great; give Sue an award!
- Next datum: 79.3
  - Get Sue out there again. She is the only one who knows how to fix the problem.
- Next data: 75.9, 75.7, 77.9, 78
  - Everything is great again!

A plot of this information is shown in Figure 3.10. From this plot, we see that the previously described reaction to the out-of-specification conditions individually did not improve the process or prevent the likelihood of having problems in the future. The firefighters did not fix anything.

> Reaction to the out-of-specification conditions individually did not improve the process or prevent the likelihood of having problems in the future. The firefighters did not fix anything.

Figure 3.11 shows a re-plot of the data as an individuals control chart. The control limits in this figure are calculated from the data. Specifications in no way affect the control limits. This chart is a statement of the VOP relative to whether the process is considered in statistical control or not, stable or not. Since people often have difficulty in understanding what *in control* means, I prefer to use the term *predictable*.

These lower and upper control limits (LCL and UCL, respectively) represent a ±3 sampling standard deviation around the mean ($\bar{x}$). For this type of chart, the ±3 sampling standard deviation is usually considered to be 2.66 times the mean of the adjacent-time-value moving range (see Volume III). Since the up-and-down movements are within the UCL and LCL and there are no unusual patterns, we would conclude that there are no special-cause data

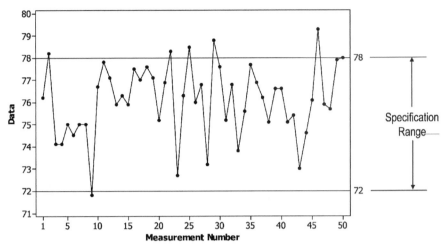

**Figure 3.10:** Reacting to common-cause variability as though it were special cause.

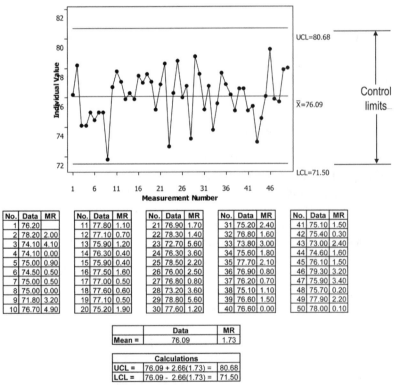

| No. | Data | MR | No. | Data | MR | No. | Data | MR | No. | Data | MR | No. | Data | MR |
|----|-------|------|----|-------|------|----|-------|------|----|-------|------|----|-------|------|
| 1 | 76.20 | | 11 | 77.80 | 1.10 | 21 | 76.90 | 1.70 | 31 | 75.20 | 2.40 | 41 | 75.10 | 1.50 |
| 2 | 78.20 | 2.00 | 12 | 77.10 | 0.70 | 22 | 78.30 | 1.40 | 32 | 76.80 | 1.60 | 42 | 75.40 | 0.30 |
| 3 | 74.10 | 4.10 | 13 | 75.90 | 1.20 | 23 | 72.70 | 5.60 | 33 | 73.80 | 3.00 | 43 | 73.00 | 2.40 |
| 4 | 74.10 | 0.00 | 14 | 76.30 | 0.40 | 24 | 76.30 | 3.60 | 34 | 75.60 | 1.80 | 44 | 74.60 | 1.60 |
| 5 | 75.00 | 0.90 | 15 | 75.90 | 0.40 | 25 | 78.50 | 2.20 | 35 | 77.70 | 2.10 | 45 | 76.10 | 1.50 |
| 6 | 74.50 | 0.50 | 16 | 77.50 | 1.60 | 26 | 76.00 | 2.50 | 36 | 76.90 | 0.80 | 46 | 79.30 | 3.20 |
| 7 | 75.00 | 0.50 | 17 | 77.00 | 0.50 | 27 | 76.80 | 0.80 | 37 | 76.20 | 0.70 | 47 | 75.90 | 3.40 |
| 8 | 75.00 | 0.00 | 18 | 77.60 | 0.60 | 28 | 73.20 | 3.60 | 38 | 75.10 | 1.10 | 48 | 75.70 | 0.20 |
| 9 | 71.80 | 3.20 | 19 | 77.10 | 0.50 | 29 | 78.80 | 5.60 | 39 | 76.60 | 1.50 | 49 | 77.90 | 2.20 |
| 10 | 76.70 | 4.90 | 20 | 75.20 | 1.90 | 30 | 77.60 | 1.20 | 40 | 76.60 | 0.00 | 50 | 78.00 | 0.10 |

| | Data | MR |
|---|-------|------|
| Mean = | 76.09 | 1.73 |

| Calculations | | |
|---|---|---|
| UCL = | 76.09 + 2.66(1.73) = | 80.68 |
| LCL = | 76.09 - 2.66(1.73) = | 71.50 |

**Figure 3.11:** Control chart illustration of common-cause variability.

conditions and that the source of process variability is common cause. The process is predictable.

Some readers might think that the control limits seem too wide and wonder about tightening up the control limits. My response to that is this:

> The control limits are considered the VOP and are directly calculated from the data. In some cases the control limits could be too wide. This occurrence is typically a function of data-collection procedures or a special-cause condition. When this occurs, you would work these issues instead of changing the control limits. For this data set, this is not the case.
>
> Most think action limits (i.e., VOC), when they decide to tighten control limits. This may seem to be a good thing, but is *not*. If you tighten the control limits to be narrower than the VOP, the result is most certainly an increase in firefighting.

This organization had been reacting to the out-of-specification conditions as though they were special cause. The focus on fixing out-of-specification conditions often leads to firefighting. When firefighting activities involve tweaking the process, additional variability can be introduced, degrading the process rather than improving it.

Deming noted the following:

- "A fault in the interpretation of observations, seen everywhere, is to suppose that every event (defect, mistake, accident) is attributable to someone (usually the nearest at hand), or is related to some special event."
- "We shall speak of faults of the system as common causes of trouble, and faults from fleeting events as special causes."
- "Confusion between common causes and special causes leads to frustration of everyone, and leads to greater variability and to higher costs, exactly contrary to what is needed."
- "I should estimate that in my experience most troubles and most possibilities for improvement add up to proportions something like this: 94 percent belong to the system (responsibility of management), 6 percent [are] special."

Let's revisit the data using a Deming approach. When data are in statistical control, we can say that the process is predictable. The next obvious question is: What do you predict? When a process control chart has recently shown stability, we can lump all data in this stable region and consider that these data are a random sample of the future, assuming that nothing either positively or negatively changes the system. Using this approach, we could create the dot plot shown in Figure 3.12.

An attribute assessment (pass or fail) for this data would yield a 12 percent (6/50) defective rate. However, some of these failures or nonfailures are borderline and, if we reran this experiment, we could get a significantly different response. Also, the overall response distribution has no impact on our statement relative to nonconformance.

A better approach would be to create a probability plot of the data from this stable control chart region. Figure 3.13 shows the results, where a probability plot is an estimated cumulative percent-less-than distribution plot. For example, a best estimate for this population is that about 0.629 percent will be below 72 and 87.768 percent will be less than 78. (See Volume III for creating and interpreting probability plots.)

From this analysis, we conclude that the process has an approximate 13 percent common-cause, nonconformance rate both now and in the future, unless something either negatively or positively impacts the *overall* process. If the financial impact of this nonconformance rate is unsatisfactory, this measurement could pull for the creation of a project to improve the process.

Note, the 13 percent determination from the probability plot is the following:

- 0.629 + [100 − 87.768] = 12.861, rounded up to 13 percent where
  - 0.629 is estimated percentile below the specification limit
  - [100 − 87.768] is estimated percentile above the specification limit

Inconsistent and ineffective organizational metric reporting can lead to much waste. The methodology described above is a consistent process that can lead to fewer firefighting activities:

Reiterating, IEE scorecard/dashboard metric reporting process is the following:

1. Assess process predictability.
2. When the process is considered predictable, formulate a prediction statement for the latest region of stability. The usual reporting format for this statement is the following:
   a. When there is a specification requirement: nonconformance percentage or DPMO

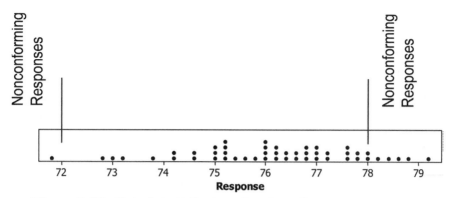

**Figure 3.12:** Dot plot attribute estimation of process percentage nonconformance rate.

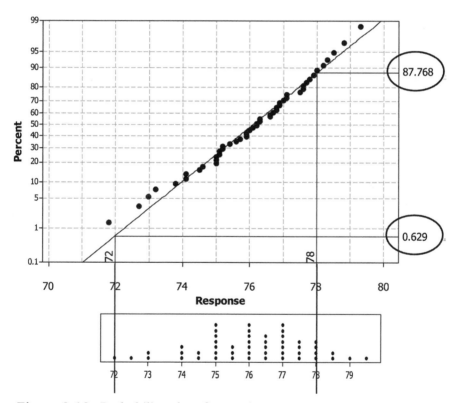

**Figure 3.13:** Probability plot of a continuous process output response from a stable process, with nonconformance rate estimation.

b.  When there is no specification requirement: median response and 80 percent frequency of occurrence rate

The described satellite-level and 30,000-foot-level control
charts and process capability/performance metric statements
can be created for a variety of situations. A process capability/
performance metric statement can quantify the magnitude of
disconnection between VOP and VOC.

It is important to note that this described prediction analysis
applies to stable processes. In the stable region of processes, data
need to be analyzed collectively for the purpose of gaining insight
to improvement opportunities. This is in contrast to attempting to
explain why one datum point is up and another point is down.

For nonpredictable processes, understanding is gained through
data examination. For example, a process change could have
resulted in a shift in the process response to a new region of
stability. For this situation, each region of stability needs to be
examined separately. Another example is when distinct multiple distributions are prevalent; for example, the holiday season
needs to be examined separately from the rest of the year. A final
example is when one point occurs beyond the control limits.
For this situation, it could be appropriate to assess that one
occurrence as an individual special-cause condition while collectively analyzing all the other points from the region of stability.

## 3.9   Creating an Enhanced Results-Achieving Culture Through Wisely Selected Performance Metrics

People often talk about wanting to make organizational cultural
change. An inordinate amount of money can be spent on workshops and consultations addressing cultural change issues, often
with questionable results.

Consider an organization that wants to create a more data-
driven, decision-making culture. Examining and reacting to these
data differently can be the impetus for making a real long-lasting
culture enhancement. In the last example, the organization reacted to every nonconformance issue as though it were a special
cause. This situation is not much different from organizations
that use war rooms to identify the problems of the day or week
so people can be deployed to firefight the latest issues. In the
previous example, Sue received an award for a long string of con-

forming production, and Harry was reprimanded for not having a long string of conforming production after his production work. In reality, these data were randomly generated. Sue was simply lucky, while Harry was unlucky. The organization culture was attacking common-cause issues as though they were special cause.

Many resources can be wasted when an organizational culture takes on corrective actions for every out-of-specification condition or individual occurrence beyond goals as though these are special-cause occurrences. Attempting to identify why individual points are beyond a specification or goal is not an effective structured root-cause-analysis approach. It does not lead to long-lasting preventive actions nor reduce the likelihood of future occurrence of a similar problem.

Consider how our organizational behavior would change were we to say that we have a predictable process where we expect to have about 13 percent nonconformance, unless we do something different to the underlying process. In this project-creation pull system, we would then follow the systematic IEE project-execution roadmap for timely resolution. In this new culture, we would focus on identifying and improving or controlling the $X$s that impact the $Y$s.

> Consider how our organizational behavior would change were we to say that we have a predictable process where we expect to have about 13 percent nonconformance, unless we do something different to the underlying process.

When a 30,000-foot-level scorecard/dashboard chart shows a need for improvement, management would be asking for project status since they understand that most recent up-and-down movements are from common-cause variability. When projects are not on schedule, management would be asking for explanations and what could be done to get back on schedule and expedite the project's completion.

Both public and private organizations frequently look at human and machine performance data similar to the situation just described and then make judgments based on the data. Production supervisors might constantly review production output by employee, by machine, by work shift, by day of the week, by product line, and so forth. In the service sector, an administrative assistant's output of letters and memos may be monitored daily. In call centers around the world, the average time spent per call could be monitored and used to counsel low-performing employees. The efficiency of computer programmers could be monitored through the tracking of lines of code produced per day. In the legal department, the number of patents secured on the company's behalf could be assessed over time. Whenever an organization reacts to individual excursions beyond requirements and specifications without examining the system as a whole, it could be reacting to common-cause situations as though they were special cause.

To illustrate this point further, I will use the example of an organization that monitored the frequency of safety memos. A safety memo is written indicating that the number of accidents involving injuries during the month of July was 16, up by 2 from 14 such injuries a year ago in July. The memo declares this increase in accidents to be unacceptable and requires all employees to watch a mandatory, 30-minute safety video by the end of August. At an average wage rate of $10 per hour, the company payroll of 1500 employees affected the August bottom line by $7500 plus wasted time getting to and from the conference room. This does not even consider the time spent issuing memos reminding people to attend, reviewing attendance rosters looking for laggards, and so forth.

I am not saying safety and productivity are not important to an organization. I am saying, as did Deming, that perhaps 94 percent of the output of a person or machine is a result of the system that management has put in place for use by the workers. If performance is poor, 94 percent of the time it is the system that must be modified for improvements to occur. Only 6 percent of the time is problems due to special causes. Knowing the difference between special-cause and common-cause variation can affect how organizations react to data and the success they achieve using the methods of a Six Sigma strategy. For someone to reduce the frequency of safety accidents from common cause, an organization would need to look at its systems collectively over a long period to determine what should be done to processes that lead to safety problems. Reacting to an individual month that does not meet a criterion can be both counterproductive and very expensive.

One simple question that should be repeated time and time again as IEE implementation proceeds is this: Is the variation I am observing common cause or special cause? The answer to this simple question has a tremendous impact on the action managers and workers take in response to process and product information. And those actions have a tremendous impact on worker motivation and worker self-esteem.

Common-cause variability of the process could, or might not, cause a problem relative to meeting customer needs. We don't know the results until we collectively compare the process output relative to a specification or requirement. This is much different from reacting to individual points that do not meet specification limits. When we treat common-cause data collectively, we focus on what should be done to improve the process. When reacting to an individual event that is beyond specification limits where only common-cause events are occurring, we focus on this individual point as though it were a special-cause condition, rather than on the process information collectively. This type of investigation wastes resources and can lead to process changes that actually degrade future system performance. It is important to note that special causes usually receive more attention because of high visibility. However, more gains can often be made by continually working on common cause.

> Common-cause variability of the process could, or might not, cause a problem relative to meeting customer needs. We don't know the results until we collectively compare the process output relative to a specification or requirement.

Reiterating, variations of common cause resulting in out-of-specification conditions do not mean that one cannot or should not do anything about it. What it does mean is that you need to focus on improving the process, not just firefight individual situations that happen to be out of specification. However, it is first essential to identify whether the condition is common or special cause. If the condition is common cause, data are used collectively when comparisons are made relative to the frequency of how the process will perform relative to specification needs. If an individual point or points are determined to be special cause from a process point of view, we then need to address what was different about them.

One of the most effective quality tools for distinguishing between common-cause and special-cause variation is the simple-to-learn and easy-to-use control chart. The problem with control charts is that they are so simple that many managers and workers misunderstand and misuse them to the detriment of product and process quality. In Chapter 7, I will elaborate on the satellite-level and 30,000-foot-level control charting procedures, which can greatly enhance an organization's success. This scorecard/dashboard format can reduce the frustration and expense associated with firefighting activities within an organization.

## 3.10 Example 3.2: Red-Yellow-Green Graphical Reporting Alternative

Figure 3.9 presented a red-yellow-green dashboard graphic report-out for this attribute situation; that is, a shipment was either on time or not. The following observations were made from the chart, where there were seven yellow and six red occurrences:

| Month | Jan-03 | Feb-03 | Mar-03 | Apr-03 | May-03 | Jun-03 | Jul-03 | Aug-03 | Sep-03 | Oct-03 | Nov-03 | Dec-03 | Jan-04 |
|---|---|---|---|---|---|---|---|---|---|---|---|---|---|
| Percent Late Deliveries | 0.38 | 3.16 | 3.59 | 1.44 | 2.86 | 3.23 | 0.88 | 3.20 | 1.64 | 0.74 | 2.11 | 1.52 | 2.45 |
| Yellow if equal to or higher than | 0 | 0 | 0 | 0 | 0 | 0 | 0 | 0 | 0 | 0 | 0 | 0 | 0 |
| Red if equal to or higher than | 2.2 | 2.2 | 2.2 | 2.2 | 2.2 | 2.2 | 2.2 | 2.2 | 2.2 | 2.2 | 2.2 | 2.2 | 2.2 |

Reiterating, the IEE analysis process that will be followed below, the IEE scorecard/dashboard metric reporting process uses the following procedure:

1. Assess process predictability.
2. When the process is considered predictable, formulate a prediction statement for the latest region of stability. The usual reporting format for this statement is the following:
   a. When there is a specification requirement: nonconformance percentage or DPMO
   b. When there is no specification requirement: median response and 80 percent frequency of occurrence rate

Applying the IEE scorecard/dashboard metric reporting process to this data set yields the following:

1. When there are no occurrences beyond the two horizontal lines (i.e., upper and lower control limits), no patterns, or data shifts, the process is said to be in control. When this occurs, we have no reason to not believe that the up-and-down monthly variability is the result of common-cause variability; the process can be described as predictable. As previously noted, the purpose of red-yellow-green charting is to stimulate improvements. The control chart in Figure 3.14 provides an IEE assessment of how well this is accomplished; that is, it appears that no improvements were made (see Volume III for chart-creation methods).
2. The next question to address is what prediction statement can be made. Since the process is predictable, we can consider the past data from the region of stability to be a random sample of the future. Unless a fundamental process improvement is made, we can expect our attribute response process output of late deliveries to be approximately 2.1

## Traditional Performance Reporting Example – Red-Yellow-Green Scorecard

## IEE Improved Reporting for Process Assessment and Improvement

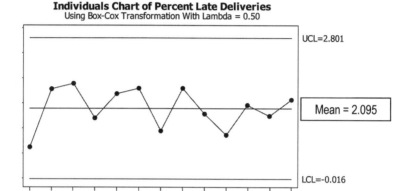

Predictable process with an approximate 2.1% non-conformance rate

(i.e., Using the current process, deliveries will be late about 2% of the time.)

**Figure 3.14:** Illustration of IEE improved attribute pass/fail process output response reporting: red-yellow-green (see Figure 3.9) versus IEE reporting.

percent, or the centerline of the control chart. An IEE statement about this process is that it is predictable with an approximate nonconformance rate of 2.1 percent.

The figure includes an alternative format statement similar to what you might hear in a news report. I prefer a consistent reporting format that makes a statement about predictability and then what is predicted; however, including this alternative format in the report-out can improve communications of the concepts. I will include this form of reporting for other volume report-outs.

Effective, long-lasting improvements to processes are not made by firefighting individual time-line conditions that are beyond a desired objective; that is, approximately 2 percent of this time for this example. Process improvements are made by examining all output data collectively to determine what should be done differently in the overall process, as opposed to assessing the points that are beyond the criteria as individual occurrences. This can be accomplished through a P-DMAIC project.

> Effective, long-lasting improvements to processes are not made by firefighting individual time-line conditions that are beyond a desired objective.

## 3.11 Example 3.3: Tabular Red-Yellow-Green Metric Reporting Alternative

Table 3.5 presented a red-yellow-green graphic scorecard/dashboard report out for a continuous response that has a criterion. The following observations were made from the chart for finance metric B, which had a target of 2.25 or higher. There were five red, two yellow, and six green occurrences:

| | Targets | Aug'04 | Sep'04 | Oct'04 | Nov'04 | Dec'04 | Jan'05 | Feb'05 | Mar'05 | Apr'05 | May'05 | Jun'05 | Jul'05 | Aug'05 |
|---|---|---|---|---|---|---|---|---|---|---|---|---|---|---|
| Finance Metric B | | 2.10 | 2.25 | 2.35 | 2.21 | 2.32 | 2.21 | 2.16 | 2.49 | 2.51 | 2.16 | 2.17 | 2.29 | 2.14 |
| Yellow if equal to or higher than | 2.20 | 2.20 | 2.20 | 2.20 | 2.20 | 2.20 | 2.20 | 2.20 | 2.20 | 2.20 | 2.20 | 2.20 | 2.20 | 2.20 |
| Green if equal to or higher than | 2.25 | 2.25 | 2.25 | 2.25 | 2.25 | 2.25 | 2.25 | 2.25 | 2.25 | 2.25 | 2.25 | 2.25 | 2.25 | 2.25 |

Reiterating the IEE analysis process that will be followed below, the IEE scorecard/dashboard metric reporting process uses the following procedure:

1.  Assess process predictability.
2.  When the process is considered predictable, formulate a prediction statement for the latest region of stability. The usual reporting format for this statement is the following:
    a.  When there is a specification requirement: nonconformance percentage or DPMO
    b.  When there is no specification requirement: median response and 80 percent frequency of occurrence rate

Applying the IEE scorecard/dashboard metric reporting process to this data set yields:

1.  As previously stated, the purpose of red-yellow-green charting is to stimulate improvements. Figure 3.15 provides

an IEE assessment of how well this is accomplished (see Volume III for chart-creation methods). This figure contains a control chart, probability plot, and histogram. As noted in the previous example, when there are no occurrences beyond the two horizontal lines (i.e., upper and lower control limits), no patterns or data shifts, the process is said to be in control. Again, when this occurs, we have no reason to not believe that the up-and-down monthly variability is the result of common-cause variability; that is, the process is predictable. Since the process is predictable, we can consider past data from the region of stability to be a random sample of the future.

2. The histogram shown in Figure 3.15 is a traditional tool that describes the distribution of random data from a population that has a continuous response. However, it is difficult to

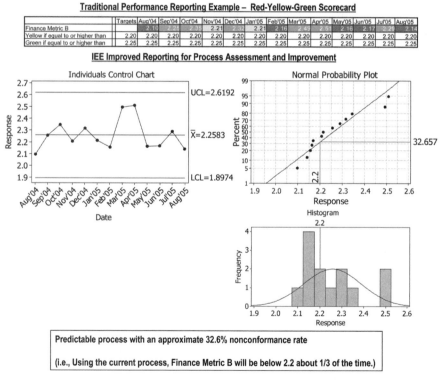

**Figure 3.15:** Illustration of IEE-improved finance metric B continuous-response reporting: red-yellow-green (see Table 3.5) scorecard versus IEE reporting (Histogram included for illustrative purposes only).

determine from a histogram the expected percentage beyond a criterion. A probability plot is a better tool to determine the nonconformance percentage. In a probability plot, actual data values are plotted on a coordinate system where percentage *less than* is on the *y*-axis. The probability plot in Figure 3.15 provides an estimate that approximately 32.6 percent of future monthly reporting will be less than the lower-bound criterion, unless a fundamental process improvement is made or something else external to the process occurs. From this figure, we also observe that this percentage value is consistent with an estimated proportion below the 2.2 reference line in the histogram graph. This percentage is also similar to the percentage of red occurrences; that is, 5 out of 13. If this nonconformance percentage of 32.6 percent is undesirable, this metric would pull for project creation.

To reemphasize, effective long-lasting improvements to processes are not made by firefighting individual time-line conditions that are beyond a desired objective. Process improvements are made by collectively examining process data over the period of stability so that insight might be gained to determine what should be done differently overall. This can be accomplished through the execution of a P-DMAIC project.

## 3.12   IEE Performance Scorecard/Dashboard Metrics that Lead to the Right Activities

The examples in the previous sections illustrate how simple goal setting does not necessarily yield improvements and, in fact, can lead to playing games with the numbers so that the company is negatively impacted. An IEE measurement-and-improvement infrastructure provides a solution to this problem.

Most first-tier companies use scorecard/dashboard metrics that seem useful and can do the following:

- Provide a uniform view of a program or process across the organization.
- Force the organization to look at the forest instead of the trees; that is, report on the overall results of a process.

- Effectively and efficiently report the state of a process to those not intimately involved such as managers, peers in other organizations, and others.
- Provide a starting point for discussions on the key issues.
- Help manage time in review meetings since only the relevant issues are discussed.
- Provide a metric, and any metric is better than no metric (note: this could be used to start non-value-added activity, which leads to ineffective resource utilization).

But think back on what comes out of these review meetings. These meetings typically have the following:

- A description of exceptions or problems.
- Half-baked plans to address both the problem and its consequences: shipments were late, not sure why, how to get on-time shipments, and how to mollify customers who received late shipments.
- Too many problems: only talk about problems and organization's apparent lack of ability to perform better makes for unhappy meetings.
- And most importantly, every meeting is the same; only the problems change. But there are always problems, always angst, always the need to fix the problem and the consequences of the problem, and always no real improvement.

Consider alternatively using 30,000-foot-level scorecard/dashboard metric reporting. Benefits include the following:

- Reduced firefighting of common-cause problems as though they were special cause.
- Reporting process performance in terms everyone understands; for example, the process is predictable with a two percent nonconformance rate that costs the business $200,000 monthly.
- Assess trends *before* they are classified as problems that need immediate attention.
- For statistically determined common-cause or special-cause problems, provides clear, specific direction for the process breakdowns. Benefits include the following:
  - Actionable activities are recognized.

– Subprocess improvements can be measured and quantified.
– Success is seen and rewarded in subsequent meetings when subprocesses are improved.
– Over time, the overall process is not only under control, but also *improves*.

It is important to keep in mind the following:

• Bad stress is when people feel they are not in control. Traditional dashboards show problems without a clear read on why or how to fix it.
• Good stress is when people feel they have control over the situation. IEE provides a high-level process view highlighting areas that need fixing with actionable tools.

In an E-DMAIC structure, high-level enterprise-process analyses can provide metric goals and a structured improvement strategy that are truly aligned to business objectives and needs. The number of these metrics and value-chain goals from this analysis may be fewer than the number of current organizational metric-improvement objectives.

Improvement goal objectives determined at the 30,000-foot-level from an E-DMAIC analysis could be placed in employees' performance plans and reported as a scorecard/dashboard metric. Whether metric improvement goals are later met, and how well, would be assessed at the 30,000-foot-level for a statistically positive metric shift. Implementation of this methodology would be creating a system and culture where metric improvement needs pull for the creation of projects that have long-lasting benefits for the company.

The Sarbanes-Oxley (SOX) Act is legislation created in 2002 partly in response to the Enron and WorldCom financial scandals. SOX was created to protect shareholders and the public from enterprise-process accounting errors and fraud. In addition, it ensures a degree of consistency in access to information and reporting of it that could impact the value of a company's stock. IEE is in direct alignment with the initial spirit of SOX.

This volume describes how to structure IEE metrics and how to utilize a no-nonsense roadmap leading to process improvement that benefits the organization as a whole. This volume describes the how-to methods to create a level five system.

# 3.13 Applying Integrated Enterprise Excellence (IEE)

Someone invites you to a seminar on trading stock options. You attend the session and the methodology sounds like a great investment opportunity. You decide to act so that you can increase the return on your investments. You decide to follow Deming's cycle of PDCA, as part of a hoshin kanri implementation. In the plan phase of the PDCA cycle, you attend training sessions, study training CDs, study software, and create your investment strategy. In the do phase you start investing. After a time you proceed to the check phase; however, your analysis indicates that things are not going well. You believe that you must be doing something wrong. The training sessions led you to believe things would be a lot better than you are experiencing. In the act phase you decide to attend more training sessions. You then return to the plan phase of the PDCA cycle, make adjustments to your investment techniques, and proceed through the remaining steps of the cycle.

After going through the PDCA cycle several times, your assessment of your overall investment returns is not good. You then decide to discuss the problems that you are having with other investors who took the training, hoping to learn something from them. In these discussions, you hear fantastic large-percentage trade-gain stories. You ask your colleagues more probing questions about how well they are doing overall. You are surprised when others provide an honest examination of their big-picture investment performance. You find that they are not doing any better than you.

In the above methodology, a plan was created from something thought to be beneficial, that is, options investing. No analyses were conducted to see if this was the best plan to achieve your overall desired objectives. Now consider what could have been done differently. Instead of starting with a plan, first define your vision, mission, and objectives. Then create performance metrics and conduct analyses that give insight to the best strategy to use.

Consider that the define phase finds you want to have sufficient savings so you don't have to worry about money in your retirement years. In the measure phase, a 30,000-foot-level scorecard/dashboard monthly tracking of rate of return for your financial holdings was not as good as you would have liked. A SMART goal was set. In the analyze phase, you make assessments for determining the best *strategy* to accomplish your defined objectives.

When conducting this analysis, keep in mind that you can't violate laws that govern the system. Determine the best approach that is not contrary to a law of physics (see Glossary). For example, Isaac Newton's second law of motion is that force equals mass times acceleration ($F = MA$). Unless you are dealing with situations where Albert Einstein's theory of relativity applies, don't try to develop a strategy that is contrary to the proven $F = MA$ law. It is important to emphasize that out-of-the-box thinking is good for problem solving and strategic development. Care simply needs to be exercised when approaching current known physical law boundaries.

Statisticians know that stock market motion is random and not predictable. Let's consider this a system law. Most options-trading models involve some form of prediction. Because of this assessment, we could conclude that options investing would not be a good strategy to pursue, since it competes against a system law.

In investing, as has been stated many times, the best way to obtain good capital growth is to make consistent, regular deposits to a balanced selection of equity funds that provide good returns. Let's consider this a proven system law. Investing in individual stocks is probably not a good idea for most investors because a stock-picking system would need to be developed. Mutual funds seem like the best alternative; however, which one should we choose? Mutual fund brochures can be very deceiving.

This task initially seems to be overwhelming. Every financial magazine has a system and funds that are proclaimed to be the best. Brochures often relay one-year, five-year, and other time-interval return statements, which can be very deceiving. Results can depend on the start and stop date for each period. This form of reporting does not provide insight into what could have happened if a large investment had been made at some other point in time during the year, when a major market correction occurred immediately after the investment.

What we would like to assess is the output of various investment processes, mutual funds, a portfolio of various exchange-traded funds (ETFs), companies that manage portfolios, and the like. We could make this assessment using a spreadsheet where the growth of a hypothetical amount of money, say $10,000, was plotted monthly over a long time for the various investment options. We would look for a fund that provides not only long-haul consistent growth but also has low month-to-month variability and small pull-backs during stock market correction periods. Since we are basically comparing investment processes, we can also make comparisons for arbitrarily chosen blocks of time that would contain major market corrections. Assuming that the funds were in existence at these times, we might compare funds during the periods 1982–1993, 1996–2003, 1999 to the present, and 1982 to the present.

What we have just done is analyze data to gain insight to the best investment process or strategy for us, given our define-phase objectives. We can also assess whether our goals for rate of investment return are reasonable. SMART goals should be consistent with the system laws of physics. If they are not, an adjustment needs to be made or a completely different strategy needs to be investigated; perhaps investing in real estate.

| SMART goals should be consistent with the "laws of physics." |
| --- |

The implementation of our strategy *at this point in time* is not inconsistent with the hoshin kanri Deming cycle of PDCA. We would start with the creation of a detailed plan for how much will be invested each month to reach our long-term objectives. The control phase of the E-DMAIC would assess the overall strategy over time to ensure that the mutual fund's performance did not degrade relative to market indexes and other competing funds.

This investment example is not much different from what happens in many companies. Are companies systematically performing analyses to choose their strategies, such as those in Tables 3.2–3.4? Do companies, such as Enron, pick strategies that are not realistically possible?

Most employees don't get involved in creating strategic plans; they implement them. This volume asks whether this is the best approach, and what is the current process for creating a strategic plan? One purpose of this chapter is to stimulate thought on this topic. In my opinion, most companies would agree that this is an area for improvement. E-DMAIC provides a systematic approach to address these opportunities, as describe in this volume.

Let's now consider the organizational metrics described in this chapter. Setting goals and reacting to individual points beyond these goals can lead to undesirable behaviors; for example, firefighting Deming's 94 percent common-cause issues as though they were special cause. Traditional scorecards encourage managers and decision makers to focus on targets at the expense of accepting measurement variability. Red-yellow-green scorecards can initially seem to be a good thing; however, this form of metric reporting can lead to a very large amount of wasted resources and playing games with the numbers.

The 30,000-foot-level metric is used in IEE to describe a high-level project or operation metric that has infrequent subgrouping/sampling so that short-term variations, which might be caused by typical variation in input levels, will result in charts that view these perturbations as common-cause issues. This objective, which is captured using 30,000-foot-level control charts, is different from traditional control-chart objectives, which mean to identify special-cause conditions so that corrective actions can be taken (see Volume III for chart-creation methods). Examples of 30,000-foot-level metrics are lead time, inventory, defective rates, and a critical part dimension. There can be a drill-down to a 20,000-foot-level metric if there is an alignment, such as the largest product defect type.

> The 30,000-foot-level metric is used in IEE to describe a high-level project or operation metric that has infrequent subgrouping/sampling so that short-term variations, which might be caused by typical variation in input levels, will result in charts that view these perturbations as common-cause issues. This objective, which is captured using 30,000-foot-level control charts, is different from traditional control-chart objectives, which mean to identify special-cause conditions so that corrective actions can be taken.

The purpose of the 30,000-foot-level chart is to view a process response from a high-level airplane view to determine whether a process is predictable or has common-cause variability. If the process output from common-cause variability is not satisfactory or what we desire, then a process-improvement effort would experience a pull for project creation. This is in contrast to traditional control charts, which are created for timely identification of when special causes occur so that adjustments can be made to bring the process back in control. As a business metric, 30,000-foot-level reporting can lead to more efficient resource utilization and less manipulation of the numbers.

> The purpose of the 30,000-foot-level chart is to view a process response from a high-level, airplane view to determine whether a process is predictable; that is, has common cause variability. If the process output from common cause variability is not satisfactory or what we desire, then a process improvement project would be pulled for creation.

Section 14.8 includes a description of the IEE DNA rules, which take Lean Six Sigma and traditional scorecards to their next level. The application of the system described in this volume can become the enabling means to "pass the test" for achieving both the Malcolm Baldrige Award and Shingo prize (see Glossary).

I suggest that you read over the following exercises, since readers often consider these questions to be thought provoking. For example, my conclusions to Exercise 5 were that corporate vision, mission, values, and strategies often either are not existent, are not communicated, or are not readily available internally/externally to the company. If this is the case, one could question corporations using these principles as the guiding light for orchestrating day-to-day and improvement activities.

I would like to get your thoughts and responses to these and other similar exercises throughout this volume. My contact information is included in the preface. The next chapter elaborates more on the IEE system, which addresses many of the issues described in this chapter.

## 3.14   Exercises

1. Describe a situation in which you think management, organizations, or society is addressing the wrong problem. Describe what needs to be done to change this.
2. You are to present the pie chart, line chart, and stack bar chart shown in Figures 3.2, 3.3, and 3.4 to your management. Summarize your presentation.
3. You are to present the year-to-year monthly revenue chart shown in Table 3.1. Summarize your presentation.
4. Compare your response to questions 2 and 3 to the IEE analysis alternative presented in Example 9.3. Comment on differences and implication of these differences in an organization.
5. It is often stated that companies are to have a vision, mission, values, and strategies. Hoshin kanri is to link organizational work to high-level missions and strategies. A logical assumption and expectation from this is that the company does a good job communicating its corporate and other missions/strategies throughout the company. One would think that the company would also make readily available

the corporate vision, mission, and values outside the company; e.g., to show their overall direction to others.

a. Select a sample of companies and visit their websites. Document the vision, mission, and values for each company. Describe where on the website the information was found; e.g., home page link or annual report.

b. Select a sample of company employees. Ask each employee to state his/her company's vision, mission, values, and strategies. Strategies were included in this list and not the previous list since companies may consider that this information is something that they do not want to share outside their company. If someone does not immediately state or does not know the answer to the question, allow him/her some time to locate a response on the intranet or elsewhere.

Describe the survey results. State your conclusions or possibilities. For those companies whose corporate principles (i.e., vision, mission, values, and strategies) were not found, consider the possibilities: principle is not communicated or poorly communicated; principle is not retained by intended audience; audience surveyed is not the intended audience; surveyed information source (e.g., annual report or website) is not to communicate principles; principles' search/survey was defective.

c. Describe your thoughts as to whether a mission is necessary and whether there is a relationship between mission and success.

d. Describe your thoughts as to whether hoshin kanri or strategic planning can succeed where there is no mission.

e. Describe your thoughts as to whether hoshin kanri or strategic planning ensures that there is a mission.

f. Describe your thoughts as to the advantages and disadvantages of implementing hoshin kanri throughout a company.

# 4

# Improving Management Governance and Innovation through IEE

The previous chapter described problems with traditional business metrics and how conventional strategic planning can lead to activities that are not in the best interest of the business as a whole. This chapter provides a high-level description of how IEE can create a culture that transitions organizations from firefighting to an orchestrated governance system that moves toward the three *R*s of business: everyone doing the Right things and doing them Right at the Right time.

> IEE can create a culture that transitions organizations from firefighting to an orchestrated system that moves toward the three *R*s of business.

In a company a governance model might define the composition of the cross-organizational or cross-functional teams who will monitor the processes, the metrics, the meeting frequency, and so on. Organizations can have governance models for key strategic areas like total customer experience, warranty, and so on. Rather than targeting key strategies, which can change over time, the IEE system focus is on the enterprise value chain, its metrics, and targeted improvement efforts. The overall governance system

99

for this focus can be achieved through E-DMAIC, which can be orchestrated by the enterprise process management (EPM) organization (see Section 7.5).

As business competition gets tougher, there is much pressure on product development, manufacturing, and service organizations to become more productive and efficient. Developers need to create innovative products in less time, even though the products may be more complex, while at the same time addressing business risks. Manufacturing organizations feel growing pressure to improve quality while decreasing costs and to increase production volumes with fewer resources. Service organizations must reduce lead times and improve customer satisfaction. Organizations can address these issues by adopting an implementation strategy that has direct linkage to both customer needs and bottom-line benefits. One might summarize this process as the following:

Integrated Enterprise Excellence (IEE) is a sustainable business management governance system, which integrates business scorecards, strategies, and process improvement so that organizations move toward the three *R*s of business (everyone is doing the Right things and doing them Right at the Right time). IEE provides the framework for innovation and continual improvement, which goes beyond Lean Six Sigma's project-based defect- and waste-reduction methods. The existence and excellence of a business depends on more customers and cash; or, $E = MC^2$. As a business way of life, IEE provides the organizational orchestration to achieve more customer and cash.

The word *quality* often carries excess baggage with some people and therefore does not appear in this definition. For example, it is often difficult to get buy in throughout an organization when a program is viewed as a quality program that is run by the quality department. IEE is to be viewed as a methodology that applies to all functions within every organization. This system can become the framework for overcoming communication barriers and building an organizational cultural norm for continuous improvement. The wise application of statistical and nonstatistical tools, including business metrics such as satellite-level and 30,000-foot-level metrics, occurs at all levels. Organizations benefit considerably when these scorecard/dashboard metrics and improvement techniques become a business way of life; however, there can be initial resistance to adopting the overall system.

The performance and improvement system of IEE basically lowers the water level in an organization, which can expose some ugly rocks. People who have been hiding behind an ineffective organizational measurement and improvement system could initially be very concern by the increased visibility to their functional performance. However, an advantage of the IEE system is that the system not only can show ugly rocks but also has a very effective step-by-step system for remove the rocks – one by one starting with the largest rocks first.

## 4.1 Processes and Metrics

Every day we encounter devices that have an input and an output. For example, the simple movement of a light switch causes a light to turn on. Input to this process is the movement of the switch. Within the switch, a process is executed whereby internal electrical connections are made, and the output is a light turning on. This is just one example of an input-process-output (IPO), illustrated in Figure 4.1.

As users of a light switch, toaster, or radio, we are not typically interested in the mechanical details of how the process is executed. We typically view these processes as a black box. However, there are other processes with which we are more involved; for example, the process we use when preparing for and traveling to work or school. For this process, there can be multiple outputs such as arrival time, whether you experienced an automobile accident or another problem, and perhaps whether your children or spouse also arrived on time. The important outputs to processes are called key process output variables (KPOVs), critical to quality (CTQ) characteristics, or Ys.

For both black-box and other processes, we can track output over time to examine the performance of the system. Inputs to processes can take the form of *inherent process inputs* (e.g., raw material), *controlled variables* (e.g., process temperature), and

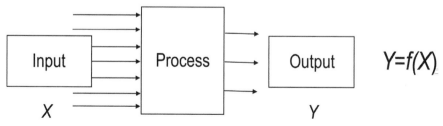

**Figure 4.1:** Input-process-output (IPO).

*uncontrolled noise variables* (e.g., raw material lots). For our example of going to work or school, consider that daily we quantified the difference between our actual and planned arrival times and then tracked this metric over time. For this measure, we might see much variability in the output of our process. We might then wish to examine why there is so much variability by consciously trying to identify the inputs to the process that can affect the process output. For reducing the variability of commuting time, we might list inputs to our process as departure time from home, time we got out of bed, traffic congestion during the commute, and whether someone had an accident along our route.

> We might see much variability in the output of our process. We might then wish to examine why there is so much variability by consciously trying to identify the inputs to the process that can affect the process output.

If we examine the inputs to our process, there are both controllable and uncontrollable, or noise, inputs. A controllable input might be setting the alarm clock, while an uncontrollable input is whether someone had an accident on our route that affected the travel time. By examining our arrival times, we might find that if we left the house five minutes earlier we could reduce our commute time by twenty-five minutes. For this situation, departure time is a key process input variable (KPIV) that is an important $X$, which affects our arrival time. When this KPIV is controlled in our go-to-work or -school process, we can reduce the amount of variability in our arrival time (KPOV).

Another tactic to reduce the variability of our arrival time is to change our process so that we can reduce the commute time or make our process robust to withstand the effect of uncontrollable input variables. For example, we might change our travel route to work or school to avoid the high traffic hours of the day. This change could also reduce the likelihood of lengthy delays from accidents. We made our process robust with respect to accidents, which was a noise input variable.

There is always a process, even though it cannot be seen or is not standardized. Manufacturing processes are easy to see. We can simply follow the product. Processes are much more difficult to see in intangible business areas such as legal and financial.

Some managerial processes are beyond the scope of producing, distributing, or selling a product or service. These include budgeting, business planning, rewards and recognition, and process reporting. Middle management typically owns the responsibilities for design and implementation of these processes. These processes should help orchestrate the business toward efficiency and effectiveness, where everyone is going in the same direction toward meeting business objectives. When they are poor processes, the organization can become dysfunctional that can result in much wasted effort and even business failure. Since the means to making improvement is through the process, understanding the process is crucial to making improvements.

Similarly, in business and other organizations we have processes or systems. For the process for going to work or school, the identification of inputs and potential process changes that positively impact our process output is not too difficult. Easy fixes can also occur within business processes when we view it systematically through an IEE strategy. However, identification and improvement systems for some business processes can be complex. For these situations, I view this search for KPIVs and process-improvement strategies as a mystery, where we uncovering clues, using a structured approach, that lead us to understanding the process outputs.

Table 4.1 example illustrates KPOVs (*Y*s) that a company could experience along with one, of perhaps many, associated KPIV (*X*s) for each of these processes.

These *Y*s are at various levels within an organization's overall system of doing business. One should note that the input to one process can be the output from another. For example, a described input for expense is work in progress (WIP), which is a high-level output from other processes.

Both customers and suppliers are involved in a process. This relationship is often expressed using a supplier-input-process-output-customer (SIPOC) diagram (see Volume III).

In IEE an enterprise cascading measurement methodology (ECMM) can be created, which aligns metrics throughout the

**Table 4.1** KPOVs (*Y*s) With a KPIV (*X*) for Each

|   | *Y*s or KPOVs | *X*s or KPIVs |
|---|---|---|
| 1 | Profits | Identification and exploitation of enterprise constraint |
| 2 | Customer satisfaction | Out of stock items |
| 3 | Enterprise goal | Development of improvement strategies from enterprise analysis |
| 4 | Expense | Amount of WIP |
| 5 | Production cycle time | Amount of internal rework |
| 6 | Defect rate | Invoices returned because they were sent to the wrong department |
| 7 | Critical dimension on a part | Process temperature |

organization to the overall organizational needs. The tracking of these measurements, over time, can then pull for the creation of P-DMAIC or DFIEE/DFSS projects, which address improvement needs for common-cause variability for the process output. Through this pragmatic approach, where no games are played with the numbers, organizations have a systematic way to improve both their bottom line and customer satisfaction. This system is much more than a quality initiative—it is a business way of life.

The IEE system uses 30,000-foot-level scorecard/dashboard metric terminology to describe a high-level view for KPOV (CTQ, or *Y* variable) responses. This high-level, in-flight airplane view for operational and project metrics has infrequent subgrouping/sampling so that short-term variations, which might be caused by KPIVs, will result in charts that view these perturbations as common-cause issues. A 30,000-foot-level individuals control chart (see Volume III for chart-creation methods) can reduce the amount of organizational firefighting when used to report operational metrics.

An alignment and management of metrics may be implemented throughout the organization so that there is an orchestration of the right activity being done at the correct time. Meaningful measurements are statistically tracked over time at various functional levels of the business. This leads to an ECMM, where meaningful measurements are statistically tracked over time at various functional levels. In this system, there is an alignment of important metrics throughout the organization. This alignment extends from the satellite-level business metrics to high-level KPOV operational metrics, which can be at the 30,000-foot-level, 20,000-foot-level, or 10,000-foot-level (infrequent subgrouping/sampling), to KPIVs at the 50-foot-level (frequent subgrouping/sampling). This metric system helps organizations run the business so there is less firefighting and it has a pull system for the creation and execution of projects whenever operational metric improvements are needed.

## 4.2   Overview of IEE

Management needs to ask the right questions; the right questions lead to the wise use of statistical and nonstatistical techniques for the purpose of obtaining knowledge from facts and data. Management needs to encourage the *wise* application of statistical techniques. Management needs to operate using the bromide In God we trust; all others bring data.

This series volume suggests periodic process reviews and projects based on assessments leading to a knowledge-centered activity (KCA) focus in all aspects of the business, where KCA describes efforts for wisely obtaining knowledge and then wisely using this knowledge within organizations and processes. KCA can redirect the focus of business so that efforts are more productive.

When implemented at GE, Six Sigma had evolved to a project-based system where emphasis was given to defect reduction. In this deployment, the quantification of project success was an improved process sigma quality level (see Glossary for sigma quality level definition) and with a quantifiable financial benefit.

Because Six Sigma projects begin with a problem statement, it is only natural that Six Sigma is considered to be a problem-solving system. The evolution from Six Sigma to Lean Six Sigma resulted in the expansion of problem statement opportunities to include the gambit of considering waste in traditional Lean deployments; that is, overproduction, waiting, transportation, inventory, over-processing, motion, defects, and people utilization.

However, often project deployments that center on the use of Lean or Six Sigma tools do not significantly impact the organization's big picture. Organizations may not pick the best projects to work on, which could result in sub-optimization that makes the system as a whole worse. In addition, Lean Six Sigma is a project-driven system, not a business system. IEE is an encompassing business system that addresses these issues, and more.

Lean Six Sigma curriculums typically don't address organizational measurements and the building of a business strategy that targets the system as a whole. DMAIC is the traditional roadmap for executing and managing Six Sigma process-improvement projects. DMAIC is used in IEE not only to describe process-improvement project execution steps but also to establish the framework for the overall enterprise process.

Figure 4.2 shows how the IEE *enterprise process* DMAIC roadmap has linkage in the *enterprise process* improve phase to the *improvement project* DMAIC roadmap and *design project* define-measure-analyze-design-verify (DMADV) roadmap. The measure phase of the improvement project DMAIC roadmap has the additional noted drill-downs.

As noted earlier, I refer to the enterprise-process DMAIC roadmap as E-DMAIC and to the project DMAIC roadmap as P-DMAIC. The high-level P-DMAIC project-execution roadmap steps are shown in Volume III. In this volume the steps of the E-DMAIC roadmap will be described sequentially. Volume III, after an introduction, sequentially describes the P-DMAIC roadmap steps.

> I refer to the enterprise-process DMAIC roadmap as E-DMAIC and to the project DMAIC roadmap as P-DMAIC.

Figure 4.3 illustrates the IEE integration of Lean, Six Sigma, and other tools and techniques at both the enterprise and process-improvement project level. In the E-DMAIC roadmap, Lean tools are specifically described in the analyze phase. In the P-DMAIC roadmap, Lean tools are specifically described in the measure and improve phases.

Excessive measurement-system error can lead to firefighting behavior and make it difficult to develop correlations that help determine what inputs drive the outputs. The focus tends to be on improving the process, when the needed effort should be on improving the measurement system. Measurement systems

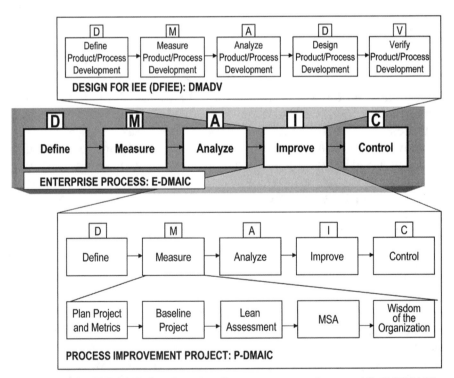

**Figure 4.2:** IEE high-level enterprise process roadmap with P-DMAIC process improvement and DMADV design project roadmaps (MSA = measurement system analysis).

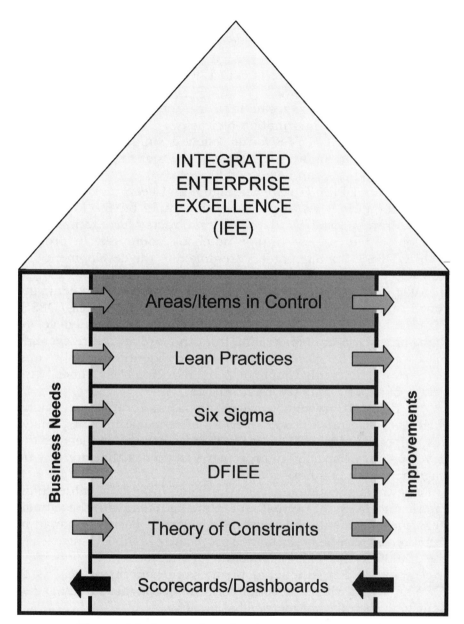

**Figure 4.3:** Integration of tools and methodologies.

analysis (MSA) addresses these issues, which are applicable as both enterprise performance metrics and project metrics (see Volume III).

There are execution steps to walk through for the organization's enterprise-process (E-DMAIC) and process-improvement-project

(P-DMAIC) roadmap. Many Six Sigma and Lean tools also apply to the design-project DMADV process, which is often called design for Six Sigma (DFSS) or design for Lean Six Sigma (DFLSS). In IEE, this design system is called design for Integrated Enterprise Excellence, or DFIEE.

DFIEE/DFSS projects can take the form of product-design, process-design, or information-technology (IT) projects. In IEE, these three DFIEE/DFSS forms follow a similar DMADV roadmap, as noted in Figure 4.2; however, the tool emphasis for each of these situations can be quite different.

In product DFIEE/DFSS, Six Sigma and Lean tools are linked to address new types of products that build on the knowledge gained from previously developed products; for example, the development of a new vintage notebook computer. In process DFIEE/DFSS, Six Sigma tools are linked to the development of a new process that has never previously been created by the organization; for example, creation of a call center within a company that in the past did not have a call center. In IT, DFIEE/DFSS, Six Sigma, and Lean tools are integrated into the overall development process. Example benefits from this are structure systems for capturing the voice of the customer, identifying risks, and perhaps significantly improving or reducing test times with design of experiments (DOE) strategies.

The E-DMAIC system provides an infrastructure for linking high-level enterprise-process-performance measurements, analyses, improvements, and controls. This framework can lead to the development of specific improvement strategies that are in true alignment with business goals.

From these created strategies, targeted functional value-chain metric improvement needs that are in alignment with these business measurement goals can be developed. Positive change in functional-baseline performance scorecard/dashboard metrics at the 30,000-foot-level is the measure of success relative to achieving targets. Each functional business-measurement goal is to have an owner whose personal performance is measured against achieving the relevant metric goal.

Long-lasting improvements in the 30,000-foot-level scorecard/dashboard metrics are the result of systematic process-improvement and design projects. This IEE improvement-metric system creates a stimulus that results in a pull for project creation. From this system, projects are created that are in true alignment to business needs. In addition, this system framework leads to the creation and execution of a long-lasting business-measurement and business-improvement organizational system.

> Long-lasting improvements in the 30,000-foot-level scorecard or dashboard metrics are the result of systematic process-improvement and design projects. This IEE improvement-metric system creates a stimulus that results in a pull, for the creation of these improvement and design projects.

This system can provide many more benefits than the push for Lean Six Sigma project creation from a list of potential projects and the execution of these projects, where the primary quantification of success is the amount of money saved. In addition, these projects might not have true alignment to business needs.

IEE's execution flow follows the overall thought process of evaluating the enterprise process (E-DMAIC) to the mechanics of executing a specific improvement project (P-DMAIC), as illustrated in Figure 4.2. Volume III provides highlights of the benefits of Six Sigma and Lean tools that are most applicable and that challenge some of the traditional Six Sigma and Lean Six Sigma techniques that can lead to questionable results. I will expand on other techniques that are beyond the boundaries of these methodologies. The reader can refer to *Implementing Six Sigma* (Breyfogle 2003a) for elaboration on the traditional methodologies of Six Sigma and Lean.

It has been my observation that many Six Sigma and Lean Six Sigma implementations have a push for a project creation system. This can lead to projects that have little, if any, value to the true bottom line of the organization or to multiple projects claiming the same savings.

> It has been my observation that many Six Sigma and Lean Six Sigma implementations have a push for a project creation system. This can lead to projects that have little, if any, value to the true bottom line of the organization or to multiple projects claiming the same savings.

The described approach in this volume goes beyond traditional techniques, so that there is a pull for project creation by enterprise-process measurements. A traditional Six Sigma model can lead to all levels of management asking for the creation of Six Sigma projects that improve the numbers against which they are measured. These projects often are not as beneficial as one might think since this project-selection approach does not focus on identifying and resolving enterprise-process constraint issues. We have had people come back to us saying that another Six Sigma provider is claiming that they have saved hundred million dollars in a company; however, no one can seem to find the money.

The IEE approach can help sustain Six Sigma or Lean Six Sigma activities, a problem that many companies that have previously implemented Six Sigma or Lean Six Sigma are now confronting. In addition, this system focuses on downplaying a traditional Six Sigma policy that all Six Sigma projects must have a defined defect. I have found that this policy can lead to many nonproductive activities, game playing with the numbers, and overall frustration. The practice of not defining a defect makes this strategy much more conducive to a true integration with general workflow-improvement tools that use Lean thinking methods.

Various steps have been proposed by organizations while executing Six Sigma. Motorola frequently referenced a six-step approach to implementing Six Sigma. I referenced a ten-step Motorola approach in *Statistical Methods for Testing Development and Manufacturing* (Breyfogle 1992), which I preferred over Motorola's more frequently referenced six-step approach, since the ten-step method linked the steps with statistical and nonstatistical application tools.

To achieve success, organizations must wisely address metrics and their infrastructure. The success of deployment is linked to a set of cross-functional metrics that lead to significant improvements in customer satisfaction and bottom-line benefits. Companies experiencing success have created an infrastructure that supports this strategy.

An IEE business strategy involves the measurement of how well business processes meet organizational goals and offers strategies to make needed improvements. The application of the techniques to all functions results in a very high level of quality at reduced costs with a reduction in lead times, resulting in improved profitability and a competitive advantage. It is most important to choose the best set of measurements for a particular situation and to focus on the wise integration of statistical and other improvement tools offered by an IEE implementation.

A mission of Six Sigma is the reduction of cost of poor quality (COPQ). Traditionally, the broad costing categories of COPQ are internal failure costs, external failure costs, appraisal costs, and prevention costs. In Six Sigma, COPQ has a less rigid interpretation and perhaps a broader scope. In Six Sigma, COPQ means not doing what is right the first time, which can encompass anything from scrap to reworks to meetings with no purpose. COPQ also encompasses the cost of process steps that do not add value to a product or service for which a customer is willing to pay. In this volume, I prefer to reference this metric as the cost of doing nothing differently (CODND). CODND has broader cost implications than COPQ, which could be perceived as a quality initiative.

Quality cost issues can dramatically affect a business, but very important ones are often hidden from view. Organizations can be missing the largest issues when they focus only on the tip of the iceberg, as shown in Figure 4.4. It is important for organizations to direct their efforts so these hidden issues, which are often more important than the readily visible ones, are uncovered. IEE techniques can help flatten many of the issues that affect overall cost. However, management needs to ask the right questions before these issues are addressed effectively. Success is the function of a need, a vision, and a plan.

This volume describes the IEE business strategy: executive ownership, a support infrastructure, projects with bottom-line results, full-time (suggested) black belts, part-time green belts, reward and motivation considerations, finance engagement (i.e., to determine the CODND and return on investment for projects), and training in all roles, both "hard" and "soft" skills.

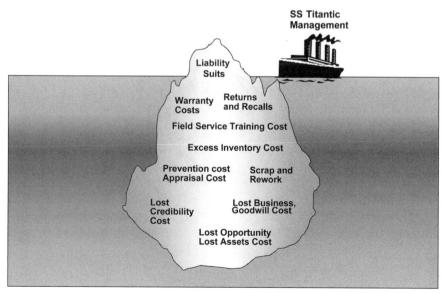

**Figure 4.4:** Cost of poor quality (COPQ), or cost of doing nothing differently (CODND).

Organizations create strategic plans and policies. They also create goals that describe the intent of the organization. These goals should have measurable results those are attained through defined action plans. The question of concern is: How effective and aligned are these management-system practices within an organization? An improvement to this system can dramatically impact an organization's bottom line.

An IEE system measures the overall organization using score-cards/dashboard metrics that report at the satellite-level and 30,000-foot-level metrics, as illustrated in Figure 4.5. Physically, these metrics can have many forms, as illustrated in Figure 4.6. Traditional business metrics that could be classified as satellite-level metrics are gross revenue; profit; net profit margin; earnings before interest, depreciation, and amortization (EBIDA); and voice of the customer. Traditional operational metrics at the 30,000-foot-level are defective or defect rates, lead time, waste, days sales outstanding (DSO), on-time delivery, number of days from promise date, number of days from customer-requested date,

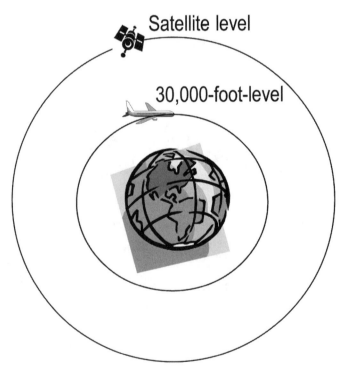

**Figure 4.5:** Satellite-level and 30,000-foot-level scorecard/dashboard metrics.

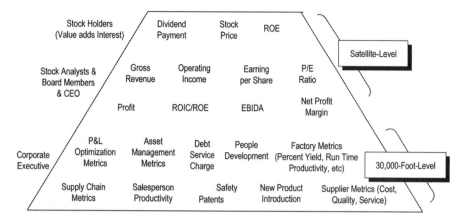

ROE = Return on Equity; OI = Operating Income; P/E = Price to Earnings; ROIC = Return on Invested Capital
P&L = Profit & Loss; EBIDA = Earnings Before Interest Depreciation, and Amortization; VOC = Voice of the Customer

**Figure 4.6:** Example satellite-level and 30,000-foot-level metrics.

dimensional property, inventory, and head count. The enterprise-process financial analysis can be linked to these metrics, leading to process-improvement projects, as described later in this volume.

Both satellite-level and 30,000-foot-level metrics are tracked over time and are not bounded by calendar year. If nothing has changed in ten years, satellite-level and 30,000-foot-level charts would present how the system performed over the past ten years. Organizations will find it very beneficial when they align project selection with satellite-level measures from theory of constraint (TOC) metrics; that is, TOC throughput (see Glossary), investment and inventory, and operating expense.

> Both satellite-level and 30,000-foot-level metrics are tracked over time and are not bounded by calendar year. If nothing has changed in ten years, satellite-level and 30,000-foot-level charts would present how the system performed over the past ten years.

Data presented in the satellite-level and 30,000-foot-level scorecard/dashboard format provide additional business insight when, for example, compared to tabular quarterly format reporting. Satellite-level and 30,000-foot-level reporting involves the creation of scorecards/dashboard metrics throughout the organization's value chain. An enterprise cascading-measurement methodology (ECMM) is a system that cascades and aligns important metrics throughout the organization so that meaningful measurements are statistically tracked over time at various functional levels of the business.

| Key process output variable – an important measurable process response |
| --- |

ECMM tracking cascades satellite-level business metrics down to high-level KPOV operational metrics. These high-level KPOV metrics might have a 30,000-foot-level, 20,000-foot-level, and 10,000-foot-level metric reporting, where all these high-level metrics are tracked using infrequent subgrouping/sampling techniques. This cascading can further progress down to 50-foot-level KPIV metrics, where frequent sampling feedback is used to determine when timely adjustments are needed to a process.

| KPIV: Key Process Input Variable – a process input that can significantly affect its response. |
| --- |

High-level KPOV metrics provide voice of the process views at various organizational levels, while low-level KPIV metrics provide the trigger for when timely process-adjustments are needed so that high-level KPOV performance is maintained. For example, in popular grocery stores, a high-level KPOV cascaded metric from an overall customer satisfaction metric could be grocery store check-out time. A related low-level KPIV to this high-level check-out-time metric would the number of people in line, which could provide a timely decision point for determining whether grocery store checkers should be added, reduced, or remain the same.

High-level ECMM metrics in conjunction with an effective process improvement system can transition a business from a culture of firefighting to one of fire prevention. Within this fire-prevention culture, business performance metric improvement needs pull for the creation of projects that lead to long-lasting, beneficial process change. The result from this is that there are less future fires to fight.

An illustration of how an organizational metric cascading environment can create a fire-prevention culture is:

An enterprise's 30,000-foot-level on-time-shipment tracking could consist of weekly random selecting 100 product shipments and then comparing how well each shipment performed relative to its due date. For this reporting, each product shipment could be viewed as an attribute; i.e., it was received on-time or not. This data would then be combined to create a weekly cumulated non-conformance rate for deliveries relative to due dates.

For this reporting format, a shipment that is one day late would carry the same delinquency severity level as a shipment that is twenty days late. Typically the reporting of these two non-compliance deliveries would not be viewed with an equivalent level of dissatisfaction. Hence, if at all possible, it would be better to convert this form of attribute conformance reporting to continuous data; e.g., a 3.0 would indicate three days late, while −1.0 would indicate one day early.

This data format could then be tracked over time using the basic IEE scorecard/dashboard metric reporting process described below. There should be ownership for each 30,000-foot-level metric. This owner would be responsible for achieving assigned future process improvement goals for his/her 30,000-foot-level performance metric(s).

During an E-DMAIC study, this metric could have been determined to be a high potential area for improvement. This volume will later show how an enterprise improvement plan (EIP) can be used to drill down from a goal to high potential areas for improvement (see Figure 12.1).

This 30,000-foot-level metric could also be cascaded downward as a 20,000-foot-level metric, 10,000-foot-level metric, etc. throughout the organization. This could be accomplished by using a similar sampling procedure to the one described above for product delivery times by sites and perhaps individual part numbers. The assignment of deliver metric ownership for the 20,000-foot-level and other components of the 30,000-foot-level organizational metrics can provide the focus needed for process measurement and improvement opportunities.

If an improvement is desired for this enterprise 30,000-foot-level metric, a Pareto chart could be useful to determine which sites and part numbers should be given focus for improving the 30,000-foot-level metric as a whole; i.e., creation of targeted projects that are pulled for creation by metric improvement needs.

The reader should note how this approach is quite different than passing down an across the board goal of "improving on-time shipments" for all sites through an organizational chart or other means. With the above approach, sites that are performing well need to only maintain their performance, while other sites that are not performing well would get the needed attention focus for determining what to do to improve their performance. In the sites that are not doing well, one or more projects would be pulled for creation by this metric improvement need.

NONCONFORMANCE: Failure to meet a specification

This individual-measurement report tracking is accomplished through the metric-reporting process for the IEE scorecard/dashboard as follows:

1. Assess process predictability.
2. When the process is considered predictable, formulate a prediction statement for the latest region of stability. The usual reporting format for this prediction statement is the following:
   a. When there is a specification requirement: nonconformance percentage or defects per million opportunities (DPMO)
   b. When there is no specification requirement: median response and 80 percent frequency of occurrence rate

In IEE, prediction statements are referred to as a process capability/performance metric. If there is a specification or requirement, IEE prediction statements usually are reported as a nonconformance proportion rate, for example, out-of-specification percentage or DPMO. In IEE, both continuous and attribute pass or fail response data use this reporting format. If there are no specifications or requirements for a continuous response, then a median response and 80 percent frequency of occurrence rate is reported. An 80 percent frequency of occurrence rate is typically used for this situation, since this percentage provides an easy-to-understand picture of the variability around the median that can be expected from the process.

It needs to be highlighted that prediction statements provide a best estimate of how the process is currently performing and what performance could be expected from the process in the future, unless something changes. Predictive processes can shift either positively or negatively at any time, in any month or day of the year. When a process shifts between two stable and predictable regions, the quantification of the before-and-after change (predictive statements difference) is a best-estimate statement for the project's benefit.

This metric tracking approach assesses the organization as a system, which can lead to focused improvement efforts and a reduction of firefighting activities. Data presented in this format can be useful for executives as an input to the creation of strategic plans and then for tracking the results from the execution of those plans. With this strategy, action plans to achieve organizational goals center on the creation and implementation of projects in the E-DMAIC system, as illustrated in Figure 4.7.

The following describes the basic thought process of an E-DMAIC execution using the steps of Figure 4.7.

- Step 1 (Define phase of E-DMAIC):
  - Define vision and mission.
- Step 2 (Define phase [value-chain steps] and measure phase [value-chain measurements] of E-DMAIC)
  - Describe value chain, including 30,000-foot-level metrics.
  - Create satellite-level metrics for the past three to ten years. We want to ensure that the selected time is long enough that multiple business cycles are captured.
  - Compile 30,000-foot-level value-chain metrics.
- Step 3 (Analyze phase of E-DMAIC)
  - Analyze satellite-level and 30,000-foot-level metrics looking for improvement opportunities.
  - Analyze the enterprise as a whole looking for constraints, improvement opportunities, and new product opportunities, which could include acquisitions or selling portions of the business.
- Step 4 (Analyze phase of E-DMAIC)
  - Establish SMART goals that are consistent with the work from step 3.
- Step 5 (Analyze phase of E-DMAIC)
  - Create strategies from analyses described in step three.

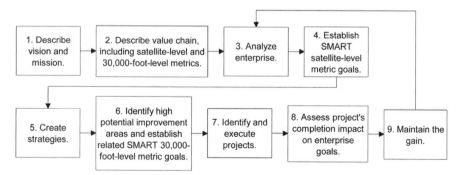

**Figure 4.7:** Aligning projects with business needs through E-DMAIC roadmap for project selection and P-DMAIC or DMADV roadmap for project execution.

- Step 6 (Analyze phase of E-DMAIC)
  - Identify high potential areas and related 30,000-foot-level scorecard/dashboard metrics for focusing improvement efforts using goals and the value-chain process map to help guide the selection process.
  - Establish 30,000-foot-level value-chain metric goals with agree-to ownership and time for achievement. The project champion should be the owner of the metric that is to be improved.
  - Identify potential projects that are in alignment with de-termined business needs.
- Step 7 (Improve phase of E-DMAIC)
  - Select and assign well-scoped projects that are not too large or too small.
  - Work for timely project completion of process using resource of champion and black belt or green belt with coaching.
- Step 8 (Improve phase of E-DMAIC)
  - Assess project completion impact on enterprise goals.
- Step 9 (Control phase of E-DMAIC)
  - Maintain the gains
- Repeat.

IEE 30,000-foot-level scorecard/dashboard metrics are high-level operational or project metrics. The right metrics are needed for the orchestration of the right activities. The E-DMAIC process just described accomplishes this by linking improvement activities to business goals and to strategies that are aligned with these goals through the use of analytics.

This strategy can also be used with other types of improvement projects such as reliability excellence and behavior-based safety. People in organizations often feel overwhelmed when facing multiple improvement activities and when resources are in competition between associated projects. This system can tie all the improvement practices together and prioritize the resources where needed. It can help organizations understand and improve the key drivers that affect the metrics and enterprise process scorecards.

## 4.3   IEE as a Business Strategy

In a work environment, tasks are completed. These tasks can lead to a response even though the procedures to perform them are not formally documented. Lead time is one potential response for the completion of a series of tasks. Another is the quality of the completed work. Reference will be made to important responses from a process as key process output variables (KPOVs), sometimes called the *Y*s of the process.

Sometimes the things that are completed within a work environment cause a problem to customers or create a great deal of waste; i.e., overproduction, waiting, transportation, inventory, overprocessing, motion, defects, and people utilization, which can be very expensive to an organization. Attempts to solve waste do not always address these problems from an overall system viewpoint. The organization might also have a variety of KPOVs, such as a critical dimension, overall lead time, a DPMO rate that could expose a hidden-factory rework issue currently not reported, customer satisfaction, and so on.

For this type of situation, organizations often react to the up-and-down movements of the KPOV level over time in a firefighting mode, fixing the problems of the day. Frequent arbitrary tweaks to controllable process variables and noise (for example, material differences, operator-to-operator differences, machine-to-machine differences, and measurement imprecision) can cause excess variability and yield a large nonconforming proportion for the KPOV. Practitioners and management might think that their day-to-day problem-fixing activities are making improvements to the system. In reality, these activities often expend many resources without making any improvements to the process. Unless long-lasting process changes are made, the proportion of noncompliance will remain approximately the same.

When we manage simply toward goals and targets throughout the organization chart, we are managing to the *Y*s in the mathematical relationship $Y = f(X)$. This can lead to the wrong behavior; that is, the Enron effect. The way to make long-lasting improvements is through process changes or improving the management of the *X*s that are shown in Figure 4.8.

> When we manage simply toward goals and targets throughout the organization chart, we are managing to the *Y*s in the mathematical relationship $Y = f(X)$. This can lead to the wrong behavior; that is, the Enron effect. The way to make long-lasting improvements is through process changes or improving the management of the *X*s.

Organizations that frequently encounter this type of situation have much to gain from the implementation of an IEE business

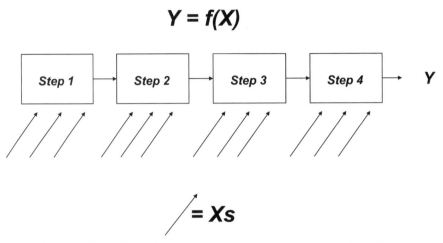

**Figure 4.8:** Magnitude of a process response as a function of its input levels.

strategy. They can better appreciate this potential gain when they consider all the direct and indirect costs associated with their current level of nonconformance.

The described methodology is a deployment system that uses both statistical and nonstatistical tools. As Figure 4.2 illustrates, an E-DMAIC system can lead to an improvement project that follows the P-DMAIC roadmap. P-DMAIC is an enhanced version of the traditional Six Sigma DMAIC roadmap. The P-DMAIC roadmap offers additional component breakdown in the measure phase and true Lean tool integration.

In this business strategy, a practitioner applies the P-DMAIC roadmap either during a workshop or as a project after a workshop. The baseline for a created project would be determined through the metric-reporting process, as noted earlier, for the IEE scorecard or dashboard as follows:

1. Assess process predictability.
2. When the process is considered predictable, formulate a prediction statement for the latest region of stability. The usual reporting format for this statement is the following:
    a. When there is a specification requirement: nonconformance percentage or DPMO
    b. When there is no specification requirement: median response and 80 percent frequency of occurrence rate

Figure 4.9 illustrates for continuous data the pull for project creation and benefit from the project as demonstrated in the 30,000-foot-level metric change. Figure 4.10 illustrates the same for an attribute response. It should be noted for continuous data that all individual values from the stable region of the process are used to create a voice of the process (VOP) distribution. The placements of specifications on this distribution provide an assessment of how well the process is performing relative to customer requirements, for example, a form of voice of the customer (VOC). While for attribute data, no distribution plot is needed since the centerline is a direct nonconformance rate estimate.

A resulting change process can have less waste and be more robust or indifferent to process noise variables. This effort can result in an improved-process mean shift or reduced variability or both, which leads to quantifiable bottom-line monetary benefits.

The success of IEE is a function of management commitment and an infrastructure that supports this commitment. However, this commitment does not need to come from the CEO level. This infrastructure can start anywhere. It can then spread throughout the company when system benefits materialize and can be shown to others.

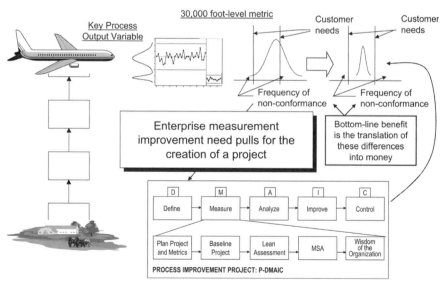

**Figure 4.9:** IEE Project creation, execution, and the benefits for a continuous response.

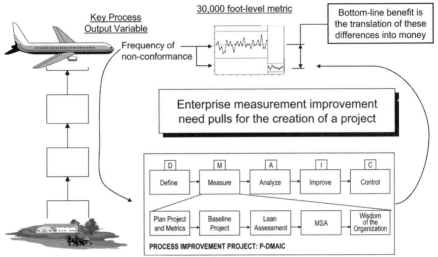

**Figure 4.10:** IEE Project creation, execution, and the benefits for an attribute response.

## 4.4   Integration of Six Sigma with Lean

There has been much contention between Six Sigma and Lean functions. I will use the terms *Lean* or *Lean thinking* to describe the application of Lean manufacturing, Lean production, or Lean enterprise-process principles to all processes. The Six Sigma community typically believes that Six Sigma comes first or is above Lean, relative to the application within an organization. Lean disciples typically believe that Lean comes first or is above Six Sigma, relative to application within an organization.

When people who have a strong foundation in Lean make the generalization that Lean improvement activities should be conducted before applying Six Sigma techniques, their thought process might be this: Lean will reduce the number of production lines producing the product. After this reduction, Six Sigma can be used to reduce variation. The reverse order may create redundant and unnecessary activities. For example, if three production lines are running, each with its own set of waste problems, it is far better to apply Lean initially to reduce the lines to one. From there, you can apply Six Sigma to reduce the variation.

I do not believe that such a generalization should be made. In some situations, Lean methods should be considered first. There are other situations where Six Sigma methods should come first. In IEE there is no preset rule for which methodology precedes the other.

> IEE integrates the two concepts, where the high-level metrics improvement need dictates which Lean or Six Sigma tools should be used at both the enterprise process and project execution level.

IEE integrates the two concepts, where the high-level metrics-improvement need dictates which Lean or Six Sigma tools should be used at both the enterprise-process and project-execution level. For example, in the P-DMAIC project-execution roadmap, Lean tools are applied in both the measure and improve phases. When a Lean or Six Sigma methodology is used to achieve the project goal, the 30,000-foot-level metric change will be used to quantify statistically the change benefit on a continuing basis.

One reason this integration works so well is that the IEE approach does not require defining a project defect, as a traditional Six Sigma deployment does, where this definition would then impact the COPQ calculation. Not requiring a defect definition is very important since Lean metrics involve various waste measures, such as inventory or lead time, which do not have true specification criteria like manufactured components. COPQ calculations cannot really be made for these situations, since there are no true specifications; however, a CODND calculation can still be determined, where the objective of an IEE project is to reduce the CODND magnitude.

It is beneficial to dissolve any separately existing Six Sigma and Lean organizational functions. Organizations should strive to have the same person use an IEE methodology in which the most appropriate tool is applied for any given situation, whether the tool is Lean, Six Sigma, or a combination of both.

## 4.5   Day-to-Day Business Management Using IEE

Organizations often experience much firefighting, where they react to the problems of the day. These organizations need a system where they can replace many of their firefighting activities with fire prevention. This can be accomplished through cascading the measures.

With this strategy, metrics are orchestrated through a statistically based, high-level measurement system. Through the alignment of the satellite-level view with the 30,000-foot-level view and other high-level metrics, organizations can create meaningful scorecard/dashboard metrics that have a direct focus on the needs of the business at the operational level. The use of these metrics can improve the orchestration of day-to-day activities.

When we view our system using a set of cascading high-level individuals control charts that have infrequent subgrouping/ sampling, behaviors can dramatically change for the better. Historically, metric systems often encouraged addressing individual day-to-day out-of-specification conditions as though they were special cause, even though they were truly common cause. This management style can lead to extensive firefighting. These fires, which often reappear after a temporary extinguishing, need immediate attention.

When there are common-cause variability problems resulting in a specification not being consistently met, the overall process needs to be changed to improve the metrics. Long-lasting improvements can be accomplished either through P-DMAIC projects, DFIEE/DFSS projects, or business-process-improvement events (BPIEs). P-DMAIC projects address the overall system's process steps and its metrics, including the measurement system itself and a control mechanism for the process that keeps it from returning to its previous unsatisfactory state. BPIEs are just-do-it improvement events that are needed by the system but do not require the formalities of a P-DMAIC project.

With this approach, process-management teams might meet weekly to discuss their high-level 30,000-foot-level scorecard/ dashboard operational metrics, while executives may review the metrics monthly. When an individuals control chart that has infrequent subgrouping/sampling shows a predictable process that does not yield a satisfactory level for the capability/performance metric , a project can be created. The P-DMAIC system experiences a pull for project creation by the need to improve the metrics.

This could become a green-belt project that is executed by a part-time process-improvement practitioner, who is within an organization's department function. The project might also become a large black-belt project that needs to address cross-functional issues. During project execution, both Six Sigma and Lean tools and methodologies need consideration to determine what needs to be done differently to achieve the desired enhanced-process response. Improvement direction might be generated quickly by executing a focused team-based kaizen event. In any case, when project improvements are made to the overall system, the 30,000-foot-level operational metric would change to an improved level.

Awareness of the 30,000-foot-level metrics and the results of project-improvement efforts should be made available to everyone, including those in the operations of the process. This information could be routinely posted using the visual-factory concept typically encountered in Lean implementations. Posting of information can improve the awareness and benefits of the system throughout the organization, which can lead to more buy in of the IEE methodology throughout the function. This can result in the stimulation of other improvement efforts that dramatically improve the overall satellite-level metrics.

This metric tracking and reporting approach along with the creation of improvement activities can alter management's focus, which might be on the problems of the day. It could lead to asking questions about the status of projects that would improve the overall operational process capability/performance metrics of the company. Behavioral changes would then start to take place that would focus on prevention rather reaction. The completion of few projects in the most beneficial area of a business can have dramatic benefits in the high-level organizational metrics.

## 4.6   Integrating Innovation and Analytics through IEE

Thurm (2007) states:

> "We've had management by objective and total quality management. Now it's time for the latest trend in business methodology: management by data. The success of enterprises as diverse as Harrah's Entertainment, Google, Capital One Financial and the Oakland A's has inspired case studies, books and consultants promising to help executives outpace rivals by collecting more information and analyzing it better.
>
> Google, the company that tracks every user keystroke on its Web site, also frees its engineers to spend 20% of their work time on self-directed projects. That has given birth to such programs as Google News, Gmail and, most significantly, AdSense for content, which places Google-brokered ads on other Web sites.
>
> Dave Girouard, vice president and general manager of the Google unit building software for businesses, encourages his several hundred employees to use their self-directed time. 'A lot of analytical stuff will give you incremental improvement, but it won't give you

a big leap,' he says. 'You can't time or plan for innovation. It can't come from customer data. It has to come from the heart of somebody with an idea'."

In addition, it is believed by some (*BusinessWeek* 2007, Hindo 2007) that Lean Six Sigma inhibits rather than encourages innovation. This could be the case in an organization's Lean Six Sigma deployment, where focus is given to the search for projects and their completion. In these organizations, primary focus can be for black-belt or green-belt certification upon project completion. With this deployment style, sight of the big picture can be lost.

In other cases, there can be a promulgation of this innovation-stifling belief by those who feel threatened. Some can be concern by the additional level of accountability and are looking for ways to undermine the deployment's implementation.

I have seen companies that were innovative; however, the organization did not benefit from the created technologies. This happens when either the technology did not fit into the company's product line or no system was in place to take the innovated product or service to market. Innovation with no framework for its creation and transition to a marketable product or service is not unlike an orchestra where every person uses his or her instrument to play individually composed musical selections at the same time. Individually, each musical presentation (innovated product or service) could sound very good but the beauty of each musical piece was not heard or appreciated at the orchestra level (organization or company); i.e., the delivery of each musical selection did not have good overall orchestration.

> Innovation with no framework for its creation and transition to a marketable product or service is not unlike an orchestra where every person uses his or her instrument to play individually composed musical selections at the same time.

The IEE system that takes Lean Six Sigma and the balanced scorecard to the next level, enhances rather than detracts from innovation. IEE addresses the issues described by Thurm (2007), *BusinessWeek* (2007), and Hindo (2007) through a governance system where organizations consciously integrate analytics and innovation to create a system blend that is right for them.

By creating a system that captures VOC in the product-development cycle, greater emphasis can be given to using innovation to create products or services that are marketable. In this system, innovation is enabled by creating an infrastructure that breaks down creativity-usage barriers, which when effective orchestrated can benefit the business as a whole.

The E-DMAIC system provides a framework for organizations to create a culture that is right for them relative to the amount of innovation nurturing and idea up-selling; i.e., some companies by the nature of the business need more out-of-the-box innovation thinking than other organizations.

For example, a company's created IEE infrastructure could include an annual get-together to stimulate or share thoughts about new product or service innovations, in addition to innovation-allocated "free time" for some people. The overall company process to encourage innovation could include TRIZ (see List of Symbols and Acronyms) and other tools as part of existing ad hoc or innovation-generation practices that enhance the opportunity for creating innovative breakthrough-formulation opportunities.

Without the rigor of creating a system that embraces the orchestration of creativity and a go-to-market execution, chaos, the archenemy of innovation, can result.

## 4.7  Infrastructure

IEE is supported by a practitioner belt structure similar to that of traditional Six Sigma and Lean Six Sigma, where the value of maintaining and improving customer satisfaction must not be overlooked by organizational activities.

Black belts (BBs) and master black belts (MBBs) are a key part of the deployment infrastructure. Not only do selected BBs and MBBs need to have the capability of learning and applying statistical methodologies, but they also need to be proactive people who are good at the soft skills needed while effectively working with others. BBs and MBBs will not only need to analyze information and use statistical techniques to get results, but also be able to work with others through mentoring, teaching, coaching, and selling others on how they can benefit from the techniques. In my experience, the most successful BBs and MBBs possess the following skill set:

- Fire in the belly: They have an unquenchable desire to improve the way an organization does its business.

- Soft skills: They have the ability to work effectively with people in teams and other organizations.
- Project management: They have the ability to get things done well and on time.
- System thinker: They have an appreciation that work is accomplished through processes and that true long-lasting results are made through systematic improvements to these processes.
- Multi-tasking: They have no problem managing and scheduling several activities in the same time frame.
- Unstructured environment management: They have the ability to work in chaotic environments and create systems within these situations.
- Big picture thinker: They focus on aligning their efforts to impact the big picture. They avoid analysis paralysis.
- Analytical skills: They have correct and valid reasoning skills and are comfortable using mathematic techniques such as algebra.
- Organizational navigation skills: They can work around barriers without invoking higher authority.
- Critical thinking skills: They are skillful at conceptualizing, applying, analyzing, synthesizing, and evaluating information from multiple sources.

All these items have more linkage to inherent natural abilities than to teachable skill sets. It is not difficult to teach statistical methodologies if a person has good analytical skills, however, the lack of other personality traits can make it difficult to achieve benefits from the deployment. When implementing an IEE Business Strategy, organizations need to create a process for selecting black belt trainees that addresses innate talent as well as these skills.

Efforts to hire previously trained BBs and MBBs are often not very successful. Hiring the right person who possesses the above skills is not an easy or mistake proof task. In addition, this new hire would need to fit into the organizational culture and know the internal structure for getting things done. Finally, one might ask how long we can anticipate this new hire will remain with the company. If the person is very good, headhunters might entice him to move onto another company—just after your company finally got him/her up to speed.

Alternatively, companies know which employees best fit the above profile. These employees already know the company protocol and how to get things done within its culture. With a little training and coaching, they can become very effective at implementing the system.

A rule of thumb for the number of black belts in an organization is 1 to 2 percent of the total number of employees. Black belts are supported technically through a master black belt and through the management chain of an organization by way of a champion. Individuals who are given IEE training to a lesser extent and support black belts are called green belts.

When an organization chooses to implement Six Sigma, Lean Six Sigma, or IEE, it is important that the organization hit the road running as soon as possible. It is important that the organization do it right the first time and not have a false start. It is important that internal organizational resources focus on creating the infrastructure and help with expediting results, not with the development of training materials.

Because of this, it is best to utilize an outside training/coaching company to get the organization started. This training/coaching company can help with setting up a deployment strategy, conducting initial training, and providing project coaching. The decision on which group is chosen can dramatically affect the success of its implementation. However, choosing the best group to help an organization implement Six Sigma can be a challenge. Some items for consideration are covered in *Implementing Six Sigma* (Breyfogle 2003a).

This volume focuses on using the E-DMAIC project execution roadmap to gain quick, repeatable results. The statistical community and others often comment that most procedures, which are suggested in these roadmaps, are not new. As a general statement, I do not disagree. However, the Six Sigma and Lean names have increased the awareness of upper level management to the value of using statistical concepts and nonstatistical concepts. The structure of the E-DMAIC roadmap provides an efficient linkage of the tools that help novice and experienced practitioners utilize both Six Sigma and Lean tools effectively.

Topic focus on executing E-DMAIC steps is given later in this volume, while Volume III focuses on the execution P-DMAIC steps. Many tools are applicable to both DMAIC methodologies; hence, in this series of volumes there is cross-referencing between the roadmaps.

# 4.8  Comparison to Total Quality Management

Often people suggest that Six Sigma is the same as total quality management (TQM). I do not agree. However, before making any generalities about the advantages of Six Sigma, it should be emphasized that there have been implementation and success/ failure differences for both TQM and Six Sigma.

In my opinion, TQM did not systematically address the following itemized list with as much detail as Six Sigma. Six Sigma addresses most of the points in this list; however, IEE addresses all these items so that the concepts in Six Sigma/Lean Six Sigma are taken to the next level.

Some inherent advantages of using an IEE implementation are:

- Focus is given to bottom line benefits for organizations, where project monetary benefits are verified by finance. At the executive level, this breeds excitement since improvement work is being aligned to their primary measure of success.
- A support infrastructure is created where specific roles exist for people to be full-time practitioners (black belts) and other support/leadership roles (champions, green belts, and others).
- Practitioners follow a consistent project execution roadmap as describe in this volume.
- Rather than a quality program, it is a business strategy that helps drive the business to the right activities correctly. This point needs to be communicated and understood at the deployment onset.
- Projects are pulled for creation by the metrics that drive the business. However, often companies a push for project creation, which may not be the best utilization of resources.
- Voice of the Customer focus is given at both the satellite-level business metrics and 30,000-foot-level project execution metrics.

When implementing IEE, we need to capitalize on the lessons learned from other Six Sigma implementations. The Six Sigma benchmark study summary shown in Section A.2 of *Implementing Six Sigma* (Breyfogle 2003a) summarizes what six benchmarked companies have done.

My experiences for the success of IEE are consistent with the summary of common case study Six Sigma deployment attributes from Snee and Hoerl (2003):

| Very Successful Case Studies | Less Successful Case Studies |
|---|---|
| • Committed leadership<br>  - Use of top talent | • Supportive leadership<br>  - Use of whoever was available |
| • Supporting infrastructure<br>  - Formal project selection process<br>  - Formal project review process<br>  - Dedicated resources<br>  - Financial system integration | • No supporting infrastructure<br>  - No formal project selection process<br>  - No formal project review process<br>  - Part time resources<br>  - Not integrated financial system |

## 4.9   Initiating Deployment

Often organizations that are considering a Lean Six Sigma, Six Sigma, or IEE deployment make the statement that before deploying the system they want to conduct a pilot improvement project. With this approach, someone is trained and then applies the methodologies to improve a specified process. The success of the improvement project on making a business financial impact would then be the deciding factor whether to pursue a deployment.

On the surface, this approach sounds reasonable. However, a pilot project can fail for numerous reasons. One reason is that nondedicated people were to complete the project but no work time was allotted for the project or there was no, or too little, instructor-trainee project-application coaching. Another reason is that the process owner had no sense of urgency for project completion; the project's success had no impact on the performance measures of the process owner. One final cause for failure is that the pilot-trained person was someone who was available but did not have the characteristics for being an effective black belt.

Even if the pilot project was a great success, consider what it proved. The described tools work. The only question is: How can the organization best get started and create an infrastructure to support it? The success of one project does not make for a successful deployment.

It has been said many times that traditional Six Sigma and Lean Six Sigma deployments need to be initiated at the executive level; a CEO project-driven deployment. Jack Welch used this approach when he initiated Six Sigma at GE. If the right people are selected to fill the roles, and a good Six Sigma infrastructure is created, there can be successful projects. However, even in the best deployment kick-offs and infrastructure, where the executive is committed, organizations have difficulty sustaining a project search-and-completion deployment.

Traditional Six Sigma and Lean Six Sigma deployments create an organization in itself to search for projects and then complete them. Traditionally, the measure of success is the financial benefits from these projects. Reward systems for individuals can even be created that encourage the hunt for and completion of projects, which can often have little benefit for the system as a whole and drive the wrong activities. Often, even in the best find-our-next-project deployments, when the person who is leading the deployment leaves the company or has a position reassignment, the deployment loses much of its effectiveness.

As a business system that draws upon the many aspects of Six Sigma and Lean Six Sigma, IEE does not have the above deployment issues. When building the IEE system, it is best to start by building the enterprise process measurement and improvement system before project selection. The best way to build this infrastructure is by starting small and growing into a bigger system where the goal is to make the concepts of IEE and tools of Six Sigma and Lean a part of how work is done and not an add-on; not something extra that needs to be done.

A start-small-and-grow-big IEE deployment provides flexibility in that implementation can originate at a lower point in the management organization chart and then later grow throughout the business. This is analogous to the spreading of a warm-weather grass that is prevalent in the southern United States. Bermuda grass can be plugged since it grows in an outward direction through runners. Similarly, high-level executives need only to be willing to introduce an IEE pilot-build in one portion of the business. Success of this business measurement and improvement system can then propagate throughout the business, similar to a Bermuda plug.

The purpose of this multi-volume series is to provide a consistent IEE message that fulfills various needs and desires. It will help bridge the gap between those who will execute the details, as described in Volume III, and those who need a higher understanding level of the concepts, as presented in Volumes 1 and 2. With the proposed start-small-and-grow-big approach, executives could abort an implementation system at any time. For executives, this overall system has minimal downside risk and huge upside potential.

This approach is very different from the previously described pilot project approach. An IEE deployment can create a business system from which system performance measures pull for creating the best projects.

The foundation and system created during this deployment can springboard an organization into:

- Enterprise-wide alignment, metrics, tracking, and reporting standards
- Focus not only on how, but also what, to measure
- Leaders are able to reduce firefighting by having the right measurements with the correct interpretations so that organizational efficiency and effectiveness improve.

IEE deployment opportunities include:

- A business is new or relatively new to Lean Six Sigma.
- A business has recently hired a deployment leader such as a master black belt to create a Lean Six Sigma infrastructure.
- A Six Sigma or Lean Six Sigma deployment has been stalled.

The basic steps for an IEE deployment are;

1. One or more black belts or master black belts work the IEE deployment as their certification project
2. The E-DMAIC structure is roughed out during a week-long, on-site workout near the end of their training
   a. Monday: Executive overview and kickoff
   b. Tuesday-Thursday: Provider facilitates with the trainee(s) and their team the building of an E-DMAIC structure tailored to their business
   c. Friday: Tailored E-DMAIC structure presentation to executive team
3. Trainee(s) moves the E-DMAIC structure to a working system, with provider's coaching
4. Build a network of resources to support the execution of the E-DMAIC business measurements and improvements

More information about an IEE deployment can be found at www.SmarterSolutions.com. Appendix A.1 includes a deployment provider selection matrix.

# 4.10   Applying IEE

When we buy a product or service, we expect good service and delivery at the right price. If we take our car to the repair shop, we want the mechanics to work on the right problem with the right tools. At the enterprise level, a system is needed to assess how well processes are delivering per customer expectations. These expectations are typically captured in VOC studies and translated to process or product requirements. The scorecard/dashboard metrics that address how well these expectations are being met should follow a consistent methodology leading to the right activities. We want to create a system that encourages data investigation that formulates an understanding, which can be readily communicated to others. We want to create a system that becomes a means to achieving enterprise objectives. The techniques described in this chapter provide a system for addressing these needs.

In traditional Six Sigma and Lean Six Sigma deployments, projects are usually selected from a steering committee list of potential projects. Created projects might sound financially worthwhile, but upon completion these projects often do not truly deliver benefits to the overall enterprise. I have seen Six Sigma deployments stall when using this push for project creation approach. It is more desirable to have measurement improvement needs pull for project creation.

When organizations use satellite-level and 30,000-foot-level metrics for their scorecards/dashboard metrics, behaviors can dramatically change. In this system, when the measures degrade or indicate that an improvement is needed, a process owner initiates a correct action that may result in a project. This would depend on whether the root-cause analysis revealed that the cause was common or special. The completion of these projects can result in fewer fires to fight and a long-term, sustainable process adjustment. With this approach, IEE is much more than doing Six Sigma or Lean Six Sigma projects. IEE is a business measurement and improvement system that builds on the strengths of the project-driven Lean Six Sigma or Six Sigma methodologies and takes business scorecards/dashboards to the next level. Figure 4.11 illustrates how the IEE infrastructure and metrics can create a long-lasting, data-driven culture.

> IEE is much more than doing Six Sigma or Lean Six Sigma projects. IEE is a business measurement and improvement system that builds on the strengths of the project-driven Lean Six Sigma or Six Sigma methodologies and takes business scorecards/dashboards to the next level.

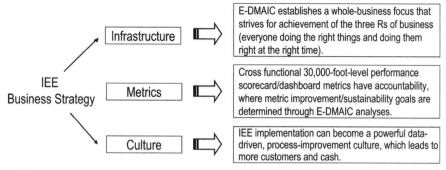

**Figure 4.11:** Creation of a data-driven and process-improvement culture through IEE.

The reader should also note how Figure 4.7 includes business analyses (step 4) before strategy creation (step 5). Often in hoshin kanri and other organizational deployments, the business jumps from step 1 to step 5. In reality, the executive team might have great insight and create the best possible strategy. However, this nine-step process formalizes the whole system so that the strategy-development process is more repeatable. This will make the system less dependent on executive team intuition; that is, the company will become more data driven.

I have heard people complain that their company wastes resources and does things that do not make sense; however, their organization is not ready for change. Organizations need to continually improve for survival. I hope this volume and other volumes in this series provide the stimulus and direction needed for making enhancements to organizational scorecards, strategy building, and improvement systems.

The next leadership chapter provides a process for selling ideas and concepts to others.

## 4.11  Exercises

1. Read Appendix Section C.1 "Sarbanes-Oxley (SOX) Act of 2002." Comment on how IEE might help address SOX needs.
2. Describe how a company, government office, or social organization might benefit from IEE.
3. Compare an organizational scorecard to an IEE alternative.

# 5

# Leadership and Building Successful Teams

The previous chapter described the IEE system and its differences from traditional systems. The implementation of this system or any new methodology involves leadership and change management. It seems that many problems are common cause but good skills and leadership are needed to understand and address these issues. This chapter describes these needs, along with people productivity, which are applicable to both managers and practitioners such as black belts.

The noise of a faulty process can deafen common sense. Of course this does not refer to the acoustic properties of the process; instead, it reflects the cascade of inputs of processes. The inputs, each represented by one or more variables, do have an effect on the process and outcomes. However, some process inputs are uncontrollable; i.e., noise inputs that are not controllable. These uncontrollable inputs may or may not adversely affect the process output. Nonetheless, these inputs compete for time and resources with value-add portions of the process (Watson 2006).

By identifying and segregating or eliminating these sources of waste, the process becomes quieter. Crises and rework disappear. Resources no longer needed to generate and fix waste are redirected to continuous improvement and increased productivity efforts. With focused effort, companies can realistically expect to drive waste from more than 40% to 20% or less within a relatively short period of time.

> By identifying and segregating or eliminating these sources of waste, the process becomes quieter. Crises and rework disappear. Resources no longer needed to generate and fix waste are redirected to continuous improvement and increased productivity efforts.

However, the stimulus and organizational orchestration for making the improvements require leadership. In addition, with these improvements come environmental and behavioral changes in the workplace that company leaders need to predict and manage. When a company experiences improvement in its processes, it will take workers time to become accustomed to the new processes which they have helped identify and create. When the waste is gone, the change is palpable. Some workers actually sense a level of discomfort with the lack of crisis—something is not right! It's too quiet. The process must have stopped, since there are no more complaints!

One company actually had to assure itself that one of its division's environmental compliance unit was still functioning correctly; over two years, the division had implemented an ISO 14000 program and had driven environmental infractions from more than one serious event per month to less than four minor events per year.

## 5.1   Advocacy Selling and the Acceptance of Change

Know who invented the commonly used computer mouse? It was Xerox. Know how much Xerox benefited financially from inventing the mouse? Since the developing engineers were not able to sell the design concept to management, Xerox had no financial gain. Do you think that the management at Xerox would have liked to have had financial gain from the mouse? I am sure that they would; management surely wants to realize financial benefit from their developed products.

Who is to blame for Xerox's not gaining financially from its unplanned developed product as 3M did when it invented Post-it® notes? One could blame management; however, John Daly, who frequently conducts an advocacy selling module in Smarter

Solutions' IEE master black belt training, blames the engineer/ engineers since he/she/they were not able to sell the concept.

Fundamental changes in how a business is conducted are important to help cope with a market environment that continually becomes more complex and challenging. Companies need to face this head-on or they will not survive. Many readers will be able to see how their company could reduce firefighting activities and increase profitability if they developed the described measurement and improvement system.

The failure of Xerox engineers to sell the concept of the computer mouse is a cautionary tale for readers to advocate for and sell the idea of evaluating IEE within their own companies; e.g., by attending a one-day public or on-site overview seminar. If these readers don't take on this leadership advocacy selling, they could be the victim of a company's cost-cutting or of a down-sizing attempt to become more profitable, even though they were doing a great job of executing all tasks given to them by their manager.

It is easy to say, "Let's change a particular business practice or procedure;" however, change is not easy. Someone who is resisting change typically uses one or several of the following "cave-speak" ("Citizens Against Virtually Everything" Speak) phrases. Lockheed created a pocket-sized card listing 50 of these statements. Referencing the card can lighten situations where change is being resisted.

(1) We tried that before.  (2) Our place is different. (3) It costs too much. (4) That's not my job.  (5) They're too busy to do that.  (6) We don't have the time.  (7) Not enough help. (8) It's too radical a change.  (9) The staff will never buy it. (10) It's against company policy. (11) The union will scream. (12) Runs up our overhead. (13) We don't have the authority. (14) Let's get back to reality.  (15) That's not our problem. (16) I don't like the idea. (17) You're right, but ... (18) You're two years ahead of your time.  (19) We're not ready for that. (20) It isn't in the budget.  (21) Can't teach an old dog new tricks. (22) Good thought, but impractical. (23) Let's give it more thought. (24) We'll be the laughingstock. (25) Not that again. (26) Where'd you dig that one up? (27) We did all right without it. (28) It's never been tried before. (29) Let's put that one on the back burner. (30) Let's form a committee. (31) I don't see the connection. (32) It won't work in our plant/ office. (33) The committee would never go for it. (34) Let's sleep on it. (35) It can't be done. (36) It's too much trouble to change. (37) It won't pay for itself. (38) It's impossible

(39) I know a person who tried it.    (40) We've always done it this way.    (41) Top management won't buy it. (42) We'd lose money in the long run.    (43) Don't rock the boat.    (44) That's all we can expect.    (45) Has anyone else ever tried it?    (46) Let's look into it further (later). (47) Quit dreaming.    (48) That won't work in our school.    (49) That's too much ivory tower.    (50) It's too much work.

Companies have undertaken various initiatives over the years in an attempt to make constructive change to their organization. Some organizations have had success with these initiatives; however, others have been very disappointed.

To understand better the implication of change, let's consider the last New Year resolution you made. If you are like the vast majority of New Year resolution makers, the change you resolved to make did not occur, at least for any length of time. Similarly, organizations have difficulty with change and with reaping expected benefits through their business change initiatives.

It is important to address both initial and sustaining change management issues during implementation. A goal of IEE is to utilize measurements and data within the company so that the right decisions are made; i.e., KCA. The IEE system is a culture that is aligned with these objectives. The system in this volume can create a culture that orchestrates the right behaviors. A force field analysis (see Appendix Section D.14) can be useful to gain insight to where targeted efforts for change buy-in should be directed.

A leader implementing IEE within an organization needs to become a change agent by walking the walk and talking the talk; i.e., applying the concepts in his/her work. Such a leader needs to be able to manage change, overcome organizational roadblocks, negotiate/resolve conflicts, motivate others, and communicate to overcome organizational barriers for success.

## 5.2   Seeking Pleasure and Fear of Pain

The motivational speaker, Tony Robbins, has suggested that the reason people change is either to seek pleasure or to avoid pain. Robbins then noted that the more powerful of these two forces for achieving change is the fear of pain. I need to note that the motivational force of this fear of pain should have a different connotation from the periodic infliction of pain upon someone being yelled at to do something differently. Let's consider these two points from a personal level and then from a business level.

The reason people change is either to seek pleasure or avoid pain.

At a personal level, I think that most people agree that people in the United States need to eat less fat and exercise more. Let's now consider what drives change on a personal level for someone who should implement a diet and exercise program. A seeking-pleasure motivation would be the encouragement from a loved one saying, "You will feel better if you exercise more and eat less fat," while a fear-of-pain motivation would be the fear of having another heart attack. Consider which one of these motivational forces is the most effective. Unfortunately, my observation is that the latter is more effective.

In business, a seeking-pleasure motivation could be the promise of a yearly bonus if corporate objectives are met. A fear-of-pain motivation could be fear of being fired for not improving processes within an area. The realism of this fear was reinforced when a friend did lose his job because he was not making long-lasting improvements within his area of the business. Again, consider which one of these motivational forces is the most effective in driving day-to-day activities.

I believe that the reason Six Sigma was so successful within GE was because the fear-of-pain stimulus described above was used as the primary driving force, with a secondary driving of the seeking-pleasure stimulus through financial benefits and recognition that were tied to Six Sigma project benefits.

I believe that it is important to have both the "fear-of-pain" and the "seeking-pleasure" motivation in putting a business strategy in place. I think that GE did an excellent job of using the "fear-of-pain" motivation for driving change within its organization. I believe that most people in GE believed that they needed to embrace Six Sigma and the concepts of Six Sigma or they would lose their jobs.

However, I am not so sure about how well GE and others have accomplished the seeking-pleasure piece of the puzzle. This piece is much harder to implement throughout an organization since the day-to-day interface between levels of management and management-to-employee needs to be changed for this motivation to be successful. I believe that the day-to-day "pats on the back" for small tasks well done is perhaps a better driving force in general than the hope for a bonus because of some arbitrary organizational goal set by high-level management. Changing this level of behavior can be very challenging. In some organizations,

I believe that the day-to-day motivational benefits from quarterly or yearly bonuses that are linked to organizational goals can be from the peer pressure. That is, well-performing peers might exert pressure on colleagues who are not performing well.

Whenever I think about the changing of day-to-day behavior, I think about a time when my wife and I enrolled our dog in obedience school. I believe I learned more than the dog did.

In this dog obedience school, a choker chain was used as a stimulus to change the dog's behavior. To some who are not familiar with the process, this might sound cruel, but it isn't, when the choker chain is used correctly.

I will use the training of one command to illustrate the training process. When walking, a dog is to heel on your left side and move at the same pace as you. When you stop, the dog is to stop and then sit at your left side without any command being given. This behavior needs to be trained since it is not natural for the dog.

The training procedure that I learned from class was to start walking with the dog heeling at your left. When you stop walking, wait to see if the dog stops and sits with no command given. If the dog does not sit, lightly jerk the choke chain once. If the dog still does not sit, push down on the rump of the dog until it sits down. When the dog does sits, compliment the dog by petting it and saying nice things.

Repeat the above procedure. It may take a few times, but the dog will sit when the choker chain is jerked after stopping from a walk. At this point in time during the training, you really compliment the dog when it has achieved this next level. Our dog then quickly proceeded to the next level where it would sit after stopping from a walk with no choker chain jerk. Again, the compliments flow to the dog.

Since my encounter with dog training and its utilization of positive reinforcement, I have wondered how we might use these techniques more in perhaps the most challenging and important role many people ever encounter: parenting. When raising children, it is easy to get in the habit of correcting children for everything that they don't do correctly as opposed to praising them for when they do things right; e.g., picking up one toy and returning it to its toy box when finished. If the primary stimulus in parenting a child is negative, it should be no surprise that an early word out of the mouth of a young child is "No."

My conclusion is that the process of parenting would be improved if couples bought a dog and took the dog to training before they have any children. Future parents would learn firsthand from their dog the power of positive reinforcement and then later apply the techniques to their children.

I think that this timely positive feedback technique is useful in many areas. My wife is very good at this. She will often give me a timely thank you or affectionate comment. For example, I have noted that my wife, when returning to the house, will thank me for putting a few dishes that had accumulated in the sink into the dishwasher. This type of behavior from her affects my behavior. Because of her actions, I am more likely to do and say things that make her feel good. She expresses these good feelings through her positive feedback. This type of relationship is far superior to the nagging husband or wife.

This is consistent with the principles of Dr. Deming. Workers know the right things that need to be done to produce and improve a process. By giving workers the opportunity to apply what they know, catching them doing the right things, and then rewarding them appropriately, a sustainable work environment is created that constantly improves itself. IEE is a methodically approach that identifies, channels, and follows through on these initiatives.

Leaders in many companies could dramatically improve their culture through this model by the giving of timely reinforcements to people even when the tasks they completed are small but aligned with the needs of the business. This type of feedback can reinforce behaviors in people so that they achieve greater things.

One challenge with this timely positive reinforcement model is that the quality of implementation of this skill by someone is not easy to measure. Hence, it is often not given the emphasis needed. Often the visibility within an organization is given to the firefighters who fixed the problem of the day rather than to the people who worked effectively together getting the job done right the first time.

One final point needs to be made. GE had a ranking system for employees where the company periodically terminated a percentage of lower-ranked people. Ranking systems can have severe problems for many reasons. One reason is that the people making the decision on the ranking of an individual often do not know all the details or might have a personality issue with the person being ranked. However, it is important to note that we cannot ignore the fact that some people will not change their behaviors to meet the needs of the business better no matter how much fear-of-pain and seeking-pleasure stimulus they are given. For these people, termination or relocation to a different position is perhaps the only answer. Keith Moe, 3M retired executive vice president, states this policy as "Change the people or change the people." At the same time that this is done, let's consider whether our current termination/assessment process and hiring process offer improvement opportunities.

The following sections describe other tools and approaches for change management.

## 5.3   Stimulating Change

You have a great idea that would be beneficial to the organization where you work; e.g., IEE implementation. Presenting simple logic about the benefits of the approach is typically is not enough to sell the concept to others. This section describes a process for stimulating acceptance of the proposed change.

Kotter (1995) lists the following eight stages for a successful change process. We will discuss the linkages of these steps to an IEE implementation strategy and how-tos of execution.

1. Establishing a sense of urgency
2. Forming a powerful guiding coalition
3. Creating a vision
4. Communicating the vision
5. Empowering others to act on the vision
6. Planning for and creating short-term wins
7. Consolidating improvements and producing still more change
8. Institutionalizing new approaches

### 1. Establishing a sense of urgency

Typically, change efforts begin after some individuals become aware of the need for change through their assessment of their organization's competitive/market/technology position and/or financial situation. To build this awareness for change throughout their organization, they need to find ways that communicate these issues so that motivation for change is stimulated. If motivation is not created, efforts will stall from lack of support.

In IEE, the satellite-level measures of a company provide an overview of the KPOVs of a company that is not restricted to accounting periods. This statistical time-series view and process capability/performance metric of the organization establish a baseline and can offer some insight to where the company has been, is currently, and is going. A satellite-level metric plot is also useful to identify when there has been either a positive or negative change within the overall system.

A focused voice of the customer examination then can give timely insight to the realities from the competition and the overall direction of the market. Wisdom of the organization tools can help identify both potential crises and major opportunities.

After this information is compiled and then presented to the management team, a high sense of urgency must be created. This act is creating the pain, as described in an earlier section. Kotter (1995) considers that this rate of urgency is high enough when about 75% of the company's management is honestly convinced that business-as-usual is totally unacceptable.

## 2. Forming a powerful guiding coalition

Typically, one or two people start major renewal efforts within an organization. When transformations are successful, this effort must grow over time. The head of the organization must share the commitment of excellent performance with 5–15 people, depending upon the size of the organization.

Within the IEE infrastructure, this guiding coalition would be the executive committee. This step would lead to the creation of a group that addresses many of the infrastructure system building needs.

## 3. Creating a vision

A picture of the future must be created that is easy to describe to stockholders, customers, and employees. Plans and directives that have no vision and focus can be counterproductive.

In IEE, the executive committee and steering committee can create a vision that is aligned with their satellite-level metrics. A strategic plan to accomplish this vision is then created by drilling down from the satellite-level metrics. The satellite-level metrics and their aligned 30,000-foot-level metrics are useful to track as a scorecard/dashboard the success of implementation to the strategic plan.

The vision for the transformation should be communicated crisply. This vision can be communicated not only through words but also through the use of graphical representations. This description must get a reaction that conveys both understanding and interest.

## 4. Communicating the vision

Communication of the vision is more than one-shot presentations given to the masses, where management retains old behavior patterns that are not consistent with the vision. Executives and those below the executive level must incorporate messages in their hour-by-hour activities. They must discuss how day-to-day activities are either in alignment or not in alignment with the vision. They must walk the walk and talk the talk. Company newsletters and other communication channels must continually convey this vision.

In IEE, one form of communication is through the day-to-day operational metrics at the 30,000-foot-level. This scorecard/ dashboard form of reporting can create an environment where firefighting activities are reduced through the institution of fire preventive actions. When there is common-cause variability, questions from these charts can lead to the inquiries about a P-DMAIC project initiation or about the status of an existing project that is designed to improve those metrics. Emphasis should be given whenever possible to how these metrics are aligned with the satellite-level metrics and vision of the organization. Project successes should be communicated throughout the organization where credit is given to the effectiveness of the team and how the effort aligns with the organizational satellite-level metrics and vision of the organization.

## 5. Empowering others to act on the vision

Organizations that are undergoing transformation need to remove the obstacles for change. For example, job categories that are too narrow can seriously undermine improvement efforts in productivity and customer interactions. Another example: Compensation and the system for making performance appraisals lead people to choose an interest that better suits them rather than aligning with the vision. Systems that seriously undermine the vision need to be changed. The taking of risks and execution of nontraditional actions need to be encouraged.

In IEE, one form of empowerment is through the execution of projects. Traditional functional boundaries within an organization can be lowered when strategically aligned projects that bridge traditional barriers are implemented in a cooperative environment. The benefits of these successes need to be communicated so that the cross-functional team that executed the project is given visible recognition for their work and the benefits of the work. P-DMAIC projects that have high-level support can improve systems that are undermining the implementation of changes that are inconsistent with the transformation vision.

## 6. Planning for and creating short-term wins

Victories that are clearly recognizable within the first year or two of the change effort bring the doubters of the change effort more in line with the effort. There is often a reluctance to force the reality of short-term wins on managers. However, this pressure can be a beneficial piece of the change effort. This is one way to overcome the perception that it takes a long time to produce a long-term gain, which results in a lack of urgency.

In an IEE strategy, the creation of well-focused projects that are in alignment with the vision and satellite-level metrics of an organization creates an environment where many short-term wins combine to make statistically significant long-term wins for the organization. Short-term wins from projects that are in areas sponsored by managers who are reluctant to the change effort can be very instrumental in changing their view of the benefits of the work.

## 7. Consolidating improvements and producing still more change

When statistically significant changes have been made, it can be catastrophic to declare victory, thereby halting the transformation efforts. Replace the victory celebration with a short-term win celebration that reinforces the efforts. Because of the credibility gained from short-term wins, bigger problems can now be addressed.

In an IEE strategy, the tracking and scorecard/dashboard reporting of satellite-level and 30,000-foot-level day-to-day operational/project metrics that are aligned encourage the asking of questions that lead to improvements within the overall system on a continuing basis. One challenge of implementation is having a project-tracking and operational metric-reporting system that is available and used by all levels of management

and employees in the company. At various points in the transformation process, it is important to celebrate short-term overall wins. Reinforcement of the long-term vision should be giv-
en so that future efforts can be directed toward problems and
systems that can be more difficult and time-consuming to
improve.

### 8. Institutionalizing new approaches

To sustain change, new behaviors need to be rooted as the social
norms and as the shared values of the organization. Until this
happens, behaviors are subject to degradation whenever pressure is eased. When institutionalizing change, it is important
to show people how the new approaches have helped improve
performance. Also, it is important for the next generation of top
management to identify with the methodology. Replacements at
the executive management level need to be in alignment with the
approach to change. Because of this, members of the Board of
Directors need to be in tune with the details of the transformation process so that executive replacements do not undermine the
changes that have been made.

## 5.4   Managing Change and Transition

The last section dealt with leadership-simulated organizational change. This section deals with the acceptance and transition change process. Leaders need to address these issues as
well.

Five stages occur when a SEE (significant emotional event) occurs in both professional and personal lives. These stages are:
1. Shock or denial, 2. Flood of emotion, usually anger, 3. Bargain-
ing, 4. Depression or grief, 5. Intellectual/emotional acceptance.
Working through the five stages takes a minimum of 1.5 years.
The results of not dealing with change in two years is burnout/
quitting job, becoming an employee who is difficult to work with,
or becoming emotionally/physically ill (Bissell 1992).

All change produces fear and distorted perceptions. Companies
need to provide a steam valve so that internal frustrations can be
openly discussed and addressed in a timely fashion. Increased information flow counteracts fear, anger, and low morale as well as
those distorted perceptions. Management needs to validate that
this information was correctly received and understood.

It is important to keep things familiar since people need to feel stable when encountering change. Grieving is normal and necessary. It is also important to build a new support system of people who are healthy for you.

To cope with the stress of change, people need to take care of themselves, both physically and mentally. Signals that accompany stress often manifest themselves as breathing problems, increased eating pace, and irregular sleeping patterns. During times of stress, it is important to play.

## 5.5 People Productivity

For organizational survival, it is important that leadership move toward an orchestration of the three *R*s of business, as described earlier; i.e., everyone doing the right things and doing them right at the right time. This form of direction can be accomplished by a dictator-management style where someone is very knowledgeable and tells everyone the right thing to do at the correct time. However, an organization can come upon very difficult times when this leader is no longer with the organization for various reasons.

What we would like to create is a leadership system that can aid with the above orchestration. IEE can help organizations accomplish this objective, where one aspect of this system is the effective use of people.

Consider the significance of the following:

- Collins (2001) in his book *Good to Great* stresses the importance of getting the right people on the bus and in the right seat.
- Keith Moe says, "Everything good or bad in business begins with people. Everything good or bad in business ends up in the financials" (Moe 2006).
- Keith Moe says that organizations should avoid "management by hope."
- As noted earlier, Keith Moe says, "Change the people or change the people" (Moe 2006).

Figure 5.1 describes the phases of people's performance over time (Moe 2006). People productivity is dependent upon how well leadership addresses the questions noted in the figure.

When people join a company they may have very little, if any, productivity. In the training phase, the organization needs to have effective training processes so that people's productivity ramps up as fast as possible. In the productive phase, people productivity increases when the organizational environment nurtures the effective use of existing skills and on-the-job training. However, unless properly managed, the problem phase described in the figure can occur in time.

Supervision can bring productivity back, if problems are identified and addressed in a timely fashion. For example, re-training can address loss of skills and computer hardware/software upgrades could address unsatisfactory employee tool effectiveness.

Organizations need to have a plan with established goals that have specific elements to achieve those goals. This plan needs to be communicated both properly and regularly. When this is not done, issues fall into the crevice and you are dealing with management by hope, as illustrated in Part A of Figure 5.2. If these issues are not properly managed, there will be performance problems. However, when communication yields

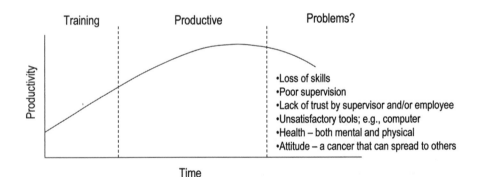

**Figure 5.1:** People productivity (Moe 2006).

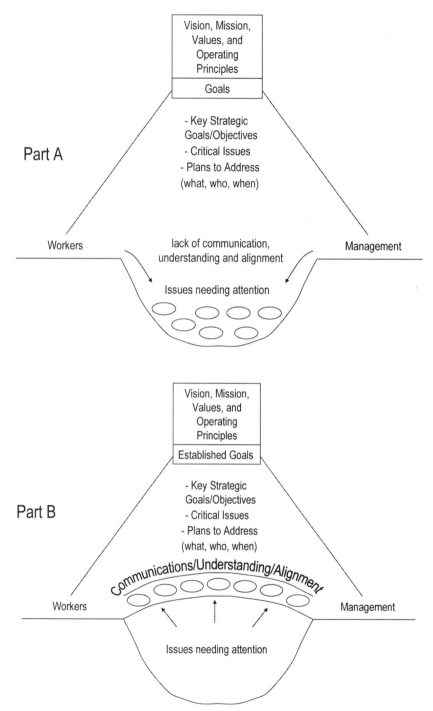

**Figure 5.2:** Build the bridge of success (Moe 2006).

understanding and organizational alignment, a bridge is built between workers and management, as described in Part B of Figure 5.2.

This organizational bridge assumes effective orchestration between workers and management. However, bridge building and maintenance need ongoing attention. If something is broken and there is no timely resolution, more issues will surface. Poor communications can lead to issues that become very significant.

A process to avoid organizational issues is illustrated in Figure 5.3 using Dr. Deming's plan-do-check-act (PDCA) model. A description for these steps is:

1.  Since everything good or bad in business starts with people, it is essential to hire the right people. This is the number one opportunity for achieving positive financial results. In *Good to Great* (Collins 2001) Jim Collins' description of effective hiring is getting the right people on the bus and in the right seat. People assignments in the organization need to match their skills, aptitude, and personal desires. The hiring and the matching of people with job assignment needs to be viewed and executed as a process. Moe (2006) lists the following skills as traits of high

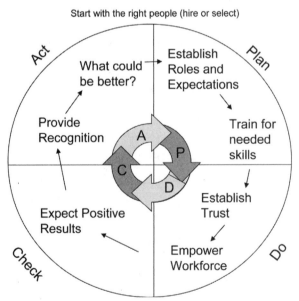

**Figure 5.3:** Achieving high-level individual performances (Moe 2006).

potential people that need to be addressed in this hiring/selection process; e.g., using a characteristic selection matrix (Table D.5):

- People skills
- Results-oriented
- Experience
- Team player and professional skills
- Good judgment
- Demonstrated leadership skills
- Self-confidence
- Strong planning and organizational skills
- Decision-making skills
- High integrity and trustworthiness
- Goals-oriented and high standards
- Self-discipline
- Good performance under stress
- Excellent oral and written communication skills
- Effectively sells ideas and proposals
- Positive attitude
- Creative skills
- Education
- Loyalty

2. After hiring the right person/people, positive performance is dependent upon clearly established roles and expectations. These established requirements become the basis for determining performance measures; i.e., tell me how I am measured, and I will tell you how I will act.
3. Checks need to be made to ensure that the person has the skills to produce the expected results. If skills are lacking, then investment is needed so that he/she learns the skills that are necessary to do the job. If the person cannot be trained, then timely corrective action needs to be taken, since the wrong person was either hired or selected for the job.
4. Is there trust between the person and his/her supervisor? If not, there is a potential issue relative to positive result expectations. This can lead to one or more issues falling into the crevice, as was described in Part A of Figure 5.2. Stephen Covey uses the term "emotional bank account" to describe the amount of trust that has been built up in a relationship. Established trust is gained through account

accumulation, which has the following types of transactions (Moe 2006):

| Deposits (Positives) | Withdrawals (Negatives) |
|---|---|
| • Be a giver | • Be a taker |
| • Tell the truth | • Lie |
| • Seek first to understand | • Seek first to be understood |
| • Make and keep promises BB | • Break or do not make promises |
| • Be kind, courteous | • Be unkind, discourteous |
| • Think win-win or no-deal | • Think win-lose |
| • Clarify expectations | • Violate expectations |
| • Be loyalty to the absent | • Be disloyal, duplicitous |
| • Apologize | • Exhibit pride, conceit, arrogance |
| • Receive feedback, give "I" messages | • Give no feedback, "you" messages |

5.  When trust is in place, the person needs to be empowered to do the jobs outlined in roles and expectations.

6.  Everyone needs to understand that positive results are now expected. This expectation needs to be communicated, as illustrated in Part B of Figure 5.2. Issues should not surface if the previous steps of this overall process are followed

7.  Recognition should be provided when positive results are achieved. Recognition can take many forms such as a pat on the back, financial bonus, dinner with spouse or significant other, or expense-paid trip. The form of this recognition should be directly related to the importance of the results. Companies that are not providing recognition need to return to the previous step and drill down to find the problem's core.

8.  If steps numbered six and/or seven are not being achieved, the whole picture is an opportunity for drill downs to resolve the issue. If results are lacking, we need to go back through the cycle to determine what should be done differently. This assessment should consider issues such as:

    •  Person selection for the position. Business is like a team sport—success depends upon getting the right people on the team.
    •  People productivity, as described in Figure 5.1.
    •  Worker trust of supervisor, and visa versa

## 5.6 Effective Teams

A major factor for an organization's success is how well teams work together. Teams are also used for IEE infrastructure building and management, along with project execution. The success of these tasks depends upon transforming a group of diverse individuals into a team that is productive and highly functional. Next few sections describe the characteristics of teams and what could be done to improve their effectiveness.

The range of commitment levels that stakeholders can have during project definition is: enthusiastic, will lend support, compliant, hesitant, indifferent, uncooperative, opposed, or hostile. An expectation for enthusiastic support by all team members for all projects is not realistic. However, team leaders can do a stakeholder analysis, quantify where each member is in the described scale above, keeping in mind the importance of moving team members toward the enthusiastic level.

The next section describes a commonly used and easy-to-follow model that can help improve team effectiveness.

## 5.7 Orming Model

It is commonly agreed that teams go through stages to become a highly effective team. In addition, it is generally agreed that teams can improve the quality of their interactions when each member of the team is aware of these stages. Tuckman (1965) described the four stages of team development as *forming, storming, norming,* and *performing.* These team stages are often collectively referenced as the orming model. Successful teams are those who transition back and forth between these stages when circumstances change. Adjourning and recognition can be considered as the final stages of the team stages.

In the *forming* stage, the team leader needs to provide structure for the team, clarifying expectations about the initiation of team processes. The work that needs to be accomplished is: team member introduction, team resource assessment, and objective definition. Issues that need to be overcome are the team leader's taking on most of the work, team members not organized around a common objective, and team not taking advantage of all the team resources. The status of the team execution process at this stage is a wait and see attitude, where the team process is usually noticed but avoided.

In the *storming* stage, the team leader coaches the team in maintaining focus on the goals and expectations, managing the team process and conflict resolution, generating ideas, and explaining decisions. The work that needs to be accomplished is: identifying team member expectations, discussing differences, and conflict management. Issues that surface are team members feeling unsatisfied and/or overburdened, and lack of contribution. The status of the team execution process at this stage is the formation of cliques because the general perception is that the effort does not require teamwork.

In the *norming* stage, the team leader primarily acts as a facilitator who provides encouragement, helps with consensus building, and gives feedback. Attention needs to be given to resolving differences through establishing ground rules, developing trust, and discussing directly how better to work together. Issues that arise are ongoing disagreements between team members and team members' working at cross-purposes. The status of the team execution process at this stage is general support for leadership, with the sharing of leadership among the team.

In the *performing* stage, the team leader facilitates the team process, where there is a delegation of tasks and objectives. Attention needs to be given to objective achievement, team member satisfaction, and collaboration. Issues that surface are unfinished work and not celebrating success. The status of the team execution process at this stage is that members are not dependent on the designated leaders, where everyone shares the responsibility for initiating and discussing team process issues.

## 5.8   Interaction Styles

Teams are made up of individuals who have different styles. Individuals may be more task oriented or people oriented. Some team members prefer to focus more on the job at hand, while others focus on relationships. People also tend to be thinkers and doers. Thinkers reflect on their work, while doers tend to discuss their work more openly. Everybody strikes his or her balance between these characteristics. This yields a distinctive profile for each individual on a team and the team as a whole.

The inherent dynamics can be quite different between teams since the styles for members of the team can be quite different. The success of a team is dependent upon how well differences between individuals are understood and capitalized upon. Teams need to have profile diversity, but the team also needs to be able to work together.

The question of concern is: What should be done to make the teams within an IEE implementation most effective? Those who are involved in creating the team should consider the interaction styles of people and how well these people's skills and styles would complement each other towards the common team goal. Secondly, after the team is formed, it is important that each team member understands and considers the difference in interaction styles between the team members so that each knows how best to interface with the team as a whole and with individuals within the team.

There are many tests that assess the personality of individuals; e.g., Myers-Briggs. It can be advantageous to take such a test and study the results to determine what each member of the team needs to do to interact better with the team as a whole or with other individuals who have a personality style that can easily conflict with their own.

One model describes the interaction styles of people as they relate to teams. These styles are driver, enthusiast, analyzer, or affiliator, where the characteristics for these styles are (Teamwork 2002):

- Driver: Someone who takes charge. Drivers focus on results. They exert a strong influence to get things done.
- Enthusiast: Someone who is a social specialist. Enthusiasts express opinions and emotions easily. They prefer a strong interaction with people
- Analyzer: Someone who likes to be well organized, thinking things out. Analyzers prefer specific projects and activities. They enjoy putting structure into ideas.
- Affiliator: Someone who is an adaptive specialist. Affiliators have a high concern for good relationships. They seek stability and predictability. They want to be a part of the bigger picture.

The potential strengths and potential weaknesses of each style are noted in Table 5.1.

**Table 5.1** Potential Strengths and Potential Weaknesses of Styles

| Style | Strengths | | Weaknesses | |
|---|---|---|---|---|
| Driver | *Determined<br>*Decisive<br>*Direct | *Thorough<br>*Efficient | *Dominating<br>*Demanding<br>*Impatient | *Unsympathetic<br>*Critical |
| Enthusiast | *Personable<br>*Enthusiastic | *Stimulating<br>*Innovative | *Opinionated<br>*Reactionary | *Undependable |
| Analyzer | *Industrious<br>*Serious   *Orderly | *Persistent<br>*Methodical | *Indecisive<br>*Critical | *Uncommunicative |
| Affiliator | *Cooperative<br>*Dependable | *Supportive<br>*Helpful | *Conforming<br>*Hides true feelings | *Uncommitted |

# 5.9   Making a Successful Team

When initiating teams, it is important to have members who have the appropriate skill sets; e.g., self-facilitation and technical/subject-matter expertise. The teams should have an appropriate number of members and representation. When launching a team, it is important to have a clear purpose, goals, commitment, ground rules, roles, and responsibilities set for the team members. Schedules, support from management, and team empowerment issues must also be addressed.

Team dynamics and performance issues must also be addressed, such as:

1. Team-building techniques that address goals, roles, responsibilities, introductions, and stated/hidden agenda.
2. Team facilitation techniques that include applying coaching, mentoring, and facilitation techniques that guide a team to overcome problems; e.g., overbearing, dominant, or reluctant participants. In addition, the unquestioned acceptances of opinions as facts, feuding, floundering, rush to accomplishment, attribution, digressions, tangents, etc.
3. Measurement of team performance in relationship to goals, objectives and metrics.
4. Use of team tools such as nominal group technique, force-field analysis, and other team tools described in Appendix D.

Ten ingredients for a successful team have been described as (Scholtes 1988):

1. Clarity in team goals
2. An improvement plan

   3.   Clearly defined roles
   4.   Clear communication
   5.   Beneficial team behaviors
   6.   Well-defined decision procedures
   7.   Balanced participation
   8.   Established ground rules
   9.   Awareness of the group process
   10.  Use of the scientific approach

I will address each of these ten points as they apply to the execution of a project within IEE. However, these ingredients also apply to the executive team and steering team.

1. *Clarity of team goals*: All team members should understand and maintain focus on the goals of the project as expressed within the IEE team charter. During the execution of projects, there will be times when it is best to redirect or re-scope a project. There will be other times when new project opportunities arise, or it appears that it would be best to abort further work on the project. All of these situations can occur during a project's execution. In IEE, it is important for the team lead to inform the project Champion and others about these issues. Until formal alterations are made to the project charter, it is important that the team maintain focus on the current project chart definition.

2. *An improvement plan*: A project execution plan should be made from the IEE project execution roadmap. This plan guides the team to determine schedules and identify mileposts. Reference is made to these documents when there are discussions about what direction to take next and about resource/training needs.

3. *Clearly defined roles*: The efficiency and effectiveness of teams are dependent upon how well everyone's talents are tapped. It is also important for members to understand what they are to do and who is responsible for various issues and tasks. Ideally, there are designated roles for all team members. The chain of command of an organization should not dictate the roles and duty assignments within a team.

4. *Clear communication*: The effectiveness of discussions is based upon how well information is transferred between members of the team. Team members need to speak with clarity and directness. Team members need to listen to others proactively, avoiding both interruptions and talking when someone else is speaking.

5. *Beneficial team behaviors*: Within teams there should be encouragement to use the skills and methodologies that make discussions and meetings more effective. Each team meeting

should use an agenda. There should be a facilitator who is responsible for keeping the meeting focused and moving. Someone should take minutes for each meeting. There should be a draft of the next agenda and evaluation of the meeting. Everyone should give his or her full attention to the meeting. No one should leave the meeting unless there is truly an emergency. During a meeting, members should initiate discussions, seek information, and clarify/elaborate on ideas. There should be focused discussions, avoiding digressions.

6. *Well-defined decision procedures*: A team should be aware and flexible in order to execute the different ways to reach a decision. Discussions should determine when a poll or consensus is most appropriate. Many of the decision-making procedures are part of the IEE project execution roadmap.

7. *Balanced participation*: Every team member should participate in discussions and in decisions. Team members should share in the contribution of their talents and be committed to the success of the project. Ideally, there should be balanced participation with the building of the styles offered by each team member.

8. *Established ground rules*: Every team should establish ground rules that address how meetings will be run. Norms should be set for how members are to interact and what kind of behavior is acceptable. Some important ground rules for meetings are: high priority on attendance, promptness for meeting start/stop times with full attendance, clear indications of meeting place and time along with how this notification is communicated.

9. *Awareness of the group process*: Team members should be aware of how the team works together where attention is given to the content of the meeting. Members should be sensitive to non-verbal communication and to the group dynamics. They should feel free to comment and intervene when appropriate to correct a process problem of the group.

10. *Use of the scientific approach*: Teams need to focus on how they can best use the IEE project execution roadmap for their particular situation. They should focus on the when and how to implement the best tool for every given situation.

## 5.10   Team Member Feedback

Teams need to work both smart and hard at completing their tasks. However, the team needs to support the needs of individual members. To understand the needs of team members, there has to be feedback. The most common form of this feedback is a one-on-one conversation.

We want feedback to be constructive. For this to happen, we must acknowledge the need for both positive and negative feedback, know when and how to both give and receive feedback, and understand the context (Scholtes 1988). Feedback should be descriptive, relating objectively to the situation, giving examples whenever possible. The basic format for such a statement follows, where descriptive words could be changed for the particular situation.

"When you are late for meetings, I get angry because I think it is wasting the time of all the other team members, and we are never able to get through our agenda items. I would like you to consider finding some way to plan your schedule that lets you get to these meetings on time. That way we can be more productive at the meetings, and we can all keep to our tight schedules."

Additional guidelines for giving feedback are: don't use labels such as immature, don't exaggerate, don't be judgmental, speak for yourself, and talk about yourself, not about the other person. In addition, phrase the issue as a statement rather than a question, restrict feedback to things you know for certain, and help people hear/accept your compliments when positive feedback is given.

Guidelines for receiving feedback are: breathe to relax, listen carefully, ask questions for clarification, acknowledge the understanding of the feedback, acknowledge the validity of points, and, when appropriate, take time out to sort what you heard before responding.

Within a team, it is best to anticipate and prevent problems whenever possible. However, whenever a problem occurs, it should be thought of as a team problem. It is important to neither under-nor over-react to problems. Typical decisions that need to be made by the team leader for problems are: do nothing, off-line conversation, impersonal group time (e.g., start of meeting describing the problem with no mention of name), off-line confrontation, in-group confrontation, and expulsion from the group, an option that should not be used. These options are listed in order of preference and sequence of execution. That is, off-line confrontation would typically be used only if a less forceful off-line conversation earlier did not work.

# 5.11   Reacting to Common Team Problems

Ten common group problems have been described as (Scholtes 1988):

1.   Floundering
2.   Overbearing participants
3.   Dominating participants
4.   Reluctant participants
5.   Unquestioned acceptance of opinions as facts
6.   Rush to accomplishment
7.   Attribution
8.   Discounted values
9.   Wanderlust: digression and tangents
10.   Feuding members

1. *Floundering*: Teams often experience trouble starting or ending a project, and/or addressing various stages of the project. Problems occurring at the beginning of a project can indicate that the team is unclear or overwhelmed by its task. When this occurs, specific questions should be asked and addressed by the team such as: "Let's review our project charter and make sure it's clear to everyone." "What do we need to do so that we can move on?"

2. *Overbearing participants*: Because of their position of authority or area of expertise, some members wield a disproportionate amount of influence. This can be detrimental to the team when they discourage discussion in their area. When this occurs, the team leader can reinforce the agreement that no area is sacred and a team policy of "In God we trust. All others must have data!"

3. *Dominating participants*: Some team members talk too much, using long anecdotes when a concise statement would do. These members may or may not have any authority or expertise. When this occurs, the leader can structure discussions that encourage equal participation using such tools as nominal group technique. The leader may need to practice gate-keeping using such statements as "Paul, we've heard from you on this. I'd like to hear what others have to say."

4. *Reluctant participants*: Some team members rarely speak. A group can have problems when there are no built-in activities that encourage introverts to participate and extroverts to listen. When this occurs, the leader may need to divide the tasks into individual assignments with reports. A gate-keeping approach

would be to ask the silent person a direct question about his experience in the area under consideration.

5. *Unquestioned acceptance of opinions as facts*: Team members sometime express a personal belief with such confidence that listeners assume that what they are hearing is fact. When this occurs, the leader may ask a question such as, "Is your statement an opinion or fact? Do you have data?"

6. *Rush to accomplishment*: Often, teams will have at least one member who is either impatient or sensitive to the outside pressures to such a level that he/she feels that the team must do something now. If this pressure gets too great, the team can be led to unsystematic efforts to make improvements that lead to chaos. When this occurs, the leader can remind the members of the team that they are to follow the systematic IEE roadmap, which allows for the possibility of executing quick "low-hanging fruit fixes" when these fixes are appropriate for a project.

7. *Attribution*: There is a tendency to attribute motives to people when we don't understand or disagree with their behavior. Statements such as "They won't get involved since they are waiting their time out to collect their pension." can lead to hostility when aimed at another team member or someone outside the team. When this occurs, the leader could respond by saying, "That might well explain why this is occurring. But, how do we know for sure? Has anyone seen or heard something that indicates this is true? Is there any data that supports this statement?"

8. *Discounted values*: We all have certain values and perspectives which may consciously or unconsciously be important to us. When these values are ignored or ridiculed, we feel discounted. A discounted statement "plop" occurs when someone makes a statement that no one acknowledges, and discussion picks up on a subject totally irrelevant to the statement. The speaker then wonders why there was no response. The speaker needs feedback whether such a statement is or is not relevant to the conversation. When this occurs, the leader can interject conversation that supports the discounted person's statement. If a team member frequently discounts people, the leader might give off-line constructive feedback.

9. *Wanderlust: digression and tangents*: Meetings that have unfocused conversations are an example of wanderlust conversation. When this happens, team members can wonder where the time went for the meeting. To deal with this problem, the team leader can write an agenda that has time estimates for each item, referencing the time when discussions deviate too far from the current topic.

10. *Feuding members*: Within a team, sometimes there are members who have been having feuds long before the team creation. Their behavior can disrupt a team. Interaction by other team members could be viewed as taking sides with one of the combatants. It is best that feuding members not be placed on the same team. When this is not possible, the leader may need to have offline discussions with both individuals at the onset of the team's creation.

## 5.12   Applying IEE

It is important to keep team focus so that everyone is going in the right direction for timely project execution. The chapter after the next chapter discusses the project execution plan. The described project execution roadmap steps in Volume III can be used as a guideline for creating this plan and providing overall project direction. The project checklists in Volume III can be used during meetings to provide project status against roadmap steps execution.

This chapter described many aspects of effective leadership. Other leadership aspects described in Volume III are effective presentations and project management.

## 5.13   Exercises

1. Create a force field analysis (see Appendix Section D.14) for the implementation of IEE in an organization.
2. Create a plan to sell the benefits of IEE to an organization which you believe could benefit from the techniques but is not sold on the approach and/or need.
3. Consider the following meeting dynamics of a team in the P-DMAIC analyze phase. The team is behind schedule and has a presentation to upper management due next week. An agenda has been set to determine where to focus improvements and to calculate the CODND. The last few meetings have seemed like re-runs with no clear direction on where to drill down and focus low-hanging fruit improvements. During the meeting, various group members share conflicting opinions about what area of the process should be the point

of focus for improvements. Team members are complaining that nothing is getting done and are losing momentum to work on the project. The team leader will not budge on the direction in which he thinks the team should go, although most members are in disagreement with his perception. Discuss and record what went wrong, how the facilitator could have acted differently in order to gain team consensus, and what tools/actions are most appropriate for this scenario.

# PART II
## Enterprise Process Define-Measure-Analyze-Improve-Control (E-DMAIC) Roadmap

The logic and flow of the E-DMAIC steps are different from the P-DMAIC steps. However, tools commonly associated with P-DMAIC execution can be very useful in the overall enterprise process. These tools can help organizations utilize data more effectively when making business decisions.

# 6

# E-DMAIC—Define Phase: Vision, Mission, and Voice of the Customer

## 6.1    E-DMAIC Roadmap Component

The previous chapters described how an organization can benefit from an IEE system through the establishment of specific functional performance metric improvement needs that are linked back to overall business goals. Chapters 6–14 will describe the framework of this business system.

This chapter includes capturing and utilizing voice of the customer inputs, as a process, in the define phase of the E-DMAIC roadmap, as noted in the define phase checklist in the next section. Chapter 7 will then describe the building of the organizational value chain and its 30,000-foot-level performance measurement system. Chapter 8 will then describe goal setting and strategy building.

The *Disciple of Market Leaders* (Treacy and Wiersema 1997) message is that companies must determine the unique value that it alone can deliver by having a discipline in operational excellence, product leadership, or customer intimacy. The described E-DMAIC system in the next sections initiates this process with voice of the customer or a system of creating more customer

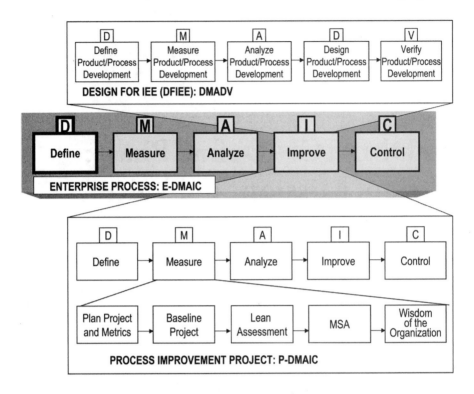

intimacy. By following described system of continuous improving processes, organizations will at the same time be improving operational excellence and product leadership.

## 6.2   Checklist: Enterprise Process Define Phase

E-DMAIC define phase activities include:

- Describe and document organization's vision, mission, and values.
- Describe and document Jim Collins' three circles (see Glossary).
- Describe enterprise system and work flow in a value chain that has appropriate information linkages.
- Describe how business process improvement events (BPIEs) are captured and implemented (see Section 13.3).
- Define a system to update the value chain and its linkages, as needed, to reflect current operating procedures.

- Describe in the value chain the conducting of team meetings to discuss value-chain scorecard metrics, area-projects, BPIEs, and concerns/issues.
- Describe in value chain a system used to capture and analyze voice of the customer inputs.
- Upload changes to allow interactive access by others.

## 6.3 Vision, Mission, and Values

An organization's vision statement describes expected benefits to customers, employees, shareholders and/or society. A well-stated vision statement is brief, catchy, inspirational, and believable. In addition, a visions statement serves as a rallying point that clearly states what the organization must become, allowing for execution flexibility.

A mission statement is a descriptor of why an organization exists and its business intent. As a charter, the mission identifies fundamental customer and market needs that are to be fulfilled. Missions can be created to describe existence purpose not only for the corporate level but also for the organizational level. Mission statements should identify our customers, their needs, offered products/services, and success performance measurements. Missions should be short and memorable to such an extent that people can recite their mission.

The term *values* encompass core values and governing values. Value statements describe the worthwhile traits and qualities, which are the organizational driving force. They are organizational statements about customers, suppliers, and the internal community valuing, which defines how people behave with each other.

An Internet search located the following statements:

- Toyota Industrial Equipment
  - Vision statement: To become the most successful and respected lift truck company in the United States
  - Mission statement: To sustain profitable growth by providing the best customer experience and dealer support.
- AMD
  - Vision statement: A world where the amazing power of AMD technology improves the quality of people's lives.

- Mission statement: Lead through innovative, customer-centric solutions that empower businesses, enhance the digital lifestyle, and accelerate global digital inclusion.
- Values: Respect for people, integrity, our customers' success, customer-centric innovation, initiative and accountability, fair and open competition.

Often what happens after a vision statement has been determined is the development of key strategies for attaining that vision. This topic will be addressed in the next section.

## 6.4 The Three Circles

Isaiah Berlin in his essay "The Hedgehog and the Fox" divided the world into hedgehogs and foxes. Based on an ancient Greek parable the fox knows many things, but the hedgehog knows one big thing. Collins (2001) notes how good-to-great companies were not unlike hedgehogs. These companies used a hedgehog nature to drive toward what Jim Collins calls a company's Hedgehog Concept. Those who led comparison companies in the study that was described in Jim Collin's book tended to be foxes. These companies were diffused, scattered, and inconsistent, never gaining the clarifying advantage of a Hedgehog Concept.

Good-to-great and comparison companies differed in two fundamental distinctions. First, the good-to-great companies founded their strategies on deep understanding along three key dimensions; i.e., three circles. Secondly, good-to-great companies transitioned this understanding into a simple, crystalline concept that guided all their efforts. This hedgehog concept is a simple focused concept that flows from a deep understanding about the intersection of these three circles:

1.  What you can be the best in the world at (and, equally important, what you cannot be the best in the world at): It is important to realize that just because an organization possesses a core competence doesn't necessarily mean that it can be the best in the world at it. On the other side of the coin, what an organization might be best at might not even be something that they are currently engaged.

2. What drives your economic engine: All the good-to-great companies gave intense focus as to how to most effectively generate sustained cash flow and profitability.
3. What you are deeply passionate about: The good-to-great companies gave focus to the activities that sparked their passion. This concept is not how to stimulate passion but instead discover what makes one passionate.

A three-circle introspection as part of the E-DMAIC roadmap can provide insight to whether an organization is currently going in the direction that best aligns with its strengths.

## 6.5 Where Are Organizations Going and How Are They Going to Get There?

Executives often establish strategic plan action items for the purpose of directing organizational work focus. It has been my experience that often the resulting strategic plan items from these sessions are not specific and could lead to different interpretations throughout the company of the directive intent and how to accomplish these plans. In addition, I often ask the question in my workshops: "Do you think that the strategic plan directives could be significantly different if the executive team that created the plan were different?" The response to the inquiry is typically a resounding "Yes."

I suggest that it can be very difficult for a level five leader to create a self-sustaining level five system when work directives and measurements are initiated through a strategic plan that it is very dependent upon the executive leadership team composition.

Consider the utopian situation where a country is ruled by a dictator who knows and executes the best possible policies throughout the country. This ideal dictator does not need any assistance because he always knows the best thing to do and has dependable people to execute his commands. Life under these ideal circumstances could be very good. However, what happens when the dictator is no longer able to rule? Since the dictator did not create a system that describes what he did if he were not present, chaos or a degraded system would probably result. The dictator's overall decision-making and execution process were not described in his tenure so that the system could be self-sustaining after his departure.

This can also happen in companies. A strong leader at the helm of a company or a Six Sigma program can be analogous to a dictator who gives direction on what tasks should be performed in the company and when. Life in this company can be good when these leaders make the right decisions. However, what happens when the company leader is no longer with the company? Often the organization experiences chaos or a decay from previous performance levels.

Having the right people on the bus (Collins 2001) can make the company much more productive and can reduce the risk of turmoil when leadership changes. However, getting the right people on the bus is just part of the formula for creating long-lasting company success. What is needed is a formula that helps companies achieve greatness both now and after leadership changes; i.e., a level five system. The implementation of IEE provides a roadmap to accomplish this.

Instead of using the strategic plan up front to direct organizational activities and metrics, IEE places strategic planning in the analyze phase of the E-DMAIC roadmap. This system, which is described in Chapter 8, leads to more specific and measurable actions than most traditional strategic plan outputs. In E-DMAIC, the value chain and its metrics are analyzed prior to strategic plan creation so that additional insight is gained before goal setting, strategic plan creation, and project selection (see Figure 12.1). This E-DMAIC process gives focus to ensuring that a strategic plan is created, which is consistent with the company's goals, vision, mission, and value proposition.

It is also essential to create a system that captures the voice of the customer at the enterprise process level. It is important that we align our processes with voice of the customer inputs, as illustrated in Figure 6.1. This figure's voice of the customer U-shape can be considered an analogy to Taguchi's loss function. In this loss function, there is a cost associated with not exactly meeting the target specification, as described in Volume III. In this model, a quadratic function usually describes Taguchi's increasing loss to society cost departure from a zero $y$-value at the target value.

At this organizational level, voice of the customer addresses more than simple surveys of how the company is doing relative to customer satisfaction. This voice of the customer input system describes what is needed at the enterprise process level not only to keep up with but also to exceed the competition.

However, we need to consider that customers can also be challenged by their organization's struggle to convert needs and wants to actionable specifications through their procurement model. Organizations need to institutionalize a system that helps identify and communicate true customer needs, which is often not the same as an original request. A company can create a differentiation for its services when it learns how to understand true customer needs and communicates how is services effectively address these needs.

Let's describe customer satisfaction as a $Y$ response. This response is the sum of both product desirability and its affiliated service, which would be the collective assessment of how well the product met accuracy, performance, consistency, price, and servicing. IEE assesses how well these metrics are achieved through a value-chain customer-centered measurement system. We seek to maximize these desirable metric attributes, as perceived by the customer, though the adjustment and control of key process $X$s. Major adjustment improvements are accomplished by systematically executing IEE projects, as described later in this volume.

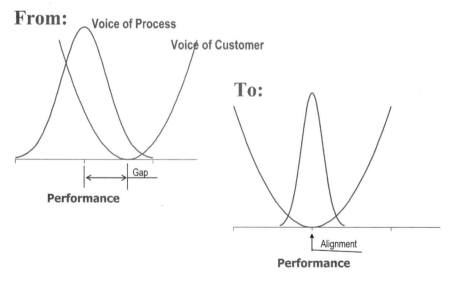

**Figure 6.1:** Alignment of voice of the customer and voice of the process (Moe 2006).

## 6.6   Voice of the Customer

Consider products that a customer has purchased that do not meet his or her expectations. Perhaps a product or service has many "bells and whistles" but does not meet his or her basic needs, or perhaps the product is not user-friendly or has poor quality. Will a customer take the time to complain about the product or service? Will the customer avoid purchasing products from the same company in the future? Achieving customer satisfaction is an important attribute of an IEE implementation.

Key marketplace points that apply to many consumer and industrial products are (Goodman 1991):

- Most customers do not complain if a problem exists (50 percent encounter a problem but do not complain; 45 percent complain at the local level; 5 percent complain to top management).
- On problems with loss of over $100 and where the complaint has been resolved, only 45 percent of customers will purchase again (only 19 percent if the complaint has not been resolved).
- Word-of-mouth behavior is significant. If a large problem is resolved to the customer's satisfaction, about 8 persons will be told about the experience; if the customer is dissatisfied with the resolution, 16 other persons will be told.

These realities of business make it important to address customer satisfaction, along with customer retention and loyalty. Organizations should address the cost to keep customers and the value of word-of-mouth referrals. A calculation for the economic worth of a loyal customer is the combination of revenue projections with expenses over the expected lifetime of repeated purchases. The economic worth is calculated as the net present value (NPV) of the net cash flow (profits) over the time period. This NPV is the value expressed in today's money of the profits over time (see Chapter 9).

> Important to address customer satisfaction, along with customer retention and loyalty. Organizations should address the cost to keep customers and the value of word-of-mouth referrals.

With regard to customers, it should be emphasized that the end user of a product is not the only customer. For example, a supplier that manufactures a component part of a larger assembly has a customer relationship with the company responsible for the larger assembly. Procedures used to determine the needs of customers can also be useful to define such business procedural tasks as office physical layout, accounting procedures, internal organization structure, and product test procedures. Focusing on the needs of customers goes hand in hand with "answering the right question" and the IEE assessments throughout this volume. In an IEE strategy, the voice of the customer is assessed at two levels: the high-level of the organization (satellite-level) and the project-level (e.g., 30,000-foot-level).

Customer needs are dynamic. The quantification of customer satisfaction relative to the presence of a characteristic was modeled by Noritaki Kano. Figure 6.2 describes the Kano model as it relates to three factors and their degree or level of implementation: basic—must exist; expected—more is better; delighter—excitement.

A basic factor is something that a customer expects. The presence of this factor results in a neutral customer response, while its absence generates dissatisfaction. Examples include a heater in automobiles, safe air travel, and clean towels in hotel rooms. Basic factors do not imply easy fulfillment; e.g., air travel security. With these factors, market surveys have little value, since basic factors are expected. Because of this, design requirements need to build upon past experience, feedback, and observation.

An expectation factor can cause much dissatisfaction at one extreme and delight at another extreme. These more-is-better type factors are typically already in existence. The question is how to identify the factor and improve its performance. Examples include higher automobile gas mileage, improved on-time airline departure, and speedy hotel registration. Market surveys can identify these factors, but observation is also needed to, for example, identify dissatisfaction features. Improved performance often requires improved processes or a creative new design.

A delighter factor is an unexpected factor that increases delight; i.e., a wow factor. At one point in time the following were considered delighter factor: the replacement of the automobile crank start with an electronic starter, the initial installation of airport terminal televisions, and the introduction of hotel in-room coffee makers. Product features that were in the past considered wow features can transition quickly to basic features; i.e., we do not expect to crank-start our automobile in the morning. Market surveys have little value in identifying these features. It is critical to stay up to date with customer expectation changes. A blending of creativity with a true appreciation of customer needs can provide breakthroughs; however, wow features need to be provided at minimal extra cost. Benchmarking and other tools such as quality function deployment (Breyfogle 2003b), and TRIZ (see Volume III) can help facilitate this development.

To capture voice of the customer at the satellite-level, organizations need input from a variety of sources such as audits, management systems, unbiased surveys and focus groups, interviews, data warehouse, and complaints. Organizations need a process that captures and integrates this information so that they are going in the right direction and have the best focus relative to customer requirements. This assessment needs to lead to targeted improvement activities, where organizations need first to ensure that customer basic requirements are satisfied. Secondly, organizations need to assess how well asked-for performance requirements are being met. Thirdly, organizations need to determine what can be done to capture customer wow perceptions.

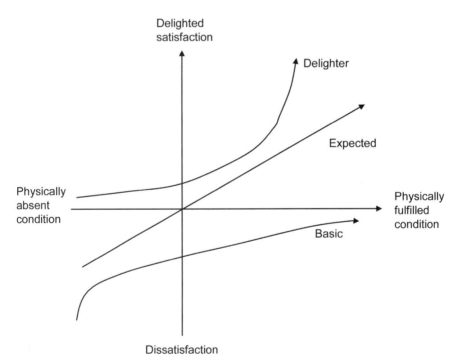

**Figure 6.2:** Kano diagram. Satisfied feeling versus condition.

Quality function deployment (QFD) is often used to address voice of the customer needs. *Implementing Six Sigma* (Breyfogle 2003a) describes the mechanics and some of the challenges when conducting a QFD.

## 6.7 Customer Value—A Framework For Enterprise Excellence

Value fulfillment drives human behavior and decision making (Ekstrom 2006). This is true for individuals as well as for businesses. The more value we get, the better we feel about ourselves. Great companies realize this and focus on providing value to their customers. Higher customer value results in higher company value. That is why the focus of any enterprise strategy needs to be customer value. Great enterprises have a passion for what they do in ways that exceeds the expectations of their customers and thus provide higher value. All decision making within the enterprise can be measured against this. How will our actions improve customer value? So it follows that, if a company provides more customer value relative to their competitors in one form or another, that company will attain what it wants, which is More Customers and Cash ($MC^2$).

Enterprise excellence depends on having a solid strategy for satisfying customers. This strategy must include an understanding of the customers to achieve success, and understanding the customers means that companies need to listen to them. The voice of the customer is important for aligning the company with its customers. For the company, the issue then becomes one of determining what their customers really value in the products and services they purchase and then providing more of it overall than their competitors. This is where the voice of the customer comes into play. Those companies which do not know who their customers really are and what they really want are at a distinct disadvantage. They are the followers of the true innovators in the market and they often end up competing primarily on cost.

> Enterprise excellence depends on having a solid strategy for satisfying customers. This strategy must include an understanding of the customers to achieve success, and understanding the customers means that companies need to listen to them.

Few companies actually measure customer value based on their customer's wants and needs. More often than not, they impute customer value from customer satisfaction. They do periodic customer surveys, summarize the data, and reactively improve their products and services based on issues and problems that arise. Products and services are more often than not developed as trial-and-error solutions to customer's wants and needs. They are a result of some data, some conjecture, some intuition, and just plain luck. This is not to say that trial and error won't produce good products because they do. The problem is in what it costs in both time and money to do it.

## Key Questions

The key to higher customer value comes from answering some basic questions before the right products and services can be provided to the market:

1. Who are our customers?
2. What do they want?
3. Why do they want it?
4. How do they know they have it when they get it? (How would they recognize it?)
5. How important is each of the benefits relative to each other?
6. How satisfied are they that our company or a competitor company is satisfying each benefit?

The extent to which a company knows the answer to these questions will be a good indicator of its success in the market.

## Identifying the Customers

For a company truly to satisfy its customers, it must know who the customers are. Needless to say, companies trying to be all things to all people usually have a difficult time in developing products and services because they are being pulled in too many directions and end up not being good in any of them.

There are typically three types of customers:

- Buyers        Those that make the buying decision.
- Doers        The middlemen.
- Users        Those who interact directly with the product or service.

The important thing to remember when obtaining the voice of the customer is that each of these customer types has a distinctly different list of requirements that they are trying to satisfy. It is important therefore to identify them separately and not let one customer type speak for another.

*Buyers*
Knowing who makes the buying decision is a critical first step in collecting the voice of the customer. Buyers may never use the product or even see the product but it is they who control the money. Their perception of value must be understood to achieve sales. They may be influenced by the doers and users, but, in the end, they will have their own buying criteria which must be satisfied. Their requirements often center on price, delivery, terms and conditions of the contract, quality level, etc. because these are the buyers' organizational performance metrics.

*Doers*
The middlemen don't make the buying decision and typically don't use the product. Their role is to provide functions such as distribution, training, customer support, repair, maintenance, etc. Satisfaction of these requirements is typically needed to achieve low cost. Their wants and needs are quite different from those of either the buyers or users, and they can have a big impact on overall customer value. For example, products that are low cost to purchase and that users prefer may require a great deal of maintenance, repair, or consumables to maintain their usefulness.

*Users*
Those who actually use the end product or service initially get the most attention from developers. End users must be satisfied to achieve value through high productivity or psychographics.

# Identifying What the Customers Want

If customer value drives the strategy, then the voice of the customer will drive an understanding of customer value. Knowing how to collect the voice of the customer and what to do with the information after it is collected is how enterprise excellence is achieved. Many companies test their completed designs with key customers. This is a good idea, but it is still trial and error. Great enterprises ensure customer satisfaction by collecting requirements before any design work and then confirm the design with customers prior to production or delivery.

*Buyers*
Key questions for buyers are typically:

- Why do customers buy?
- What is the basis of comparison for buying?
- Why do customers choose one brand relative to another?
- Where is the buying decision made?
- How do customers buy the product or service?
- What buying criteria are used?
- How much are buyers willing to spend?
- How often and how much do customers buy?

*Doers*
Key questions for doers are typically:

- What functions should the middlemen perform?
- Where are the bottlenecks in the process?
- What do the middlemen want to make their job easier?
- What takes the most time in performing the middlemen functions?
- What tools/software/services/training are needed?
- How can the products/services be changed to facilitate the middlemen functions?

*Users*
Key questions for users are typically:

- What functions should the product or service deliver?
- What style or image fits best?
- What problems or issues need resolution?
- What is the basis of comparison for the product or service?

As customers are expressing their wants and needs, it is important to ensure that the underlying benefit is obtained rather than a solution. When a customer provides a solution, they often have difficulty expressing the real underlying benefit of it and are often unaware of alternative solutions that could deliver the same benefits equally well or better. It is important to keep asking "why" customers want what they want until the underlying benefit is revealed. Whereas the list of wants and needs for delivering a combination of benefits can be unlimited, the list of benefits is a relatively small number. For example, a list of 100 wants and needs expressed by customers may reduce to typically fewer than 15 benefits at the level of the topic being discussed. This list of wants and needs is typically boiled down by using the affinity diagram (see Appendix Section D.11), where each want and need is placed in a group with similar wants and needs, all with an affinity for a distinctly different benefit. An example list of customer benefits is:

The *Ideal* Customer Services Terminal...

- Is intuitive to use
- Is sheltered from the weather
- Is quick to use
- Provides a wide range of services
- Helps me complete my tasks
- Is always available
- Has a low cost to use
- Lets me send information anywhere
- Prints any of the information I want
- Makes it easy to input information

The customer requirements (benefits) always seem obvious after they are finally identified, but getting to this final list requires asking "Why?" several times. Note that the list contains no solutions or specifications. The alternative solutions for satisfying these benefits are infinite and the extent to which one company does it relative to another is what determines the overall customer value.

## Measuring Importance of Customer Requirements

Obtaining answers to the questions above will yield a more in-depth understanding of each customer type, including a list of benefits. Following the collection of this information and the summary list of benefits for each customer type, the next step is

**Figure 6.3:** Measurement methods and their relative ranking for producing useful results.

to determine how important each of the requirements is relative to each other (comparative data) from the customer's viewpoint. As stated above, the affinity grouping exercise separates the unimportant from the important so that at this stage we already know that all of the benefits on the summary list are important. What we need to do now is to establish their importance relative to each other from the customer's viewpoint. This must be done using a comparative measurement method. If a non-comparative method such as a direct rating scale is used, the only thing that will be confirmed is that all of the benefits are important. Figure 6.3 illustrates various measurement methods and their relative ranking for producing useful results.

A description of each of these measurement methods is:

### Direct Rating Scales

Direct Rating Scales are often used in market research studies for a variety of applications but they are NOT appropriate for this application. Direct Rating Scales compare the importance of the item to a scale such as 1–10 but do not compare the items relative to one another. A typical question using this technique might be:

*On a scale from 1–10, how important is item n?*

A tendency of customers using this technique is to rate all of the items high. This is of little use in prioritization since we already know at this point that everything on the list is important. What we are attempting to do is to distinguish between the important items so that we need a technique that compares the items to each other and therefore helps to spread the data over more of a the range of the scale.

### Forced Ranking

Force Ranking is a comparative technique that compares the items and ranks them relative to one another. A typical question using this technique might be:

> *Number the following list of items in order of importance beginning with 1 being the most important and* n *being the least important.*

The drawback of this technique is that it assumes that the distance between each item is equal. It does not indicate how much more important one item is than another. Also, for customers using this technique it is often easy to determine the most important item(s) and the least important item(s), but the remaining items are usually thrown into the middle without much thought. Therefore, a good perception of relative importance is difficult to come by.

### Forced Choice Paired Comparisons

Forced Choice Paired Comparisons help to provide a more accurate perception of relative importance because it ensures that each item is compared with each other item in a systematic way. A typical task to rate importance of a list of items might be the following:

> *Each of the items described in the previous section are matched in pairs below. Each item is compared to each of the others at some point and there are no duplications. Please compare the items in each pair and place an X beside the item which is most important to you. That is, if you could only have one of the two items, which one would it be? Examples of this are:*

| ___ Keeps me informed about the production<br>_X_ Operates efficiently | _X_ Has reliable equipment and tooling<br>___Manufactures high-quality products |
|---|---|

This technique is a comparative one, but it still does not indicate how much more important one item is than another, and therefore it produces a ranking rather than a rating. It merely indicates the percentage of time one item is chosen over another.

### Anchored Scales

Anchored scales assist respondents in spreading their responses over a specified range. This method anchors both ends of the scale and places each requirement relative to those endpoints. Respondents are first asked to choose the most important requirement on the list and assign it a value of 10. Next, they are asked to choose the least important requirement on the list and assign it a value of 1. Finally, they are asked to review each of the remaining requirements and assign values from 1 to 10 based on their relative importance to the two endpoints. Multiple values are allowed for any given number

Example:

| *Requirement* | *Rating* |
|---|---|
| 1. Makes it easy to learn the system | 3 |
| 2. Is easy to qualify for operation | 1 *Least important* |
| 3. Helps me efficiently manage my workload | 5 |
| 4. Is always available | 10 *Most important* |
| 5. Is easy to use | 8 |

### Constant Sum

The constant sum scale is a technique that overcomes the problem of having the respondents evaluate objects two at a time. Rather, respondents are instructed to allocate a number of points or dollars—say for example $100—among requirements or alternatives according to some criterion; e.g., preference or importance. Respondents are instructed to allocate the points or dollars in such a way that if they like Item A twice as much as Item B, they should assign twice as many points or dollars.

Example:

| *Requirement* | *Number of Points* |
|---|---|
| 1. Makes it easy to learn the system | 10 |
| 2. Is easy to qualify for operation | 5 |
| 3. Helps me efficiently manage my workload | 20 |
| 4. Is always available | 40 |
| 5. Is easy to use | 25 |
| | ____ |
| Total | 100 |

### Forced Choice Graded Paired Comparison

The Forced Choice Graded Paired Comparison provides the most accurate estimate of the true priorities. It not only ranks the requirements but also rates how much more or less important they are relative to each other. Each of the requirements is matched in pairs. Each requirement is compared to each of the others at some point and there are no duplications. To evaluate the list, first compare the requirements in each pair and identify the requirement that is most important. Circle how much more important that requirement is than the other by using the scale below. If they are equal, circle the "E" in the center.

E—Equally important
1—Weakly more important
2—Moderately more important
3—Strongly more important
4—Extremely more important

Example:

| Keeps me informed about the production | 4  3  2 1  **E**  1  ②  3  4 | Has reliable equip- ment and tooling |
|---|---|---|

The analytical hierarchy process (AHP) described in Appendix Section D.10 is another form of forced choice graded paired comparison.

To ensure that companies are working on solutions that emphasize the most important attributes, the forced choice graded paired comparison method produces the highest quality data for this application. This method compares each benefit against the other benefits and measures the extent to which one is more important than the other.

All the benefits may need to be delivered to some degree for each customer type and it is the relative importance that will help developers decide that degree when they are establishing their targets and specifications. In addition, the various market segments may often prioritize the same list of benefits much differently. For example, low cost may be the highest priority for one segment and the lowest for another. Market segmentation based on customer benefits can be very useful for further characterizing each customer. An illustration of benefit segmentation is illustrated in Figure 6.4.

In this example, Product Segments cross several Market Segments to create Customer Segments. Each Product (Platform) Segment may need one or more products to satisfy the key market segments and the objectives are to:

- identify the total number of products that could reasonably satisfy the key Market Segments for each Product Segment;

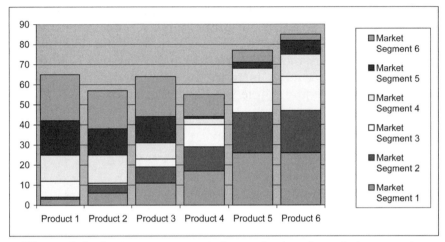

**Figure 6.4:** Customer segments by product and market segments.

- reduce the total number of products to the minimum number of product platforms; and
- reduce/optimize the number of products to satisfy the most customers at the minimum cost to the company.

## Measuring Customer Satisfaction

Measurements of customer satisfaction should also be made on each of the benefits listed for each customer type. This information will provide companies an indication of how they compare to their competitors and can be used to exploit competitors' weaknesses as well as correct weaknesses in their own products and services. To be useful, the degree of satisfaction relative to the customer's expectations must be measured and therefore must be determined in a way that will provide ratio data. It is also important that customers rate only their satisfaction with the product or service they use and with which they are familiar. These data combined with the importance ratings described previously can be summarized in a table like that of the example in Table 6.1.

The above data can be plotted on a Market Opportunity Map using importance and satisfaction as the axes as illustrated in Figure 6.5. This is useful for interpreting where a company stands relative to the competition and for determining actions which they may want to take to reposition them. Customer requirements

**Table 6.1** Voice of the Customer Data

| | Importance Rating | Satisfaction | | |
|---|---|---|---|---|
| | | * | A | B |
| The *Ideal* Customer Services Terminal... | | | | |
| Is intuitive to use | 8.5 | 3.5 | 7.0 | 5.5 |
| Is sheltered from the weather | 5.5 | 4.0 | 5.0 | 8.0 |
| Is quick to use | 7.5 | 7.0 | 5.0 | 6.0 |
| Provides a wide range of services | 6.1 | 2.0 | 7.0 | 1.0 |
| Helps me complete my tasks | 2.1 | 4.0 | 1.0 | 1.0 |
| Is always available | 9.1 | 6.0 | 5.0 | 8.0 |
| Has a low cost to use | 4.4 | 1.0 | 3.0 | 1.0 |
| Lets me send information anywhere | 7.1 | 1.0 | 1.0 | 3.0 |
| Prints any of the information I want | 1.3 | 9.0 | 3.5 | 3.0 |
| Makes it easy to input information | 3.6 | 8.0 | 6.0 | 7.0 |

**Legend**

*   Our company
A   Competitor A
B   Competitor B

(benefits) in the lower left quadrant are called Emerging Opportunities. They are not yet that important to the customer either because he/she really doesn't care about that particular benefit or doesn't recognize the benefit on that application. Emerging requirements are important because they are often the basis for expanding the market. Customer requirements for new products and innovations usually start out in this area and then move up to the top left quadrant. These are called Market Opportunities because they are important to the customer and none of the competitors is satisfying the requirement to suit the customers at this time. If a company can develop a solution to satisfying a requirement in this quadrant, it can gain a competitive advantage.

Requirements in the top right quadrant are called Market Requirements. They are being satisfied by at least one company so that they become requirements that must be satisfied by other companies if they intend to be competitive in the market on the most important customer requirements. The longer a product stays on the market, the more of these requirements become satisfied by most competitors. Then they tend to drift to the lower

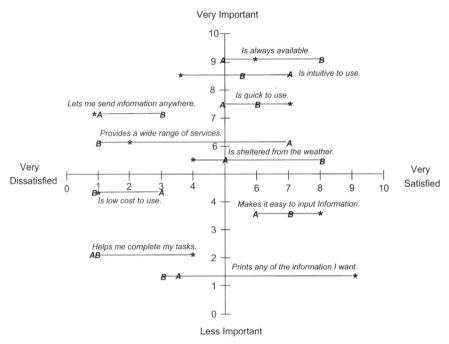

**Figure 6.5:** Example market opportunity map.
Legend A = Competitor A; B = Competitor B; * = Our performance.

right quadrant and become what are called Expected Requirements. These requirements must be satisfied as a minimum. The
four quadrants shown in Figure 6.6 illustrate these four types of
requirements.

An understanding of this map for each customer segment can
provide companies with a distinct advantage over their competitors. It will guide them in focusing their efforts in maximizing
customer value.

## 6.8 Exercises

1.  State the reported vision, mission, and values for a com-
    pany, government office, or social organization. Comment
    on the statements and any other observations that you had
    when collecting the information.
2.  Comment on a voice of the customer survey that you either
    took or had the opportunity to take.

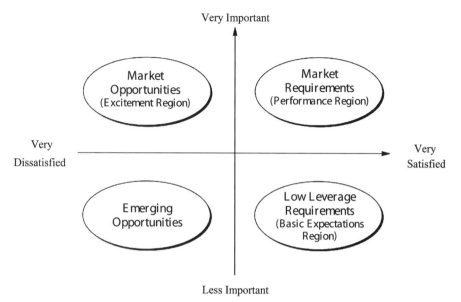

**Figure 6.6:** Market opportunity map.

3. Describe a situation where you were either very satisfied or very dissatisfied with a service. Describe the effectiveness of the organization's mechanism for capturing your feedback. Describe what the company could have done better to capture your inputs or thoughts.

# 7

# E-DMAIC—Define and Measure Phases: Enterprise Value Chain with Performance Measures

## 7.1 E-DMAIC Roadmap Component

The previous chapter described capturing voice of the customer at the enterprise level, which is the front-end of the E-DMAIC define phase. Organizations are managed in IEE through the value chain and its associated metrics. This chapter describes the value chain and its metrics, which is what the customer and business experience relative to overall deliverables and business hand-offs. These checklist activities are under the define phase and measure phase of the E-DMAIC roadmap.

This chapter illustrates at a high level the IEE scorecard/dashboard two-step creation process. Example 9.3 compares this thought process to traditional scorecard/dashboard annual or quarter calendar-based statement reporting. As earlier described:

IEE scorecard/dashboard metric reporting process

1. Assess process predictability.
2. When the process is considered predictable, formulate a prediction statement for the latest region of stability. The usual reporting format for this statement is:

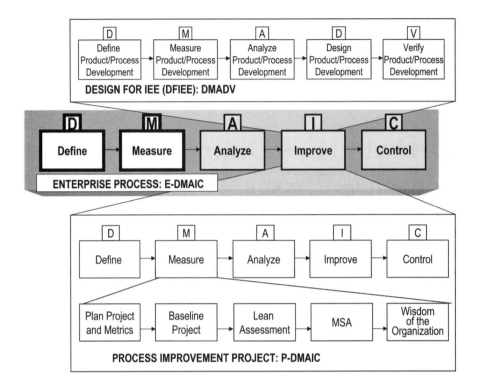

a.   When there is a specification requirement: nonconformance percentage or defects per million opportunities (DPMO)

b.   When there are no specification requirements: median response and 80% frequency of occurrence rate

Volume III chapters 12 and 13 describe the mechanics of creating the described satellite-level/30,000-foot-level control charts and formulating process capability/performance metric statements for a variety of situations.

## 7.2   Checklist: Enterprise Process Measure Phase

E-DMAIC measure phase activities include:

*   Establish agreed-to scorecard/dashboard satellite-level and 30,000-foot-level value-chain metrics, which are not bounded by calendar years or quarters in their reporting.

- Ensure that appropriate value-chain metrics are captured, reported, and used effectively, including between-product, IT, and development metrics.
- Define/ensure ownership of all scorecard/dashboard 30,000-foot-level metrics.
- For each agreed-to value chain metric, assess process predictability. For processes that are currently predictable, formulate a prediction statement for the latest stable region.
- Establish a system to capture and report value-chain scorecard/dashboard metrics.

The enterprise process value chain was included in the E-DMAIC define phase, which was described in the last chapter. I am including the detailed discussion about the value chain in this chapter since the value chain and 30,000-foot-level/satellite-level metrics are so closely integrated.

## 7.3  Enterprise Process Value Chain

Most organizations create an organizational chart and then manage through that chart. However, the enterprise-process customer can experience something quite different; that is, the impact from the fundamental flow of what is being done. The steps of the value-chain capture at a high level what we do and how we measure what is done. The metrics that are aligned to steps of the value chain need to be tracked and reported at the satellite- or 30,000-foot-level as a scorecard/dashboard. The shading on two functional steps in Figure 7.1 indicates these steps have drill-down procedures, as described in the next section.

> Most organizations create an organizational chart and then manage through that chart. However, the enterprise process customer can experience something quite different; that is, the impact from the fundamental flow of what is being done.

An organizational value chain can begin at the corporate level, site level, or other level throughout the company. As previously demonstrated, this value chain can also become the linkage to all standard operating procedures and processes. An example of a partially constructed value chain is shown in Figure 7.1. Notice how the main flow describes at a high level what the organiza-

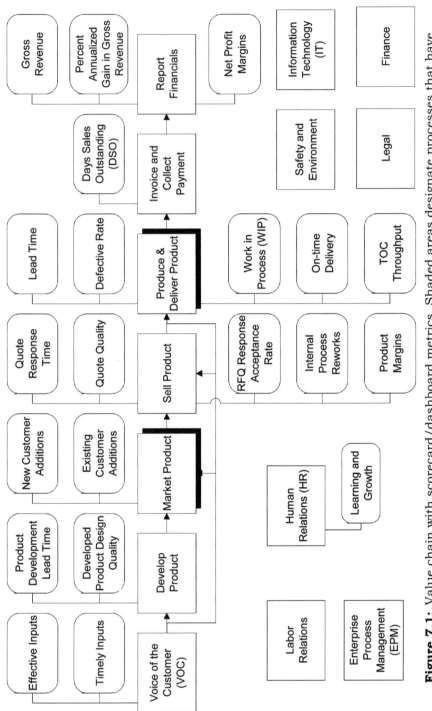

**Figure 7.1:** Value chain with scorecard/dashboard metrics. Shaded areas designate processes that have sub-process drill-downs.

tion does, where separate functions such as Human Relations (HR) and IT could be described as separate entities. In all cases, created metrics describe what is important to the business and where these metrics should address Lean E-DMAIC issues such as quality, waste, lead time, and total costs.

As was noted earlier, in the early 1990s the balanced scorecard was introduced, which addressed at the same time finance, customer, internal business processes, and learning and growth. Achieving scorecard balance is important because if you don't, you could be giving one metric more focus than another, which can lead to problems. For example, when focus is given to only on-time delivery, product quality could suffer dramatically to meet shipment dates. However, you have to be careful in how you achieve this balance. A natural balance is much more powerful than one that forces an inappropriate structure throughout the organization. All the characteristics of the balanced scorecard are naturally covered in this value chain, noting that learning and growth was assigned to HR.

A value chain can be created so that a simple double-click on a performance metric will present the 30,000-foot-level or satellite-level scorecard/dashboard metric. This performance-metric format can lead to improved behavior over the previously described metric reporting systems in Sections 3.3, 3.6, and 3.7.

Previously a good metric was described as having the characteristics of:

- Business alignment
- Honest assessment
- Consistency
- Repeatability and reproducibility
- Actionability
- Time-series tracking
- Predictability
- Peer comparability

Cunningham and Fiume (2003) provide metric guidelines as:

- Support the company's strategy
- Be relatively few in number
- Be mostly nonfinancial
- Be structured to motivate the right behavior
- Be simple and easy to understand
- Measure the process, not the people

- Measure actual results versus goals
- Do not combine measures of different things into a single index
- Be timely; weekly, daily, or hourly
- Show trend lines
- Be visual

The following figures later present various aspects of the value chain:

- Figures 7.2–7.5 illustrate how value-chain linkage of processes and procedures creates an easy accessible documentation repository.
- Figure 7.6 illustrates where organizationally the overall E-DMAIC process management orchestration can reside in the value chain, noting that this is where existing enterprise process analysis and improvement procedures could reside.
- Figure 7.7 exemplifies value-chain linkage with organization's satellite-level metrics.
- Figures 7.8–7.10 exemplifies value chain linkage with 30,000-foot-level functional performance metrics.

The reporting of business metrics at the satellite-level is included in the last value-chain step. These business metrics are to reflect important business financial metrics, where this satellite-level reporting does not have calendar boundaries such as year and month. Examples of satellite-level metrics are the following:

- Gross revenue
- Net profit margin
- Profit
- Earnings before interest, depreciation, and amortization (EBIDA)
- Voice of the customer (VOC)

Operational metrics are also reported throughout the value chain. As in hoshin kanri, each function in a value chain could have a generic mission definition that addresses quality, cost, and delivery. The measurements for each generic mission should not change as a function of the overall organization mission changes. However, goals for these metrics could change depending on business inputs and VOC. E-DMAIC analyses can provide insight as to where directed improvement efforts would have the most benefit to the overall enterprise. Improvement measurement needs would pull for project creation.

These metrics provide no-nonsense scorecard/dashboard business tracking at the 30,000-foot-level. They assess how the organizational functions are performing over time relative to predictability, along with appropriate prediction statements; that is, functional-process capability/performance metric statements.

> These metrics provide a no-nonsense scorecard/dashboard business tracking at the 30,000-foot-level. They assess how the organizational functions are performing over time relative to predictability, along with appropriate prediction statements.

These VOC internal and external metrics need to have an owner responsible for performance of these functions and meeting of agreed-to metric goals. Value-chain scorecard/dashboard metrics that should be reported in the 30,000-foot-level metric format, as opposed to the tables and chart formats previously described, include the following:

- Defective and defect rates
- Lead times
- Number of days sales outstanding
- Customer satisfaction and loyalty
- On-time delivery
- Unplanned downtime as percentage of total available time
- Injury rate; total employee work hours between injuries
- Medical costs per employee
- Lost-time accidents as a percentage of total possible employee work time
- Number of days from promise date
- Number of days from customer requested date
- Raw material inventory
- WIP inventory
- Finished goods inventory
- Performance to customer demand rate
- Sales per employee
- Market share
- Absenteeism as percentage of workforce
- Product-development lead time
- Operating cost as a percentage of sales
- Research and development as a percentage of sales
- Percentage of sales from new products
- Capital investment as percentage of sales
- Working capital as a percentage of sales

# 7.4 Value Chain Drill-Downs

A readily available format may be created to describe each step's value creation so that standard operating procedures, process inputs, and such are easily understood.

Organizations have procedural documents; however, there is often no single repository for locating procedural flowcharts and associated documents. The following web-based value chain with drill-downs addresses this issue, where a simple click on a value-chain step leads to its drill-down subprocess, attached documents, or website options.

Figure 7.2 uses Figure 7.1 to illustrate the creation of a subprocess that can have procedural linkages and further sub-process drill-downs. All new IEE project procedures and BPIEs should be linked to the value chain. Figure 7.3 illustrates how "swim lanes" can be used to describe different subprocess procedures.

Figure 7.4 shows the linkage of value stream mapping (VSM) to the value chain. VSM can address both product and information flow, along with the reporting of lead time versus value-added time, as described later in this volume. From this model, we can also run simulations to address what-if possibilities. The customer value stream is very important since it is a basis for organizational improvements.

Figure 7.5 shows how a simple value-chain click can lead to a procedural document and website option linkage.

# 7.5 Enterprise Process Management (EPM)

It is unfortunate that many companies compile VOC data without having an overall plan that addresses what they will do with the data once they receive it. Organizations need a sustainable governance system for not only capturing customer data but also conducting competitive new-product-development analyses, reporting metrics, creating strategic plans, and so forth. Organizations need a sustainable system that captures KPIVs and translates this input into both real products or services and actionable items.

As organizations move forward, it can be healthy to honestly assess the effectiveness of existing systems based on auditable results. This assessment can address whether these systems are

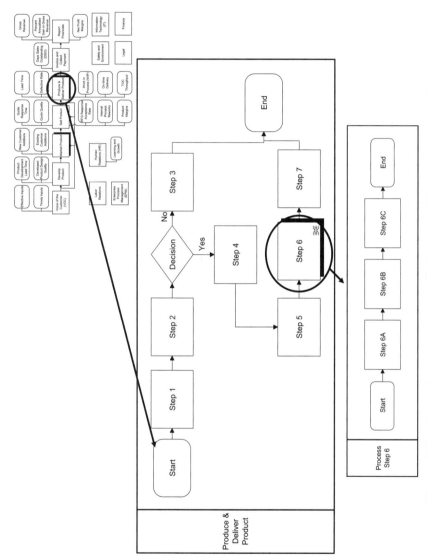

**Figure 7.2:** Example subprocess drill-down and linkage to value chain.

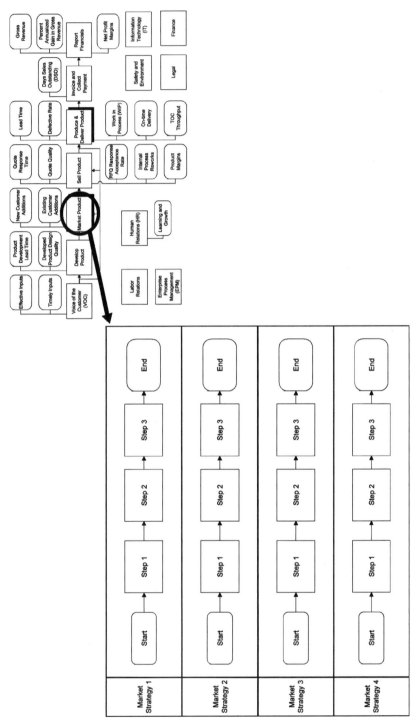

**Figure 7.3:** Example subprocess swim-lane drill-down.

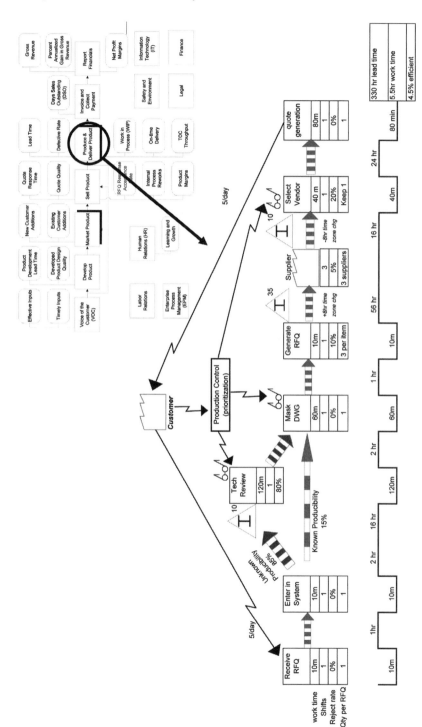

**Figure 7.4:** Example subprocess value stream map drill-down.

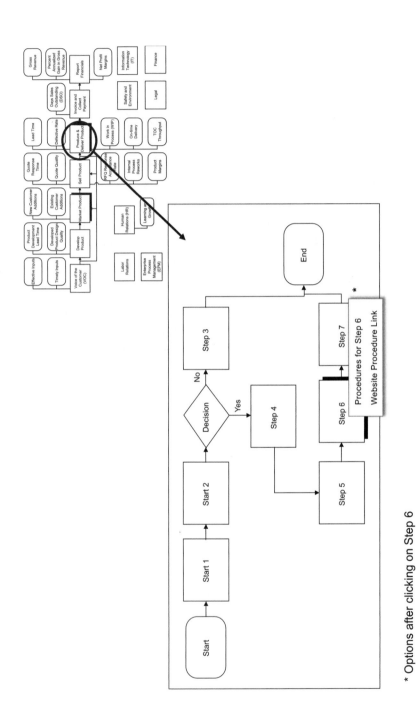

**Figure 7.5:** Example linkage in a process step.

* Options after clicking on Step 6

being executed consistently and effectively, where executed procedures are part of an overall procedural repository. Often there are indications for improvement opportunities.

Rather than having a model for governance that addresses initiatives as separate entities, a value-chain enterprise process management (EPM) function can provide orchestration to this system. The EPM function, as shown in the value chain in Figure 7.6, is responsible for integrating, overseeing, and improving the execution of these processes using an E-DMAIC roadmap.

> Rather than having a governance model that addresses initiatives as separate entities, a value-chain Enterprise Process Management (EPM) function can be created that orchestrates this system.

The EPM function can orchestrate the integration of existing enterprise procedures with the appropriate overall E-DMAIC functions described in this volume, where ownership assignments can be made. In a one-week workout, we have helped organizations successfully create the drill-down structure for each of the enterprise-process steps shown in Figure 7.6. The detail for each of these steps is refined over time.

The integration of the E-DMAIC methodologies with existing procedures can lead to an improved overall enterprise system that is more data driven and sustainable. Improved measurements from this implementation can lead to a significant reduction in waste and reduce firefighting activities. Activity checks and balances that ensure continuing improvements through timely project completions are part of the E-DMAIC control phase.

This EPM function implementation can lead to the creation of an enterprise system that consistently allows a company to retain its current customer base with no added expense, while maximizing its resources to attract and secure new ones.


# 7.6 Technical Aspects of Satellite-Level and 30,000-Foot-Level Charting

The primary intent of traditional control charting is to timely identify when a special cause condition occurs and take appropriate action. This is not the case with satellite-level and 30,000-foot-level control charting. Because of this, there are several technical

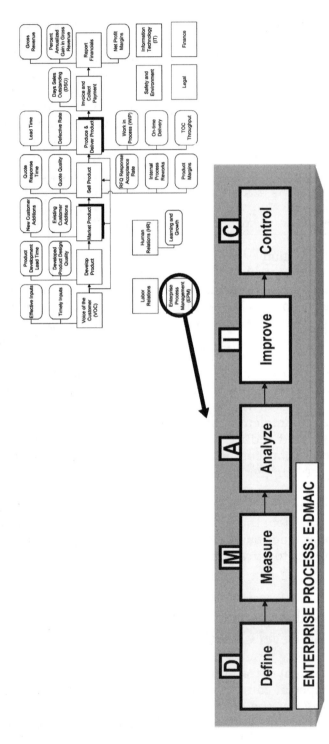

**Figure 7.6:** Enterprise process management drill-down.

issues to address when creating these charts. The purpose of this section is to provide chart-creation highlights.

Satellite-level and 30,000-foot-level charting focus is the providing of a high-level view for what the internal or external customer of the process is expected to experience. As noted earlier, the two basic objectives for satellite-level and 30,000-foot-level reporting is:

1. Assess process predictability.
2. When the process is considered predictable, formulate a prediction statement for the latest region of stability. The usual reporting format for this statement is the following:
   a. When there is a specification requirement: nonconformance percentage or DPMO
   b. When there is no specification requirement: median response and 80 percent frequency of occurrence rate

Because of these charting objectives, the mechanics to create these charts is often different than traditional control charting (Breyfogle 2003b, 2004b, 2005b, 2006). Volume III elaborates more on the details of this statement and provides the chart-creation details for various situations. Highlights of issues that need addressing when creating satellite-level and 30,000-foot-level charts are:

- The reporting and use of probability plots is different for attribute and continuous data (see Appendix E.1), as demonstrated in the following examples.
- Control charting subgroups are created using infrequent subgrouping/sampling techniques so that short-term variations, which might be caused by typical variation in input levels, will result in charts that view these perturbations as common-cause variability sources.
- Individuals control charts can trigger false special-cause conditions when plotted data are from a distribution that is not normally distributed (see Appendix E.2).

# 7.7 Example 7.1: Satellite-Level Metrics

This example gives focus to the interpretation and use of satellite-level metrics. The mechanics of creating these charts is described in Volume III.

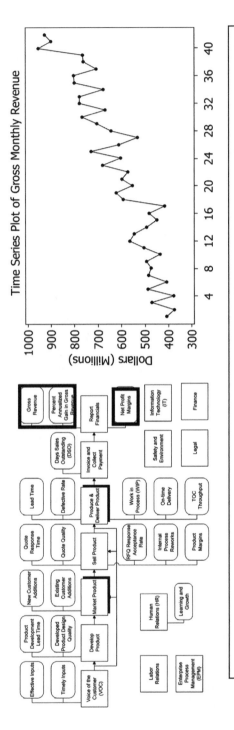

**Figure 7.7:** (Part A) Comparison of traditional performance reporting with an IEE value-chain satellite-level score-card/dashboard report.

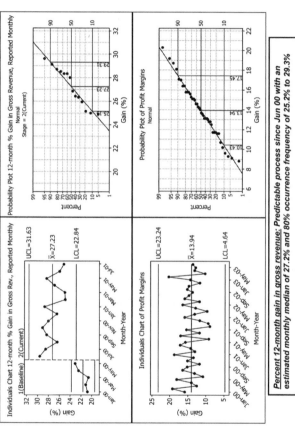

**Figure 7.7:** (Part B) Comparison of traditional performance reporting with an IEE value-chain satellite-level score-card/dashboard report. Stage 1 (Baseline) and Stage 2 (New) process levels are designated are at the top of the graphs.

We want to satisfy stakeholders with our products and services. To accomplish this, we need to define and observe key metrics and indicators. Let's start with the financials those provide a business-health picture of how well objectives and stockholder expectations are being met.

Organizations often establish annual gross-revenue growth-and-profit-margin objectives. Earlier it was illustrated how simply focusing on quarterly numbers often leads to the wrong activities. This example provides an alternative system-focused methodology that can provide more timely information on how good performance is relative to business goals.

Consider that the satellite-level metrics for Acme Medical are gross revenue, percentage annual gain in gross revenue, and net-profit margins. The report-out of these satellite-level metrics in Figure 7.7 shows a time-series plot of monthly gross revenue. The reader should note that no curve has been fitted to this line for making future-revenue projections. Time-series projections can be very dangerous. Building an accurate time-series model requires a great deal of data. Because it would take one year to capture only twelve data points, this analysis could easily miss a timely statement about nonlinearity or a flattening of a growth curve. Because no statement was made relative to predictability, extrapolations could be very deceiving.

One might ask: why not simply report total revenue growth for each month, instead of including percent gain in gross revenue, which the figure includes? For one thing, a total revenue plot does not directly address a common organizational goal; i.e., grow the business by a certain percentage year over year. Also, a simple monthly total revenue growth report-out offers no statement about future output expectations from the current process.

In the IEE satellite-level report-out in Figure 7.7, the 12-month percentage gain in gross revenue (GR; monthly reporting) is determined by calculating the annual percentage gain as if the yearly financial statements were closing that month. For example, a March 2008 percentage-gain point would be determined as

$$
\frac{\text{GR \% annual gain}}{\text{plot point for 3/08}} = \frac{GR_{[4/1/07\text{ to }3/31/08]} - GR_{[4/1/06\text{ to }3/31/07]}}{GR_{[4/1/06\text{ to }3/31/07]}} (100)
$$

If a goal is to increase annual gross-revenue growth, detecting a process shift can take some time. However, this tracking procedure is in true alignment with the organizational annual-revenue-growth goal statement and can provide a monthly feedback assessment on the impact of efforts to achieve this goal.

With this form of reporting, management should not be reacting to the up-and-down control chart variability as though it were special cause. This does not mean that one should ignore the variation and simply talk it away as common cause variability. What it does mean is that we do not react either positively or negatively to individual common-cause datum points; that is, we would examine the data collectively. If the numbers were down below what is desired, focus would be given to process-improvement effort, as opposed to spending a lot of time explaining what happened last month.

A detailed interpretation of the annualized percentage gain in gross revenue and profit margin plots is shown in Figure 7.7 using the IEE scorecard/dashboard metric reporting process:

1. Assess process predictability.
2. When the process is considered predictable, formulate a prediction statement for the latest region of stability. The usual reporting format for this statement is the following:
   a. When there is a specification requirement: nonconformance percentage or DPMO
   b. When there is no specification requirement: median response and 80 percent frequency of occurrence rate

An interpretation of the *annual-gross-revenue-growth plots* shown in Figure 7.7 using this process follows:

1. A control chart test on the annual-gross-revenue data indicated a shift about Jun 00. Perhaps another company was acquired at this time. Since then, the process has experienced only common-cause variability. Even though the control chart appears to have some trends from this point in time, the rules of control charting would have us conclude that the process is now predictable.
2. From the probability plot, we estimate that since Jun 00 a monthly median of 27.2 percent and an 80 percent occurrence frequency of 25.2–29.3 percent has occurred; that is, we expect that 80 percent of the future monthly reporting will be between these two percentages.

An interpretation of *profit-margin plots* shown in Figure 7.7 using this process follows:

1. Even though the control chart of profit appears to have trends, the rules of control charting would have us conclude that the process was predictable.

2. From the probability plot, we estimate a monthly median of 13.9 percent and an 80 percent monthly occurrence frequency of 10.4 percent to 17.4 percent; i.e., we expect that 80 percent of the future monthly reporting will be between these percentages.

After all value-chain metrics are collectively examined, realistic goals can be set to improve the satellite-level metrics. A strategy could then be created to improve these metrics, which is part of the E-DMA-IC process analyze phase. As part of this enterprise decision-making process, areas thought to drive higher net-profit margins might be the reduction of defects and the creation of a new product line.

Specific goals can be established for improvements to the 30,000-foot-level scorecard/dashboard metrics. The 30,000-foot-level metric's owners would be responsible for making targeted improvements in the allotted time frame; for example, shift the process mean to the desired goal in six months. For the 30,000-foot-level metric to improve its level of performance, a fundamental improvement is needed in the process.

These metric improvement needs would pull for P-DMAIC project creation. Managers would then assign black belts or green belts to these projects who would follow the IEE project-execution roadmap described in Volume III. Since these managers are measured against the success of the metric shift, they will want to have frequent updates about the status of the project. The overall system that accomplishes this is part of the E-DMAIC analyze and improve phases.

One should note how this form of management focuses on improving the systems of doing things, as opposed to firefighting the process common-cause ups and downs or targeting tabular outputs that do not meet expectations, for example, red-yellow-green metric reporting.

This E-DMAIC reporting at the satellite-level and 30,000-foot-level can lead to a very positive governance model that moves organizations toward achieving the three $R$s of business: everyone doing the Right things and doing them Right at the Right time. This is in contrast to a business governance model that encourage the executive team to do whatever it takes to achieve the next calendar-based financial target; that is, trying to manage the $Y$ output of a process rather than giving focus to improving the process or its $X$ inputs, which either positively or negatively impact the $Y$ output.

Many practitioners would be hesitant to present this type of satellite-level and 30,000-foot-level (later examples in this chapter) metric report-out to their management. This is understandable since this report-out is probably quite different than what has been previously presented and requested.

For those readers who see the benefit in this type of reporting and do not know how to get their management's interest, I suggest using advocacy selling and stealth training techniques. For the advocacy selling portion of this strategy, you could describe the charts off-line to a leading-thinking influential person, who is on the executive team. After taking the time to understand the IEE reporting methodology off-line, he/she could then support the creation of an opportunity where you give a short presentation to the executive team. In this presentation, you could select data sets from your business where you compare your current methods with the described IEE methodology.

Now comes the stealth training. During the meeting you should give focus to the prediction statement, which is highlighted at the bottom of the presentation slide. You should not make any statement about the graphs per se, which is the stealth-training portion of this presentation. What you want is someone to ask a question about the charts and variation swings. In most of these type meetings, someone will ask about the data variability that is conveyed in the charts.

When responding to this and other initial questions, don't try to give too much initial explanation—more detailed information can come in another presentation. You might simply say that all the up and down motion in the control chart is common-cause variability, which indicates that the process is predictable. Pointing now to the probability plot you could then show how the prediction statement was determined.

I suggest that you also have a slide that compares this IEE report-out methodology to your traditional reporting methodology, which makes no prediction statement. During this presentation you might be able to demonstrate that your organization's many firefighting skirmishes have not really fixing much, if anything, long term.

I have had practitioners say that there is no way that their management would ever accept satellite-level and 30,000-foot-level reporting. However, these practitioners did try and now they say that their management is requesting this form of reporting.

## 7.8   Example 7.2: 30,000-Foot-Level Metric with Specifications

This example focuses on the interpretation and use of 30,000-foot-level metrics. The mechanics of creating these charts is described in Volume III.

Let's say that on-time delivery is considered one of the greatest customer satisfiers to sales of products and services in Acme Medical's business value chain. This example provides a high-levelview of the output from IEE 30,000-foot-level scorecard/ dashboard metric reporting. For the purpose of illustration, the following data were randomly generated from a normal distribution.

In Acme Medical's value chain, the on-time delivery 30,000-foot-level scorecard/dashboard metric performance was tracked by randomly selecting one shipment weekly. Results from this analysis are shown in Figure 7.8, where +1 indicates one day late and −1 indicates one day early.

A detailed interpretation of this figure follows from the IEE scorecard/dashboard metric reporting process:

1. Assess process predictability.
2. When the process is considered predictable, formulate a prediction statement for the latest region of stability. The usual reporting format for this statement is the following:
   a. When there is a specification requirement: nonconformance percentage or DPMO
   b. When there is no specification requirement: median response and 80 percent frequency of occurrence rate

Interpretation of Figure 7.8 using this process:

1. Even though the control chart in Figure 7.8 appears to have trends, the rules of control charting would have us conclude that the process was predictable. As a reminder, these data were randomly generated and all variability was due to chance.
2. The agreed-to shipping requirement was that shipments were not to be late (i.e., >+1.0) and no earlier than five days (i.e., <−5.0) from their due date. The value-chain manager responsible for producing and delivering the product is responsible for this metric relative to current level of performance maintenance and any desired improvements. Acme's current performance and predicted future performance is that about 6.1 percent of all shipments will be earlier than the agreed-to date and about 7.6 percent of all shipments will be later than the agreed-to date (100 − 92.433 = 7.567 rounded off). This leads to the expectation that about 13.7 percent (6.1 + 7.6) will be either earlier or later than the agreed-to delivery date.

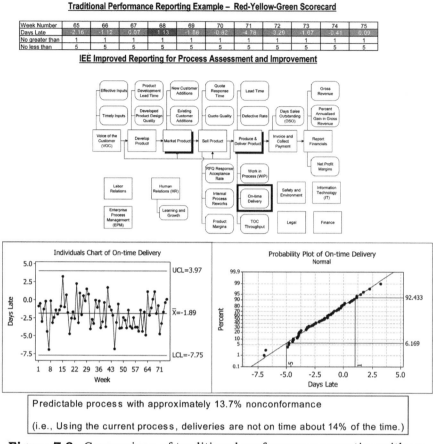

**Figure 7.8:** Comparison of traditional performance reporting with an IEE value chain 30,000-foot-level on-time delivery performance scorecard/dashboard report. The traditional performance reporting example contains the most recent eleven data points.

Often, on-time-delivery metrics are reported as attribute data; that is, each shipment was received within the agreed-to time interval or not. It is hoped that the reader will appreciate the value of using the above continuous-response data-analysis approach over attribute reporting. With continuous data, much more insight is gained with a significantly smaller sample size. As illustrated in the example above, we not only estimate the proportion of shipments that are both early and late but also describe the distribution of delivery times.

Using control charting rules, we have no reason to infer that the apparent short-term trends in the 30,000-foot-level control chart were from chance and should not be reacted to as individual values. Long-lasting improvements to this metric can be made through fundamental process changes.

When all value-chain metrics are collectively examined in the E-DMAIC analyze phase, this metric could be chosen as one that needs improvement because of its anticipated impact on gross-revenue goals, net-profit improvement goals, or customer retention. If this were the case, this metric would be creating a pull for project creation. The owner of this "produce and deliver product" metric would be responsible for making the targeted improvements in the allotted time frame, for example, shifting the process mean to the desired goal in six months. This manager would then assign a black belt or green belt to the project, where he would follow the IEE project-execution roadmap described in Volume III. Since this manager is measured against the success of the metric shift, he will want to have frequent updates about the status of the project.

> When all value-chain metrics are collectively examined in the E-DMAIC analyze phase, this metric could be chosen as one that needs improvement because of its anticipated impact upon gross-revenue and net-profit improvement goals. If this were the case, this metric would be pulling for an improvement project creation.

Note how this form of management focuses on improving the systems of doing things, as opposed to firefighting the common-cause ups and downs of processes or point tabular values that do not meet expectations, such as red-yellow-green metric reporting.

## 7.9    Example 7.3: 30,000-Foot-Level Continuous Response Metric with No Specifications

This example gives focus to the interpretation and use of 30,000-foot-level metrics. The mechanics of creating these charts is described in Volume III.

Days sales outstanding (DSO) is important to business cash flow in Acme's business value chain. DSO is typically the average number of days it takes to collect revenue after a sale has been made. For purposes of this study we defined DSO as the number of days before or after the due date that a payment is to be received. A +1 would indicate that an invoice receipt was one day after the due date, while a −1 would indicate that receipt was one day before the due date.

This example gives a high-level view of the output from this 30,000-foot-level scorecard/dashboard metric reporting. The following data were randomly generated from a normal distribution. We could select more for each subgroup; however, I want to start with a simple illustration. In this fictitious example, consider that some invoices had 90-day payment terms.

A detailed interpretation of this figure follows from the IEE scorecard/dashboard metric reporting process:

1. Assess process predictability.
2. When the process is considered predictable, formulate a prediction statement for the latest region of stability. The usual reporting format for this statement is:
   a. When there is a specification requirement: nonconformance percentage or defects per million opportunities (DPMO)
   b. When there are no specification requirements: median response and 80 percent frequency of occurrence rate

Interpretation of Figure 7.9 using this process:

1. Even though the control chart in Figure 7.9 appears to have trends, the rules of control charting would have us conclude that the process was predictable. As a reminder, these data were randomly generated and all variability was due to chance.
2. Since there are no true specification requirements, a 50 percent and 80 percent frequency of occurrence reporting gives a good feel for what to expect from the process, including its variability. For this process, we estimate a median (50 percent frequency of occurrence) of about 4.8 days late with an 80 percent frequency of occurrence of 18.2 days early to 27.9 days late.

With this form of reporting, anyone, whether familiar with this process or not, has a general understanding of what to expect from it. To quantify better the impact of this tardiness, we can also report the impact in financial terms such as a cost of doing nothing differently (CODND) metric.

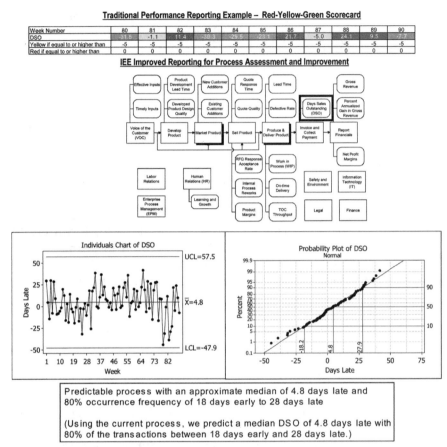

**Figure 7.9:** Comparison of traditional performance reporting with an IEE value-chain 30,000-foot-level DSO performance scorecard/dashboard report. The traditional performance reporting example contains the most recent eleven data points.

As in the previous example, it is important to note that the apparent short-term trends in the 30,000-foot-level control chart were all from chance and should not be reacted to as an individual value. Long-lasting improvements to this metric are achieved only through fundamental changes to the process.

When all value-chain metrics are collectively examined in the E-DMAIC analyze phase, this metric could be chosen as one that needs improvement because of its anticipated impact to grossrevenue and net-profit business goals. If this were the case, this metric would create a pull for a project creation. The owner of this "invoice and collect payment" metric would be responsible for making the targeted improvements in the allotted time frame, for example, shifting process mean to an EIP goal in six months. The manager would then assign a black belt or green belt to this project, where he would follow the P-DMAIC execution road map described in Volume III. Since this manager is measured against the success of the metric shift, he will want to have frequent updates about the status of the project.

One should note how this form of management focuses on improving the systems of doing things, as opposed to firefighting the common cause ups and downs of processes or point tabular values that do not meet expectations; for example, red-yellow-green metric reporting.

## 7.10   Example 7.4: 30,000-Foot-Level Attribute Response Metric

This example focuses on the interpretation and use of 30,000-foot-level metrics. The mechanics of creating these charts is described in Volume III.

As in our previous example, let's say that low defective rate is considered one of the greatest customer satisfiers to sales of products and services in Acme's business value chain. This example gives a high-level view of the output from 30,000-foot-level scorecard/dashboard metric reporting with randomly generated data. For illustration purposes, the following data were randomly generated from a normal distribution.

Acme Medical produced a certain amount of product daily. The defective rate 30,000-foot-level metric performance was tracked over time. Results from this analysis are shown in Figure 7.10. The "produce and deliver product" value-chain manager is responsible for this metric relative to current level of performance maintenance and to any desired improvements.

A detailed interpretation of this figure follows from the IEE scorecard/dashboard metric reporting process:

1. Assess process predictability.
2. When the process is considered predictable, formulate a prediction statement for the latest region of stability. The usual reporting format for this statement is:
   a. When there is a specification requirement: nonconformance percentage or defects per million opportunities (DPMO)

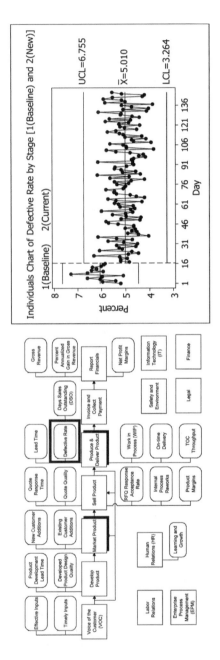

**Figure 7.10:** Comparison of traditional performance reporting with an IEE value-chain 30,000-foot-level defective rate performance scorecard/dashboard report. Stage 1 (Baseline) and Stage 2 (New) process levels are designated at the top of the graphs. The traditional performance reporting example contains the most recent eleven data points.

b.   When there are no specification requirements: median response and 80 percent frequency of occurrence rate

Interpretation of Figure 7.10 using this process:

1.   The individuals control chart of defective rate by stage
indicates a process shift on day 16 establishing a new level
of predictive performance.
2.   Since we are tracking defective rate, we can use the mean
response from this chart to estimate the current and future level of performance, which is about 5 percent defective rate. The centerline shift of 1 percent is an estimate of
the process improvement on day 16.

Since day 16, this process has been experiencing common
cause variability. These are best estimates of the performance of
this process. If this process response is not satisfactory, something needs to be done to improve the process, that is, a pull for
project creation.

Effort was made to improve this enterprise process step.
A hypothesis test of the equality of the failure rate from stage
1(Baseline) to stage 2(Current) in Figure 7.10 indicates a significant improvement was made. The control chart was constructed
to denote this shift, where the process has stabilized and now
has a new process capability/performance metric. The current
performance and predicted future defective rate is that of about
5 percent (5.01 rounded-off). Since these data are attribute and
assumed subgroup sizes are equal, the centerline of the stable
process region is the estimated future defective rate.

It is important to note that the apparent short-term trends
in the 30,000-foot-level control chart were all from chance and
should not be reacted to as an individual value. Long-lasting
improvements to this metric can be made through fundamental
changes to the process.

When all the value-chain metrics were collectively examined in
the E-DMAIC analyze phase, this metric could have been chosen
as one that needs improvement. If this were the case, a financial
analysis would have indicated that a reduction in internal re-
work/reject rates would be an important step toward achieving a
net-profit margin business goal; that is, this metric improvement
need would create a pull for project creation. The owner of this
"produce and deliver product" metric would be responsible for
making the targeted improvements in the allotted time frame, for

example, shift process mean to the desired goal in seven months. The manager would then assign a black belt or green belt to this project, where he would follow the project execution road map and checklists described in Volume III. Since this manager is measured against the success of the metric shift, he will want to have frequent project status updates.

One should note how this form of management focuses on improving the systems of doing things, as opposed to firefighting the common-cause ups and downs of processes or point tabular values that do not meet expectations, for example red-yellow-green metric reporting.

# 7.11   CEO's Role, Compensation, and Communication

An organization should consider addressing not only the following items in their value chain but also what needs to be done for the organization to truly embrace implementation of the concepts.

## Team Meetings

Communication is essential in an organization. Teams need to understand the business purpose and how it is performing. Structured monthly hour-long team meetings presenting financials, scorecards/dashboards, and BPIEs (see Section 13.3) are a way to accomplish this objective. During this meeting, team members can present, if applicable, their scorecard/dashboard metric in a 30,000-foot-level/50-foot-level format along with any project status to improve these metrics. Team members can also present BPIEs that involve them from either a creation or implementation point of view.

Each person is encouraged to ask questions and suggest improvements. These team meetings can be used to discuss issues and offer suggestions on how work flow can be improved. These meetings are very beneficial in building knowledge about system measurements and improvements. So that there is enterprise consistency when conducting these meetings, the generic meeting flow can be described in an EPM drill down (see Figure 7.6).

## CEO'S Role and Compensation System

I agree with the following points that Fiume (2006) makes, except that I would replace Lean with IEE.

CEO's role:

- Learn Lean (i.e., IEE) thinking
- Out front—hands on—don't delegate
- Lots of leaps of faith
- Change metrics and set stretch goals
- Create an environment where it's okay to fail
- Provide air cover for early adopters
- Eliminate concrete heads
- Have a "no-layoff" policy
- Organize around value streams

Change compensation systems that don't support Lean (i.e., IEE):

- Factory:
  - Piece work incentives
  - Narrow job classifications and many pay grades
- Middle management:
  - Bonus based on individual performance
- Sales:
  - Bonus based on meeting quota
- Senior Management:
  - Incentive compensation based on individual performance

## 7.12  Malcolm Baldrige National Quality Award, Shingo Prize, and IEE

The foundation for the Malcolm Baldrige National Quality Award was established in 1988. The Baldrige Award is given by the President of the United States to businesses—manufacturing and service, small and large—and to education, health care and non-profit organizations that apply and are judged to be outstanding in seven areas: leadership; strategic planning; customer and market focus; measurement, analysis, and knowledge management; human resource focus; process management; and results. (See www.quality.nist.gov.)

The Shingo Prize was established in 1988 to promote awareness of Lean manufacturing concepts and recognize companies in the United States, Canada, and Mexico that achieve world-class manufacturing status. The Shingo Prize recognizes organizations and research with three types of prizes, which are business prize, research prize, and public sector prize. The five categories of the Shingo Prize are: leadership culture and infrastructure; manufacturing strategies and system integration; business functions and process integration; quality, cost, and delivery; customer satisfaction and profitability. (See www.shingoprize.org.)

The E-DMAIC system, which starts with the define and measure phases, provides a framework for implementing practices that are consistent with the Baldrige Award and the Shingo Prize criteria. When building an IEE structure, use of the concepts described in the Baldrige Award and Shingo Prize applications can help an organization create a *Level Five System*.

## 7.13  Exercises

1. Select a for-profit company, non-profit organization, school, religious organization, or political organization. Define its satellite-level metrics.
2. Create a value chain for a selected organization or a company that owns your favorite grocery store. Include representative 30,000-foot-level metrics.
3. Describe the benefits when managing to value-chain 30,000-foot-level metrics, as opposed to the traditional scorecard/dashboards.

# 8

# E-DMAIC—Analyze Phase: Goal Setting, Business Fundamentals, and Strategy Development

## 8.1  E-DMAIC Roadmap Component

Some might feel that it would be more appropriate to position the enterprise analyze phase before the define phase and measure phase. However, in the E-DMAIC system, it is suggested that the leadership of existing businesses start by defining and presenting what the organization does in the define phase, e.g., its vision, mission, and value-chain process.

The measure phase would then present a tracking of the value-chain metrics at the satellite-level and 30,000-foot-level. This business foundation then would be assessed as a whole in the analyze phase to create an iterative process from which refinements can be made to the value chain and then validated through 30,000-foot-level metric improvement analyses.

To be successful, organizations need to make high-level business decisions. These decisions can be made through instincts and/or data analyses. People can be very successful leading a company by relying heavily on their instincts using minimal data analyses. However, often what might be thought as the best approach or strategy may be found not true if there were data analy-

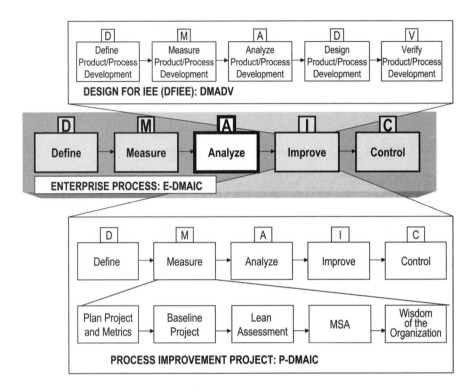

ses. In addition, if the lead person for historically making beneficial instinct-based decisions is no longer available, bad things can
occur.

The E-DMAIC analyze phase does not suggest that the use of
instincts is bad and should be avoided. However, what is suggested is that effort be given to create a system that efficiently and
effectively structurally combines data with instincts and organizational wisdom. In this system, data analyses can later provide insight to which decisions were beneficial and which ones were not.
Through these analyses, an organization can learn what could be
done differently the next time to create better results. The overall
goal of this integration is to create a Results Orchestration (RO)
system that moves toward achieving the three *R*s of business,
i.e., everyone doing the right things and doing them right at the
right time.

For most organizations, many business analyze systems already
exist. However, these systems may often be ad hoc, dependent
upon a particular person to execute the process, or have a large
opportunity for improvement. Davenport and Harris (2007) stated,
"We discovered a significant statistical association between an

organization's commitment to analytics and high performance. Companies with strong analytical orientations (those who answered with a four or five on all our questions) represented 25 percent of the sample (93 companies), and their orientations correlated highly with financial out performance in terms of profit, revenue, and shareholder return. In fact, one of the strongest and most consistent differences between low- and high-performance businesses is their attitude toward, and application of analytics." Results from a study on importance of analytical orientation indicated:

- Have significant decision-support/analytical capabilities: low performers = 23%, high performers = 65%
- Value analytical insights to a very large extent: low performers = 8%, high performers = 36%
- Have above-average analytical capability within industry: low performers = 33%, high performers = 77%
- Use analytics across their entire organization: low performers = 23%, high performers = 40%

Davenport and Harris (2007) provide the following illustrations of analytics use as part of an organization's enterprise:

- Marriott embeds analytics into several customer-facing processes. The most profitable customers are identified through its Marriott Rewards loyalty program so that marketing offers and campaigns can be targeted to them. Sophisticated Web analytics has led to a four-billion-dollar annual business through its online channel. The company, partly as a result of its wise use of analytics, has been named *Fortune* magazine's most admired firm in its industry for seven straight years.
- Best Buy increases subsequent sales after an initial purchase through a predictive model. For example, a digital camera purchase could trigger a timely e-coupon for a photo printer.
- Sprint uses analytics to better understand customer life cycles. In this life-cycle model, forty-two attributes are used to characterize interactions, perceptions, and emotions of customers from initial product awareness through service renewal/upgrade. This analytics is integrated into operational models to determine the best ways to maximize, over time, customer loyalty and spending.
- Google has a very large commitment to experimentation before making any search-site change. Search-engine algo-

rithm changes need to pass through a test funnel and demonstrate substantial improvements with high quality.

Davenport and Harris (2007) highlight the three critical types of outcomes to measuring the performance of an initiative as: behavior, processes and programs, and financial results. The financial results, which matter in the end, probably will not be achieved without focusing on intermediate outcomes, that is, the Xs in the relationship $Y=f(X)$.

- Behavior of employees, to a large extent, is a major driver of improved financial outcomes. For example, new analytical pricing strategies can require the behavior change of thousands of employees.
- Process and program changes are often required to improve results through fact-based analyses. For example, insights to deter the loss of wireless customers to another carrier need translation into actions, perhaps through a new training program for employees who face customers. The integration of analytics into business applications and work processes is a means to ensure that data-driven insights are incorporated into the business.
- Financial results may include goals to improve profitability or higher revenue. Cost savings are initially the most frequent justification for an analytical initiative because it is much easier in advance to specify how to cut costs. It is more difficult to predict and measure increased revenue; however, analytical models can be developed from small tests and pilot studies. With increased analytical maturity, organizations can become more willing to invest in initiatives that have the target of exploiting growth and revenue-generating opportunities.

The E-DMAIC analyze phase provides a framework for the repository of a company's existing systems and the ongoing enhancement of these systems through the use of analytics. In the next section, a checklist of action items is presented for this phase. I am providing this list up front in the road map phase so that the reader can view the big picture objectives of this phase. The reader can reference this checklist as needed when progressing through the phase. This chapter then proceeds to describing a structured strategic analysis system that can improve organizational focus.

# 8.2 Checklist: Enterprise Process Analyze Phase

Currently, organizations have systems that address many of the following items. The E-DMAIC analysis phase is the focal point for system identification, coordination, and improvement.

E-DMAIC analyze phase activities include:

- Assess business fundamentals for providing the best customer value/price on a consistent basis.
- Conduct a strategic analysis, which addresses industry, competitor analysis, customer/marketplace trends, environmental forecast, and internal strength/weakness/resources.
- Revisit organization's vision, mission, and value proposition.
- Assess alignment of organizational direction to defined Jim Collins's three circles.
- Conduct an environmental scan checking market conditions (see Section 8.8).
- Conduct FMEA (see Volume III) to identify enterprise risks.
- Examine satellite-level metrics and establish SMART goals for these metrics.
- Assess effectiveness of prior strategic plans and the direct impact that these plans have upon the improvement of the enterprise's satellite-level metrics.
- Conduct SWOT analysis (see Section 1.7).
- Create the enterprise's five strategic development elements (see Figure 8.1).
- Analyze satellite-level metrics and 30,000-foot-level scorecard/dashboard metrics reporting to identify improvement opportunity focus areas.
- Analyze the satellite-level, 30,000-foot-level metrics, financial equation components (e.g., ROI), and enterprise processes to identify constraints and improvement opportunities. For this data analysis, utilize financial, statistical, nonstatistical, simulation, TOC, and Lean tools (e.g., value stream mapping and time value diagramming).
- Analyze product development and IT project execution effectiveness. Consider whether reliability, DOE, Design for $X$, and other tools could be applied more effectively to streamline the design process.
- Use benchmarking to gain process knowledge and external best practices.
- Analyze BPIE inputs for project opportunities or just-do-it actions.

- Obtain inputs through one-on-one meetings with area managers for a description of process-improvement opportunities.
- Present compiled data analyses to executive team. Conduct an executive brainstorming session for potential causal issues and improvement opportunities, conducting data analyses to test developed hypotheses, when appropriate, for statistical significance.
- Create or modify existing strategic plan, as needed.
- Create organizational 30,000-foot-level scorecard/dashboard metric goals that are consistent with the delivery of established satellite-level metric goals.
- Drill down to project opportunities using an enterprise improvement plan (EIP) template (see Figure 12.1), showing 30,000-foot-level metric goal linkages, when appropriate.
- Create business cases for new product/service development opportunities, considering portfolio management, design modularity, reuse of existing designs, axiomatic design, and TRIZ.

The following sections of this chapter and the next four chapters will elaborate on many of the above items. Additional information about the application of statistical, nonstatistical, and Lean tools is described in the P-DMAIC roadmap execution, Appendix, and through information at www.SmarterSolutions.com.

## 8.3   Business Fundamentals and Public Financial Projections

To achieve more customers and cash, we need to provide the best customer value/price on a consistent basis. The three fundamental ingredients to becoming the best customer supplier are people relationships, timely differentiation, and cost control (Moe 2006). Components of people relationships and timely differentiation that need to be managed are:

- People relationships
  - Organization teamwork
  - Customers
  - Suppliers
  - Contractors
  - Channel partners
- Timely differentiation
  - Product (Performance)
  - Quality (Consistency)

- Service(s)
- Marketing
- Total cost of ownership
- Ease of use
• Cost control

Not only should the value chain, its metrics, and policies describe how these issues are addressed, but also the organizational culture needs to embrace the concepts.

Dr. Lloyd S. Nelson stated: "The central problem of management in all its aspects, including planning, procurement, manufacturing, research, sales, personnel, accounting, and law, is to understand better the meaning of variation, and to extract the information contained in variation" (Deming 1986).

In the United States, public companies often provide quarterly financial projections. A stock's price can experience a dramatic positive or negative impact when the reported company's performance is not consistent with its projections.

One given is that it is very unusual that a projection is exactly correct. The question is: how wrong is the projection? In companies, we want to drive the right kind of behavior. Consider the position of a CEO whose company missed previously projected earnings by a large amount. Since a CEO's job could be dependent upon this reporting, do you think that there might be a natural tendency before the earning's announcement to see what could be done to shift money around to make things look better or to skirt the issues with the media?

What is the value of all the expended effort to create financial quarterly projections and then be fearful that they will not be met? Public financial projection statements can lead to short-term thinking and actions that can be very detrimental to the company; i.e., what can be done to meet the short-term numbers? Companies should not provide public financial projection statements. Companies need to focus on what should be done to improve the long-term health of the company, not create and then test the company against short-term public financial projections.

---

Public financial projection statements can lead to short-term thinking and actions that can be very detrimental to the company; i.e., what can be done to meet the short-term numbers? Companies should not provide public financial projection statements.

Short-term financial $Y$s in the equation $Y=f(X)$ should be whatever they are using as sound financial accounting. Long-lasting improvements are made by focusing on what can be done to improve the $X$s that impact the $Y$ financials. Executives need to create a culture that nurtures this measurement and thought process throughout the company.

## 8.4   Do You Have a Strategy?

In the article "Are you sure you have a strategy?" Hambrick and Fredrickson (2001) describe shortcomings with developed frameworks for strategic analysis. They point out that what is missing is guidance for what constitutes a strategy and what should be the outcome. This chapter blends article highlights within E-DMAIC.

"Strategy has become a catchall term used to mean whatever one wants it to mean. Executives now talk about their 'service strategy,' their 'branding strategy,' their 'acquisition strategy,' or whatever kind of strategy that is on their mind at a particular moment. But strategists—whether they are CEOs of established firms, division presidents, or entrepreneurs—must have a strategy, an integrated, overarching concept of how the business will achieve its objectives."

> What is missing is guidance for what constitutes a strategy and what should be the outcome.

Consider these statements of strategy drawn from actual documents and announcements of several companies:

"Our strategy is to be the low-cost provider."
"We're pursuing a global strategy."
"The company's strategy is to integrate a set of regional acquisitions."
"Our strategy is to provide unrivaled customer service."
"Our strategic intent is to always be the first mover."
"Our strategy is to move from defense to industrial applications."

"What do these declarations have in common? Only that none of them is a strategy. They are strategic threads, mere elements of strategy. But they are no more strategies than Dell Computer's strategy can be summed up as selling direct to customers, or than Hannibal's strategy was to use elephants to cross the Alps. And their use reflects an increasingly common syndrome—the catch-all fragmentation of strategy" (Hambrick and Fredrickson 2001). These described strategic elements are not inconsistent with the strategy in Figure 3.4, which a corporation stated on its webpage.

"Executives then communicate these strategic threads to their organizations in the mistaken belief that doing so will help managers make tough choices. But how does knowing that their firm is pursuing an 'acquisition strategy' or a 'first-mover strategy' help the vast majority of managers do their job or set priorities?" (Hambrick and Fredrickson 2001)

Business leaders must have a strategy to meet their objectives. Without a strategy, time and resources can be wasted on piecemeal, disparate activities. Without a strategy, mid-level managers will fill the void with their interpretation of what the business should be doing, typically resulting in a disjointed set of activities.

The define phase of E-DMAIC includes the company's vision, mission, values, and Jim Collins' three circles: What can you be the best in the world? What drives your economic engine? What are you deeply passionate about? (Collins 2001). The organization's value chain along with satellite-level and 30,000-foot-level scorecard/dashboard metrics are created in the measure phase of E-DMAIC.

With IEE, organizations are now in a position to assess the current state of the high-level value-chain metrics to determine the most appropriate goals for an organization. These goals blended with a strategic analysis can then provide inputs to a strategy, which is a centrally integrated, externally oriented concept on what tactics can be created to achieve the desired results.

## 8.5   Enterprise-Process Goal Setting

Vince Lombardi changed the National Football League (NFL) Green Bay Packers, who were perpetually losing at the time, into an NFL dynasty. Coach Lombardi said, "If you are not keeping score, you are just practicing."

Deming (1986) states: "If you have a stable system, then there is no use to specify a goal. You will get whatever the system will deliver. A goal beyond the capability of the system will not be reached.... If you do not have a stable system, then there is again no point in setting a goal. There is no way to know what the system will produce: it has no capability."

Dr. Lloyd S. Nelson (Deming 1986) stated: "If you can improve productivity, or sales, or quality, or anything else, by (e.g.,) five percent next year without a rational plan for improvement, then why were you not doing it last year?"

When organizations establish scorecard goals, much care needs to be exercised. Goals should be SMART. However, these guidelines are often violated. Arbitrary goals set for individuals or organizations can be very counterproductive and costly.

The implication of Deming's statement is that simple goal setting alone will not yield an improved output. For an improved output, organizations need to give due diligence to bettering the process. This volume focuses on the creation of more customers and cash ($MC^2$) not the simple creation of arbitrary goals throughout the organization which can lead to the wrong activities or strategies that often lead to misinterpretation and action-item inconsistencies.

> The implication of Deming's statement is that simple goal setting alone will not yield an improved output. For an improved output, organizations need to give due diligence to bettering the process.

In E-DMAIC, satellite-level and 30,000-foot-level scorecard/ dashboard metrics are examined over time before financial goals are established. The assessment of these noncalendar bounded metrics helps with the creation of SMART goals. This assessment could lead to the following mean monthly satellite-level metric goals:

- Sales growth: 10 percent
- Operating margins: 20 percent
- ROCE (return on capital employed): 20 percent

Other organizational goals that could be tracked at the 30,000-foot-level scorecard/dashboard metric level are the following:

- Environmental: Energy cost reductions of at least 25 percent over three years
- New products: 30 percent of products sold have been available five years or less

Satellite-level enterprise-process goals can be drilled down to 30,000-foot-level goals and then to specific projects that facilitate the process of achieving these goals, which will be described later in this volume.

## 8.6   Strategic Analyses

Strategic thinking is important to the business. A strategic analysis includes (Hambrick and Fredrickson 2001) the following:

- Industrial analysis
- Customer or marketplace trends
- Environmental forecast
- Competitor analysis
- Assessment of internal strengths, weakness, resources

Organizations often build strategies around statements such as develop strategic relationship with industry leaders. How does an organization interpret and measure success against a statement like this? What makes matters worse is that these strategies are then cascaded throughout the whole organization and functional goals are set against them. Could there be different interpretations for these strategies? Of course. What happens when leadership changes? Do the strategies change? I would again say yes, and the change could lead to havoc with a redo of many organizational metrics.

The E-DMAIC system described later overcomes these issues.

## 8.7   Strategy Development

A strategy needs to be dynamic so that it can address timely changes, flexible so that it can address multiple options. It needs to be able to form an effective assessment of current conditions for the creation of a meaningful 2 to 3-year plan. Most strategic plans emphasize only one or two components of what is truly needed.

Figure 8.1 describes a process that organizations can walk through to execute the five critical elements for strategy development (Hambrick and Fredrickson 2001). These five elements, requiring choice, preparation, and investment, also need alignment with the conclusions from a SWOT analysis and developed strategy.

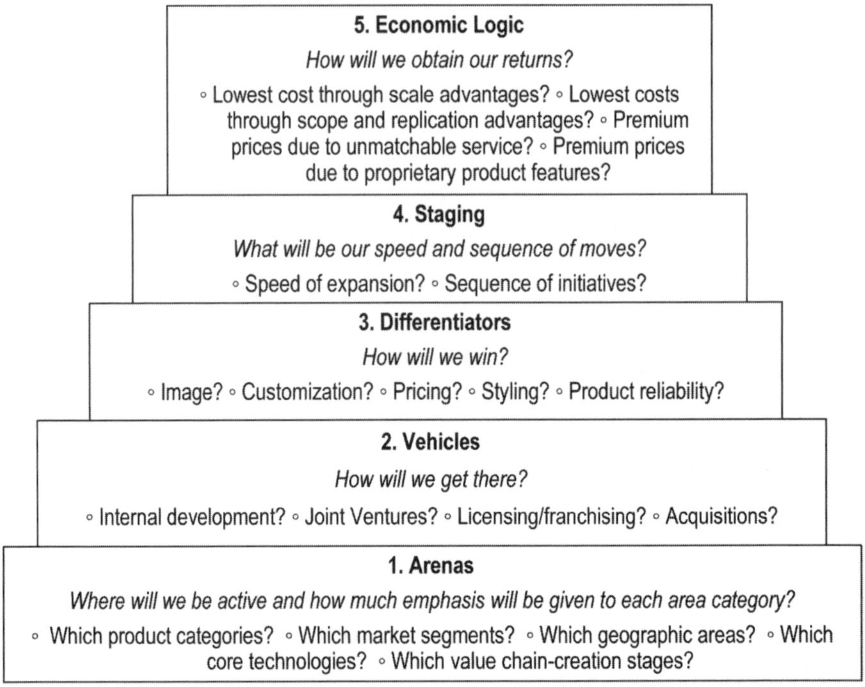

**Figure 8.1:** Five strategic development elements.

Criteria for testing the quality of a strategy (Hambrick and Fredrickson 2001) are the following:

1. **Does your strategy fit with what's going on in the environment?**
   Is there healthy profit potential where you're headed? Does your strategy align with the key success factors of your chosen environment?

2. **Does your strategy exploit your key resources?**
   With your particular mix of resources, does this strategy give you a good head start on competitors? Can you pursue this strategy more economically than your competitors?

3. **Will your envisioned differentiators be sustainable?**
   Will competitors have difficulty matching you? If not, does your strategy explicitly include a ceaseless regimen of innovation and opportunity creation?

4. **Are the elements of your strategy internally consistent?**
   Have you made choices of areas, vehicles, differentiators, staging, and economic logic? Do they all fit and mutually reinforce each other?

5. **Do you have enough resources to pursue this strategy?**
   Do you have the money, managerial time and talent, and other capabilities to do all you envision? Are you sure that you're not spreading your resources too thin, only to be left with a collection of feeble positions?
6. **Can your strategy be implemented?**
   Will your key constituencies allow you to pursue this strategy? Can your organization make it through the transition? Are you and your management team able and willing to lead the required changes?

Creating a vision begins with an understanding of the current situation. An organization needs to understand the hundreds of controllable and uncontrollable forces that pull them in multiple directions so that they can make appropriate adjustments. Organization's success depends upon how well they accomplish these. Some basic *today* and *in the future* strategic planning questions are (Hamel and Prahalad 1994):

- Describe customers that you serve? (today and the future)
- What channels are used to reach your customers? (today and the future)
- Describe your competitors? (today and the future)
- Describe your competitive advantage basis? (today and the future)
- Describe the source for your margins? (today and the future)
- What are your unique skills or capabilities? (today and the future)

# 8.8   Hoshin Kanri Tools: Environmental Scan Checking Market Conditions

The previous section provided self assessment for building a strategy. This section provides six hoshin kanri midterm-strategic-planning tools, which can be used to check market conditions (Jackson 2006). This analysis can provide insight to markets and competitive resources, which should then be fed into an Enterprise improvement plan (EIP) creation (see Section 12.3).

These tools are:

- The *Porter matrix* is a tool for displaying your company's position relative to competitors. In this matrix, the left-axis measures market segment degree from narrow at the matrix bottom to broad at the matrix top. The horizontal axis measures product differentiation from low on the left to high on the right. Each company position in this matrix is displayed as a circle with the company name inside the circle. Example: A company's Porter matrix highlighted new competition and competitive forces that needed to be addressed.

- The *product/market matrix* provides insight to relative product or product group market-segmentation valuation. In the matrix, your major products are listed down the left-hand side and your major customers across the top. At each matrix row-to-column intersection classify the value of the product to the customer as either high (H), medium (M), or low (L). Example: A company's product/market matrix suggested a mass customization strategy, where the combination of design modularity and flexibility could lead to the offering of a wide variety of products at relative low cost.

- The *market/technology matrix* can identify market breakthrough opportunities in current markets or technology and management methodologies. In this matrix, your existing market, related market, and new market are listed down the left-hand side. In the top matrix row, columns have the title hard and soft technologies with a pre-title of existing, related, or new. At each matrix row-to-column intersection, a product(s) or technique description(s) is listed. Example: A company's market/technology matrix highlighted an opportunity to expand from its existing product market to a related market. In addition, this matrix highlighted an opportunity to enhance the current management system process through E-DMAIC.

- The *value stream profit and loss statement* provides insight to a product or product family's raw profitability. In this value stream accounting, differences between direct and indirect labor are ignored. In addition, there is no differentiation between administrative and shop floor waste. Section 9.6 provides more information on Lean accounting. Example: A company's value stream profit and loss statement analysis indicated that a five percent reduction of both materials and conversion costs was achievable over the next three years, which would result in an average return on sales of about 9%.

- The *value stream map* provides current state understanding (see Section 11.19). This mapping technique could be used to map the entire product lifecycle. This map could incorporate flow of information and material through marketing, engineering, and supply chain. Example: A company's value stream maps of their order entry process, engineering process, and manufacturing supply chain identified problems that could be resolved through projects.

- The *president's diagnosis* highlights progress that is being made in developing internal capabilities to become an IEE system. Similar to the Shingo Prize or Baldrige Award, diagnosis begins with a judgment criteria set. A radar chart (see Glossary) can be used to compare your company to major competitors in several areas on a scale of one to five. Comparison areas to address are: business operating system; finance and accounting system; human resource system; supply chain system; information system; quality system; sales and marketing system; engineering system; manufacturing operations system; maintenance system; materials and logistics system. Example: A company's president's diagnosis indicated that competitors have superior sales and marketing strengths. Process improvement focus was planned for this area.

Creating a journal of events is one way to keep abreast of changes and the dynamics in the targeted industry and market. Emphasis should be given to business areas or issues identified using the above six tools. The journal should capture your observations, thoughts, and feelings about the country and global future.

Basic rules for creating a journal are:

- Select the best time and place.
- Select tools that encourage reflection and creative thinking; e.g., computer, notebook, colored pencils, scissors/tape for attaching articles into journal.
- Determine research data source; e.g., leading industry publications to read.
- Create consistency; e.g., conduct research the same time every day where there is a weekly number of entries goal.
- Execute informally and reflectively; e.g., neatness of journal entries should not impact the process.
- Establish creativity; e.g., describe alternative viewpoints by asking "what if?"
- Discuss your perspectives; e.g., create an observation list to share with your team.

## 8.9   Exercises

1. Use the Internet to determine strategies for a company, government office, or social organization. Using the points described in this chapter, comment on these strategies.
2. Create the five strategic development elements for an organization.

# 9

# E-DMAIC—Analyze Phase: Financial and Data Analyses

## 9.1    E-DMAIC Roadmap Component

In the enterprise analyze phase, we want to assess the overall system to determine what we should do to improve. The previous chapter described a strategic planning system as part of the enterprise analyze phase. This chapter focuses on financial and data analysis.

In Section 8.2, the analyze phase E-DMAIC checklist included financial and data analyses. This chapter provides a high-level description of financial analysis and reporting, along with data analyses. An appreciation and understanding of these basic techniques can improve the communications between managers, practitioners, and accounting; e.g., project determination and valuation.

This understanding helps move an organization toward improved goal-setting and process improvement activities, which have direct alignment to true long-lasting financial business objectives. Project benefits need to be felt by the entire company, not just sound good at a sub-process level.

This volume provides only a high-level financial analysis discussion. Finance books need to be referenced for more detailed information.

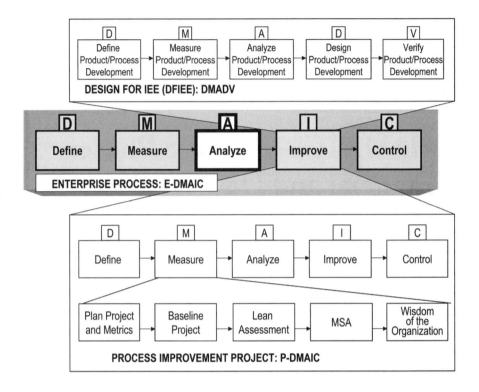

## 9.2    Current Accounting and Finance Systems

Organizations are to follow generally accepted accounting principles (GAAP) in their tax and shareholder financial accounting, including the following four basic tenets of reporting (Cunningham and Fiume 2003):

- Materiality: A matter is considered material if there is a substantial likelihood that a reasonable person would consider it important.
- Conservatism: Good news should not be over emphasized, and bad news should not be under emphasized.
- Consistency: Facts are to be presented consistently over time so that trends will have meaning.
- Matching: Any significant cost must be included as an expense as soon as the cost is realized.

Organizations must fulfill GAAP requirements; however, managing the business with a primary focus on these reported financials can lead to the wrong behavior. For example, throughout this volume inventory is described as being a very undesirable waste source that should be minimized; however, in financial accounting, inventory is considered an asset. Because of this financial accounting procedure, an organization might choose to manufacture product that was not needed so that they could make their financial statements look better. The Lean accounting system described in Section 9.6 provides an alternative system.

Cunningham and Fiume (2003) state: "In too many organizations, accounting teeters on the brink of irrelevancy. Accounting departments produce information that arrives late and is often misleading. Few managers fully understand the columns of numbers and variances presented in these reports. Instead, they have learned to accept that most accounting is impenetrable. Lack of clarity, however, creates an atmosphere of distrust. That same distrust further isolates the accountant, who has become marginalized, operating behind a veil of mystery.

> In too many organizations, accounting teeters on the brink of irrelevancy. Accounting departments produce information that arrives late and is often misleading.

Improvement programs have offered businesses new paths.... Accounting, however, has largely been left in the cold.... we believe that accountants must become a fundamental part of the team-based improvement efforts.... When accountants are excluded from team-based improvements, they become barriers to change because they cannot approve what they do not understand. If accountants are not involved in change, they remain mired in the old culture, along with batch processing and standard cost accounting. Once involved, however, they use their skills to help accelerate change throughout the organization.

Accounts must change focus from Cost Accounting to Cost Management. We must abandon our obsession with developing a unit cost for each of our products, and lose the associated horrors created by standard cost accounting and its related concepts of absorption and variance analysis. Unit costs are truly only an estimate, given the number of subjective allocations that go into the sum, and often lead to poor decisions. Understanding costs at a higher level and providing tools to manage them better should be our real goal."

The triangle in Figure 9.1 is a simple way to describe the work content in an accounting team. In the largest part of the first triangle are the ubiquitous transactions. Probably two-thirds of the people in most accounting departments are working on transactions: paying bills, collecting money, filing taxes, and paying people. Then there are a few cost accountants, fixed-asset accountants, and someone responsible for creating the financial statements. There might be a couple of financial analysts checking to see how much is being spent and evaluating capital investments. Finally there is probably a controller or CFO who goes to the business planning meetings and works on the budget and planning. We'll refer to that last category as consultants or business partners. If the area in the triangle represents time spent, the base of the first triangle shows that the largest amount of total time is spent in transactions.

Then we need to ask: "What does the business need from us (accounting and finance)? What does the CEO value enough to pay our salaries? Unfortunately, those CEOs probably want help understanding the numbers. But, they also need our help growing the business profitably.... On the other hand, what are most businesses paying for now? Sure the bills need to be dealt with, money collected and people paid. Taxes must be paid to keep us all out of jail. But the first triangle must be turned upside down without necessarily adding new staff."

I agree with Cunningham and Fiume that accounting and finance need to be an integral part of the business decision-making process. However, it is not only a matter of accounting/finance

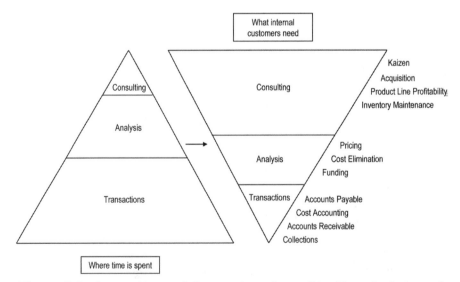

**Figure 9.1:** Accounting and finance transformation (Cunningham and Fiume 2003, with modification).

involvement but also the question of how the team can most effectively measure and improve the business. The E-DMAIC system offers a unified system to accomplish these objectives.

## 9.3 Financial Analyses

Earlier I quoted Keith Moe: "Everything good and bad in business starts with people. Everything good and bad in business ends up in the financials" (Moe 2006). In this earlier section, I elaborated on the people reference in this quote. In this chapter, I will focus on the financial portion and the creation of a system for the development of "good" business results.

An IEE system addresses both of Keith's points. Organizations who utilize IEE evaluate data wisely so that they improve their decision-making process. IEE organizations create and evaluate metrics so that organizations ask the right questions of their associates. Asking the right questions can result in a more orchestrated fire prevention culture.

With a good data assessment system, organizations gain more insight as to what direction targeted improvement activities would be most beneficial. Determining and assessing the cost of doing nothing differently (CODND), implications from the current 30,000-foot-level scorecard/dashboard metrics, can show where improvement efforts should focus and what goals are reasonable for these efforts.

Focus needs to be given to value-chain activities and metrics, while avoiding process sub-optimizations. Within this phase, tools such as time value diagramming and value stream mapping can help identify process constraints and improvement opportunities for day-to-day operations and product, process, and IT project execution.

> Focus needs to be given to value-chain activities and metrics, while avoiding process sub-optimizations.

Within this phase, strategic analyses can address industry, competitor analysis, customer/marketplace trends, environmental forecast, and internal strength/weakness/resources issues. A system for structured executive brainstorming sessions helps identify improvement opportunities. This work could then lead to setting organizational goals and/or determining what should be done differently to achieve them. When determining this goal, the organization needs to focus on creating an expected rate of return; e.g., 12%. If this is not done, ROI and rate of return become just numbers with no reference.

As needed, we must then assess and revisit any existing Strategic Plan relative to areas in which there will be activity, vehicles on how to get there, differentiators on how to win in the marketplace, staging relative to speed/sequence of actions, and economic logic to address ROI (see Section 9.8).

An alignment assessment relative to the organization's vision, mission, and value proposition can lead to the highlighting of disconnects that should be addressed. Another assessment that can prove enlightening is re-assessment of the organization's alignment against Jim Collins' three circles, which were previously created. An FMEA provides a structure means to reveal overall business risks; e.g., our sole supplier is in an area that is susceptible to hurricanes.

This phase assesses the timeliness and quality of product, process, and IT projects. Perhaps our design process needs to utilize DOE or Design for $X$ (see Glossary) tools more effectively to improve meeting desired objectives. In addition, the analyze phase addresses the effectiveness of processes that include business cases for new product/process development opportunities considering portfolio management, design modularity, reuse of existing designs, axiomatic design, and TRIZ.

Finally, we need to assess generic improvement ideas that originated within the organization to determine which of these ideas should be addressed as just-do-it projects or other more involved detailed project activity.

## 9.4 Financial Metrics

Two types of costs are fixed and variable costs. Fixed costs are constant costs regardless of the product volume. When volume increases, the per-unit fixed-cost declines. Salaries, rent, and equipment depreciation are fixed-cost expenses. Variable costs change as a function of sales. When more items are sold, variable costs rise proportionally. Raw material, commissions, and shipping are variable cost expenses. Total costs are a combination of variable and fixed costs.

The number of units ($N$) required to achieve a profit of $P$ is

$$N = \frac{F + P}{U - V}$$

where $F$ is the total fixed costs, $U$ is the unit price, and $V$ is the variable cost per unit.

For example, if a company wants to make $400,000 profit selling a product that has fixed costs of $100,000, a unit price of $500 and a variable cost of $300, it would need to sell 2500 units. That is,

$$N = \frac{F + P}{U - V} = \frac{100,000 + 400,000}{500 - 300} = 2500$$

The number to sell for breakeven would be 500. That is,

$$N = \frac{F + P}{U - V} = \frac{100,000 + 0}{500 - 300} = 500$$

If you deposit $1000 into a money market account, you would expect your deposit to grow as a function of time. Because of this, we say that money has time value. *Present value* and *future value* describe the time value of money and have the relationship

$$FV = PV(1 + i)$$

where PV is the present value of money, FV is the future value of money, and $i$ is the interest rate expressed as a proportion.

If interest were to be credited monthly to an account that had a deposit of $1000, the monetary value of the account would be compounding during each monthly compounding period. For $N$ accounting periods, future value could now be expressed as

$$FV = PV(1 + i)^N$$

Repeat purchases by a loyal customer can be very large over the years. For example, a frequent flyer of an airline might spend $100,000 in three years. The economic worth of this customer can be determined by combining revenue projections with expenses over some period of time. The net present value (NPV) of the net cash flow, that is profits, describes this economic worth. NPV describes the value of the profits over time in terms of today's dollars. The knowledge of NPV can lead to the evaluation of alternative marketing and of other strategies to attract and retain customers.

NPV calculations can also be used within the selection process of IEE projects and the determination of the value for these projects. However, both costs and benefits often have a cash flow stream, rather than lump sums. In addition, these cash flow streams can be uneven. These added complexities make the calculation for NPV tedious. However, most spreadsheets have a function to address these calculations. For example, someone could enter a desired rate of return along with the net revenue (e.g., yearly benefits less costs) for several years. He could then execute a function that calculates the NPV for these inputs.

Interest rate paid on a loan and rate of return (ROI) are both computations from the annual cost of money expressed in percentage units. However, they differ in that one is the investor, and the other is the borrower. For an investment period of one year, the computation is simply

$$ROI = \frac{S - P}{P}$$

where $S$ is the amount collected or paid back and $P$ is the amount borrowed or invested. Computations for ROI increase when other factors are considered, such as increase in the number of interest periods, compounding of interest, and taxes. Companies can use complex models to make this calculation.

For example, if a company invests \$200,000 in a new machine and its increase in sales that year is \$100,000, the ROI would be –50%.

$$ROI = \frac{100,000 - 200,000}{200,000} = -50\%$$

And if after two years the total increase in sales was \$250,000, the ROI for the piece of equipment would be 25%.

$$ROI = \frac{250,000 - 200,000}{200,000} = 25\%$$

Internal rate of return (IRR) is the rate of return that equates the present value of future cash flows with investment costs. IRR could be determined using an IRR function within many spreadsheets. For example, annual price and cash flows for a project could be entered into a spreadsheet, where expenditures are minus and receipts are positive. The IRR function would then make iterative calculations to determine the project IRR. Another application of IRR is within the project selection process, where projects are prioritized according to their expected IRR.

Payback period is the time necessary for net financial benefits (inflows) to equate to the net costs (outflows). The equations are simplistic, where typically the time value of money is ignored. Projects can be compared using this approach; however, financial benefits beyond the payback period are not addressed. When there is an initial investment and an inflow of cash that is fixed, the payback period can be calculated from (Johnson and Melicher 1982)

$$\text{Payback Period} = \frac{\text{Initial}\,(\&\,\text{Incremental})\,\text{Investment}}{\text{Annual}\,(\text{or Monthly})\,\text{Cash Flow}}$$

The overall financial attractiveness of a project depends on future cash flows generated and opportunity costs. Sunk costs are irrelevant. To illustrate this, consider a company which spent $400,000 on research for product A and $100,000 on product B. In deciding between producing A or B, sunk costs should not be included at all; i.e., this money has already been spent. Only the future cash flows generated by the projects should be considered.

Incremental Cash Flows attributable to a project are caused by resulting changes in revenue, expenses, taxes, and depreciation. Generally, a project has three types of cash flows:

- Initial: expenditures to acquire property, plant or equipment
- Operating: net benefits or expenses over the life of the project
- Terminal: recovery of salvage value of assets and net working capital

The net benefits over the life of the project are expressed as the change in cash flow after taxes:

$$\Delta CFAT = (\Delta S - \Delta C - \Delta D)(1 - T) + \Delta D - \Delta B$$

where

- $\Delta CFAT$ is incremental cash flow after taxes
- $\Delta S$ is incremental sales
- $\Delta C$ is incremental costs

- $\Delta D$ is incremental depreciation, where depreciation is defined as [(purchase price − salvage value)/useful life]
- $\Delta B$ is incremental cost of principle on financed loan (interest included in $\Delta C$)
- $T$ is tax rate

For example, if a company has $100,000 in sales, $30,000 cost, $30,000 depreciation, principle payments totaling $40,000, and is taxed at 25%, they would then have cash flow of $20,000.

$\Delta$CFAT = (100,000 − 30,000 − 30,000)(1 − 0.25) + 30,000 − 40,000 = $20,000

Operating Cash Flows often occur as annuity streams; i.e., same dollar payback over a period of months. If this is not the case, the $\Delta$CFAT for each month must be considered separately. The periodic $\Delta$CFAT is discounted to present value using the appropriate discount rate, $i$, and time period, $n$.

$$PV = \frac{FV}{(1+i)^n}$$

The following project evaluation methods are used for calculating hard financial savings. Black belts and master black belts need to work with Finance to determine the appropriate methods that are used in the company.

Historical methods are payback period and accounting rate of return. Financial methods are net present value (NPV), internal rate of return (IRR), and profitability index (PI).

Payback period is determined from the equation:

$$\text{Payback Period} = \frac{\text{Initial Investment}}{\text{Annual Cash Flows}}$$

This relationship is popular in many companies due to its simplicity. Lower numbers are better since there is a faster investment payback, where companies usually set a minimum required payback period of investment. Problems with this method are that cash flows beyond the payback period are not considered, opportunity costs and risks are ignored, and pattern of cash flows is irrelevant.

Accounting rate of return is determined from the equation:

$$\text{Accounting Rate of Return (AROR)} = \frac{\text{Annual Profit}}{\text{Average Investment}}$$

In this relationship, the average investment is the beginning value plus the end value divided by two, where larger numbers are better. Problems with this method are that it uses profits rather than cash flow, ignores time value of money, and has no relationship to market-determined returns. As well, choosing a project with the highest AROR does not mean that it has the highest market value.

Net present value is determined from the equation:

$$NPV = PV_{\text{inflows}} - PV_{\text{outflows}}$$

This relationship focuses on the cash flows generated by a project. It capitalizes cash flows at a required rate of return, RRR. The RRR is the minimum expected rate of return which a project must earn to justify acceptance. If the NPV is positive, it earns more than the RRR and produces economic profit; hence, the project would be accepted. If the NPV is negative, the project earns less than the RRR and produces economic losses; hence, the project would not be accepted. NPV is the financially sound method for ranking and approving projects.

Internal rate of return (IRR) calculations consider the time value of money and are based on profits. The IRR is the discount rate that makes the NPV = $0. A project is accepted or rejected by comparing IRR to RRR. A project is accepted if IRR is greater than RRR. A project is rejected if IRR is less than RRR. One problem with this method is that it assumes that all intermediate cash flows are reinvested at the IRR, rather than at the opportunity cost of capital. Another problem is that this method is an iterative process and requires a financial calculator or spreadsheet.

Profitability Index is determined from the equation:

$$PI = \frac{PV_{\text{inflows}}}{PV_{\text{outflows}}}$$

This methodology is also called the benefit-to-cost ratio. It is a different way to present the same information as the NPV provides. If PI is greater than one, the project would be accepted. If PI is less then one, the project would be rejected. The problem with this relationship is that, since PI is a ratio, it is a relative measure, giving benefits per dollar of investment, adjusted for time value (NPV is an absolute measure), and this relation can lead to conflicting results when ranking projects.

A survey of 100 companies in the Fortune 500 (Bierman 1993) found:

- 99% used NPV or IRR either as their primary or secondary evaluative method.
- 84% used some form of payback method, but none used it as the primary evaluative method.
- About 50% used some form of Accounting Rate of Return.
- 87% of the firms surveyed used at least three different methods.
- In 1955, only 4% of managers used some form of NPV analysis, compared with 85% in 1992.

Only hard benefits appear on the financial statements. Hard benefits are quantifiable and permanently change the cost or income structure, which would directly impact operating profit or cash flow positively if all else were to be held equal. Hard benefits can be supported by rigorous calculations based on the defect reduction, units, unit costs/profit margins, and other economic factors that result in tangible dollars. Projects must be supported by a control plan to sustain the benefit year after year.

Soft benefits indirectly impact business results. Soft benefits are quantifiable through inferred calculation and may not be directly measurable as the change in one or more expense categories or revenue lines. Soft benefits may be more important in the long-term for the survival of the business.

Once project benefits are calculated, it is important to determine where they will appear on the company's financial statements. Basic financial statements are balance sheet and income statement plus statement of retained earnings. Derivative financial statements are the cash flow and common size statement.

The balance sheet (see Table 9.1) provides a statement of the firm's assets and the claims against those assets at a particular time, typically the end of the year. Names of the assets are listed in descending order of liquidity, usually divided into current and long-term assets.

- Current assets: those that could be converted to cash within one year.
- Long-term assets: usually fixed assets.
- Shareholders' equity (net worth) is the residual difference between assets and liabilities.

Assets must equal liabilities plus shareholders' equity.

The income statement (see Table 9.2) summarizes the performance (profitability) of the firm over a certain period of time (quarterly or annually), where income equals revenue minus expenses. Statement of retained earnings shows the addition to the book value of the shareholder's equity. Retained earnings in this statement, for example, could be tracked monthly year after year as a satellite-level metric. The assessment and management of this metric could lead to significant improvement projects, especially for start-ups and small businesses. This metric could be a primary running scorecard for the company.

The cash flow statement (see Table 9.3) addresses the total dollar amount of funds available to the firm to put to productive uses. The cash flow statement determines the firm's cash inflows and outflows based on operational, financial, and investment decisions, thus allowing analysis of how management's decisions have affected the firm's net cash flows. Firms that appear very profitable "on paper" can suffer if they ignore cash flow metrics.

**Table 9.1** Example Balance Sheet

| Balance Sheet - XYZ Corporation | | |
|---|---|---|
| (millions of dollars) | 12/31/2001 | 12/31/2000 |
| **ASSETS** | | |
| **Current Assets** | | |
| Cash | 40 | 37 |
| Marketable securities | 3 | 3 |
| Accounts receivable, net | 96 | 89 |
| Inventory | 111 | 92 |
| Prepaid expenses | 7 | 9 |
| **Total Current Assets** | **257** | **230** |
| **Long-Term Assets** | | |
| Property, plant, and equipment | 85 | 63 |
| Less accumulated depreciation | (26) | (22) |
| Net property, plant, and equipment | 59 | 41 |
| Other long-term assets | | |
| **Total Long-Term Assets** | **59** | **41** |
| **Total Assets** | **316** | **271** |
| **LIABILITIES AND SHAREHOLDERS' EQUITY** | | |
| **Current Liabilities** | | |
| Accounts payable | 77 | 63 |
| Notes payable:bank | 31 | 46 |
| Income taxes payable | 3 | 3 |
| Accrued liabilities | 24 | 21 |
| **Total Current Liabilities** | **135** | **133** |
| **Long-Term Liabilities** | | |
| Bonds outstanding | 49 | 33 |
| Deferred income taxes | 12 | 10 |
| **Total Long-Term Liabilities** | **61** | **43** |
| **Owners' Equity** | | |
| Common stock | 25 | 25 |
| Additional paid-in capital | 22 | 22 |
| Retained earnings | 73 | 48 |
| **Total Owners' Equity** | **120** | **95** |
| **Total Liabilities and Owners' Equity** | **316** | **271** |

Assets tell us what the firm owns

Liabilities and Owners' Equity tell us how it was financed

$$A = L + OE$$

**Table 9.2** Example Income Statement

| Income Statement - XYZ Corporation | | |
|---|---|---|
| | **12/31/2001** | **12/31/2000** |
| **Sales** | | |
| Net Sales | 801 | 720 |
| **Total Sales** | **801** | **720** |
| Less **Cost of Goods Sold** | 492 | 468 |
| **Gross Profit** | **309** | **252** |
| **Operating Expenses** | | |
| Salaries and wages | 87 | 63 |
| General and Administrative | 126 | 115 |
| Rent | 40 | 30 |
| Depreciation | 4 | 3 |
| **Total Operating Expenses** | **257** | **211** |
| **Net Operating Income (NOI)** | **52** | **41** |
| Interest income (expense) | 18 | 21 |
| Other income (expense) | 4 | 5 |
| **Net Profit (Loss) Before Taxes (NPBT)** | **38** | **25** |
| **Income Taxes** | 6 | 4 |
| **Net Income (Loss) (NI)** | **32** | **21** |
| **Cumulative Net Income (Loss)** | **32** | **53** |
| | | |
| **Statement of Retained Earnings** | | |
| Beginning balance | 48 | 32 |
| Add: Net Income | 32 | 21 |
| Less Dividends | 7 | 5 |
| **Ending Balance** | **73** | **48** |

Gross Profit is Revenue minus Expenses from production activities

Salaries and wages, Employee benefits, Payroll taxes, Rent, Utilities, Repairs and maintenance, Insurance, Travel, Telephone, Postage, Office supplies, Advertising, Marketing/promotion, Professional fees, Training and development, Bank charges, Depreciation, Miscellaneous

Financial Expenses

Based on current tax laws

Retained Earnings are Net Income minus dividends to stockholders

**Table 9.3** Example Cash Flow Statement

| Net Cash Flow Statement | Dec, 2001 |
|---|---|
| **Operating Cash Flows** | |
| Net Sales | 801 |
| Less: Increase in Receivables | 7 |
| **Cash from Sales** | **794** |
| Cost of Goods Sold | 492 |
| Plus: Increase in Inventories | 19 |
| Less: Increase in Payables | 14 |
| **Cash Production Costs** | **497** |
| **Gross Cash Margin** | **297** |
| Operating Expenses (ex. Depreciation) | 253 |
| Less: Decrease in Prepaid expenses | 2 |
| Less: Increase in Accruals | 3 |
| Plus: Increase in Other Current Assets | 0 |
| **Cash Operating Expenses** | **248** |
| Cash from Operations | 49 |
| Less: Income Taxes Paid | 4 |
| **Net Cash Flow from Operations** | **45** |
| | |
| **Financial Cash Flows** | |
| Financial outflows | |
| Interest Expense | 18 |
| Cash Dividends Paid | 7 |
| Decrease in Notes Payable | 15 |
| **Total Financial Outflows (neg.)** | **(40)** |
| Financial outflows | |
| Nonoperating Income | 4 |
| Increase in long-term debt | 16 |
| Increase in new equity | 0 |
| **Total Financial Inflows (pos.)** | **20** |
| **Net Financial Cash Flows** | **(20)** |
| | |
| **Investment Cash Flows** | |
| Investment Outflows | |
| Less: Increase in marketable securities | 0 |
| Less: Increase in gross Plant and Eqpt. | 22 |
| **Net Investment Cash Flows** | **(22)** |
| | |
| Change in Cash Position | 3 |
| Plus: Beginning Cash Balance | 37 |
| **Ending Cash Balance** | **40** |

Gross cash margin (GCM) = cash from sales – less cash production costs

Cash from Ops= GCM- cash operating expenses

The ending cash balance will match the figure in the Balance Sheet

Common Size Statements allow for the comparison of the firm with other firms or with an industry average, by converting all the statement amounts into percentages of a base number. For the Balance Sheet, all items are shown as a percentage of total assets. For the Income Statement, each item is shown as a percentage of sales.

## 9.5 Cost Management Versus Cost Accounting and Activity-Based Costing (ABC)

The success of cost management in a company depends upon how well everyone contributes. Operations cost minimization involves producing to customer demand. Maximization efforts for equipment utilization can lead to over production and increased storage/inventory costs.

When analyzing the cost management system for improvement opportunities, both operations and design processes should be considered. Organizations should consider annual versus life-of-product costing so that they avoid knee jerk reactions to common-cause variability from their system.

Conventional costing or mass costing systems have had problems in recent manufacturing since overhead costs are sometimes inappropriately allocated, which leads to misleading product costs. Conventional cost accounting has a two-stage allocation process for overhead costs. The first stage is an allocation to costs centers or departments followed by a second stage reallocation to products, typically based on labor or machine hours of product consumption. With this approach, there is typically a uniform cost center distribution rate.

Unlike the past, overhead now contributes the major cost proportions, while direct labor and machine hours have little contribution. Because of this, major distortions can easily occur, especially when there is a large product complexity mix from a process.

An alternative to conventional costing is activity-based costing (ABC). ABC allocates cost elements to activities that in turn make an allocation to products through cost drivers, where this allocation is based upon consumption quantity; e.g., inspection activity. Raw material, direct labor, and other similar costs would have direct product allocation.

In ABC, salaries, machines, power, and rent are examples of activity-traceable cost elements. A repetitive operation such as inspecting, receiving, shipping, storage, accounting, and materials handling, which has direct value stream linkage, is consider a primary activity. Secondary activities such as personnel or training should be recovered by the primary served activities. Floor space and activities that support production are cost drivers which have allocation according to the volume of the activity. Categories such as postage that is difficult to have particular activity trace can be allocated using a conventional rule such as direct machine hours.

Dividing the total activity cost by activity volume yields the unit cost per activity. Products consume these cost drivers unlike conventional costing systems which do not cost activities. ABC can provide underlying business cost structure before calculation of product costs.

Because of traceability, more accurate costs can be achieved with ABC; however, ABC is a fairly complex system that still involves judgment. Both ABC and conventional costing make assumptions about the future, which are not likely to be exact and may not be worth tracking. Accuracy versus system complexity needs to be considered, since scores of drivers for a complex system may have little value when considering speed and expense impact. When improperly used, ABC can be very wasteful; hence, an organization might choose to use it periodically instead of continually. A benefit assessment might lead to the conclusion that little is gained from continuously running an ABC system. Cunningham and Fiume (2003) state, "The problem with ideas like ABC is one of narrow vision: they are based on old accounting concepts and a greater sense of the limits of accounting than real creative thought. We believe that the natural evolution of the Lean movement is toward streamlining and simplicity, and that accounting systems can and should become simple and even elegant."

Cunningham and Fiume (2003) state, "Instead of cost accounting, the Lean accountant's focus should be on cost management, which includes a different kind of cost accounting. We have learned that it is far less important to know the cost of making an individual product than it is to manage the costs of the business as a whole. In short, traditional cost accounting is narrow-minded. Managers and accountants accustomed to the old system may balk at this, but ask why they need to know the cost of making an individual product or service and you will most likely get some combination of three answers: to determine the selling price, to reduce costs, and to value inventory. The fact is however, that except for government cost-plus contracts or where a monopoly exists, the market determines the selling price—not the accountant. Regarding cost reduction, any business should be concentrating on reducing costs for the entire enterprise, not for individual products. And there are alternative methods for inventory valuation in a Lean environment."

> We have learned that it is far less important to know the cost of making an individual product than it is to manage the costs of the business as a whole.

With a shift from cost accounting to cost management, there often is focus redirection to product design. Costs allocation during the product design process involves target pricing, target costing, and value engineering. For a new service/product, target pricing addresses an organization's costs, customers, and competition. Pricing can impact sales volumes, which will impact production volumes. Rising and falling production volume has an impact on both variable and fixed costs, which affects the bottom line. Target costing addresses the future service/product costs for desirable profit generation. Value engineering addresses cost factors that consider target quality and reliability along with price relative to customer wants and needs.

# 9.6   Lean Accounting and IEE Accounting

Management accounting, as opposed to financial accounting, should be used for decision making. Lean Accounting is a management accounting category that gives focus to operational value streams and their metrics. This form of accounting focuses on the elimination of accounting and control transactions such as labor tracking and shop floor control that drive the wrong activity.

Cunningham and Fiume (2003) state, "In a traditional manufacturing environment, an attempt is made at cost control using standard cost and variance analysis.... The problem is that, except for those companies that exercise lot identification—as in the pharmaceutical industry—it is virtually impossible to trace an unfavorable variance to its root cause.... The role of cost control in a Lean environment is to reduce cost by eliminating waste…. Therefore, it is important to think in terms of presenting information that minimizes and segregates allocated costs…. One effective way of doing this is to move away from looking at profitability by individual product. Instead, look at profitability in groups or families of products." The IEE measurement and improvement system can yield a better cost control system than a variance analysis.

Aspects of Lean Accounting include (Bicheno 2004):

- Working toward direct costs. Rather than trying to solve the overhead allocation problem by some elegant procedures such as ABC, decentralize overhead functions to be directly associated with cells or products.
- Eliminate variance reporting.
- Eliminate detailed product cost reporting.
- Transform accountant thinking to variation of costs rather than cost variances.
- Transform accountant thinking to common-cause and special-cause variation.
- Clarify the presentation of accounts so that all can read them. The word variance should not appear on a Profit and Loss statement.
- Record only raw material value in inventory valuations. Do not accrue value. Do not show deferred labor and overhead as costs, which were accrued into inventory.
- Concentrate on cash flows.
- Focus costs around the company's constraint resources. Determine the opportunity cost per unit of time at the constraint so that accountants can cost it.
- Involve accountants in the creation of current and future state maps.

Cunningham and Fiume (2003) provide the following comments relative to a Lean transformation: "Make no mistake: there will be barriers. Once a company dramatically lowers inventory, the financial statements will get confusing, especially if standard cost and variance-style income statements are still used. The cost from the old inventory must be included in the expense column. The result will be opposite of what most organizations would expect. For a time, profits will look lower and the results will look worse from doing the right thing. Just remember the real expense of carrying inventory was hidden under the old system. That's one more barrier to advancing toward Lean management accounting.

The pressure to make the month is another barrier. For public companies, there is terrific pressure to meet the projected numbers every quarter. Even the smallest reduction in your earnings, compared to projections or prior quarter results, can mean a death toll for the stock price. Sometime, it means the job of the CFO. And this is not just a problem for public companies. Often there are bonus programs tied to profits or sales, or bank loans tied to results or inventory balances. These are real issues and must be considered, not as a road block but as a factor to include as you make necessary improvements.

> The pressure to make the month is another barrier. For public companies, there is terrific pressure to meet the projected numbers every quarter. Even the smallest reduction in your earnings, compared to projections or prior quarter results, can mean a death toll for the stock price.

As you work through the barriers, take courage from knowing that many obstructions are of our own making. Over time, you have become locked into certain measures and those same measures have very likely become improvement barriers for other departments. Consider accounting's complicated ways of figuring the worth of a machine, for instance. Our measures—our rows of logical numbers—keep a piece of equipment constantly utilized. Accounting said this machine must be run constantly to make it profitable, keep unit cost low, and keep from having unfavorable variances. Therefore, the company buys materials it doesn't need, pays an operator to run parts that are not needed and puts unnecessary wear and tear on the machine. This is all done because accounting blessed the machine's purchase base on specific parameters, which included sales projections that were too optimistic. Now we say, if you don't need the parts, don't run the machine. We need a new mindset regarding idle time."

IEE accounting embraces the Lean accounting concepts described in this chapter. The difference is that, in IEE, performance measurements and improvement strategy follow the E-DMAIC and P-DMAIC roadmaps.

## 9.7 Project Benefits

This section describes some enterprise process financial considerations in the E-DMAIC system, while Volume III elaborates more on the financial benefits for specific projects. Section 12.10 shows the linkage of these financial considerations to effective project selection through an Enterprise Improvement Plan (EIP).

One way in which Six Sigma differs from many prior business improvement efforts is its focus on rigorous calculation and tracking of financial benefits delivered by projects. To measure consistently the benefits of IEE projects, a uniform set of guidelines must be developed by each business, in alignment with internal finance policies.

Project benefits are usually classified as hard or soft savings. Hard savings are either above or below the operating profit line. Above the operating profit line examples are cost reduction and revenue enhancement. Below the operating profit line examples are working capital reductions and cost avoidance. The quantification of these benefits is typically expressed as cost of doing nothing differently (CODND). Soft savings, as described below, have indirect benefits.

Categories of hard savings are:

- Revenue Increase (collections, sales, capacity, lead time)
- Labor reduction (salary, wages, overtime, benefits)
- Material Savings
- Reduction or Elimination of Contracts with Outside vendors
- Reduction in Warranty Claims (errors, write-offs, services, leases)
- Other Fixed Savings (travel, communications, pagers, cell phones, shipping, utilities)

Working capital benefit improvements produce real money, but below the operating profit line. Generally, project benefits are calculated using a cost of money approach that utilizes a cost of debt calculation, with the concept being that improvement in these areas equates to financing that is avoided. The financial analysis can tell the black belt the appropriate cost of capital for their company.

Inventory reduction addresses:

- Finished Goods: Completed product or service that is available for purchase
- WIP: Products that are not yet available to the customer for purchase
- Parts: Items that are available to be used in the production of a product or service

- Maintenance and Repair—Equipment Spares: Items that are available to be used in repair or maintenance
- Accounts Receivable Reduction
- Money due to the firm from its customers

Soft benefits are less tangible. It is often difficult to assign specific monetary value to them. Examples of soft benefits are:

- Customer Satisfaction
- Employee Morale
- Reputation of the company or brand
- Regulatory Compliance
- Legal Exposure
- Safety

Some companies attempt to evaluate and track soft benefits because they feel that soft benefits are just as important as the hard benefits.

The project prioritization of project in categories such as legal, regulatory, social or customer satisfaction reasons could be addressed through an FMEA assessment.

## 9.8 Enterprise Data Analytics

ROI at the company level is a complex reflection of all individual activities over the reflected time period. A graphic representation of this ROI is shown in Figure 9.2. I agree with Cunningham and Fiume (2003) who state: "If a company is constantly improving its processes, the results in ROI will come. This focus on improving the individual elements of the process, by eliminating waste and increasing velocity, has great impact on the bottom line, but only when we are not focused exclusively on that bottom line. The winners will be companies that focus on process first, not results."

Consider that the goal of an organization is to increase ROI. For this to occur, the ROI numerator increases relative to the denominator, the ROI denominator decreases relative to the numerator, or both occur. The following analyses can provide insight to where improvement efforts should focus.

Much insight can be achieved into what an organization can do to improve through a systematic analysis of the existing enterprise system and improvement possibilities with linkage to enterprise voice of the customer inputs. This analysis can involve the financials either directly or indirectly. The insight gained from an

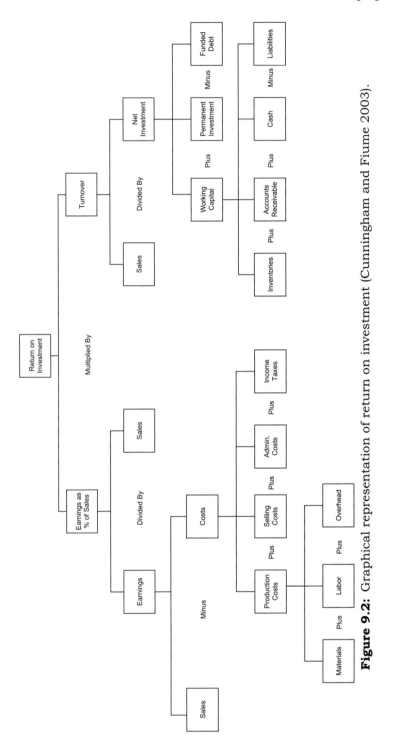

**Figure 9.2:** Graphical representation of return on investment (Cunningham and Fiume 2003).

effective enterprise analysis can enhance a company's strategic planning direction.

At the enterprise level, there are many potential analysis paths. An approach to funnel down these many options is the scoping down of work through an enterprise brainstorming session. Wisdom of the organization tools that are a part of an improvement project execution roadmap could be used to facilitate this information collection process; e.g., cause-and-effect diagram and cause-and-effect matrix (see Appendix Sections D.9 and D.10).

This wisdom of the organization work could then lead to hypothesis tests that would again utilize tools that are often associated with improvement project execution. The importance of getting to know your data through graphing and statistical analyses is an essential part of this overall process. People can get themselves into trouble when they just look at the results of a statistical analysis without plotting the data; i.e., plotting and statistical analyses should both be used when appropriate. A systematic utilization of data analyses tools, such as those used in the P-DMAIC roadmap, helps orchestrate organizational strategic direction and improvement focus efforts. Areas to consider for this segmentation and analysis for differences and trends include: Sales source

- Customer satisfaction/needs assessment
- External force assessment; e.g., changes in technology, competition, and government regulations
- Internal force assessment; e.g., core competencies, supplier and process assessments

Let's now consider analyses' potentials for these areas. Example sales source assessments are:

- Statistical and graphic assessment of sales by sales personnel, department, managers, or regions
- Pareto chart (see Appendix Section D.13) showing generated sales by customer/customer segment or product/service
- Matrix showing sales or percent of sales from market segment versus product type.

Data for a customer satisfaction/needs assessment can originate from the first value-chain step. Brainstorming and an affinity diagram (see Appendix D.11) can be used to describe whether there is a want, need, or desire at each matrix intersection point of a customer needs versus market segment matrix. Another matrix can then be created to address how well your company and competition are addressing those needs.

Success depends on the nimbleness of an organization to identify and respond to forces beyond its control. Organizations need to create a system to stay abreast of changes in technology, competition, government regulations, and other forces. One approach to accomplish this is to:

1. Use a cross-functional brainstorming session to create a list of external forces.
2. Compile literature that supports each external force item.
3. Use literature to predict each force impact on the current state.
4. Identify areas that could be threatened.
5. Identify areas that could be exploited.
6. Develop strategies to address threatened and exploited areas.

An internal force assessment could address how well the identified core competencies exist and are being utilized to address customer needs. An assessment could be made by creating a matrix to show the relationship between core competencies, supplier fulfillment, and key processes to customer satisfaction.

The results from the sales source, customer satisfaction/needs assessment, external force assessment, and internal force assessment can be synthesized in a strengths–weakness–opportunities–threats (SWOT) analysis. The point where most employee process activities impact ROI can be five or six levels deep. An ROI component contribution analysis from these processes/opportunities can provide direction as to where improvement efforts would have the largest big-picture metric impact. A simulation model can help with this determination by assessing the impact of considered changes through what-if analyses. This accumulated analysis can then become data-driven input for the Enterprise Improvement Plan (EIP) creation (see Section 12.10).

# 9.9   Example 9.1: Enterprise Process Financial Analysis

This example illustrates a company's business unit application of E-DMAIC analyze and improve phase methods. In this example, financial business measurement improvement needs can lead to the creation of projects (Moe 2006).

The competitive forces for a company's business unit were intensifying. Some very high-volume accounts demanded price reduction. Prices breaks were being conceded to these accounts because their account volume justified adjustments. The general situation in the company was not as good as it could have been, and improvements were needed.

Companies are in business to create customers and cash; however, companies typically have competition. It is important that organizations understand these competitive forces so that they can create product/service differentiation. The success of an organization depends on how well improvement principles and tools are applied to create this differentiation.

If an organization is improving, the package value prices can be raised because of this differentiation, but for the described competitive situation, price concessions were needed. Along with dealing with the financial top line, this business unit needed to uncover ways to deal with cost structure. The strategy used was based upon Deming's principles and utilized IEE methodologies to improve processes so that the common-cause key process response levels would be more in line with customer and business needs.

Customers generally judge companies and their products/services relative to quality, cost, and service. For example, a target is established when someone orders a medium-cooked steak. Expectations are not met if the restaurant delivers an over/under cooked steak, the delivery is slow, or the charges are excessive. When customer expectations are not satisfied, the service/product provider will not be a likely candidate for future purchases. Unsatisfied customers can also significantly impact the purchase decisions of others through bad-will stories about the company's products or services. In business, we need to focus on the alignment of process outputs to targets so that process variability is minimized. The understanding of current performance and improvement opportunities is through data analyses.

From data, organizations can determine what they like and don't like about current conditions. If a big picture financial metric assessment, as described in Figure 9.3, conveys a satisfactory picture, improvement efforts are not needed. However, if the picture is not desirable, targeted drill downs are needed

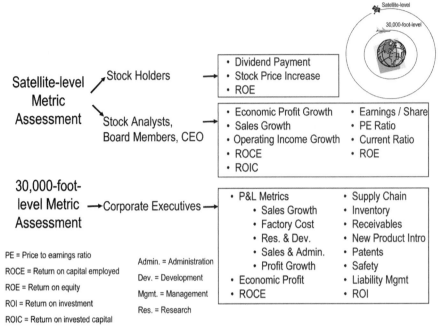

**Figure 9.3:** Corporate financial metric assessment.

to determine what should be done differently to improve the picture.

A profit and loss (P&L) statement data analysis of the following areas can provide insight to opportunities for targeted drill-downs. These efforts need to be in alignment with the previously described metrics and improvement strategy:

- Increase sales
  - Introduce more new products on time
  - Increase penetration into existing markets
  - Create new markets and max market share
  - Price customer solutions on value as well as cost
  - Improve customer service
  - Price to cover inflation
  - Reduce customer complaint adjustments to gross sales
  - Improve sales productivity
- Decrease factory cost
  - Reduce raw material (RM) prices, waste
  - Improve productivity
  - Reduce operating expenses
  - Reduce dead inventory

- Effective Sales and Administration (S&A) costs
  - Improve unit cost/quality
  - Increase people productivity
  - Recruit and develop top-notch people
  - Manage and control discretionary costs
- Increase operating income
  - Maximize total revenue and profit margins
  - Eliminate loss commodities/products
  - Reduce need for accruals

Current pricing pressures in this business unit yielded unsatisfactory general metric trends. Factory costs were rising, and there were productivity issues. The asset management side of the business describes cash usage and management issues. Both P&L and asset management needed assessment because organizational cash-tight situations can significantly curtail efforts to pave for the future. Cash-tight organizations are going be restricted unless they seek bank loans, resulting in additional cash outlay through interest and servicing payments. Because of this, organizations need to quantify the current high-level metrics and determine where efforts can have the most opportunity to improve the P&L bottom-line.

General categories for P&L statement improvements include increased sales and reduction of factory and S&A costs. To address these opportunities, a good starting point is to understand the customer needs and any disconnections relative to fulfilling those needs. If complaints are received, somebody is not happy with the delivered product or service. For this situation, it was found that the business unit was maximizing margin and giving up share. After this balancing and the according price adjustments, product share and cash flow increased.

When addressing how to increase operating income, it was discovered that a number of business-unit products were losing money. The sales force said that they needed a full menu of commodities even though some commodities lost money. An analysis indicated that this was true in some situations but not true in most situations. This data analysis not only uncovered the current problem but also exposed this as being a multi-year problem. Decisions had to be made whether to stop these commodity losses either by turning the commodity around or eliminating the commodities from the product-offering portfolio. Many commodity offerings were removed.

When addressing how to increase operating income, it was discovered that a number of business-unit products were losing money. The sales force said that they needed a full menu of commodities even though some commodities lost money.

As noted above, another strategy to increase operating income is the reduction of accruals. Accruals are often considered okay; however, they are not good. Obsolete inventory accruals, for example, quantify the number of problem items that need resolution. When these types of issues are resolved, inventory accruals can be lowered, leading to the freeing-up of cash and an increased bottom line.

Investigation into the sales force led to the commonly used day-to-day metric of number of sales calls. This metric is not necessarily in alignment with the objective of a sales force; i.e., sell products. A top-line, financial focus can give insight to appropriate metric considerations, along with productivity. Calls per day could be a productivity element; however, that alone does not yield success. For example, care needs to be exercised so that the sales force is provided the best tools and training. When this training was implemented with a feedback system, the selling process became more effective. This training included an easy-to-understand process that increased customer communications relative to proposed product value and tangible benefits, along with supplying appropriate sales personnel tools; e.g., computers and software.

Simply approaching the sales force to state the desire for more sales does not make it happen. It is important for the sales force first to know the new product portfolio and existing product differentiation. If an assessment indicates that this knowledge is not satisfactory, these issues must be addressed.

Organizations need to focus efforts on determining what needs to be done so that everyone throughout the enterprise process works smarter; however, this does not always happen. When organizations arrive at the point where everyone recognizes how to work smarter, it can become fun.

In an economic profit analysis, both asset management needs (business cash tie-up) are considered in addition to the P&L statement. The hypothetical example in Table 9.4 addresses cash generation, which is the P&L side, where a hundred billion dollars was placed on the bottom line. The tying up of cash affects what can be done to create the future. Economic Profit Calculations

**Table 9.4** Economic Profit Analysis (ROCE = Return on capital employed)

| *Millions of dollars* | | | | | |
|---|---|---|---|---|---|
| *P&L* | | | *Asset Management* | | |
| Sales | - | | Accounts Rec | - | |
| Factory Cost | - | | Inventory | - | |
| S&A Costs | - | | Fixed Assets - Net | - | |
| Freight & Other | - | | Other Assets | - | |
| Operating Income | - | | Less Liabilities | - | |
| Less: Operating Tax | - | | Net Operating Capital | $750 | |
| Net Operating Income | $100 | | Cost of Capital | 10% | |
| | | | Capital Charge | $75 | |
| Economic Profit | $25 | | | | |
| ROCE | 13% | | | | |

(EPC) or Economic Value Add (EVA) calculations address cash tie-up issues. To illustrate how organizations can use these calculations, consider that 750 million dollars was the total capital investment. Consider that there was a 10% self-charge for the cost of this money, which yielded a capital charge of 75 million. The subtraction of this amount from the operating net income yields a 25 million dollar economic profit.

A ROCE calculation is determined by dividing the 100 million net income by 750 million. If this value of 13% were not larger that the cost of capital or the rate of return that we could receive from the bank, then one can question why your cash was not just deposited in a bank.

When these numbers are not favorable in companies, this can result in other companies' examination of the effectiveness of current operations to determine whether the company might be a good possible takeover. The examining company could believe that it would manage the organization better than the current organization.

From the annotated value chain shown in Figure 9.4, developed improvement opportunities can be initiated. For example, consider if we could reduce customer complaints to zero, customers would be happier, and they would have more positive conversations about the company's products and services. Moving from the left side of the chart, we note that there are other opportunities relative to the lab, suppliers, carriers, factories, order entries, and the closed loop system in general.

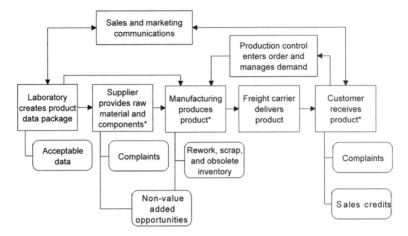

\* Delivers/receives: product performance, consistent quality, correct quantity, on-time service, and satisfactory pricing

**Figure 9.4:** Annotated value chain illustration (Moe 2006).

A good starting place for improving the enterprise process financials is by focusing on the customer. When customer problems are solved, satisfaction is increased. When both internal and external customers are happy, things can really start to happen. For this example, analysis and improvement efforts resulted in a significant reduction in sales credits. Moving to the left in the value-chain factory, suppliers, and the lab, other opportunities for improvement can become apparent.

> An enterprise process assessment of the supplier situation uncovered the fact that most problems were caused by the lab's providing poor specifications, test methods, and other information.

An enterprise process assessment of the supplier situation uncovered the fact that most problems were caused by the lab's providing poor specifications, test methods, and other information. When suppliers need to provide something beyond the normal for no good reason, the charges for the part or service is greater; i.e., there is a negative impact to the bottom line. This analysis indicated that many supplier issues originated with our organization.

One of the major problems uncovered was that the lab enjoyed working to create a design solution. However, the lab did not enjoy the work that it took to provide high-quality raw material and process documentation/specifications, along with accompanying test methodologies. Factories need this information to operate efficiently with new and modified product introductions. For a supplier, this information is essential to provide a high-quality service or product. Much non-productive work and wasted time resulted. The highlighting of these lab issues stimulated the placement of tools and procedures for the lab to do a better job, including the improved use of statistical design of experiments (DOE). This lab assessment also uncovered the fact that specifications were often too tight. Opening up these tolerances led to better prices and a better product because standard product raw materials were utilized, rather than some special made-to-order materials that could have quality issues.

Organizations that are not structurally observing data using IEE techniques can be oblivious to product/service issues. While these issues can be very important to customers, they can also result in unnecessary activities or internal waste. In either case, these issues can have a dramatic negative impact on the bottom line.

For example, an enterprise process analysis uncovered in the following situation two bottom-line issues. First, excessive air freight was used to address not having the right product on time at a customer's facility. Secondly, sales promotions at the end of the quarter drove the factory crazy with excessive over time, inventory build-ups, and finished goods that were not being sold. Policies were established in the business unit to address these unsatisfactory conditions.

Organizations that initiate an enterprise process macro financial and value chain, as highlighted in this example, can lead to effective targeted improvement activities. One should realize that the quantification of customer complaints is often only the tip of the iceberg (see Figure 4.4). The described analysis reflects all real transaction costs; however, controller feedback has indicated that there is perhaps another 75% intangible cost implication below the waterline. This estimate does not include lost customers. For every dissatisfied customer who gives feedback, there are probably ten who do not give feedback.

In this business unit, the execution of this systematic enterprise process analysis and improvement strategy led to significant growth and profitability so that this unit became the company's performance leader.

# 9.10   A 30,000-Foot-Level Metric's Improvement Opportunity Prioritization

A Pareto chart (see Appendix Section D.13) is a tool that can be helpful in identifying the source of common causes in a manufacturing process. The Pareto principle basically states that a vital few of the manufacturing/service process characteristics affect most of the line quality problems, while a trivial many of the manufacturing process characteristics cause only a small portion of the quality problems. The Pareto chart is a tool that is used to identify the most likely candidates or areas for improvement. Within a given area of improvement, DOE techniques, as part of an IEE improvement project, can often be used to determine efficiently which of the considered changes are most important for implementation within the process.

## 9.11    Example 9.2: Improving a Process that Has Defects

As noted earlier, 30,000-foot-level process control charts are useful for monitoring the process stability and identifying the point at which special-cause situations occur. A process is generally considered in-control/predictable whenever it is sampled periodically, and whenever the measurements from the samples are within the upper control limit (UCL) and lower control limit (LCL), which are positioned around a centerline (CL). Note that these control limits are independent of any specification limits.

Figure 7.10 in Example 7.4 showed that the overall process defective rate improved some time ago; however, the current and predicted process defective transaction rate is still about 5%. A value-chain CODND analysis indicated that costs for these defective units had a high adverse impact on the organization's net profit margins. A Pareto analysis was conducted to determine whether there were one or more opportunities for IEE projects.

Two Pareto charts of the transaction failure types since the improvement are shown in Figure 9.5, where one Pareto addresses the frequency of occurrence by type of transaction failure and the other by CODND impact for each transaction failure type. Even though the type 3 defect had the largest frequency of occurrence, the financial impacts from types 4 and 2 transaction defects impact the financial bottom line the most. Hence, a reduction of type 4 and 2 failures would be likely candidates for a few projects. These projects should be considered along with other projects when putting together a plan for executing the projects in the E-DMAIC improve phase.

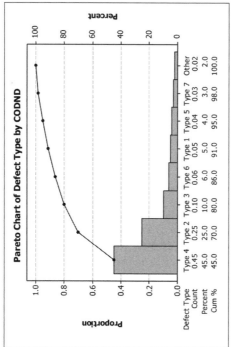

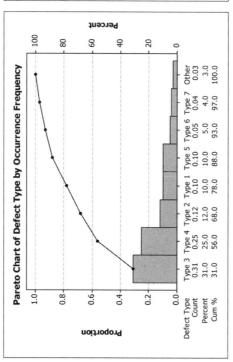

**Figure 9.5:** Pareto charts of defect type by occurrence frequency and CODND impact.

## 9.12   Example 9.3: Sales Personnel
## Scorecard/Dashboard and Data Analyses

This example illustrates an IEE alternative to traditional score-card/dashboard reporting and analyses described in Sections 3.3, 3.6, and 3.7. More specifically, this example focuses on alternatives to the charting described in Figures 3.1 to 3.3 for the Table 9.5 data. Volume III describes the mechanics to create these charts and conduct these analyses.

As was noted earlier, Figures 3.1 to 3.3 charts report formats typically lead to *stories* about the past. The chart presentation format will dictate the presented *story* type. For example, the calendar boundaries in Figure 3.3 bar-chart reporting format will surely lead to adjacent-month and previous yearly-month comparisons. Consider how accurate is a year-based reporting if something changed during the year? For example, if there was a fundamental sales process change in July, then we would be including old information with the latest information when examining annualized data in a pie chart. Wouldn't it be better to first identify if and when a change occurred and then either compare new to old process responses, or describe what is happening most recently?

Also consider, which interests us the most: the past or the future? Most often the response to this question is "the future." Reporting individual up-and-down historical movement or arbitrary-time-based comparisons do not provide insight to future process-output expectations, assuming that the process experiences no dramatic positive or negative change. However, if we could somehow estimate the future and we then don't like the resulting prediction, we gain insight to improvement focus opportunities; i.e., the metric improvement needs pull for process improvement project creation. What is next described is an IEE metric reporting alternative that provides insight that these forms of reporting do not.

Figure 9.6 describes the results of a business area drill down of the gross revenue satellite-level metric. From this 30,000-foot-level scorecard/dashboard reporting analysis, we are able to identify a process shift in Oct. 03. This was when a team made a change and they could now see the impact from this change by the shift in the 30,000-foot-level control chart. The process reached an improved performance level, where the noted predictability state-

**Table 9.5** Sales Scorecard/Dashboard Data

| Month Count | Year | Month | Revenue | Sales Person | Stage |
|---|---|---|---|---|---|
| 1 | 1 | 1 | 34969 | 1 | 1 |
| 1 | 1 | 1 | 88135 | 2 | 1 |
| 1 | 1 | 1 | 51123 | 3 | 1 |
| 1 | 1 | 1 | 50845 | 4 | 1 |
| 1 | 1 | 1 | 131719 | 5 | 1 |
| 2 | 1 | 2 | 54926 | 1 | 1 |
| 2 | 1 | 2 | 157637 | 2 | 1 |
| 2 | 1 | 2 | 95178 | 3 | 1 |
| 2 | 1 | 2 | 69030 | 4 | 1 |
| 2 | 1 | 2 | 117008 | 5 | 1 |
| 3 | 1 | 3 | 42623 | 1 | 1 |
| 3 | 1 | 3 | 93521 | 2 | 1 |
| 3 | 1 | 3 | 63296 | 3 | 1 |
| 3 | 1 | 3 | 53634 | 4 | 1 |
| 3 | 1 | 3 | 90716 | 5 | 1 |
| 4 | 1 | 4 | 53981 | 1 | 1 |
| 4 | 1 | 4 | 67017 | 2 | 1 |
| 4 | 1 | 4 | 85399 | 3 | 1 |
| 4 | 1 | 4 | 69865 | 4 | 1 |
| 4 | 1 | 4 | 152789 | 5 | 1 |
| 5 | 1 | 5 | 57628 | 1 | 1 |
| 5 | 1 | 5 | 47585 | 2 | 1 |
| 5 | 1 | 5 | 21212 | 3 | 1 |
| 5 | 1 | 5 | 41716 | 4 | 1 |
| 5 | 1 | 5 | 78185 | 5 | 1 |
| 6 | 1 | 6 | 95744 | 1 | 1 |
| 6 | 1 | 6 | 3936 | 2 | 1 |
| 6 | 1 | 6 | 62703 | 3 | 1 |
| 6 | 1 | 6 | 32950 | 4 | 1 |
| 6 | 1 | 6 | 96591 | 5 | 1 |
| 7 | 1 | 7 | 79108 | 1 | 1 |
| 7 | 1 | 7 | 94614 | 2 | 1 |
| 7 | 1 | 7 | 106464 | 3 | 1 |
| 7 | 1 | 7 | 46893 | 4 | 1 |
| 7 | 1 | 7 | 110152 | 5 | 1 |
| 8 | 1 | 8 | 64376 | 1 | 1 |
| 8 | 1 | 8 | 27319 | 2 | 1 |
| 8 | 1 | 8 | 47222 | 3 | 1 |
| 8 | 1 | 8 | 63039 | 4 | 1 |
| 8 | 1 | 8 | 121866 | 5 | 1 |
| 9 | 1 | 9 | 105821 | 1 | 1 |
| 9 | 1 | 9 | 22965 | 2 | 1 |
| 9 | 1 | 9 | 57262 | 3 | 1 |
| 9 | 1 | 9 | 56388 | 4 | 1 |
| 9 | 1 | 9 | 95788 | 5 | 1 |
| 10 | 1 | 10 | 83282 | 1 | 1 |
| 10 | 1 | 10 | 48811 | 2 | 1 |
| 10 | 1 | 10 | 57556 | 3 | 1 |
| 10 | 1 | 10 | 1088 | 4 | 1 |
| 10 | 1 | 10 | 83161 | 5 | 1 |
| 11 | 1 | 11 | 49674 | 1 | 1 |
| 11 | 1 | 11 | 57223 | 2 | 1 |
| 11 | 1 | 11 | 55203 | 3 | 1 |
| 11 | 1 | 11 | 77731 | 4 | 1 |
| 11 | 1 | 11 | 65248 | 5 | 1 |
| 12 | 1 | 12 | 2000 | 1 | 1 |
| 12 | 1 | 12 | 110131 | 2 | 1 |
| 12 | 1 | 12 | 29210 | 3 | 1 |
| 12 | 1 | 12 | 1200 | 4 | 1 |
| 12 | 1 | 12 | 84348 | 5 | 1 |
| 13 | 2 | 1 | 101319 | 1 | 1 |
| 13 | 2 | 1 | 61193 | 2 | 1 |
| 13 | 2 | 1 | 59790 | 3 | 1 |
| 13 | 2 | 1 | 23991 | 4 | 1 |
| 13 | 2 | 1 | 104281 | 5 | 1 |
| 14 | 2 | 2 | 161092 | 1 | 1 |
| 14 | 2 | 2 | 28392 | 2 | 1 |
| 14 | 2 | 2 | 56699 | 3 | 1 |
| 14 | 2 | 2 | 62438 | 4 | 1 |
| 14 | 2 | 2 | 99260 | 5 | 1 |
| 15 | 2 | 3 | 79160 | 1 | 1 |
| 15 | 2 | 3 | 32581 | 2 | 1 |
| 15 | 2 | 3 | 62689 | 3 | 1 |
| 15 | 2 | 3 | 87080 | 4 | 1 |
| 15 | 2 | 3 | 111742 | 5 | 1 |
| 16 | 2 | 4 | 98524 | 1 | 1 |
| 16 | 2 | 4 | 46928 | 2 | 1 |
| 16 | 2 | 4 | 80334 | 3 | 1 |
| 16 | 2 | 4 | 50350 | 4 | 1 |
| 16 | 2 | 4 | 107349 | 5 | 1 |
| 17 | 2 | 5 | 56133 | 1 | 1 |
| 17 | 2 | 5 | 53586 | 2 | 1 |
| 17 | 2 | 5 | 54897 | 3 | 1 |
| 17 | 2 | 5 | 88038 | 4 | 1 |
| 17 | 2 | 5 | 95695 | 5 | 1 |
| 18 | 2 | 6 | 46721 | 1 | 1 |
| 18 | 2 | 6 | 32251 | 2 | 1 |
| 18 | 2 | 6 | 74020 | 3 | 1 |
| 18 | 2 | 6 | 71424 | 4 | 1 |
| 18 | 2 | 6 | 103391 | 5 | 1 |
| 19 | 2 | 7 | 88761 | 1 | 1 |
| 19 | 2 | 7 | 67731 | 2 | 1 |
| 19 | 2 | 7 | 36421 | 3 | 1 |
| 19 | 2 | 7 | 3010 | 4 | 1 |
| 19 | 2 | 7 | 101091 | 5 | 1 |
| 20 | 2 | 8 | 30112 | 1 | 1 |
| 20 | 2 | 8 | 34052 | 2 | 1 |
| 20 | 2 | 8 | 78787 | 3 | 1 |
| 20 | 2 | 8 | 81508 | 4 | 1 |
| 20 | 2 | 8 | 69549 | 5 | 1 |
| 21 | 2 | 9 | 95727 | 1 | 1 |
| 21 | 2 | 9 | 62510 | 2 | 1 |
| 21 | 2 | 9 | 88725 | 3 | 1 |
| 21 | 2 | 9 | 19078 | 4 | 1 |
| 21 | 2 | 9 | 147451 | 5 | 1 |
| 22 | 2 | 10 | 101962 | 1 | 1 |
| 22 | 2 | 10 | 53754 | 2 | 1 |
| 22 | 2 | 10 | 96651 | 3 | 1 |
| 22 | 2 | 10 | 54919 | 4 | 1 |
| 22 | 2 | 10 | 120358 | 5 | 1 |
| 23 | 2 | 11 | 38956 | 1 | 1 |
| 23 | 2 | 11 | 39521 | 2 | 1 |
| 23 | 2 | 11 | 125041 | 3 | 1 |
| 23 | 2 | 11 | 74804 | 4 | 1 |
| 23 | 2 | 11 | 83914 | 5 | 1 |
| 24 | 2 | 12 | 48009 | 1 | 1 |
| 24 | 2 | 12 | 100034 | 2 | 1 |
| 24 | 2 | 12 | 111232 | 3 | 1 |
| 24 | 2 | 12 | 68673 | 4 | 1 |
| 24 | 2 | 12 | 102650 | 5 | 1 |
| 25 | 3 | 1 | 75178 | 1 | 1 |
| 25 | 3 | 1 | 102110 | 2 | 1 |
| 25 | 3 | 1 | 80236 | 3 | 1 |
| 25 | 3 | 1 | 40957 | 4 | 1 |
| 25 | 3 | 1 | 103049 | 5 | 1 |
| 26 | 3 | 2 | 49872 | 1 | 1 |
| 26 | 3 | 2 | 45034 | 2 | 1 |
| 26 | 3 | 2 | 71657 | 3 | 1 |
| 26 | 3 | 2 | 61589 | 4 | 1 |
| 26 | 3 | 2 | 113439 | 5 | 1 |
| 27 | 3 | 3 | 103052 | 1 | 1 |
| 27 | 3 | 3 | 52918 | 2 | 1 |
| 27 | 3 | 3 | 130968 | 3 | 1 |
| 27 | 3 | 3 | 21527 | 4 | 1 |
| 27 | 3 | 3 | 145602 | 5 | 1 |
| 28 | 3 | 4 | 78929 | 1 | 1 |
| 28 | 3 | 4 | 34991 | 2 | 1 |
| 28 | 3 | 4 | 98408 | 3 | 1 |
| 28 | 3 | 4 | 77927 | 4 | 1 |
| 28 | 3 | 4 | 131056 | 5 | 1 |
| 29 | 3 | 5 | 56053 | 1 | 1 |
| 29 | 3 | 5 | 51731 | 2 | 1 |
| 29 | 3 | 5 | 46524 | 3 | 1 |
| 29 | 3 | 5 | 82588 | 4 | 1 |
| 29 | 3 | 5 | 64808 | 5 | 1 |
| 30 | 3 | 6 | 45440 | 1 | 1 |
| 30 | 3 | 6 | 68631 | 2 | 1 |
| 30 | 3 | 6 | 50595 | 3 | 1 |
| 30 | 3 | 6 | 32913 | 4 | 1 |
| 30 | 3 | 6 | 81762 | 5 | 1 |
| 31 | 3 | 7 | 35650 | 1 | 1 |
| 31 | 3 | 7 | 58252 | 2 | 1 |
| 31 | 3 | 7 | 129721 | 3 | 1 |
| 31 | 3 | 7 | 100734 | 4 | 1 |
| 31 | 3 | 7 | 116974 | 5 | 1 |
| 32 | 3 | 8 | 106538 | 1 | 1 |
| 32 | 3 | 8 | 89405 | 2 | 1 |
| 32 | 3 | 8 | 53907 | 3 | 1 |
| 32 | 3 | 8 | 85316 | 4 | 1 |
| 32 | 3 | 8 | 135957 | 5 | 1 |
| 33 | 3 | 9 | 16504 | 1 | 1 |
| 33 | 3 | 9 | 51972 | 2 | 1 |
| 33 | 3 | 9 | 18991 | 3 | 1 |
| 33 | 3 | 9 | 44125 | 4 | 1 |
| 33 | 3 | 9 | 94590 | 5 | 1 |
| 34 | 3 | 10 | 84307 | 1 | 1 |
| 34 | 3 | 10 | 62449 | 2 | 1 |
| 34 | 3 | 10 | 84446 | 3 | 1 |
| 34 | 3 | 10 | 63752 | 4 | 1 |
| 34 | 3 | 10 | 103945 | 5 | 1 |
| 35 | 3 | 11 | 99710 | 1 | 2 |
| 35 | 3 | 11 | 108526 | 2 | 2 |
| 35 | 3 | 11 | 93391 | 3 | 2 |
| 35 | 3 | 11 | 104531 | 4 | 2 |
| 35 | 3 | 11 | 106597 | 5 | 2 |
| 36 | 3 | 12 | 79179 | 1 | 2 |
| 36 | 3 | 12 | 110223 | 2 | 2 |
| 36 | 3 | 12 | 108309 | 3 | 2 |
| 36 | 3 | 12 | 57019 | 4 | 2 |
| 36 | 3 | 12 | 126439 | 5 | 2 |
| 37 | 4 | 1 | 61433 | 1 | 2 |
| 37 | 4 | 1 | 130435 | 2 | 2 |
| 37 | 4 | 1 | 107330 | 3 | 2 |
| 37 | 4 | 1 | 106640 | 4 | 2 |
| 37 | 4 | 1 | 118398 | 5 | 2 |
| 38 | 4 | 2 | 65322 | 1 | 2 |
| 38 | 4 | 2 | 80393 | 2 | 2 |
| 38 | 4 | 2 | 119582 | 3 | 2 |
| 38 | 4 | 2 | 104869 | 4 | 2 |
| 38 | 4 | 2 | 97565 | 5 | 2 |
| 39 | 4 | 3 | 113024 | 1 | 2 |
| 39 | 4 | 3 | 122048 | 2 | 2 |
| 39 | 4 | 3 | 143169 | 3 | 2 |
| 39 | 4 | 3 | 102895 | 4 | 2 |
| 39 | 4 | 3 | 109127 | 5 | 2 |

ment reflects the last five months of stability. A detailed interpretation of this figure follows:

IEE scorecard/dashboard metric reporting process

1. Assess process predictability.
2. When the process is considered predictable, formulate a prediction statement for the latest region of stability. The usual reporting format for this statement is:

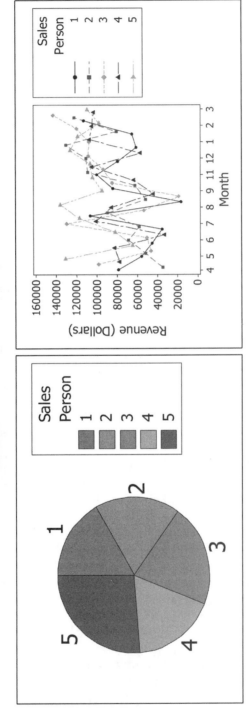

**Figure 9.6:** (Part A) Drill down to generated revenue from five sales persons, where the probability plot of individual salesperson revenue (see Part B) is from the last five months of stability.

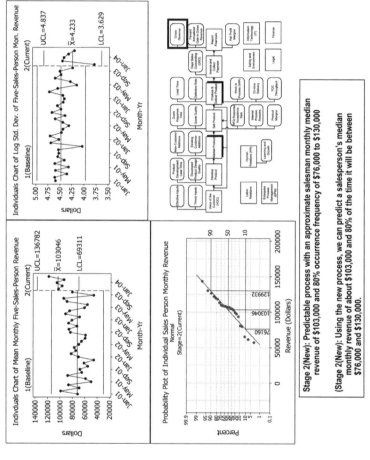

**Figure 9.6:** (Part B) Drill down to generated revenue from five sales persons, where the probability plot of individual salesperson revenue is from the last five months of stability.

    a.   When there is a specification requirement: nonconformance percentage or defects per million opportunities (DPMO)

    b.   When there are no specification requirements: median response and 80% frequency of occurrence rate

Interpretation of Figure 9.6 using this process:

1.   Monthly subgrouping/sampling was chosen (see Glossary subgroup and infrequent subgrouping/sampling). Since there are multiple samples in the subgroups, two control charts are needed to assess within subgroup change over time. One control chart assesses whether the within subgroup mean response changes over time, while the other control chart address whether within subgroup variability changes over time. Volume III describes why it is often best to track subgroup variability as the log of the subgroup standard deviation. For this example, the individuals control chart of the mean sales from the five sales persons indicates that the between subgroup mean response shifted and established a new level of predictive performance in October 2003. The Individuals control chart of log standard deviation indicates that the between subgroup variability differences by sales person (as tracked by the logarithm of standard deviation—See Appendix Section C.2) shifted and established a new level of predictive performance in October 2003.

2.   From the probability plot of individual sales person monthly revenue, a prediction statement for the new level of process performance is that the approximate expected sales person's performance will be mean monthly revenue of $103,000 and 80% frequency of occurrence by month of $76,000 to $130,000; i.e., 80% of all individual monthly sales performances is expected to be between these two estimates.

Since October 2003, this process has been experiencing common cause variability. These are best estimates of the performance of this process. If this process response is not satisfactory, something needs to be done to improve the process; i.e., a pull for project creation.

Figure 3.1 was included in Figure 9.6 for illustrative purposes to compare IEE 30,000-foot-level metric reporting against one form of traditional performance measures reporting. The reader should compare this report-out format to other options shown in Figures 3.2 and 3.3.

For example, consider the month-year bar chart reporting format illustrated in Figure 3.3. I suspect that the stories typically conveyed from Figure 3.3 report-out format would be quite different from the conclusions presented during an IEE performance metrics report-out. The stories that are conveyed from traditional reporting can often lead to resource-draining activities that have little value. For example, Joe might be told to investigate why September revenues are down when this reported value was from common-cause variation, not a special-cause condition.

I should point out that all data for this illustration were randomly generated, where the only process special cause occurrence was the process shift that occurred on Oct. 03. That is, except for this shift, all data up-and-down movements were what we could expect from common-cause variability.

In Figure 9.6, we note that the estimated mean monthly revenue for the five sales personnel is $103,046. Five times this mean response is greater than $500,000 mean monthly goal. Hence, our scorecard/dashboard prediction statement indicates that with the current process we expect to meet in the future the sales goals for the five salesmen. This statement also implies that any new higher goal for these five salesmen would require additional process change.

It should also be highlighted that when a process change does not occur on January 1 of a year, there will always be some bridging of old and new process levels with annual reporting. This phenomenon does not occur with IEE reporting, since process capability/performance metric statements can be made at any point in time during the year.

In addition, when process input comparisons are assessed over an arbitrary interval such as annual, conclusions about the impact of these inputs can be distorted. To illustrate this, consider the pie chart in Figure 3.1, which compared monthly salesman revenue for the last 12 months. From this chart, it appears that salesman number five contributed more revenue than the other salesmen. I will now illustrate an IEE approach to make these assessments using both visualization and hypothesis statements in regions of stability.

> ... when process input comparisons are assessed over an arbitrary interval such as annual, conclusions about the impact of these inputs can be distorted.

An E-DMAIC analysis was to test the hypothesis that generated monthly sales from the five salesmen were equal. Instead of making an annual or some other arbitrary timeframe comparison, it is better to make comparisons within stable/predictable regions; e.g., something could have changed between regions of stability. Figure 9.7 shows a dot plot visualization and a statistical analysis that indicates a statistically significant difference in mean stage response. Because of this, each stage was analyzed separately.

Figures 9.8 and 9.9 show visualization and statistical analysis for both stage 1(Baseline) and stage 2(Current). The marginal plot in each figure gives a visual representation of not only mean responses but also the accompanying variability that each sales person is delivering. In the analysis of means (ANOM) in these figures five hypothesis tests are present; i.e., the mean of each salesperson was compared to the overall mean. When a plotted mean value in an ANOM plot is beyond one of the two horizontal decision lines, significance is stated at the charted risk probability, 0.05 in this case.

From Figure 9.8 before change analysis [i.e., stage 1(Baseline)], it appears that salesperson number five generated significantly larger revenue than the other sales personnel. It appears that this larger revenue shifted the overall to a level that sales personnel number two and four were significantly lower than the overall mean.

From the after change Figure 9.9 analyses [i.e., stage 2(Current)], no salesperson mean revenue could be shown statistically different from the overall mean. It was noted that between stage 1(Baseline) and 2(Current) a project had changed the sales process of sales personnel 1, 2, 3, and 4 to be consistent with the most successful sales person; i.e., number 5.

The reader should compare the thought process and conclusions from this analysis to the stories that would have been created from Figures 3.1–3.3. With the traditional report-out systems, there is no structured process to identify and react to the October shift.

To some readers, IEE performance metric reporting might look very complex with the additional fear that they would need to create a similar chart. These types of charts are not difficult to create with statistical software. Volume III describes the mechanics of setting up these charts for a variety of situations. It is important to also realize that typically only a few people in the organization would need to create these charts. Managers and other leaders in the organization would only need to be able to interpret the chart and create or address appropriate action plans from the charts.

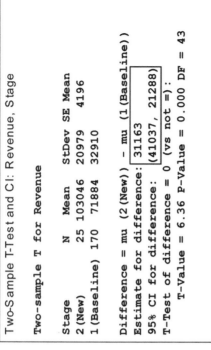

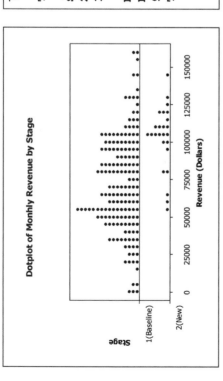

**Figure 9.7:** Visually and statistically comparing stage 1(Baseline) with stage 2(New) mean monthly sales personnel revenue.

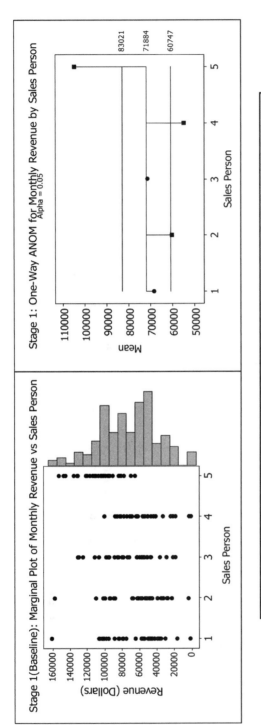

**Figure 9.8:** Stage 1 (Baseline): Mean monthly revenue visualization and statistical analysis by sales person.

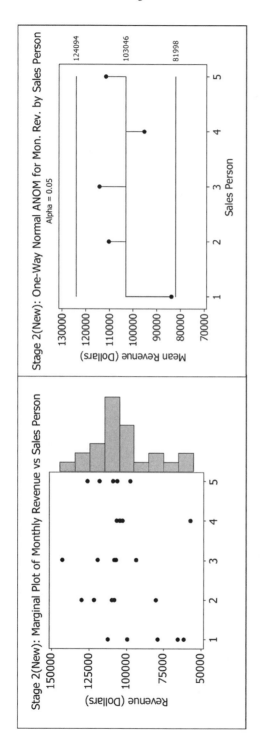

## Stage 2(New)

**Observation: From the ANOM mean plot, it is noted that no sales person mean revenue plot point is beyond the two horizontal decision lines.**

**Conclusion: There was no significant difference in any sales person's mean monthly generated revenue from the overall monthly mean. That is, we have no reason to believe that the graphically-illustrated marginal plot differences in means are what might be expect from sampling variability.**

**Figure 9.9:** Stage 2: Mean monthly revenue visualization and statistical analysis by sales person.

This form of reporting and chart interpretation could transform the workplace culture from firefighting to fire prevention. Management might now be asking Sue (See Example 3.1) when her process improvement project is to be completed, since project completion is expected to decrease a mean process 30,000-foot-level metric response to a more desirable level. This is in contrast to a daily meeting in the company's war room where direction is given to Joe to "fix" the latest problem of the day.

## 9.13   Example 9.4: Making the Numbers Assessment

Cunningham and Fiume (2003) state: "Compare these simple measures (customer service and inventory turns) with the one big hammer of a metric many companies use: Make the Month. There are businesses that expend tremendous amounts of energy and resources toward the end of the month in one mad scramble to live up to whatever numbers were budgeted or promised. Make the month might seem like a rather simple trap to avoid, but most typical results-oriented companies end up in the make-the-month category. These businesses may get results in the short term—much as fad diets get results—but in most cases, the practice creates significant waste that can seriously damage a company in the long term.

> There are businesses that expend tremendous amounts of energy and resources toward the end of the month in one mad scramble to live up to whatever numbers were budgeted or promised.

How can we tell if a company has fallen into this trap? If we use the example of shipments, look at whether shipments reflect substantially more than 25 percent of monthly sales in the last week of a typical four-week month. If the answer is yes, make-the-month syndrome is at play. We have seen companies that regularly ship 50 percent to 80 percent of their monthly volume in the last week of the month. The resource implications of this are staggering. What are the resources, such as overtime, that are needed to process 80 percent of the volume in 25 percent of the time? Or, if the organization has staffed to comfortably handle that higher volume, then what amount of resources are sitting idle or involved in make-work activities the other 75 percent of the time?"

The financial impact from these situations could be quantified as the CODND, which could then pull for project creation to improve the metric. An analysis of this situation might find that the sales department is offering discount incentives near month, or quarter, end to stimulate sales so that their numbers will be met. The question then becomes what could be done differently to address this behavior. Perhaps an improvement project could create a new sales personnel compensation policy that led to improved sales throughout the month and discouraged their previous end-of-the-month behavior, which had been adversely affecting manufacturing.

This form of detrimental business-making policy is not restricted to monthly manufacturing activities. Consider the resulting havoc when companies restrict travel near year end to meet annual budgeted or promised numbers. The impact from this type of policy can be very large; e.g., perhaps a customer was lost because a travel restriction impacted client servicing.

Organizations need to assess what changes are needed at the day-to-day process level to avoid short-term reactions to meet objectives that could have been arbitrarily set. A systematic assessment of data can provide insight into what should be done differently in policies and procedures to avoid future occurrences of these problem types. For this travel illustration, a company might find that significant throughout-the-year airline costs are occurring because there are many last-minute-called crisis travel meetings, which result in high air travel costs. This analysis result could then lead to the question: What can be done at the process level to reduce last-minute-called travel meetings throughout the year? A Pareto chart of meeting types could pull for the creation of several process improvement projects.

## 9.14 Applying IEE

My intent in this chapter was to provide some IEE financial foundation components. This chapter challenged some finance norms. The purpose of this section is to provide additional stimulus for extending this challenge to other financial processes; e.g., budgeting and capital planning processes.

For years I have questioned the effectiveness of the budgeting and capital planning processes in organization. In my opinion, these processes typically drive the wrong kind of activities. I think that it is refreshing that Cunningham and Fiume (2003) address this issue head-on when they state: "In many companies, budget season begins months in advance of the financial year's end and has all the trappings of a Senate confirmation. Executives use the process to jockey for position, to gauge status in the company and, in some cases, to actually get projects funded. Meanwhile, the CFO dons the robes of a frantic St. Peter, seeming to judge the worthiness of all who pass before her even while scrambling to gather all possible useful financial information and make it balanced and coherent. Capital requests fly in from all corners, each request padded against the arbitrary percentage cuts that people expect from accounting and upper management. A CFO can make enemies without even trying in budget season."

"I don't think budgets are worth a hill of beans, personally," says Cold Spring Granite's CFO, Greg Flint (Cunningham and Fiume 2003). "They're based on guesswork and politics. Every year, you see financial guys negotiating for a tough budget and operations guys negotiating for an easy budget so they can look good. In the end, the financial guys own the budget. Operations can say, 'It's not my fault. You gave me a bad budget.' So, we got rid of budgets. "What we do now is... and tell every department they must improve.... Their goals are purely based on improvement, and we do not insist on arbitrary percentages for improvement."

> I don't think budgets are worth a hill of beans.... They're based on guesswork and politics. Every year, you see financial guys negotiating for a tough budget and operations guys negotiating for an easy budget so they can look good ... so we got rid of budgets.

One final chapter point is that often people say that many taught Six Sigma statistical tools are not often utilized in transactional project execution. For many organizations and situations, this observation is probably true. However, in both transactional and manufacturing processes, statistical analyses and visualization tools can very beneficial when analyzing the enterprise as a whole for improvement opportunities. Well-trained black belts and master black belts using the techniques described in this volume can provide very useful enterprise-wide data analyses so that executives can gain insight, which helps them improve their direction on what specifically should be done to achieve their goals.

## 9.15   Exercises

1. Describe a company and how its reported financials are leading to the wrong activities.

2. Describe a situation where a project could initially appear important but did not impact the overall company's bottom line.

3. A project requires an initial investment of $23,000 and training costs of $6,000, which are spread over six months. Beginning with the third month, the expected monthly project savings are $3,000. Ignoring interest and taxes, determine the payback period (Quality Council of Indiana 2002).

# 10

# E-DMAIC—Analyze Phase: Theory of Constraints (TOC)

## 10.1   E-DMAIC Roadmap Component

The previous chapter described financial considerations in the enterprise analyze phase. This chapter extends the enterprise analysis to the overall system flow.

An analyze phase E-DMAIC checklist item described in Section 8.2 was theory of constraints (TOC). From a TOC analysis, we can gain direction on where a bottleneck or system constraint occurs that negatively impacts the enterprise financials. This thinking-process-tool analysis might identify that the sales process or operational step number two is the system constraint. From this analysis, we can gain important direction on where an improvement project should be targeted to improve the system output as a whole, as illustrated in Example 12.1.

TOC techniques described in this enterprise-process section of this volume are also applicable at the project level. This chapter will describe the whole methodology, even though some of the steps in TOC involve improvements.

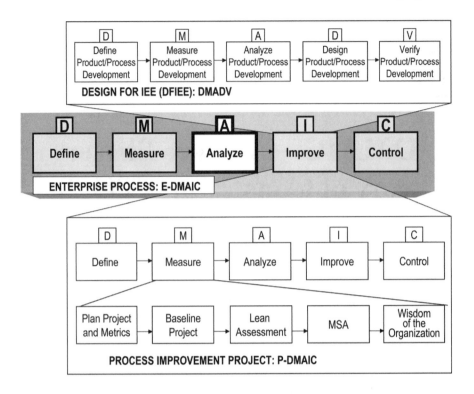

## 10.2   Theory of Constraints (TOC)

The outputs of a system are a function of the whole system, not just individual processes. When we view our system as a whole, we realize that the output is a function of the weakest link. The weakest link of the system is the constraint. If care is not exercised, we can be focusing on a subsystem that, even though improved, does not impact the overall system output. We need to focus on the orchestration of efforts so that we optimize the overall system, not individual pieces. Unfortunately, organization charts lead to workflow by function, which can result in competing forces within the organization. With TOC, systems are viewed as a whole, and work activities are directed so that the whole system performance measures are improved. To illustrate this, consider the system that is shown in Figure 10.1. Similar to water flow through a garden hose, the squeezing of one portion of the hose reduces water flow volume; i.e., step 5 in the figure.

Without considering the whole system, we might be spending a great deal of time and effort working on process step 2 because this

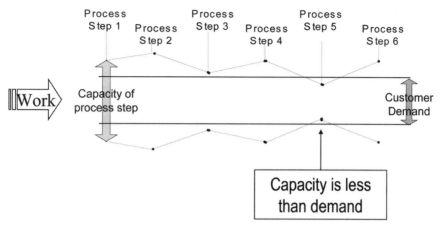

**Figure 10.1:** Identifying the overall system constraint.

step is not meeting its localized-created target objectives relative to operating efficiencies, equipment utilization, etc. From this figure, we note that improvements to process step 2 would not significantly impact the overall system and could actually degrade the overall metrics if additional WIP is created from the improvements.

The TOC system chain extends from market demand through the organization chain to suppliers. Let's consider an example when this high-level view of the overall system is not addressed. An organization works at improving internal process efficiencies. Capacity then increases. Excess inventory is then created because there is not sufficient demand. It was then discovered that the constraint is really the sales and marketing process.

Within an organization, there are often constraints that we may or may not consider. Types of constraints include market, resource, material, supplier, financial, and knowledge/competency. We need to look at the rules (i.e., policies) that drive the constraints.

## 10.3    Example 10.1: Theory of Constraints

In this example, I will use terms typically associated with manufacturing; however, the concepts apply equally to transactional processes.

A simple system is shown in Figure 10.2. Raw materials are processed through four component steps to produce a finished product. Each process step is an overall value stream link. The capacity of each step is described in the figure along with the

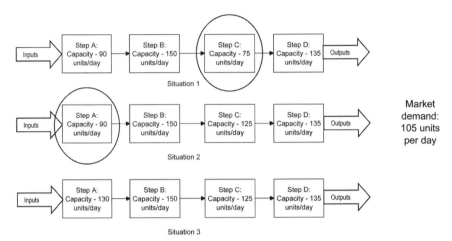

**Figure 10.2:** System constraint identification and resolution.

market demand of 105 units per day. The goal is to make as much money as possible from the process.

From the examination of situation 1 in the figure, it is noted that the capacity of Step C is 75, which is less than the market demand of 105. Even though other steps in our value stream process may not be performing up to their equipment utilization and efficiency goals, focus should be given first to increasing the capacity of Step C. From this E-DMAIC analysis, Step C would be an opportunity for a P-DMAIC project.

Upon completion of the P-DMAIC project for Step C, the process then exhibited the characteristics of situation 2 shown in the figure. An analysis of this situation indicates that the constraint is now at Step A. From this E-DMAIC analysis, it would now be appropriate for a P-DMAIC project to focus on Step A.

Upon completion of a P-DMAIC project of Step A, the process then started exhibiting the characteristics of situation 3. An analysis of this situation indicates that all four steps of the process have enough capacity to meet the market demand. The internal system constraints relative to satisfying a market demand of 115 units per day have been removed. The constraint has moved outside the system to the market place. The next P-DMAIC project should focus on determining what can be done to increase product demand through improvements in the marketing and sales processes.

This example illustrated the importance of starting by analyzing the big picture to determine where efforts should focus when creating P-DMAIC projects. Loosing sight of the big picture can lead to the ineffective utilization of resources and the suboptimization of processes.

## 10.4 Discussion

The implementation of traditional Total Quality Management (TQM) has often been implemented by dividing the system into processes and then optimizing the quality of each process. This approach is preferable to chasing symptoms; however, new problems can be created if the individual process is not considered in concert with other processes that it affects.

The theory of constraints presented by Goldratt (1992) focuses on reducing system bottlenecks as a means to continually improve the performance of the entire system. Rather than viewing the system in terms of discrete processes, TOC addresses the larger systematic picture as a chain or grid of interlinked chains. The performance of the weakest link determines the performance of the whole chain. According to Goldratt, the vast majority of constraints results from policies (e.g., rules, training, and other measures), while few constraints are physical (e.g., machines, facilities, people, and other tangible resources). For example, a large portion of highway road repair seems initially to be physically constrained by traffic flow. But the real constraint could also be government acquisition policy, which mandates the award of contracts to the lowest bidder. This drives contractors to the use of low-quality materials with shorter life in an effort to keep costs down and remain competitive.

> The theory of constraints presented focuses on reducing system bottlenecks as a means to continually improve the performance of the entire system. Rather than viewing the system in terms of discrete processes, TOC addresses the larger systematic picture as a chain or grid of interlinked chains.

TOC considers three dimensions of system performance in the following order: throughput (total sales revenues minus the total variable costs for producing a product or service), inventory (all the money a company invests in items it sells), and operating expense (money a company spends transforming inventory into throughput). Focus on these dimensions can lead a company to abandon traditional management cost accounting while at the same time causing an improvement in competitive price advantage.

## 10.5   Measures of TOC

Traditional financial measures (net profit, ROI, and cash flow) don't tell us what to do daily at the operational level. It is not easy for first or second line managers to decide how their actions might affect net profit, ROI, or cash flow. The TOC measures of throughput, inventory, and operating expense are more easily understood in relationship to operational decisions. With the IEE approach, we can view these as satellite-level metrics that drive project selection.

Throughput (T) as a TOC measure is the rate of generating money in an organization. This is a financial value-add metric which equates to revenues minus variable costs. Levels of measures/assessments are unit, product, and organization. Investment or inventory (I) as a TOC measure is money tied up within an organization. This includes capital assets, facilities, equipment, and materials. Operating expense (OE) is the money flowing out of system to generate throughput. This is the fixed expense or the overhead of the organization. These TOC metrics have the relationships described below:

$$\text{Return on Investment } = \frac{T{-}OE}{I}$$
$$\text{Net Profit} = T - OE$$
$$\text{Cash Flow (CF)} = T - OE \pm \Delta I$$

Throughput is limited by the system constraint. Operating expense is primarily generated by non-constraints. Using a TOC approach, focus is given to improve the overall system by making changes to the constraint.

## 10.6   Five Focusing Steps of TOC

The five focusing steps of TOC for addressing constraints (Schragenheim and Dettmer 2001) are:

1. Identify
2. Exploit
3. Subordinate
4. Elevate
5. Go back to step 1, but beware of the inertia

Step 1: Identify the system's constraint. Consider what is limiting the performance of the system. Determine whether the restraint is inside (resource or policy) or outside the system (market or supplier). Assess the difficulty of breaking the constraint. If the constraint can easily be broken, break it and then look for the next constraint. If it is hard to break the constraint, proceed to step 2.

Step 2: Decide how to exploit the system's constraint, where exploit means to get the most from the constraining element without additional investment. Consider what operational changes can be made to maximize productivity from the constraining element. For example, for a market demand constraint cater to the market to win more sales. If there is a resource constraint, determine the best approach to maximize its contribution to profit.

Step 3: After making a decision on how to exploit the system, subordinate everything else to that decision. This requires that other parts of the system be put in second place relative to their own measures of success. All nonconstraints are to be placed in a support role to the constraint, which can be difficult to accomplish. For example, if market demand is the only constraint, incoming orders should trigger the release of material. If there are no new orders entering the system, manufacturing managers often want to continue working so that their efficiencies remain high. For this situation, the material release process must be subordinated to the needs of the constraint.

Step 4: If the system constraint is broken by subordination, go back to step 1. If the system constraint is not broken, determine other ways to elevate the constraint, where elevate means to increase capacity. For example, if the constraint is internal, additional capacity for the resource could be achieved through acquiring more machines or people or the addition of overtime. If there is a market demand constraint (i.e., lack of sales), elevation might be achieved through an advertising campaign.

Step 5: Even when subordination does not break the constraint elevation will likely break it, unless there is a conscious effort to stop short of breaking it. After the subordinate or elevate steps are competed, step 1 needs to be repeated to determine the location of the new constraint. Sometimes a constraint moves not as a result of our intentional actions but because there is an environmental change. An example of this is the change in market demand for product mixes. One must not become complacent with their actions since inertia can change things. When a constraint moves, previous actions for subordination and elevation may no longer be the best solution. Other alternatives might need to be investigated.

# 10.7   IEE TOC Application and the Development of Strategic Plans

Theory of constraints (TOC) can be useful in helping organizations get out of the firefighting mode. TOC measures can be the satellite-level metrics that drive IEE projects. In lieu of attempting to drive improvements through traditional measures of capital utilization, growth, or revenue, a TOC satellite-level metric strategy would focus on throughput, investment/inventory, and operating expense.

Organizations can have satellite-level metrics, which are in alignment with

- 30,000-foot-level scorecard/dashboard operational metrics such as defective/defect Rates, lead time, waste, Days sales outstanding (DSO), customer satisfaction, on-time delivery, number of days from promise date, number of days from customer requested date, dimensional property, inventory, and headcount.
- A methodology to build strategic plans and then track how well results are achieved against this plan.
- The IEE project selection process.

Perhaps you have seen balance scorecard metrics for an organization presented as dashboard metrics. Dashboard metrics can present what the organization is doing at any point in time in the format of a dial. If the needle on the dial is within the green area, no action is to be taken. If the needle is in the yellow area, caution should be taken since the current response is near specification limits. If the needle is in the red region, corrective action should be taken since specification limits are not being met. Data presented in this manner tend to result in firefighting activities directed toward common cause, treating them as though they were special cause.

An IEE strategy using a TOC approach would be to track balance scorecard metrics using TOC satellite-level measures. These measures would lead to a strategy for improvement. Operational 30,000-foot-level control chart measures would then be created and tracked. IEE projects would be prioritized and then selected based upon a screening criteria to yield projects that have a high likelihood of success of achieving significant bottom-line and improved customer satisfaction benefits.

# 10.8   TOC Questions

We can use the following questions to help determine if local decisions are being made positively relative to overall system success TOC measures (Schragenheim, 2001)

Positive response will improve throughput

- Will the decision result in a better use of the worst constrained resource?
- Will it make full use of the worst constrained resource?
- Will it increase total sales?
- Will it speed up delivery to customers?
- Will it provide a characteristic of product or service that our competitors don't have?
- Will it win repeat business for us?
- Will it reduce scrap or rework?
- Will it reduce warranty or replacement costs?

Positive response will decrease inventory or investment

- Will we need fewer raw materials or purchased parts?
- Will we be able to keep less material on hand?
- Will it reduce work-in-process?
- Will we need fewer capital facilities or equipment to do the same work?

Positive response will decrease operating expense

- Will overhead go down?
- Will payments to vendors decrease?
- Will we be able to divert some people to do other throughput-generating work?

The TOC described by Goldratt (1992) presents a system thinking process where the focus is on the system's bottlenecks. This results in continual improvement of the performance of the entire system. Rather than viewing the system in terms of discrete processes, TOC addresses the larger systematic picture as a chain or grid of inter-linked chains. The performance of the whole chain is determined by the performance of its weakest link.

## 10.9   Applying IEE

TOC applies not only to manufacturing but also to transactional processes. TOC can identify bottlenecks in health care, insurance, financial, and other industries. Metrics at the 30,000-foot-level and/or satellite-level provide a good view of TOC overall performance. Pareto charts and the other statistical analysis tools described in this volume provide the means to examine the system systematically with the intent to identify where inventory, cycletime, defects, and other issues reside. This identification can lead to improvement opportunities.

## 10.10   Exercises

1.  Describe any bottlenecks that you have in the time it takes for you to go either to work or to school; i.e., from planned arise time to work/school arrival time.
2.  Describe a process where projects are selected that does not address potential bottleneck issues.

# 11

# E-DMAIC—Analyze Phase: Lean Tools and Assessments

## 11.1  E-DMAIC Roadmap Component

Previous chapters of the enterprise analyze phase described strategic analysis, financials, and TOC. An analyze phase E-DMAIC checklist item described in Section 8.2 was Lean tools. This chapter describes the application of Lean to gain insight to where improvement efforts should focus.

Womack and Jones (1996) state that lean thinking can be summarized in five principles: precisely specify *value* by specific product, identify the *value stream* for each product, make value *flow* without interruptions, let the customer pull value from the producer, and pursue perfection. The intent of this chapter is to stimulate Lean enterprise-system improvement thinking for both manufacturing and transactional processes.

The next few sections contain more detail on this evolution (Womack et al. 1990) and enterprise Lean thinking. The referenced examples are primarily manufacturing; however, the concepts apply equally to transactional processes. These sections will be followed by Lean thinking as part of IEE.

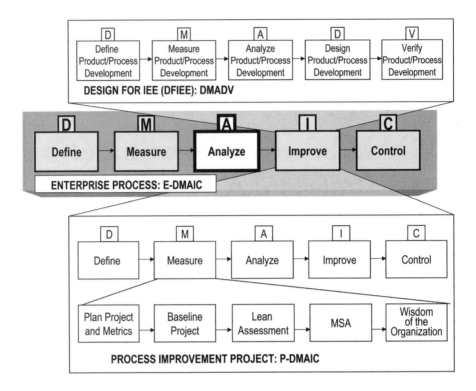

Examples 12.1 and 12.3 illustrate the application of Lean in the E-DMAIC roadmap. Execution details for the described Lean tools are in Volume III. This chapter describes both the current and future state value stream map; however, quantifiable benefits from the future state map show up in the E-DMAIC improve phase.

## 11.2   IEE Enterprise Process Roadmap

The four goals of a Lean Enterprise process are to improve quality, eliminate waste, reduce lead time, and reduce total costs MacInnes (2002), where:

- Quality examines how well products and/or services address the wants and needs of customers.
- Waste includes activities that consume resources, time, or space but is not value added relative to meeting customer requirements. The seven types of waste discussed later in

this chapter are overproduction, waiting, transportation, inventory, over-processing, motion, and defects.

- Lead time is the total time for completion of a series of process steps; e.g., customer order receipt to customer payment. Lead time consists of the cycle time, which is the task time completion of a single transaction; batch delay time, which is the wait time for other transactions within a batch; and process delay time, which is the time batches wait from the completion of one operation to the start of another operation.
- Both direct and indirect costs comprise total costs. The balance of product pricing and of operating costs is essential for an organization's success. Cost reduction involves focusing on the reduction of organizational waste and lead times.

All these measures need to be an integral part of the value chain and its performance metrics.

The techniques discussed in this chapter are applicable not only in the E-DMAIC analyze phase for project identification but also P-DMAIC. This chapter describes both the current and future state value stream map; however, quantifiable benefits from the future state map show up in the E-DMAIC improve phase.

Lean methods can assess the operation of the factory, supply chain, and transactional processes with an emphasis on the reduction of wasteful activities like waiting, transportation, material hand-offs, inventory, and overproduction. Lean co-locates the process in sequential order and, in so doing, emphasizes the reduction of variation associated with manufacturing routings, material handling, storage, lack of communication, and batch production.

The application of Lean techniques can reduce inventory value by reducing WIP, which can be tracked as a 30,000-foot-level scorecard/dashboard metric. This can be accomplished by focusing on smaller job sizes and quicker processing times. By decreasing WIP at the operational level, inventory is turned over more rapidly; i.e., inventory turns are increased. In a transactional process, WIP could be the number of uncompleted transactions in a process.

In IEE, the improvement needs of satellite-level and 30,000-foot-level scorecard/dashboard metrics (*Y*s or KPOVs) pull for the appropriate Lean and Six Sigma application tools. From a 30,000-foot-level view of a KPOV, a black belt can pick the right tool for the right situation when working a project. When a particular 30,000-foot-level metric involves the lead time or WIP of a process, Lean manufacturing tools would be very likely candidates to consider within this improvement process, along with other appropriate Six Sigma tools.

## 11.3   Resource Utilization

One view of Lean production is that Lean is an innovative system for making things. To describe Lean thinking, let's compare Lean with craft and mass production alternatives.

In craft production, highly skilled workers met customer desires by using simple tools to create customized products. These skilled workers gathered the parts and tools necessary to do the job, making adjustments or repairs as needed. In the early 1900s, these skilled workers might perform the entire complex fitting and assembly of an entire automobile and then check the completed vehicle before transferring it to the shipping department.

Crafted products can include the creation of fine paintings, furniture, and automobiles; however, most potential customers will consider the accompanying product-specialization price tag to be excessive. The per-unit craft production costs are basically the same whether one unit is built or one hundred thousand units are built. Because of this, additional customers will not be enticed through price declines to purchase the product as the result of fundamental price-reductions resulting from the spreading of production costs over a large volume of produced units.

Mass production on the other extreme uses narrow-range skilled professionals to design products made by unskilled or semiskilled workers who watch over expensive, single-purpose machines. In Ford's early mass production a line-worker might simply put a wheel on the automobile. The line-worker did not need to procure/tools, order/parts, conduct quality inspections, or repair equipment. The line-worker's only job was to do his assigned task without understanding any other job.

This mass-production system created the need for newly created support staff that included quality engineers, industrial engineers, production engineers, maintenance engineers, house cleaning and reworks specialists. Manufacturing engineers designed the equipment, industrial engineers, among other things, addressed assembly operations, and product engineers designed/

engineered the product. In this environment, it was understood that the line worker would not volunteer any information.

These machines create standardized products in high volume, where machinery costs are high and intolerant to disruption. Because of these mass-production characteristics, many buffers are created in supplies, workers, and space to ensure smooth production. New product change-over in a mass production system is costly; hence, standard designs are produced as long as possible. This all leads to lower consumer costs but at the expense of low consumer product variety. In addition, workers often find their work boring and dispiriting.

In contrast, the Lean producer integrates the beneficial aspects of craft and mass productions. Lean avoids the high costs of crafting and the rigidity of mass production. Lean employs multi-skilled workers at all organizational levels and utilizes highly flexible increasingly automated machinery to create a large variety in varying product volumes.

The term Lean describes a system that uses less resource than mass production; e.g., less human effort, new-product development time, manufacturing/office space, and tool investment. Much Lean focus is also given to inventory reduction, error-proofing, and increased flexibility. This focus enhances an organization's flexibility to meet customer changing needs better.

A Lean implementation can change how people work and think. In Lean, a key objective is to push responsibility down the organization ladder. This responsibility means that front-line workers can enjoy more individual-work freedom with the downside of being held responsible for their costly mistakes. Front-line workers can find their jobs more productive and challenging.

## 11.4  Origins of Toyota Production System (TPS)

The Toyoda family founded the Toyota Motor Company in 1937. After a turbulent beginning, in 1946 the company found itself in a depression and a worker revolt. The result of this was a compromise, where employees receive a lifetime employment guarantee. In addition, compensation was steeply graded by seniority, rather than specific job functions, and tied to company profitability through bonus payments. Employees also agreed to be flexible in work assignments and actively promote company interests by initiating improvements, rather than just responding to problems.

The implications of this settlement were huge. The work force was now as much a short-term fixed cost as machinery and, in the long term, workers had even more significant fixed-cost implications. In addition to utilizing workers to accomplish the task at hand, it now made a lot of sense to enhance worker skills continually and benefit from their knowledge and experience.

As a young engineer, Eiji Toyoda spent three months studying Ford's Detroit Rouge plant in 1950, the largest and most efficient manufacturing facility in the world. His conclusions were that there were improvement opportunities for the system. Later, Eiji Toyoda and Taiichi Ohno, a production genius, concluded that mass production would not work in Japan. This was the beginning of what is now know as the Toyota production system (TPS).

After repeated post-war visits to Detroit, Ohno concluded that there was much muda, the Japanese term for waste, throughout the process. The process contained much wasted effort, materials, and time. Ohno also concluded that only the assembly workers actually added value to the automobile. In addition, he believed that the assembly worker could do much of the support and process improvement work since they were most familiar with the process.

Ohno observed that the typical western practice required hundreds of stamping presses to make all of the parts in car and truck bodies, while Ohno's capital budget would only allow the entire car to be stamped from a few press lines. The development of simple die-change techniques and the frequent changing of die addressed this problem; e.g., every two to three hours versus two or three months. He used rollers to move dies in and out of position and simple adjustment mechanisms. In addition, he came up with the idea of letting production workers perform the task since they were idle during the changeover anyway. This was the origin of the single-minute exchange of die (SMED) concept.

To improve the process, Ohno created teams with a group lead who was not the foreman. The group was then given a portion of the assembly process and told to work together on how best to perform the necessary operations. The team lead would not only coordinate the team but also do assembly operations as well and fill in for absent workers.

Ohno assigned the team house keeping tasks, minor repair, and quality checks. In addition, after team processes were running smoothly, he allotted team time for collective suggesting process improvements. This continuous, incremental improvement process in collaboration with industrial engineers was called kaizen in Japanese.

In addition, Ohno reasoned that the mass-production practice of passing errors down the line in order to keep the line running caused errors to multiply. This practice could result in an enormous amount of rectification work. Mass-production workers believed that any action that they did to stop the line would be cause for discipline and that these errors would be later identified and reworked. In mass-production plants, line stoppage decisions were the responsibility of senior line management.

In mass-production plants, problems were treated as random events, which led to simple repairs and the hope that the problem did not resurface. In contrast, Ohno instituted the five why's problem-solving system (see Appendix Section D.15). In this system, line workers were taught to trace every error systematically to its cause and then to devise a fix so that the problem did not reoccur.

This TPS system was known as Jidoka or autonomation. Jidoka is a term used in Lean meaning automation with a human touch. This approach applies the following four principles:

- Detect the abnormality.
- Stop.
- Fix or correct the immediate condition.
- Investigate the root cause and install a countermeasure.

The conversion to a system of immediate problem identification and root-cause rectification can lead to a dramatic increase in line stoppages, which can be very discouraging. However, as experience is gained in identifying problems and tracking these problems to their source, the number of errors can lead to a steep decline. In Toyota plants where every worker can stop the line, up-time approaches 100 percent. In contrast, plants where only the line manager can stop the line, stoppage frequently occurs to resolve material supply and coordination; i.e., a 90% up-time can be considered good management.

In addition, a large amount of rework still occurs at the end of the line. However, in Ohno's system the amount of pre-ship rework dropped, and the quality of shipped cars steadily improved. This occurred since even the most diligent quality inspection will not detect all defects in today's complex products.

Ohno executed systems thinking. IEE integrates this system thinking with a structured measurement and high-level improvement system that applies in both manufacturing and transactional processes.

## 11.5   Supply Chain

Ford in the early 1900s created a complete vertical integration system where everything connected to the production of automobiles from basic raw material was handled in-house. This approach permitted less dependence upon supplier quality relative to closer tolerances and tighter delivery schedules.

In time, two fundamental supplier-sourcing philosophies evolved. In the so-called visible hand methodology, raw materials, services, etc. were obtained through internal operating divisions that were coordinated by senior executives. In contrast, an invisible hand strategy leads to purchasing parts and services from independent firms where there was no financial relationship to the buyer. In this system, transactions were to be passed on price, delivery time, and quality with no expectations of long-term relationships between buyer and seller. It was argued that the visible hand was essential for corporations to operation predictability; however, this vertical integration created vast bureaucracy with no obvious solutions.

In vehicle assemblies, only about 15 percent of the total manufacturing processes involve major components. The bulk of the process involves engineering and fabrication of over 10,000 parts and assembling these into perhaps 100 major components. It is a challenge for process coordination to ensure that everything comes together on time with high quality and low cost. Under mass production, the initial intent was for the integration of the entire production system into one huge, bureaucratic system driven from the top. Automobile manufacturers later adopted varying degrees of integration, where in-house production typically ranged from 25 to 70 percent.

At Ford and GM, central engineering staffs designed most of the 10,000-plus vehicle parts and component systems. Outside firms and internal division suppliers were then asked to bid, where there was a specified quality; e.g., maximum number of defective parts per 1000. The low bidder was then rewarded the business. For part categories such as tires and batteries and specialized technology areas such as engine computers, the bidding process depended upon price, quality, and delivery. Car makers frequently switched suppliers on short notice.

Ohno and Toyota consider the frequent make-or-buy decisions at mass-production firms to be largely irrelevant relative to the question of how the assemblers and suppliers worked together. What was important was smooth coordination to reduce costs and improve quality through whatever formal and legal relationships were needed.

Ohno and others saw many problems with the current system. Supplier organizations which worked to drawings had little or no incentive to suggest improvements based on their own experience. In addition, there was no system for suppliers who offered their own standardized designs to make implementation suggestions, since they had no information about the rest of the vehicle, which was often considered proprietary.

In addition, organizations played their suppliers against each other searching for the lowest bidder. This stifled horizontal information flow between suppliers. The assembler might ensure that supplier profit margins were low but not work with them to decrease production costs steadily through process improvements. The assembler knew little about its supplier's processes; hence, improving quality was difficult except through the establishment of acceptable defect levels.

Finally, coordinating day-to-day part-flow in the supply system was a problem. Inflexibility of supplier tools and erratic orders from assemblers responding to market-demand shifts resulted in suppliers' carrying a large amount of one part type before changing the production machine to produce another part type. This policy led to high inventory costs and the risk of producing many defective products, which were not discovered until assembly, which might be a long time after the parts were produced. The supplier did not meet a customer need and risked losing the contract.

To address these issues, Toyota in the 1950s began establishing a new Lean-production supply-chain approach for procuring components. A first step was to organize suppliers into functional tiers in relationship to the assembler. Each tier was assigned different responsibilities. The responsibility of first-tier suppliers was to be an integral part of the overall development process. They would be instructed to develop, for example, an electrical system that would work harmoniously with other systems. These suppliers were given only performance specifications and physical dimensions. These suppliers then delivered prototypes for testing. Satisfactory prototype assessments led to orders.

First-tier suppliers were encouraged to collaborate on what could be done to improve the design process. Since each of these suppliers specialized in one component type, information sharing was not an issue and was mutually beneficial. First-tier suppliers then formed their own second-tier suppliers who had expertise in process engineering and operations. Since second-tier suppliers were specialists and did not compete on a specific component type, the sharing of information on manufacturing techniques was prevalent and beneficial.

Toyota had neither a vertical integration of suppliers nor a completely independent company relationship. Instead, Toyota created quasi-independent first-tier supply companies from both previous in-house supply operations and previous independent companies. In this relationship, Toyota retained or established a fraction of the company equity.

In addition, Toyota instituted personnel sharing with supplier group firms either by lending them personnel to deal with demand peaks or by transferring senior management personnel when mutually beneficial. This management system led to a separate book-accounting system, rather than the profit centers of many vertically integrated mass-production centers, where reported results can be questionable. Toyota also encouraged these suppliers to perform considerable work for other assemblers and other industry firms. This outside work could generate significantly higher profit margins.

Ohno developed a new way to have day-to-day coordination of part flow in the supply system. This just-in-time (JIT) system is called kanban. The basic idea is to simply transition all suppliers and plants that manufacture parts into one large machine. This system dictates that parts would only be produced at each previous step to the next step's immediate demand. Ohno used the containers carrying the parts to the next step as the trigger signal for making more parts, since containers that had no more parts were sent back to the previous step.

This kanban system was difficult to implement in that it eliminated practically all inventories and meant that even one small part problem could stop the whole system. Ohno thought this was the strength of the system in that all safety nets were removed, and focus would be given on problem anticipation before the occurrence of a catastrophic event.

Collaboration is a very important aspect of successful supply-chain execution. The technology of today provides increased data usage opportunities in this collaboration. We can see and use information that had not been visible in the past to improve on time delivery and reduce inventory.

## 11.6 Product Development and Engineering

The process of engineering a complex system such as today's automobiles requires a broad range of skills. It is easy to make a mistake in organizing the process so that the desired results are not achieved.

Mass-production companies work to solve this complexity by finely dividing labor among many engineers with their variety of specialties. Often the best derived solution was using a product-development team with a leader/coordinator, whose members reported to a senior executive of their individual technical specialty. With this approach, job advancement was typically made within their specialties until they might reach the position of chief product engineer. This was the point when ensuing discussions to any disagreements between product engineers, manufacturing-process engineers, and industrial engineers led to the resolutions of issues.

By contrast, in Toyota the decision was made early that product engineering inherently contained both process and industrial engineering. Strong leaders then led cross-functional teams that contained all relevant expertise. The career path structure was framed so that strong team players received the awards. This Lean engineering significantly impacted productivity, product quality, and customer-changing-demand responsiveness.

In the early 1900s, Ford experienced large global expansion. Ford's mass-production system of focusing on producing one standard product was not well suited for all world markets. Because of gasoline prices, Europeans vocalized their desire for smaller cars, which Ford did not want to supply. This phenomenon was only the beginning. By the 1960s, consumers were placing changing demands on their cars and upon changing vehicle technology. Almost everyone was dependent upon the automobile for daily activities.

At the same time, vehicle features made automobiles quite impossible to repair. By the 1980s, automobile-repair skills of the past were not very beneficial for problems like an engine-management computer failure. The increased reliability from the systems that Toyota introduced made their products attractive to consumers.

By 1990, Toyota offered world-wide consumers as many options as General Motors, even though the company was half its size. Toyota needs half the time and effort required by a mass-producer such as General Motors to design a car.

## 11.7 Customer Interaction

By the 1920s, Ford had created small, financially independent dealers who maintained a large inventory of cars and trucks. Relationships between the factory and dealer were usually strained. The factory often tried to force cars on dealers to smooth production. Dealer to customer relationships were also strained because dealers continually adjusted prices and made deals to adjust demand with supply, trying to maximize profit.

In time, Toyota worked to create a sales network similar to its supplier group with a focus on establishing great customer relationship. The Toyota Motor Sales Company built a distributor network where some were wholly owned by Toyota and in others Toyota had a small equity stake. Effort was given to create a life-long relationship among the assembler, dealer, and buyer. To accomplish this, they worked at placing the dealer in the production system and involving the buyer in the development process.

The dealer became the first step of the kanban system. Toyota gradually stopped building cars for unknown buyers and switched to a build-to-order system. Dealers sent orders for pre-sold cars to the factory for delivery to specific customers in two to three weeks. Ohno's product system was adept at building products for specific orders; however, it could not accommodate large peaks or valleys in total demand or abrupt shifts between products that could not be addressed with the same tools.

To accomplish order sequencing so that there was a relative constant order demand, the sales staff did not wait in the show-room for orders. Instead they used a massive database accumulated over the years on households and their previous buying preferences to target efforts to the most likely buyer candidates.

Mass-producers' approach to obtaining voice of the customer was to conduct survey research of randomly selected buyers, who probably have little brand loyalty. However, Toyota went directly to its existing customer base in planning new products. Toyota worked to treat customers as members of the Toyota family and created brand loyalty.

## 11.8 Thinking Small

The general principle is to use the smallest machine possible consistent with quality requirements (Bicheno 2004). Several smaller machines instead of one bigger, faster machine allows for flexibility.

Schonberger (1987) offers excellent advice in what he terms Frugal Manufacturing. In essence:

- Get the most out of conventional equipment and present facilities before implementing large-scale automation projects.
- Keep control over manufacturing strategy rather than turn it over to newly hired engineers and computer technicians or to a turnkey automation company.
- Build up your capability to modify, customize, and simplify your machines. Do not expect commercially available general-purpose equipment to be right for your products. The ability to modify continually is becoming increasingly important as materials, technologies, quality standards and products change and improve.
- Approach bigger, faster machines and production lines with caution. High capability and cost tend to dictate production policies, and immobility and inflexibility do not accommodate shortening product life cycles.

## 11.9 Demand Management

In general, a smoother demand produces better flow (Bicheno 2004). Demand cannot be entirely smooth; however, we should work so that we do not make the situation worse by our actions. Described below are a few considerations for internal demand and external/supply chain demand, where we note that it is equally important for a company to have a supply management system that is based on the demand.

External Demand Management

- Avoid whenever possible quantity discounts or monthly sales incentives. Instead, provide regular-order discounts or regular-order incentives.
- Offer variety only at the last possible moment.
- Create a build-to-order policy with trigger points.
- Utilize yield management techniques like airlines, where early flight bookings get a better rate than late bookings.
- Offer customers free or bargain upgrades to help smooth variety and shift inventory.
- Manage, report, discuss, and setup responsibility for demand management, especially in sales and marketing. Understand the impact between "everyday low prices" and promotions.
- Create measures that encourage the right behaviors; e.g., avoid games where inventories are run up so that quarterly statement looks more favorable.
- Work at creating open communication between supply-chain partners.

> Avoid whenever possible quantity discounts or monthly sales incentives. Instead, provide regular-order discounts or regular-order incentives.

Internal Demand Management

- Aggregate similar erratic-demand subassemblies, which collectively may experience more repeatable demand.
- Use supermarkets (see Glossary) to stabilize manufacturing operations.
- Utilize a single pacemaker (see Glossary), preferably in the whole supply chain.
- Reduce changeover times to increase effectiveness of customer pull.
- Assess demand predictability at 30,000-foot-level so that common cause variations are not treated as though they were special cause.
- Schedule for under capacity to ensure that the production target is met; i.e, allow a buffer period for catching up if problems occur.
- Understand that takt time is partly under the manufacturer's control since it is a function of both customer demand

and available production time. Also, avoid reacting to customer-demand changes.

- Prioritize regular orders, filtering out erratic orders by placing them in a lower slot with their own frequency. Avoid large orders disrupting the regular schedule; ask customers if a large order can be spread over a longer period of time.
- Create distributor incentives to encourage smooth demand.
- Strive for frequent small-batch, single-vehicle, multi-location deliveries, as opposed to the same number of vehicles delivering large loads less frequently.
- Avoid temptation of overproduction, even though things seem to be going well.
- Institute a vision of regular, smooth demand. Identify and resolve barriers for this occurrence.

## 11.10  Waste Identification and Prevention

If we consider that waste is being generated anywhere work is accomplished, we can create a vehicle through which organizations can identify and reduce it. The goal is total elimination of waste through the process of defining waste, identifying its source, planning for its elimination, and establishing permanent control to prevent reoccurrence.

Muda is the Japanese term for waste. Seven elements to consider for the elimination of muda are correction, overproduction, processing, conveyance, inventory, motion, and waiting. Initiatives to consider for reducing waste include the 5S method that focuses on improvements through sorting (cleaning up), storage (organizing), shining (cleaning), standardize (standardizing), and sustaining (training and discipline). Since 5S is a Lean improvement vehicle, it is described in more detail as part of the IEE project execution roadmap improvement phase.

In the financials of a business, inventory appears as an asset, which can lead to the wrong activities. In practice, however, inventory is a detriment to business interests for the following reasons:

- Space: Wasted space and hidden cost for area maintenance
- Material handling: Moving stock around or sorting to get the right part/transaction
- Investment: Investment cost that does not earn interest

- Hidden operations: Difficult to see what is being produced because of the stacking of parts
- Quality: Hidden rejects in inventory
- Batched parts: Promote further excessive production batching
- Equipment: Large inventories hide frequent maintenance emergencies

## 11.11   Principles of Lean

Companies often try to emulate the Toyota production system (TPS) by conducting Kaizen events and other improvement activities on a project-by-project basis. These improvement activities can be beneficial; however, what is often missing in these deployments is the big-picture application of Lean concepts. This is what the TPS system does very well and is often not addressed in Lean deployments.

To illustrate this point, consider the refinishing of a piece of furniture. Someone might start by polishing a handle then sanding a leg of the furniture. Much effort can be spent using this approach; however, after much work the furniture still would probably not look very good. An alternative is to start by sanding the whole furniture with course sand paper and then move to finer grit sandpaper over time.

Let's consider that furniture represents the business. It has been my experience that in most Lean deployments focus is given to improving various components of the business; i.e., in the furniture analogy, sanding a leg and polishing a handle. With this approach, similar to the piece of furniture, the business might not look much better after a lot of work.

To effectively move toward creating a TPS system, organizations need to start with the big picture relative to Lean tool application; i.e., start sanding the whole piece of furniture with course sandpaper. Since this Volume is not just about teaching the tools but also the thought process, I am including in the next few sections many details about Lean tool applications. I have done this to illustrate how these tools can be used at the system level to improve the business as a whole.

To reiterate, Lean techniques apply at both the project and enterprise level. The next few sections provide many details of these techniques as part of the E-DMAIC system, which can be used to identify focus areas for potential P-DMAIC and DMADV project executions.

Earlier in this volume the principles of Lean were described as: (1) define customer value; (2) focus on the value stream; (3) make value flow; (4) let the customer pull product; and (5) pursue perfection relentlessly. Lean is an answer to a customer need or desire. The product or service is provided in a timely manner and at an appropriate price. You or I don't determine value; value is in the eyes of the customer.

Within Lean, we identify the value stream. This might be a process or series of process steps from concept to launch to production, order to delivery to disposition, or raw materials to customer receipt to disposal. It consists of steps that add value to a product. Within Lean, we eliminate steps that do not add value, where a product can be tangible or intangible.

When working on the product/service, we start at receipt of customer request and end at delivery to customer. We strive for no interruptions. That is, we strive for no muda. We work to avoid batch processing and strive for one-piece flow. We want a pattern of processing that accomplishes smooth flow through the process without stacking of material between process steps. We want to minimize WIP and develop standard work processes.

We strive to have just-in-time workflow, which yields exactly the right product in the exactly the right place at exactly the right time. With this approach, nothing is produced until the downstream customer requests it. An application example is a made-to-order sandwich shop versus a fast food hamburger shop that makes a batch of hamburgers in anticipation of customer demand.

Waste is anything other than the minimum number of people, the minimum amount of effort, material, information, and equipment necessary to add value to the product. We will now consider the following attributes of waste: value added, required non-value added, manufacturing waste, waste in design, and waste in administration. We will also consider what we might do to hunt for waste.

> Waste is anything other than the minimum number of people, the minimum amount of effort, material, information, and equipment necessary to add value to the product.

When there is a value-added action, the customer recognizes its importance and is willing to pay for it. Value-added actions transform the product in form, fit, or function, where the product could be information or physical product. Work is done right the first time. Required non-value-added activities do not increase customer-defined value. However, the activity may be a required business necessity (e.g., accounting), employee necessity (e.g., payroll), or process necessity (e.g., inspection).

Manufacturing waste includes:

- Overproduction: Making more than you need
- Waiting: People or product waiting
- Transportation: Moving materials
- Inventory: Having more than you need
- Overprocessing: Taking unnecessary steps
- Motion: People moving
- Defects: Making it wrong, fixing it

Waste in design includes:

- Overproduction: Un-launched designs
- Waiting: Waiting for signatures, approvals, data
- Transportation: Handoffs to other organizations
- Inventory: Backlogs, outdated designs
- Overprocessing: Approval routings, excessive analysis
- Motion: Obtaining forms, paperwork
- Defects: Incorrect drawings, data

Waste in administration and transactional processes include:

- Overproduction: Excessive reporting
- Waiting: Waiting for signatures, approvals, data
- Transportation: Handoffs to other organizations
- Inventory: Backlogs
- Overprocessing: Approval routings, signature requirements
- Motion: Obtaining forms, paperwork
- Defects: Incorrect data, missing data

Traditionally within Lean, an organization might form hunting parties to identify waste. With this approach, an individual can use a notepad to identify and record waste in his/her assigned area, sharing the findings with the team.

In IEE, the following Lean metrics, when tracked at the 30,000-foot-level, can give insight to where the overall enterprise can best target its improvement efforts:

- Inventory
  - Finished goods (FG)
  - Work in progress (WIP)
  - Raw material (RM)
- Scrap
- Headcount
- Product changeover time
- Setup time
- Distance traveled
- Yield
- Cycle time (C/T): In Lean, C/T is considered to be how often a part or transaction is completed (time for one piece). Also, duration of operator time for the completion of work before repeating the steps.
- Average completion rate (ACR): Number of things completed per unit of time.
- Takt time: Customer demand rate (your available work time per shift divided by customer demand rate per shift). Metric is expressed in units of time to produce one unit of product.
- Lead time (L/T): Time for one piece or transaction to move completely through a process or value stream to the customer
- Value-added time (VA): Work that a customer is willing to pay for
- Inventory turns: Annual cost of goods sold/average value of inventories during the year
- Little's law: Lead time = WIP (# units)/ACR (# units/time)
- Process cycle efficiency = value-added time divided by lead time

Another aspect of Lean is the visual factory, which involves management by sight. The creation of a visual factory involves the collection and display of real-time information to the entire workforce at all times. Work cell bulletin boards and other easily seen media might report information about orders, production schedules, quality, delivery performance, and financial health of business.

Continuous flow manufacturing (CFM) within Lean consists of the efficient utilization of operations and machines to build parts. Non-value-added activities in the operation are eliminated. Flexibility is a substitute for work-in-process inventory. A product focus is established in all areas of operation. Through CFM, organizations have simplified manufacturing operation into product or process flows, organized operations so that there is similarity between days, and established flow or lead times.

Within an IEE roadmap, Lean tools should be considered if the 30,000-foot-level scorecard/dashboard metric ($Y$ variable or KPOV) implies the need for improved workflow; for example, the time it takes to complete a task or reduce WIP. In Appendix D, Lean tools are described that can be used in both the enterprise analyze phase assessment and process improvement project execution. Tools included in this appendix are process observation, logic flow map, spaghetti diagram, cause-and-effect diagram, and the why-why diagram or five whys/fault tree analysis.

> Within an IEE roadmap, Lean tools should be considered if the 30,000-foot-level scorecard/dashboard metric (Y variable or KPOV) implies the need for improved workflow; for example, the time it takes to complete a task or reduce WIP.

## 11.12 Enterprise Lean Assessment

As Yogi Berra, retired baseball player and later team manager, said, "You can observe a lot by watching." This Yogiism might sound silly, but it is sure applicable to business and its improvement. Similarly, a first step to understand a process is to observe it.

Process observation involves walking the actual process while taking notes to describe what is actually occurring. This step-by-step documentation includes a description, distance from last step, estimated task time, observations, and return rate. In the Appendix, both the observation worksheet in Table D.5 and the standardized work chart (or standard work sheet) in Table D.7 can become the template for this documentation. A link in the overall enterprise value chain, as illustrated in Figure 7.5, is a potential repository for standardized work charts.

Observations during process assessments could be summarized and/or compared by simply counting the number of steps, times work is transferred, or times work is picked up or put down.

Table 11.1 summarizes Lean focus opportunities for the identification of targeted areas to improve the value-chain performance

**Table 11.1** Lean Principles

| Workplace | People | Systems |
|---|---|---|
| ◆ Workplace organization | ◆ People effectiveness | ◆ Workstation tool reliability |
| ◆ Standardized work | ◆ Quality at the source | ◆ Cellular flow |
| ◆ Visual controls | | ◆ Batch reduction or elimination |
| | | ◆ Pull versus push systems |
| | | ◆ Point of use systems |

metrics. Upon completion of this observation, the Lean assessment matrix shown in Appendix Section D.6 can provide a prioritization of improvement focus area opportunities. This same assessment is suggested in the P-DMAIC Lean assessment phase. I will now elaborate on each Lean principle area.

The workplace should be organized. It should be a neat, clean, and safe environment with an arrangement that provides specific locations for everything with the elimination of anything that is not required. Materials should be stored close to where they are used.

The workplace should have standardized work. Everyone in operations should follow the best known sequence. This best known sequence involves deviation detection from standards with timely resolution, ideally in real time. These deviations include product defects (e.g., quality, cost, delivery, inventory, and regulatory compliance), human errors, and abnormal conditions (e.g., equipment, safety, or general business conditions). Standardization is not easy. Organizations often have difficulty allotting the time to standardize, and even if they do, sustaining the standardization can be very difficult. Utilization of standardization work charts such as the one shown in the Appendix Section D.7 can be beneficial in describing what is being done and in giving insight to what should be done to improve.

In the workplace, visual controls signals provide immediate understanding of situations and/or conditions. These controls need to be simple, efficient, self-regulated, and worker-managed. Examples include schedule/status boards, color-coded files, and good directional signals.

People are an important ingredient to the success of an organization. The effective use of people and of their talent is essential. For this to occur, highly specific jobs need the flexibility of team-task rotation. Team members need to be cross-trained and multi-skilled so that they can work many operations in multiple areas. People need to be given high responsibility and authority.

Organizations need to create a quality-at-the-source discipline. People need to be certain that high-quality information and/or products are passed on to the next area. Adequate inspection tools need to be provided, along with visual tools that demonstrate acceptable standards. Systems need to have workstation tool reliability. Operations' tools and equipment need to be efficient and effective. Computer system response time needs to be good, and tool down time needs to be minimal.

Systems that have cellular flow can be very beneficial. The physical linkage of people and of supporting hardware/software in the most efficient and effective combination minimizes waste and maximizes value-add activities.

Batch systems can cause a large amount of WIP. Procedures that reduce or eliminate batching can be very beneficial. Pull systems can yield very large benefits over push systems. Pull systems control the flow of resources over time based on rules and system status. Push systems that are based on schedules, forecasts, or when time is available to perform activities should be avoided. It is also very desirable to create systems that are available where needed; i.e., point-of-use systems.

The above points can provide insight to where focus should be given when assessing an overall enterprise and initiating a process improvement project. The project Lean assessment matrix, as shown in Appendix Table D.6, can help guide this assessment.

Another approach to identify improvement opportunities is to videotape an operation, play back the recording, and document sequence times through work element. This document could follow the combination work table format in Appendix Table D.8.

Analysis of these work times can lead to effective focused improvement efforts.

## 11.13   Example 11.1: Takt Time

As noted earlier, takt time is customer demand rate. That is, the available work time per shift divided by customer demand rate per shift. This metric is expressed in units of time to produce one unit of product.

Determine the takt time, given the following:

- 1000 parts or transactions per day; i.e., customer requirements, not capability
- 8 hour shifts

- Two 15 minute breaks per shift
- 2 shifts per day

$$\text{Takt time} = \frac{(8.0\,\text{hr.} - .50\,\text{hr.}) \times 60\,\text{min.}/\text{hr.} \times 60\,\text{sec.}/\text{min.} \times 2\,\text{shifts}/\text{day}}{1000\,\text{transactions}/\text{day}}$$

$$= 54\,\text{sec. per transaction}$$

The comparison of takt time to production capacity can highlight when either excess or insufficient process capacity exists. Takt time is important since it should be used to set the tempo of the organization.

## 11.14 Little's Law

Little's law is:

$$\text{Lead time} = \frac{\text{WIP}}{\text{ACR}}$$

where ACR = average completion rate.

This equation quantifies the average length of time it takes to complete any work item or work items (lead time) from the amount of work that is waiting to be completed (WIP) and the average completion rate (transactions per day or week completed).

This relationship is more useful than one might initially think. Consider that we would like to get the lead time or average delivery time, but often it is very difficult to track individual transactions through all the process steps and then average these values.

For example, the average duration to compete an insurance claim could be determined by dividing the number of claims in the overall system (WIP) by the average completion rate; i.e., average number of claims completed in a given period of time.

## 11.15 Example 11.2: Little's Law

Determine the average wait time at a call center when, for a given day at 10 random times, the number of people observed waiting on hold averaged 12. For the same 24-hour day, 1000 calls were received.

$$\text{ACR} = 1000/24 = 41.67 \text{ calls/hour}$$

Lead time = WIP/ACR = 12/41.67 = 0.288 hrs. or 17.3 min.

## 11.16   Identification of Process Improvement Focus Areas for Projects

Examine the E-DMAIC 30,000-foot-level scorecard/dashboard value-chain metrics collectively to gain insight to project improvement opportunity areas for quality improvement, waste elimination, lead time reduction, and/or total costs reduction. For waste elimination, overproduction focus can be a most beneficial starting point, since this is often the largest waste source.

Quality improvement assessment

1.  Report-out 30,000-foot-level scorecard/dashboard metric from the value chain that is being assessed for improvement opportunities.
2.  Describe both internal and external customer wants and needs; i.e., expectations and requirements.
3.  Conduct a gap analysis of differences between products and services offerings relative to customer wants and needs. This assessment can address the 30,000-foot-level process capability/performance metric (see Glossary) relative to desired levels along with product/process design effectiveness.
4.  Identify high impact areas of the business that have the most leverage for reducing the gap between performance and customer needs.
5.  Compile and prioritize process improvement opportunities using a cause-and-effect matrix (see Appendix Section D.10).
6.  Combine the cause-and-effect matrix items from this business area with other business areas.
7.  Determine a potential improvement goal for the 30,000-foot-level scorecard/dashboard metric.
8.  Describe resulting IEE process improvement quality projects along with other IEE projects.

Waste elimination assessment

1.  Within IEE, general waste reduction areas are created through the initialization and institutionalized system, where individuals propose a business process improvement

event (BPIE) when waste removal opportunities are identified in real time. This is different from the search for waste removal activities. The other improvement area opportunities described in this section involve the pull for project creation from 30,000-foot-level scorecard/dashboard metric improvement needs.

Lead time assessment

1. Report-out 30,000-foot-level scorecard/dashboard metric from the value chain that is being assessed for improvement opportunities.
2. Initiate the construction of a value stream map or time value diagram of the business area.
3. Use Little's law to determine lead times for each step.
4. Calculate value-added time for each process step.
5. Determine the total value-added time for the overall process.
6. Determine overall process cycle efficiency (value-added time divided by lead time).
7. Determine the process cycle efficiencies by step and Pareto chart the results.
8. Consider process simulation to model process variability for the purpose of exposing waste and testing proposed changes.
9. Brainstorm for improvement opportunities to improve cycle efficiencies, targeting a ratio of 1 (i.e., 100% efficiency), considering that lead time consists of the three components: cycle time, batch delay, and process delay. In product design, one opportunity for improvement is the simplification of products or services so that there is more direct alignment with customer wants and needs. In supply, one opportunity for improvement is that an upstream/downstream analysis of the demand/supply-chain indicates that logistic practices create waste in the form of inventory. In manufacturing, potential process improvement opportunities are standardizing best practices, reducing changeover time (expedites build-to-customer-order fulfillments), one-piece/continuous flow (eliminates both process and batch delays), technology (hardware and software implementations can reduce cycle time and error frequency), and product customization earlier within overall process (which can improve implementation efficiency).

10. Identify process constraints.
11. Establish appropriate in-process metrics.
12. Compile and prioritize process improvement opportunities using a cause-and-effect matrix.
13. Combine the cause-and-effect matrix items from this business area with other business areas.
14. Determine a potential improvement goal for the 30,000-foot-level scorecard/dashboard metric.
15. Describe resulting IEE process improvement lead time projects along with other IEE projects.

WIP reduction assessment

1. Report-out 30,000-foot-level scorecard/dashboard metric from the value chain that is being assessed for improvement opportunities.
2. Initiate the construction of a value stream map of the business area.
3. Determine takt time.
4. Determine mean WIP for each process step.
5. Determine mean WIP for the overall process.
6. Pareto chart WIP by process step.
7. Consider process simulation to model process variability for the purpose of exposing waste and testing proposed changes.
8. Brainstorm for improvement opportunities to reduce WIP, targeting a value of zero.
9. Identify process constraints.
10. Establish appropriate in-process metrics.
11. Compile and prioritize process improvement opportunities using a cause-and-effect matrix.
12. Combine the cause-and-effect matrix items from this business area with other business areas.
13. Determine a potential improvement goal for the 30,000-foot-level scorecard/dashboard metric.
14. Describe resulting IEE process improvement WIP projects along with other IEE projects.

Total cost reduction

1. Report-out 30,000-foot-level scorecard/dashboard metric from the value chain that is being assessed for improvement opportunities.

2. For established services/products, initiate with high-cost products and processes, where an ABC and cost maintenance may be beneficial. For new services/products, consider process improvement efforts relative to target pricing, target costing, and value engineering.

## 11.17 Time-Value Diagram

I will first discuss the time-value diagram; however, a given situation may benefit more from a value stream map, which will be discussed later in this chapter.

In a time-value diagram, times for process steps can be considered as calendar time, work time, and value-added time. With this information, effort is focused on what changes should be made to reduce non-value-added times, which result in an improvement in the overall lead time.

Figure 11.1 shows one format of a time-value diagram. Figure 11.2 will later illustrate another format. Steps to create such a diagram such as the one shown in Figure 11.1 are:

1. Determine total lead time.
2. Determine queue times between steps.
3. Create step segments proportional to the task times.

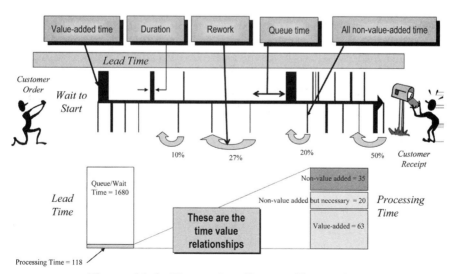

**Figure 11.1:** Time-value diagram illustration.

4.  Place steps and queues along the line segment in the order they happen.
    — Place value-added steps above the line.
    — Place non-value-added steps below the line.
    — Separate with queue times.
5.  Draw in rework loops and label with rework percentage (items sent back/items that reach that step).
6.  Indicate percentage of time in queue vs. time in activity.
7.  Indicate percentage of activity time that is value-added versus non-value-added.

When a time-value diagram includes the distribution of times for each step, simulation models can be built to understand better the impact of various process conditions on the overall output. This information can help determine where improvement efforts should be made.

## 11.18   Example 11.3: Development of a Bowling Ball

This example shows both the integration of Lean and Six Sigma tools, along with an application of product DFIEE.

An eight-month development process of bowling balls is to be reduced. A time-value diagram with calendar times and work times is shown in Figure 11.2 (Part A).

From Figure 11.2 (Part B), we note that the IEE team reduced the development lead time by 1 3/4 months (i.e., 8 months – 6.25 months = 1.75 months). The team combined two prototype definition steps through design of experiments (DOE) statistical techniques. This DOE step optimized the bowling ball core and shell requirements simultaneously. By considering manufacturing factors within this development DOE, we can also expect to produce a ball that has less variability.

Volume III, Example 37.1 illustrates another application of the simplified time-value diagram, as part a sales quoting improvement project report-out.

## 11.19   Enterprise Process Value Stream Mapping

When the 30,000-foot-level scorecard/dashboard measures for lead time and other Lean metrics are not satisfactory, the value

Part A: Before Change

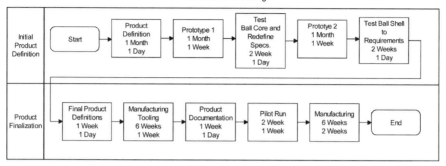

Part B: After Change

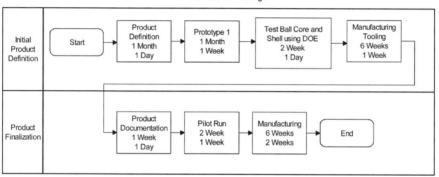

**Figure 11.2:** Simplified time-value diagram for developing a bowling ball, before change and after change.

stream mapping approach described in this section can create insight to where efforts should be placed to improve the overall enterprise process. Focused IEE projects can result from this activity. Examples 12.1 (Volume II) and 37.2 (Volume III) describe this application for transactional processes.

In Toyota, value stream mapping is known as "material and information flow mapping." In the Toyota production system, current and future states/ideal states are depicted by practitioners when they are developing plans to install Lean systems. Much attention is given to establishing flow, eliminating waste, and adding value. Toyota views manufacturing flows as material, information, and people/process. The value stream mapping methodology described in this section covers the first two of these three items (Rother and Shook 1999). This section is an overview of the methodology described in this reference.

A value stream map can trace both product and information flow across organizational boundaries of a company. A value stream manager, who is responsible for the entire value stream and reports to senior management, can be a great asset to an organization. This person can take ownership of the overall system 30,000-foot-level scorecard/dashboard metric and lead a focus effort to improving the overall system to avoid the suboptimizing of individual processes. The value stream manager can be responsible for the prioritization and orchestration of IEE projects, which have a specific focus to improve the overall value stream.

The type of value stream map described in this section utilizes symbols such as those illustrated in Figure 11.3. These symbols represent various activities when conducting value stream mapping.

Those who create a current-state map, such as the one shown in Figure 11.4, need to walk the actual pathways of material and information flow. This should begin with a quick walk of the entire value stream. One should start at the end and work upstream, mapping the entire value stream, using a pencil and paper for documentation and a stop watch to record times that were personally observed. Appendix Section D.5 includes a template that can be used to record these observations. The investigation results are then documented in a current-state value stream map.

Things to consider when creating a value stream map:

- Team members individually create a value stream map. The most accurate map is then created through consensus after collectively examining all maps.
- The value stream map creation tools are paper, pencil, eraser, and stop watch.
- After describing typical customers, compile 30,000-foot-level data that address order quantities, delivery frequency, and product mix.
- Before beginning a detailed study, initially walk the process quickly to gain high-level insight to the overall value stream steps.
- When creating the value stream, each person should interview all shift workers, verify observations against document procedures, and record all as-is observations.

| Material Icons | Represents | Notes |
|---|---|---|
| 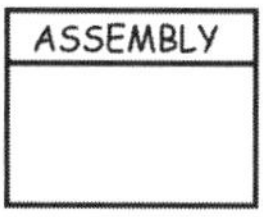 ASSEMBLY | Manufacturing Process | One process box equals an area of flow. All processes should be labeled. Also used for departments, such as Production Control. |
| 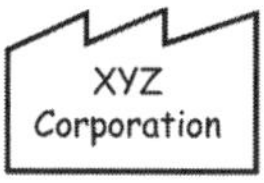 XYZ Corporation | Outside Sources | Used to show customers, suppliers, and outside manufacturing processes. |
| 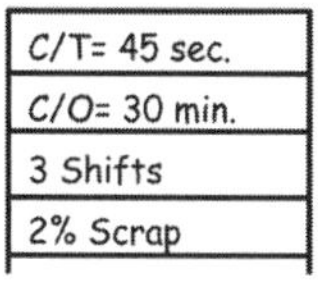 C/T= 45 sec. / C/O= 30 min. / 3 Shifts / 2% Scrap | Data Box | Used to record information concerning a manufacturing process, department, customer, etc. |
|  I / 300 pieces / 1 Day | Inventory | Count and time should be noted. |
|  Mon. & Wed. | Truck Shipment | Note frequesncy of shipments. |
|  (striped arrow) | Movement of production material by PUSH | Material that is produced and moved forward before the next process needs it, usually based on a schedule. |
|  (open arrow) | Movement of finished goods to the customer | |
|  (supermarket icon) | Supermarket | A controlled inventory of parts that is used to schedule production at an upstream process. |

**Figure 11.3:** Material flow, information flow, and general icons [From Rother and Shook (1999), with permission.].

| Material Icons | Represents | Notes |
|---|---|---|
| (withdrawal icon) | Withdrawal | Pull of materials, usually from a supermarket. |
| max. 20 pieces −FIFO→ | Transfer of controlled quantities of material between processes in a "First-In-First-Out" sequence. | Indicates a device to limit quantity and ensure FIFO flow of material between processes. Maximum quantity should be noted. |

| Information Icons | Represents | Notes |
|---|---|---|
| (arrow) | Manual information flow | For example: production schedule or shipping schedule. |
| (arrow) | Electronic Information flow | For example via electronic data interchange. |
| Weekly Schedule | Information | Describes an information flow. |
| 20 | Production Kanban (dotted line indicates kanban path) | The "one-per-container" kanban. Card or device that tells a process how many of what can be produced and gives permission to do so. |
| (withdrawal kanban icon) | Withdrawal Kanban | Card or device that instructs the material handler to get and transfer parts (i.e. from a supermarket to the consuming process). |
| (signal kanban icon) | Signal Kanban | The "one-per-batch" kanban. Signals when a reorder point is reached and another batch needs to be produced. Used where supplying process much produce in batches because changeovers are required. |

**Figure 11.3(B):** *Continued*

| Information Icons | Represents | Notes |
|---|---|---|
| | Sequenced-Pull Ball | Gives instruction to immediately produce a predetermined type and quantity, typically one unit. A pull system for subassembly processes without using a supermarket. |
| | Kanban Post | Place where kanban are collected and held for conveyance. |
| | Kanban Arriving in Batches | |
| OXOX | Load Leveling | Tool to intercept batches of kanban and level the volume and mix of them over a period of time. |
| | "Go See" Production Scheduling | Adjusting schedules based on checking inventory levels. |

| General Icons | Represents | Notes |
|---|---|---|
| | "Kaizen Lightening Burst" | Highlights improvement needs at specific processes that are critical to achieving the value stream vision. Can be used to plan kaizen workshops. |
| | Buffer or Safety Stock | "Buffer" or "Safety Stock" must be noted. |
| | Operator | Represents a person viewed from above. |

**Figure 11.3(C):** *Continued*

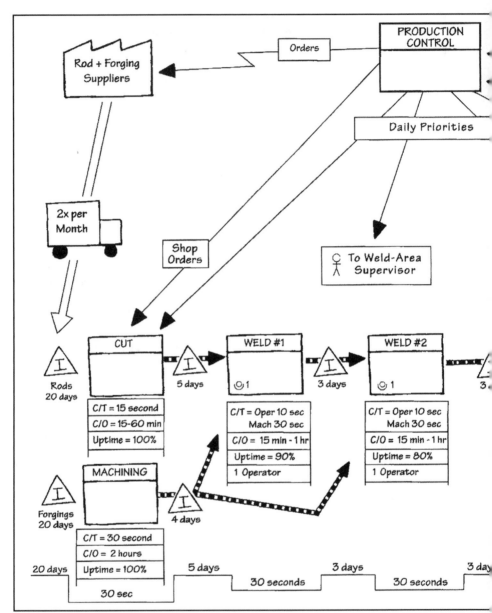

**Figure 11.4:** Current state value stream exam

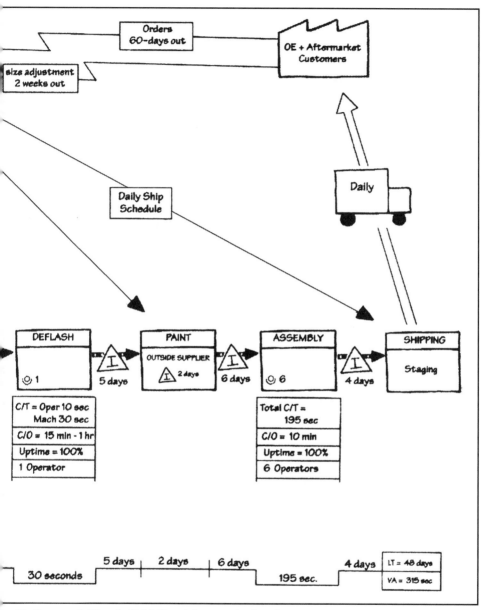

Orders
60-days out

OE + Aftermarket
Customers

size adjustment
2 weeks out

Daily Ship
Schedule

Daily

| DEFLASH | | PAINT | | ASSEMBLY | | SHIPPING |
|---|---|---|---|---|---|---|

DEFLASH

⚙ 1        5 days

PAINT

OUTSIDE SUPPLIER

⚠ 2 days    6 days

ASSEMBLY

⚙ 6        4 days

SHIPPING

Staging

C/T = Oper 10 sec
    Mach 30 sec

C/O = 15 min - 1 hr

Uptime = 100%

1 Operator

Total C/T =
    195 sec

C/O = 10 min

Uptime = 100%

6 Operators

30 seconds    5 days | 2 days | 6 days    4 days    LT = 48 days

195 sec.    VA = 315 sec

m Rother and Shook (1999), with permission.].

A value stream creation process:

1. Position customer icon in the upper right corner with customer requirements.
   • Insert the customer name in an "outside sources" (factory) icon that is placed at the upper right corner of the sheet of paper.
   • Below the "outside sources" box, draw a data box, recording customer requirements; e.g., number of pieces weekly of each product type, batch/tray size, number of shifts.
2. Create process boxes, moving from left to right, documenting below each process relevant data within data boxes.
   • Document process name in process box.
   • Create a process box wherever there is a disconnection of the process, and material flow stops.
   • Example recordings are C/T, C/O, number of people, available work time in seconds (minus time for meetings, breaks, and cleanup) and EPE.
   • When multiple flows merge, draw one flow over another. When there are many branches, initially focus on key components.
3. Record inventory and its position, using a triangle icon.
   • Document amount of inventory and duration of time for a part/transaction.
4. Describe transportation to the customer and from suppliers using a truck or airplane icon, describing material quantity or number of transactions in a data box and movement with a broad arrow.
   • Do not draw map for every purchased part. Draw flow for one or two main raw materials.
5. Place production control department icon at the top center of the diagram, including any notes where systems such as Materials Requirements Planning (MRP) exist.
   • Use go see icon, if appropriate.
6. Describe manual or electronic information flows with straight/lightning bolt arrows.
   • Separate line for forecasts and daily orders.
7. Describe material flow, using either a push arrow or pull arrow.
   • Push arrow: process produces independent of needs of downstream customer.
   • Pull arrow: parts produced as specified by the Kanban.

8. Draw a timeline that takes one part/transaction throughout its value stream.
9. Record inventory lead times, which are calculated as inventory quantity divided by daily customer requirements.
10. Record process times.
11. Estimate total production lead time by adding the lead times through each process and inventory triangle.
12. Add up the value-adding times or the processing times for all processes in the value stream.
13. Compare value-added to total lead time.

When creating a future state map for a value stream (and to improve phase action), one should keep in mind some important Lean principles. Overproduction can be created with a batch-and-push mass production system. This can occur when production is created by commands from production control instead of needs by the downstream customer of the process. Defects can remain as part of the hidden factory until discovered downstream in the process. This can result in a very long total time for a part to get through the production process, while value-added time for producing the product is very small. The most significant source of waste is overproduction, which can cause various types of waste from part storages, additional part handling, additional sorting, and rework to shortages at some production steps because the factory needs to produce parts to maintain its efficiency, even though no parts are needed. Mass production thinking implies that it is cheaper to produce if you produce more and at a faster rate. However, this is true from traditional accounting practices only where there is a direct-cost-per-item perspective that ignores all other real costs associated with direct and indirect production costs.

A Lean value stream strives for the following characteristics:

1. Produce to takt time (described later and See Glossary). For industries such as distribution, customer products, and process industries, a unit of customer demand for a takt time calculation could be the amount of work that can be accomplished by the process bottleneck during a fixed time interval; e.g., 1 hour.
2. Whenever possible, develop continuous flow, where continuous flow refers to the production of one piece at a time and the immediate passing of this part to the next step.

It might be best to have a combination of continuous flow with a FIFO (first-in-first-out) pull system.

3.   A supermarket is an inventory of parts that are controlled for the production scheduling of an upstream process. When continuous flow does not extend upstream, use supermarkets to control production. This might be needed when a machine creates several part numbers, supplier's location is distant, or there is a long lead time or unreliable process interface. Control by scheduling to downstream needs, as opposed to an independent scheduling function. A production kanban (described later and see Glossary) should trigger the production of parts, while a withdrawal kanban instructs the material handler to transfer parts downstream.

4.   Attempt customer scheduling to only one production process or subprocess in the overall production process; i.e., the pacemaker process (see Glossary). Frequently, this process is the most downstream continuous flow process in the value stream.

5.   Use load-leveling at the pacemaker process so that there is an even distribution of production of different products over time. This improves the flexibility of the overall process to have a short lead time when responding to different customer requirements, while keeping finished goods inventory and upstream supermarkets low.

6.   Release and withdraw small consistent work increments at the pacemaker process. This creates a predictable production flow, which can yield to quick problem identification and resolution. When a large amount of work is released to the shop floor, each process can shuffle orders, which results in increased lead time and the need for expediting.

7.   In fabrication processes that are upstream to the pacemaker process, create the ability to make every part every day; i.e., EPE day. We would then like to reduce EPE to shorter durations; e.g., shift. This can be accomplished by the shortening of changeover times and running smaller batches in upstream fabrication processes. An approach to determining initial batch size at fabrication processes is by determining how much time remains in a day to make changeovers. A typical target is that there is 10% of the time available for changeovers.

A future-state value stream map minimizes waste by addressing the above issues. An example future-state map is shown in Figure 11.5. From this future-state value stream map, an implementation plan is then created.

## 11.20   Value Stream Considerations

Everyone in the entire value stream should be aware of rate of customer consumption at end of value stream. For value stream creation and analysis, consider:

- Market and customers: Nimbleness to respond to market changes
- Flexibility: Low times for changeover/setup times and computer system changeovers
- Activities: Avoidance of time traps; e.g., many products flow through a single step
- Cost and complexity: Reduced complexity and number of offerings reduce cost and WIP
- Little's law (i.e., speed of process is inversely related to amount of WIP): Reduction of WIP

## 11.21   Additional Enterprise Process Lean Tools and Concepts and Examples

The following Lean tools that are described in Volume III have applicability not only in the P-DMAIC improve phase but also in the E-DMAIC analyze phase: learning by doing, standard work, one-piece flow, poka-yoke, visual management, 5S, Kaizen events, Kanban, demand management, level production, continuous flow, changeover reduction, and total productive maintenance.

Additional transactional Lean examples are:

- Example 12.2 (improve quote response)
- Volume III: Example 37.1 (sales quoting process)
- Volume III: Example 37.2 (sales quote project)

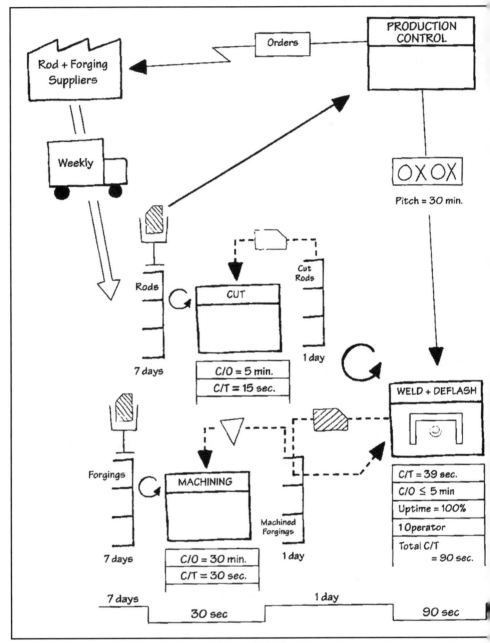

**Figure 11.5:** Future state value stream exam[

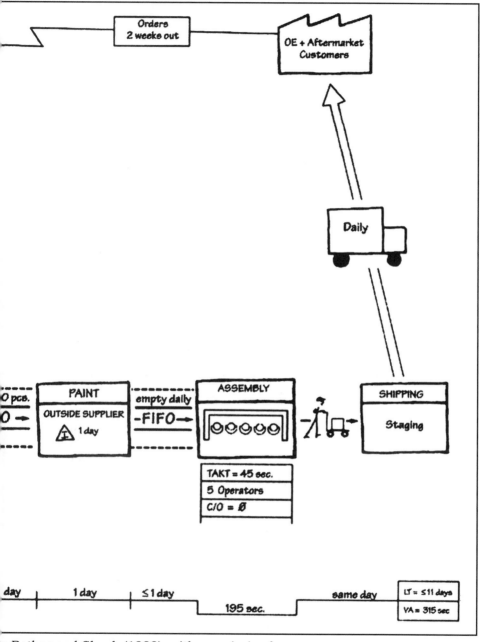

n Rother and Shook (1999), with permission.].

Volume III provides application illustrations of 5S Lean concepts to situations that could be considered transactional; i.e., inventory, suppliers, computer systems, and costing systems.

## 11.22   Applying IEE

Lean methodologies are very powerful concepts; however, care must be given to where improvement efforts should focus. Most Lean deployments don't seem to view the overall enterprise system systematically as a whole to determine what should be done to improve the overall business metrics. I have heard organizations boast that they do one kaizen event every week. One of the main principles of Lean is creating a customer pull system. When an organization sets a goal for the number of kaizen events for a period of time, I think that a tool is being pushed into the system.

> Lean methodologies are very powerful concepts; however, care must be given to where improvement efforts should focus. Most Lean deployments don't seem to view the overall enterprise system systematically as a whole to determine what should be done to improve the overall business metrics.

The Toyota production system (TPS) is typically considered the Lean benchmark. TPS is much more than just doing kaizen events when they seem appropriate. TPS is a big-picture system that manages the full value chain. In TPS, key suppliers are physically located next to manufacturing facilities to improve flows and reduce WIP both at the supplier and customer facilities. This is quite different than a company demanding that suppliers build a warehouse outside their facility so that the company does not have to carry subassemblies and parts inventory costs. The described E-DMAIC system offers the framework for measurements and improvement that has alignment with TPS. IEE can become the enabling system for organizations to move toward a TPS implementation.

In IEE, satellite-level metric goals are to lead to 30,000-foot-level scorecard/dashboard goals. The needs of a project to achieve measurement goals then pull for use of the right tool. If the goal is a reduction in lead time or inventory, then lean tools need to be considered and a kaizen event may be the best means to obtain timely results.

As noted earlier, a paper and pencil approach is typically suggested for the collection and analysis of information for the above procedure. Better information can be gained by walking the process, rather than just examining database information in an "ivory tower." However, when a value stream map includes the distribution of times for each activity, simulation models can be very useful to understand better the impact of changing conditions on the overall output and the impact of various "what-if's" on the process. This information can lead to better focused improvement efforts.

Viewing the enterprise as a whole can lead to a different behaviors. For example, one supplier of automobile parts described to me how one of its customers routinely required tightly tolerance parts, which often leaded to scrap and tooling breakages. This supplier described how a second customer visited his facility and asked him to make some sample parts. This customer took the parts and then designed his products around the tolerance capabilities of their processes. Interestingly, the second supplier is typically considered to have higher automobile product quality. Viewing the enterprise as a whole can lead to activities where suppliers and their processes are considered to be a partnership for overall business success.

The techniques described in this chapter can be used as part of P-DMAIC. Likewise, the Lean tools described in the project execution roadmap can be used at the E-DMAIC level.

## 11.23 Exercises

1. Describe an application of Lean in your everyday processes.
2. Describe how a company is claiming that they have a Lean program; however, the company is not seeing the benefits from the deployment. If desired, you may change the previous sentence wording from "company is claiming" to "company could be claiming."
3. Within a 24-hour period, an emergency room treats an average of 100 patients. From thirty random observation times, an average number of people in the waiting room was determined to be five. Determine the takt time and how long on average people spend in the waiting room.

# 12

# E-DMAIC—Analyze Phase: Innovation and the Identification of Project Opportunities

## 12.1   E-DMAIC Roadmap Component

As described earlier, traditional Six Sigma and Lean Six Sigma deployments could be viewed as a push for project creation. Consider the following:

- The success of a Six Sigma or Lean Six Sigma deployment is often measured by the total reported financial benefits of the projects. However, as noted earlier, an honest assessment can often yield a statement like, "We have supposedly saved 100 million dollars, but no one can seem to find the money." This may sound absurd, but I have heard this comment and similar comments many times.
- It is not uncommon for organizations to report the training of many people (e.g., over 500 green belts), where perhaps only 10% of those trained have completed even one project. This type of report tells me that the planned projects are not really important to management.

IEE is more of a business system than traditional Six Sigma and Lean Six Sigma deployments. With this approach, we focus on a

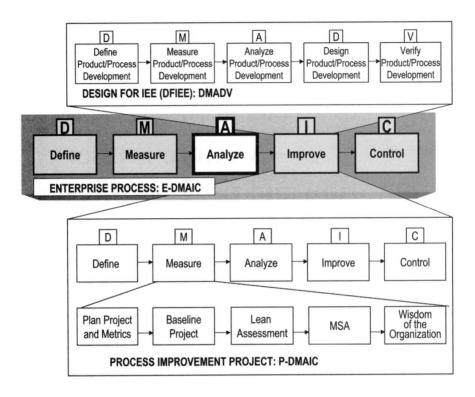

system that has measures and goals so that projects experience a pull for creation as a means to meet these goals systematically. In this system, emphasis is given to creating financial benefits that are felt by the entire company, not just at the individual sub-process measurement level. It is also important that expectations and developed strategies are consistent with the "laws of physics," as described earlier; e.g., Enron problem avoidance.

The past few chapters described various analysis techniques that indicate where improvement efforts should focus. One analyze phase E-DMAIC checklist item (see Section 8.2) was project opportunity identification. This chapter considers the previously described enterprise analyses and risk assessments for the determination of specific actionable improvement items for an organization to undertake, along with the use of creativity to help formulate innovation. In an organization, this effort could be orchestrated by the EPM function (see Figure 7.6).

From this analysis, an enterprise improvement plan (EIP) can be created to identify potential project opportunities that are in direct alignment with business goals and voice of the customer inputs. These identified projects are important to the process owner who understands that the only way for him/her to meet his/her specific measurement goals is by completing identified projects that impact these metric.

In the E-DMAIC improve phase, EIP results orchestrates project selection.

From this analysis, an enterprise improvement plan (EIP) can be created to identify potential project opportunities that are in direct alignment with business goals and voice of the customer inputs.

## 12.2 Creativity and Innovation

Analytics within E-DMAIC can provide sufficient direction to an obvious improvement solution. However, in other cases a solution is not so obvious and analyses needs to be combined with creativity for the creation of an innovative solution. The next few sections touch on some innovation generating concepts.

Creativity is a process of creating unusual associations among mental objects. Invention is a result of creative problem solving. Creativity can sometime result when there is an association of the right combination of objects. One frequently described example of association effect of the right objects is the exhaustive search of Thomas Edison during the development of a durable filament for a light bulb. In other cases, the objects are known, but an unusual association type becomes creative. An example of this is the creation of music from a fixed set of notes.

Creativity facilitates the success of brainstorming and allows out-of-the-box ideas and solutions to be considered. Without an emphasis on creativity, most improvement teams only find evolutionary improvements and conventional causes. It is the creativity that increases the chance of finding unconventional causes and revolutionary improvements.

Many team exercises are available to enhance creative behavior. With respect to process improvement efforts, the best ones focus on breaking the conventional paradigms. This can be done by starting the brainstorming of causes or solutions by setting a ground rule that some current policy(s) or current barrier(s) does not exist. The benefit of this method is that it may generate a cause or solution that is so revolutionary that the organization will set aside the barrier or policy to allow the process improvement to occur.

Another common method to spur greater creativity is to perform a creativity exercise with the team prior to the tools that benefit from greater creativity, such as brainstorming and solution selection. These may be simple exercises such as connecting the nine dots in a square without lifting your pencil (there are at least three ways) or making multiple patterns with straws.

Another stimulus for creative thought is provided in the article "A Modern Parable" (Callandra 1968). The question is how do you measure the height of a tall building using a barometer? This question has led to the creation of a list of more than 40 different methods. The methods extend from the simple physics based pressure measurement to geometric based methods using shadows or perspective, to everyone's favorite which is to use bribery by offering to give the barometer to the building superintendent if he/she will tell you the building height. This ten minute discussion will generate laughs and creativity, but it also provides a lead in to a discussion on unspoken paradigms and their hidden inhibitions on creativity.

## 12.3   Alignment of Creativity with IEE

From a how-to create perspective, Jones (1999) states that to encourage creativity we need to put ourselves in the place of most potential. Where, the place of most potential gives us insight to process improvement or breakthrough improvements. For example, conducting an experiment using DOE techniques often provides a fresh perspective that can become "the place of most potential".

Jones lists nine points for creativity:
1. Creativity is the ability to look at the ordinary, and see the extraordinary.
2. Every act can be a creative one.
3. Creativity is a matter of perspective.
4. There's always more than one right answer.
5. Re-frame problems into opportunities.
6. Don't be afraid to make mistakes.
7. Break the pattern.
8. Train your technique.
9. You've got to really care.

The IEE approach described in this volume aligns with these points. IEE creates an environment that encourages the implementation of creative solutions that are aligned with the needs of the business. Satellite-level metrics can track overall value to an organization both from a financial and customer point of view. A closer view of the value from processes can then be obtained from operational and project 30,000-foot-level metrics. Creativity activities are then to be a very integral part of the IEE project execution roadmap.

This IEE implementation process is a procedure for putting ourselves in the place of the most potential for the execution of projects that create value for the organization and its customers. One example of this occurrence: A colleague of mine executed in two stages a design of experiments (DOE) that I had designed for him because a new assembly factor was not available. The first stage had the old assembly, while the second stage had a new assembly. An analysis of this DOE indicated that the statistical significant difference between the two types of assemblies was large. I raised suspicion about the execution of this experiment when a follow-up experiment did not indicate significance of this factor. Upon further investigation, my colleague discovered that the first test had been executed using a different procedure for mounting the machine. My colleague was very apologetic about his oversight. I indicated that this was a blessing in disguise since this uncovered a testing problem we would later have within manufacturing. From this test we discovered, before product start, that the test figure yields an erroneous response relative to how a customer would experience the machine function. Through the execution of this DOE, we put ourselves in "a place of most potential" for discovery/creativity.

## 12.4  Creative Problem Solving

Teams might find that a less rigid creative approach to solving problems yields the best solutions (Teamwork 2002). With this *association of ideas* approach, one needs to understand the factors that make creative thinking work best. Through this process, imagination feeds off memory and knowledge, resulting in one idea leading to another.

This creative thinking process is dependent upon the execution of the following factors within the process.

- Suspend judgment: An open mind is an important characteristic to the success of this process.

- Self-assessment: It may be helpful for team members to conduct a self-evaluation of their tendency to cling to dogmatic ideas and opinions so that they can better assess how much work they need to do in this area.
- Develop a positive attitude: We need to develop an attitude that all ideas are good ideas.
- Use checklists: All ideas should be written down. This sends the message that all ideas are good. It also ensures that nothing is forgotten.
- Be self confident: Great ideas often can initially be ridiculed. Be confident in ideas that are different from the traditional approach.
- Encourage others: The fuel for creativity is praise and encouragement.

Five steps to solving problems creatively are:

1. Orientation: Set the stage for a productive session.
2. Preparation and analysis: Gather facts without getting into too much detail. Research for successful past solutions to problems that are similar.
3. Brainstorming: Conduct a brainstorming session where many ideas are created.
4. Incubation: Disperse the group for a period of time to let ideas grow. This time could be after a lunch break or a good-night's sleep.
5. Synthesis and verification: Construct a whole out of the ideas generated by brainstorming. To stimulate this process, the team might create a list of the desirable and undesirable qualities of the solutions. Another approach is to synthesize ideas through the creation of an outline or grouping of ideas together with similar ideas assigned to the same group. Relationships between these groups can then be mapped out.

## 12.5  Inventive Thinking

The purpose of this section is to present some background information that might be used to initiate the creation of a more rigorous inventive process within organizations.

*System* Inventive Thinking is a problem-solving methodology developed in Israel and inspired by the Russian TRIZ methodology. Innovations were added that simplified the learning and application of the problem solving methodology. These included the closed-world diagram, the qualitative-change graph, the particles method (an improvement on "smart little people" of the TRIZ method), and a simplified treatment of the solution techniques (which the Israelis call "tricks"). Whereas TRIZ stresses the use of databases of effects, the Israeli method stresses making the analyst an independent problem solver (Sickafus 1997).

*Structured* Inventive Thinking (SIT) is a modified version of the Israeli systematic inventive thinking problem-solving methodology. The methodology, sometimes referenced in the 8D problem-solving methodology, develops creative solutions to technical problems that are conceptual. Focus is given to the essence of the problem by the problem solver. The method efficiently overcomes psychological barriers to creative thinking, enabling the discovery of inventive solutions.

Unified Structured Inventive Thinking (USIT) was developed by E. N. Sickafus while teaching an elementary form of SIT at Ford Motor Company in Dearborn, Michigan (Sickafus 1997).

# 12.6   TRIZ

TRIZ states that some design problems may be modeled as technical contradiction. Creativity is required when attempts to improve some functional attributes lead to deterioration of other functional attributes. Design problems associated with a pair of functional contradiction can be solved by making trade-offs or by overcoming the obstacle. TRIZ stresses that an ideal design solution overcomes the conflict, as opposed to making a trade-off.

Problems can be grouped into those with generally known solutions and those with unknown solutions. Solutions to problems come in levels:

- Standard: uses methods well known in the profession.
- Improvement: uses methods from inventor's own industry and technology. Improves an existing system.
- Within existing paradigm: uses methods from other fields and technologies. Improves an existing system.

- Outside existing paradigm: uses little-known and under-stood physical effects (physics, chemistry, geometry).
- Discovery: goes beyond contemporary scientific knowledge. Creates a new discovery or new science.

Those problems with known solutions can usually be solved by currently available information. Those with no known solution are called inventive problems. These problems often contain contradictory requirements.

TRIZ is the Russian acronym that means *The Theory of inventive problem solving.* Genrich Altshuller, a Russian mechanical engineer is credited with the creation of TRIZ. While analyzing patents for the Russian Navy, Altshuller noticed patterns in the inventive process that he developed into a set of inventive tools and techniques for solving problems.

Instead of classifying patents by industry, such as automotive or aerospace, Altshuller removed the subject matter to uncover the problem-solving process. Altshuller found that often the same problems had been solved over and over again using one of only forty fundamental inventive principles, e.g., transformation of properties, self service, do it in reverse, and nesting.

Altshuller also classified engineering system development into eight laws:

- Law of completeness of the system: Systems derive from synthesis of separate parts into a functional system.
- Law of energy transfer in the system: Shaft, gears, magnetic fields, charged particles, which are the heart of many inventive problems.
- Law of increasing ideality: Function is created with minimum complexity, which can be considered a ratio of system usefulness to its harmful effects. The ideal system has the desired outputs with no harmful effects, i.e., no machine, just the function(s).
- Law of harmonization: Transferring energy more efficiently.
- Law of uneven development of parts: Not all parts evolve at the same pace. The least will limit the overall system
- Law of transition to a super system: Solution system becomes subsystem of larger system.
- Law of transition from macro to micro: Using physically smaller solutions, e.g., electronic tubes to chips.
- Law of increasing substance-field involvement: Viewing and modeling systems as composed of two substances interacting through a field.

Most effective solutions come from resolving contradictions without compromise. When improving some part or characteristic of our system causes deterioration in another that is contradiction. Altshuller states that invention surmounts the contradiction by moving both characteristics in a favorable direction. For example, to increase the capacity of an air conditioner, we can increase weight, price, and power consumed. However, a better solution is the use of a new technology that improves efficiency and capacity.

Altshuller thought that if only later inventors had knowledge of earlier work, solutions could have been discovered more quickly and efficiently. His approach was to use the principle of abstraction to map the problems to categories of solutions outside of a particular field of study. Conflict can be resolved through the Principle of Abstraction; that is, classification of problems in order to map the problems to categories of solutions.

When solving problems typically some feature or parameter is selected and then changed to improve the process. TRIZ formalizes this thought process by starting with a list of 39 parameters/features such as waste of time, force, speed, and shape.

TRIZ then facilitates the solution process through abstraction. Problems are stated in terms of a conflict between two attributes, e.g., parts, characteristics, functions, and features. This allows seeing generic solutions that may already be documented in other industries or fields of study. This also allows for a better search in the global patent collection. The website www.SmarterSolutions.com/triz provides tools to facilitate the TRIZ execution process.

## 12.7   Six Thinking Hats

Complexity is the biggest enemy of thinking since it leads to confusion. Six Thinking Hats is a technique developed by De Bono (1999) to help clarify and simplify thinking so that it is more enjoyable and effective. Six Thinking Hats simplifies thinking by permitting a thinker to cope with one thing at a time. The thinker is able to deal with logic, emotions, information, hope and creativity individually. Emphasis is given in the Six Hats method to "what can be" rather than simply "what is." Focus is given to determining a way forward, not on who is right or wrong.

Western thinking focuses on "what is," as determined by analysis, judgment, and argument, which many world cultures, if not most, regard argument as aggressive, personal, and non-constructive. Instead of judging our way forward what is needed is a system that helps determine "what can be," not just "what is." Six Hats provides this system through parallel thinking, where everyone at any moment is looking at a situation from the same direction.

In Six Hats the colors white, red, black, yellow, green, and blue describe hat colors or role descriptions, which are to be used at various times; e.g., during a meeting. Each hat color is related to the following function:

- White Hat: White is neutral and objective; hence, the white hat objective is facts and figures.
- Red Hat: Red suggests anger, range, and emotions; hence, the red hat provides emotional view.
- Black Hat: Black is somber and serious; hence, the black hat provides caution and carefulness by providing idea weaknesses.
- Yellow Hat: Yellow is sunny and positive; hence, the yellow hat provides optimism, covering hope and positive thinking.
- Green Hat: Green is grass, vegetation, and abundant and fertile growth; hence, the green hat indicates creativity and new ideas.
- Blue Hat: Blue is cool and the sky color, which is above all else; hence, the blue hat concern is with control, the organization thinking process, and other hat usage.

Two basic ways to use hats are to singly request a thinking type or as a meeting sequence for subject exploration or problem solving. A single use might lead to the statement: I think we need some green hat thinking here. Meeting sequence can involve two, three, four, or more hats.

Meeting sequence can be evolving or preset. In the evolving sequence, hat topic selections are chosen during the meeting; while in present sequence hat topic sequence are setup under a blue hat at the meeting's beginning. Preset sequences are suggested until experience is gained in Six Hats facilitation.

Some basic Six Hats meeting protocols are:

- The chairperson or facilitator wears a blue hat and maintains hat-meeting discipline.
- There is no need to use every hat.

- Hats can be used several times during a meeting.
- Group members must stay with current hat.
- Initial time allotment for most hats is 1 minute for each attendee; i.e., five attendees would mean five minutes.
- Blue hat is always used at both meeting beginning and end.
- There is no one right hat sequence to follow; however, some sequences are appropriate for exploration, problem solving, and dispute settlement.

The white hat is about information. White hat becomes a discipline for encouraging the thinker to clearly separate fact from extrapolations or interpretations.

The red hat provides the opportunity to express feelings, emotions, and intuition with no need for explanation or justification; e.g., ... I feel that the idea has potential. This hat considers both ordinary emotions and complex judgments such as a hunch and intuition. Emotions do not need to be logical or consistent.

The black hat is logical thinking that addresses caution and survival. Black hat thinking may highlight procedural errors, but is not argumentative and must not be allowed to degenerate into argument. The black hat addresses the questions: What will happen if we take this action? What are the potential problems? What can go wrong? How will people react? Do we have the resources? Will it continually be profitable? In assessment, the black hat can address whether we should proceed with the suggestion. In the design processes, the black hat addresses weaknesses that need to be overcome.

The yellow hat is positive and constructive thinking with optimism, which focuses people to seek out value. Under this hat the thinker deliberately sets out to find whatever benefit there might be in a suggestion; e.g., if we invest heavily in promoting this product we should have success on our hands. Suggestions can be prefixed with the words proven, very likely, good chance, even chance, possible, or remote.

The green hat is where new ideas, concepts, perceptions, or possibilities are presented. The green hat is to incorporate lateral thinking, which is pattern switching in an asymmetric patterning system. Lateral thinking is to help the thinker cut across patterns instead of just following them. A key component of lateral thinking is movement where we use an idea for its forward effect. Provocation is an important part of green hat thinking and is symbolized by the word po. Provocation is used to take us out of usual thinking patterns.

The blue hat is like the orchestra conductor. The blue hat is typically worn by the facilitator or session leader. When wearing the blue hat we think about the subject exploration, not the subject. The blue hat thinker can make comments on meeting observations; e.g., we are spending too much time arguing about this point. Let us just note it down as a point on which there are conflicting views. The first blue hat indicates purpose of meeting, definition of the situation, what we want to achieve, and plan for hat sequence. The final blue hat indicates what was achieve, conclusion, design, solution, and next steps.

## 12.8   Midterm and Annual Strategy Development

Section 3.5 described hoshin kanri's planning process. Strategy building is important; however, strategies built without blending analytics, innovation, and risks can lead to activities that are not beneficial to the business as a whole. In IEE, strategy building is part of the analyze phase of E-DMAIC.

When creating a list of potential midterm strategies identified during the E-DMAIC analyze phase, consider:

- Voice of the customer inputs
- Environmental scan check of market conditions
- Overall 30,000-foot-level scorecard/dashboard value-chain metric assessment
- Financial and data analysis
- Theory of constraints analysis
- Lean assessment

Through an analytic and a prioritization matrix (see Appendix Section D.10), dominant breakthrough opportunities are highlighted; e.g., three to five.

From the midterm three-to-five year strategy horizon, develop tactics for the next 12 to 18 months. Cost cutting should not be considered a process improvement since it does not stretch capabilities (Jackson 2006). More often it destroys processes.

Cost reduction is the result of appropriate process improvements. Developed strategies serve as input to the EIP plan creation.

## 12.9   Innovation Creation Process

Innovation is the act of introducing something new, which can involve both radical and incremental change to products, services, or processes. Often the goal of innovation is considered to be problem solving. Innovation problem solving can lead to the creation of a new opportunity; i.e., the development of a new product (innovation) leads to increased revenue (problem) or resolves a customer need (problem). Innovation can lead to a process enhancement that reduces a process defective rate; i.e., a process enhancement (innovation) leads to the reduction of a defective rate (problem).

To be most effective, a rational problem-solving/opportunity-creation approach blends analytics with creativity. However, an execution structure for this blending is often lacking, which can lead to much inefficiency and ineffectiveness, resulting in a solution that is far from optimal.

This section describes the execution of a six-step innovation creation process (ICP), which adds structure to this overall blending process, without stifling the creation of innovation opportunities. Steps for this ICP event are:

1. Environmental Analysis
2. Problem Description
3. Assumptions
4. Generating Alternatives
5. Evaluation and Choice
6. Implementation Plan

ICP has several potential IEE applications. An ICP event can occur in the E-DMAIC analyze phase for project identification and scoping, P-DMAIC improve phase for solution determination, or DFIEE/DFSS for product/process design definition/creation. The Enterprise Improvement Plan (EIP) system described in the next section provides a framework for organizational ICP execution.

Steps 1 – 3 create a foundation for the generation of ideas in step 4. Highlights from each step are:

1. Environmental Analysis: Both internal and external organizations need to be assessed and documented for both problem and opportunity identification. One should look for weaknesses and environment change. An effective E-DMAIC organizational system provides a valuable information resource that can serve as the foundation for innovation development. Components for this compilation from the Define-Measure-Analyze phases of E-DMAIC include: customer value assessment (see Section 6.7), enterprise value chain with 30,000-foot-level performance metrics (see Section 7.3), five strategic development elements (see Figure 8.1), environment scan checking market conditions (see Section 8.8), Lean and IEE accounting (see Section 9.6), enterprise data analytics (see Section 9.8), TOC five focusing steps (see Section 10.6), focus areas identification (see Section 11.16), and value stream mapping (see Section 11.19).

2. Problem Description: Compiled information from the environmental analysis step can be used to formulate the problem or opportunity description, which the ICP event is to address. At an enterprise level, an ICP problem statement could center on revenue and/or profit growth, while in the P-DMAIC improve phase, this description could be more targeted than the initial project problem statement.

3. Assumptions: Listing assumptions about the condition of current and future factors in the problem situation can be beneficial for later generation of solution alternatives and the prioritization of these alternatives; however, care must be exercised not to set boundaries that are too restrictive.

4. Generating Alternatives: This step is the most creative stage of ICP. This step is to use information from the previous steps to help with the formulation of useful options. The creative idea-generation techniques described in previous sections of this chapter can help generate more possible solutions than could otherwise be derived.

5. Evaluation and Choice: Decision making needs to have a systematic evaluation of alternatives against existing criteria and goals. Key to this rational-process step is to determine possible outcomes of various alternatives and how they would impact 30,000-foot-level and satellite-level metrics. EIP can be used to help determine, describe, and balance process improvement and design project work. Whenever possible goals should be established with ac-

countability for 30,000-foot-level metric improvements; i.e.,
a pull for project-creation system. A cause-and-effect matrix (see Table D.5) and/or nominal group techniques (NGT
– see Section D.12) can be used as part of the evaluation
process.

6.  Implementation Plan: After there is a clear idea of what is
desired and a plan to accomplish the results, action needs
to be taken. A black belt or another practitioner needs to
be assigned to the project. Persistent attention is required
for implementation through weekly and monthly project
report outs with the project champion and other management. Many details need to be anticipated and addressed
along with the overcoming of obstacles. Evaluating results
is the final but often overlooked step. This evaluation is
for the determination of the extent that undertaken actions
have resolved the problem or achieved the desired results.
A 30,000-foot-level metric assessment can be useful for this
assessment.

The dynamics of executing an ICP event in a team environment can take many forms. I will now provide an accelerated ICP
event execution option. In this process, the team lead for this
process compiles a rough-cut at putting together background information before the team begins their collective work. This generic process can be especially beneficial when team members
work remotely to each other. The basic process for accelerated
ICP execution is:

1.  The team lead works with individuals or groups independently to create a first-pass document that summarizes the
results from ICP steps 1 – 3.
2.  He/she sends the first-pass ICP document with instructions that every team member is to read the document at
least one day before an ICP team event. The document is
sent ahead of time so that each team member has time to
read the information and let the concepts settle in their
mind for idea percolation.
3.  Each team member is instructed to take notes in the first-pass document before a team meeting on what they think
should be changed or added to each ICP step.
4.  During the ICP team meeting event, the team lead uses
a computer projector to display the first-pass ICP 6-step
document.

5.  The team lead uses the projector to walk through each ICP document step, making team agreed-to changes for steps 1 – 3. Team members are to use their pre-meeting notes when providing inputs; however, team members can also provide additional thoughts that could have been generated because of meeting comments from others.

6.  ICP step 4 is to contain a listing of brainstorming ideas or alternatives generated by the team. Classical brainstorming work in this step needs to follow traditional rules; i.e., there is no inappropriate idea and all ideas are recorded. The ICP document provides a media for listing all idea alternatives. At this point in the ICP event TRIZ or other creative idea development tools can used to help stimulate thought.

7.  Ideas prioritization in ICP step 5 can be done using any-one of several approaches. An affinity diagram (See Section D.11) can be a useful tool for the categorization and then prioritization of ideas. With this approach, ideas are printed out so that each idea is recorded on a small sheet of paper, which is taped to the wall. The team would then move ideas around in typical affinity diagram fashion creating a few natural groupings. NGT or a cause-and-effect matrix (See section D.10) could be used for affinity diagram category prioritization. Nominal group technique (NGT – see Section D.12) could be used to prioritize ideas within categories.

8.  The above steps can be completed in one or two team meetings. Upon completion of the above accelerated ICP team actions, the team lead can then compile the information in a prioritization format for distribution to each team member.

9.  A follow-up team meeting can be used to formulate an implementation plan; i.e., step 6.

The above described generic accelerated ICP process is not appropriate for all situation and teams. Teams need to decide the best execution approach for their situation.

## 12.10    Enterprise Improvement Plan (EIP)

A EIP format, as illustrated in Figure 12.1, helps determine and align projects to business needs, where it is most desirable if the high potential area reflects a value-chain metric that has

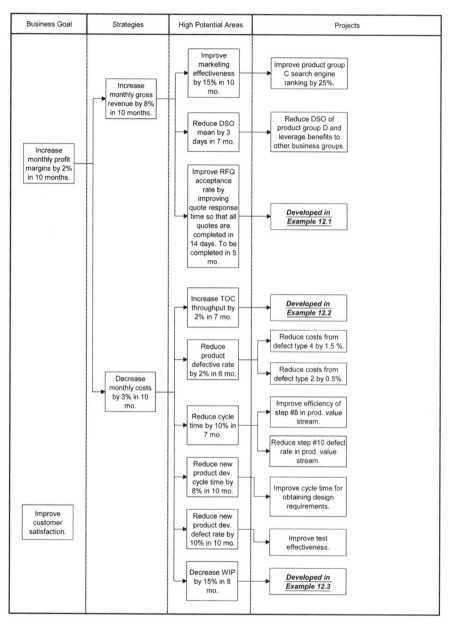

**Figure 12.1:** EIP illustration.

management ownership and specific objectives. High potential area targets need to be determined through a blending of the financials, analytics, and innovation. A strategy could include an innovation idea developed during an ICP session.

The EPM function (see Figure 7.6) could own the EIP execution. The value-chain functional drilldown could describe the ownership of various aspects of this process. The following example process has a technical team, such as master black belts, leading the EIP formulation:

1.  Compile and present the value chain and its metrics to executives.
2.  Work with executives to create SMART goals for the satellite-level metrics.
3.  Conduct an E-DMAIC analysis, working with various teams such as customer representatives, to develop various strategies that could be undertaken to meet these objectives.
4.  Summarize E-DMAIC analyses to executives and work with them to define EIP strategies.
5.  Work with teams to define EIP high potential areas and then drill down to project opportunities.

The following examples will illustrate drill downs from the three EIP high potential areas that have no project assignments in the figure.

## 12.11   Example 12.1: Project Creations for EIP High Potential Areas - Improve Quote Response Time

An EIP goal was to increase the request for quote (RFQ) acceptance rate by decreasing quote response time in five months, as shown in Figure 12.1. The VP of Sales owned this value-chain performance measurement, which is shown in Figure 12.2. The VP of Sales asked the organization's Enterprise Process Management (EPM) function (see Figure 7.6) for assistance in determining what improvement project(s) should be initiated in her area; i.e., measurement improvement needs create a pull for project creation. He/she could also be the project's champion.

As part of the organization's value-chain functional reporting, the mean and standard deviation response time for a weekly random selection of ten RFQs was tracked as a 30,000-foot-level scorecard/dashboard (see Volume III, P-DMAIC roadmap Step 3.2.4 in Appendix D).

Voice of the customer input established the requirement that RFQs needed to be completed in 14 days. Value chain reporting

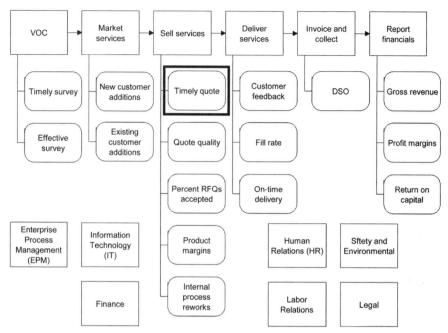

**Figure 12.2:** VP of Sales' timely quote value-chain performance metric.

was delayed by a month since most RFQs were completed in that time period. The 30,000-foot-level control chart had only 72 weeks reporting since a major process change occurred at the point in time when this chart was initiated.

The 30,000-foot-level quote response time metric shown in Figure 12.3 indicates that the process was predictable with an approximate 25 percent (100 − 74.665 = 25.335, rounded) non-conformance rate relative to customer expectations. It had been determined that not meeting a 14-day customer response time negatively impacted the RFQ response acceptance rate. One might note that the figure indicates a departure from a straight line probability plot for low-value responses. This was caused by the process rounding of response time to the nearest 0.1 day and was ignored in the 30,000-foot-level metric report-out.

The EPM function called a meeting to determine where focus should be given to meet the described objectives. In this meeting a SIPOC was created, as shown in Table 12.1. The team then created an as-is quote process flowchart followed by the value stream map, which is shown in Figure 12.4. From the flowchart and value stream map, a cause-and-effect diagram was created for excessive

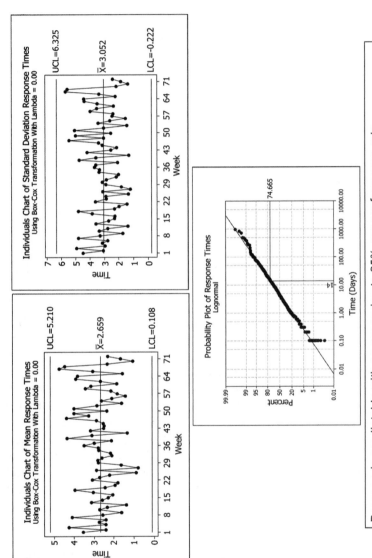

**Figure 12.3:** Quote response time 30,000-foot-level scorecard/dashboard metric.

**Table 12.1** Quote Response Time SIPOC

| Suppliers | Inputs | Process | Outputs | Customers |
|---|---|---|---|---|
| Final customer | Design drawings | Receive information | Quote (dollars, date, quantity, drawing) | Final customer |
| | Date | Conduct technical review | Advise/feasibility review | Our company |
| | Quantity | Select suppliers | Document what happened in order to move forward | |
| | | Prepare quote | Historical records | |

quote time. The cause-and-effect diagram entries were used to create a cause-and-effect matrix. A Pareto chart of the cause-and-effect matrix items' rankings is shown in the Figure 12.5.

This ranking was reduced to the following four target areas:

- Non-standard processing
- Lack of historical information
- Too many process steps
- Lack of product and supplier information by employees

In general, this type of drill down could lead to EIP projects (see Figure 12.1), subproject categories from a larger project, or just-do-it projects; i.e., BPIEs, as described in the next chapter. Targeted potential projects would then be considered in the overall project selection matrix for the entire organization, as described in the next chapter. If one or more of these projects are selected, the VP of Sales, who owns this metric, should fulfill the role of project champion.

I suggest that the reader re-read Section 3.3 to compare the measurement and improvement strategy described in this example to that described in Chapter 3.

# 12.12 Example 12.2: Project Creations for EIP High Potential Areas - Improve TOC Throughput

An EIP goal was to increase TOC throughput by 2% in seven months. The manager who owned the value-chain Produce Product and Deliver functional metric asked the EPM function (see Figure 7.6) for

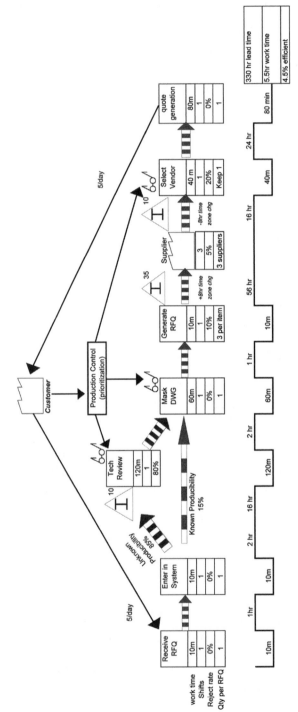

**Figure 12.4:** Value stream mapping of request for quote.

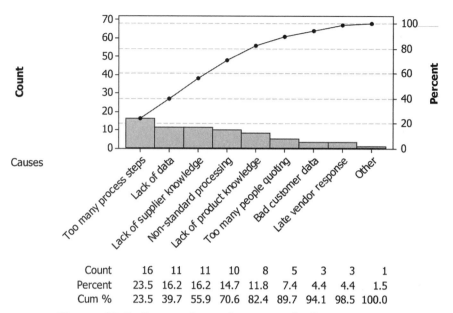

| | Count | 16 | 11 | 11 | 10 | 8 | 5 | 3 | 3 | 1 |
|---|---|---|---|---|---|---|---|---|---|---|
| | Percent | 23.5 | 16.2 | 16.2 | 14.7 | 11.8 | 7.4 | 4.4 | 4.4 | 1.5 |
| | Cum % | 23.5 | 39.7 | 55.9 | 70.6 | 82.4 | 89.7 | 94.1 | 98.5 | 100.0 |

**Figure 12.5:** Pareto chart of cause-and-effect excessive quote time causes.

assistance in determining what improvement project(s) to initiate; i.e., measurement improvement needs pull for project creation.

As noted earlier, throughput (T) as a TOC measure is the rate of generating money in an organization. This is a financial value-added metric which equates to revenues minus variable costs.

The capacity of each step of the overall process was determined. A Pareto chart of each step's capacity indicated that for the current customer demand, the facility was operating about ten percent below capacity, where step number three of the process had the lowest capacity. Because of this, increasing capacity without increased sales would not help to achieve the goal.

A Pareto analysis TOC throughput by product indicated that some products were making significantly more money than others. Further analysis indicated that the raw material costs for some products were increasing faster than the revenue generated from these products. In addition, the sales commission structure for some products was leading to the wrong sales personnel emphasis.

From this analysis, the following four target areas were chosen:

• Improve lead generation portion of sales process
• Improve sales commission structuring relative to product TOC throughput

- Improve the process for maximizing and stabilizing the difference between product pricing and variable product costs
- Increase capacity of step 3 to address potential sales increase

These four areas can be considered EIP projects for this high potential area, which were noted in Example 12.1. These targeted potential projects are later to be considered in the overall project selection matrix for the entire organization, as described in the next chapter. If one or more of these projects are selected, the Produce Product and Deliver function manager who is responsible for this metric would be the champion for project completion.

## 12.13   Example 12.3: Project Creations for EIP High Potential Areas - Reduce WIP

An EIP goal was to decrease WIP by 15 percent in eight months. The manager who owned the value-chain Produce Product and Deliver functional metric asked the EPM function (see Figure 7.6) for assistance in determining what improvement project(s) to initiate; i.e., measurement improvement needs pull for project creation. He/she could also be the champion for the project.

The mean WIP in each step of the overall process was determined. A value stream map was created for the major produce product and deliver process.

A Pareto chart of each step's WIP indicated that step seven had much larger WIP than any other step because of die change time. At step seven, line managers were building product inventory safeguards to protect against potential peak product-specific demands. A die changeover time reduction project was proposed. If this project is selected, the Produce Product and Deliver function manager who is responsible for this metric would be the champion for project completion.

## 12.14   Exercises

1. Define satellite-level metrics for a for-profit company, non-profit organization, school, religious organization, or political organization.

2. Create a value chain for one of the organizations described in Exercise 1.

3. Create 30,000-foot-level operational scorecard/dashboard metrics for the value-chain functions that are aligned with the satellite-level metrics described in Exercise 1.

4. Create a goal for improving a set of satellite-level metrics for one of the categories noted in Exercise 1.

5. Create strategies directed toward achieving the goal described in Exercise 4.

6. Define high potential areas for one of the strategies described in Exercise 5.

7. Describe a project as a problem statement that you would expect would be pulled from the activities described in Exercises 1 through 6.

8. Describe the 30,000-foot-level scorecard/dashboard metric that is to be improved for the project described in Exercise 7.

9. For the project described in Exercises 7 and 8, estimate the CODND and the impact to customers of the process.

10. Compare the business measurement and improvement methodology of Examples 12.1, 12.2, and 12.3 to that described in Chapter 3.

11. Describe your place of most creativity; e.g., showering or shaving, while commuting to work, while falling asleep or waking up, during a boring meeting, during leisure time, during exercising, on waking up in the middle of the night, while listing to an inspirational speaker, or while performing non-mental tasks.

12. Describe what you might do to stimulate creativity for yourself and your team.

# 13

# E-DMAIC—Improve Phase

## 13.1  E-DMAIC Roadmap Component

Dr. Lloyd S. Nelson stated: "In the state of statistical control, action initiated on appearance of a defect will be ineffective and will cause more trouble. What is needed is improvement of the process, by reduction of variation, or by change of level, or both. Study of the sources of product, upstream, gives powerful leverage on improvement." (Deming 1986)

From the E-DMAIC analyze phase, the improve phase takes information to develop specific action plans for the purpose of improving the overall business not only with financial savings but also with customer relations. These action plan types can be subdivided into three categories, where the graphic above visually describes the first two categories:

- Design projects; i.e., product, process, or IT
- Process improvement projects
- Business process improvement events (BPIEs)

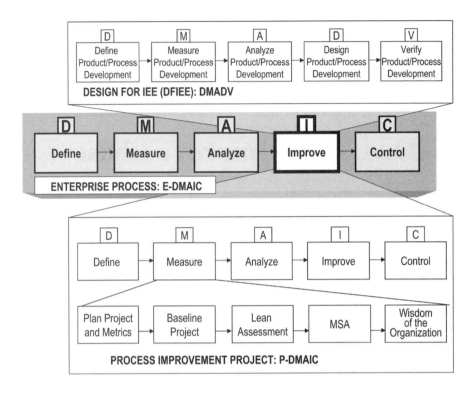

From the E-DMAIC analyze phase, the improve phase takes information to develop specific action plans for the purpose of improving the
overall business with not only financial savings but also customer
relations.

## 13.2   Checklist: Enterprise Process Improve Phase

E-DMAIC improve phase activities include:

- Suggest low-hanging-fruit actions identified in the analyze
  phase.
- Rank and select improvement projects from EIP and elsewhere using a prioritization matrix, which considers BPIEs,
  DMAIC, and DFIEE opportunities, resources, and organizational goals.
- Write business case (calculating CODND) and select most
  effective belts to drive projects; e.g., black belt or green belt.
  Suggest belt training to management, when appropriate.

- Determine appropriate belt training.
- Plan and execute just do-it projects from BPIE projects, including meetings to discuss their status.
- Plan and execute P-DMAIC projects.
- Plan and execute product, process, or IT DFIEE (DMADV) projects.
- Assess and report-out benefits from improvement efforts.

The following sections describe these categories. Later sections describe a drill-down process for creating specific projects.

## 13.3   Business Process Improvement Events (BPIEs)

Organizations need a system to identify and resolve simple reoccurring problems in a timely fashion. The resolution for these issues could involve a simple agree-to procedure change where the process change could have procedural documentation in a value-chain drill down, and people who would be impacted would receive process change notification, or the change may involve several iterations of the PDCA cycle.

> Unlike projects that go through the full P-DMAIC process, BPIEs do not need to undergo the rigor of a formal project; e.g., demonstrate a beneficial shift in the 30,000-foot-level scorecard/dashboard metric and describe the financial project benefit.

Sometimes this type of improvement effort is referred to as a mini-kaizen. I will make reference to this effort as a business process improvement event (BPIE). Unlike projects that go through the full P-DMAIC process, BPIEs do not need to undergo the rigor of a formal project; e.g., demonstrate a beneficial shift in the 30,000-foot-level scorecard/dashboard metric and describe the financial project benefit. Basic sequence steps for initiating and executing a mini-kaizen or BPIE are:

1. Employee identifies and documents a problem, waste, defect, or something that does not work correctly.
2. Employee develops and reports to immediate manager an improvement idea.
3. Manager reviews improvement idea and encourages immediate implementation, if appropriate.

4. The idea is implemented.
5. The idea is documented in a simple form.
6. Manager posts form for immediate recognition and as a stimulus for others to participate.
7. Improvement is documented in value chain, when appropriate.

BPIEs can lead to increased customer satisfaction, decreased number of processing steps/time, reduced costs, reduced waste, and improved quality. A system should be instituted to encourage employee BPIE participation. For example, a point system could be initiated where employees are given a point for BPIE creation and a point for BPIE execution. The amount of BPIE participation could be a part of an employee's performance plan. Also, the current total BPIEs' count could also be prominently posted so that results are visual to all employees. In addition, small recognition awards could be given for team/department participation.

An organization can also create a repository, where anyone can initiate a BPIE. This repository should capture both simple just-do-it process changes at a department/individual level and larger issues, such as:

• A customer wants to make a home-delivery television purchase. From a previous conversation in a competing store, the customer is certain that there are no more desired brand/size televisions in the country. However, this store's computer system indicates that there are two of the desired televisions in the warehouse. The customer asks the salesperson whether she is certain that one of those two warehouse televisions will be set aside for his delivery. Since the salesperson ensures the customer that one of the televisions would fill the order, the customer purchased the television. On delivery day, the customer waited all day for the television to arrive; however, there was no delivery. The store's response to the customer inquiry about the delivery problem was that there were no televisions in the warehouse. Apparently, the computer-identified two warehouse televisions were either delivered to someone else or the computer inventory system was incorrect. In addition, there was no system in place to work the home delivery agree-to details. The salesperson was apologetic, and the store gave additional price concessions to the customer. In an IEE deployment, the salesperson who experienced the problem would be encouraged to document the problem as a BPIE, rather than receiving retribution for highlighting the system problem(s) to management.

- After cruise ships' arrivals every Saturday morning, an in-town rental outlet experiences high demand to fill reserved car orders. Every Saturday morning for weeks, customers have been complaining about the hour-plus wait to obtain their reserved car. Rather than simply explaining to customers that this happens every time cruise ships arrive, the rental-desk-clerk should be encouraged to create a BPIE so that this common-cause customer satisfaction issue can be resolved on a going-forward basis.

For larger identified BPIEs, a reliable feedback system is needed to convey BPIE status back to the originating person.

## 13.4 Example 13.1: BPIE Improvement

Being assigned multiple tasks can be overwhelming to some people, while others do not have a problem with unorganized inputs. When leaning out organizations, the hiring process needs to be sensitive to the importance of hiring people who are not only the right person for the current job need but who are also capable of handling flexible assignments. At the same time we should strive to create processes that are robust to differing employee skill sets.

For improving administrative tasks, it can be helpful to determine what happens during a typical workday. In administration, it is typically more difficult to identify waste than in manufacturing, where workflow can be more easily examined. Example BPIE activities are

- Improving layout and labeling of drawers in a storage room
- Placing pictures on bins to match products that are inside the bins
- Improving directory system for computer files
- Improving layout of desk and office area so items can be found quicker.

## 13.5  DFIEE/DFSS: Product, Process, or Information Technology (IT) Project

For DFIEE/DFSS, the basic thought process differs from the process improvement roadmap. The process used in IEE is called DMADV (define-measure-analyze-design-verify), as illustrated in Figure 4.2. This IEE DMADV design-project approach is appropriate for product, process, or information technology (IT) projects.

> This IEE DMADV design-project approach is appropriate for product, process, or information technology (IT) projects.

For companies who develop new products, such as a new computer or insurance policy, there is typically a development process. However, much of the responsibility specifics for executing the process still reside with the product development manager. One might ask the question whether they think that the execution of a product development cycle and success of the developed product could differ dramatically if there were different product managers. The typical response to this question is affirmative.

Traditionally, products and processes were designed based on know-how and trial-and-error. However, the experiences of a designer are limited, which can lead to mistakes that are costly. Tools such as Axiomatic Design (AD) and Theory of inventive problem solving (TRIZ) can aid the design decision-making process. In addition, often there are oversights or lack of focus to important needs of the overall development process. Concurrent engineering is an approach to improve new product development where the product and its associated processes are developed in parallel. The Design for X techniques focus on the details needed within Concurrent Engineering.

What we would like is a product development process that is efficient, effective, and more robust to differences between product development managers. Implementation of the IEE DMADV roadmap addresses this by providing the opportunity for the wise integration of Lean and Six Sigma tools such as DOE with existing development process requirements. This system can provide a more effective product-to-product development process learning-bridge framework so that products can be developed better, faster, and more in alignment to customer needs. This system can enhance product development and at the same time yield a system that is more robust to product manager-to-manager differences.

Another application of the fundamental IEE DMADV roadmap is new process development. This same basic IEE DMADV roadmap can be applied to the creation of a process or system that the organization has never done before or has not done recently; e.g., building of a new call center, acquiring a company, or setting up a new facility. This system can complement a project manager's skills for the task at hand. This is done through tool applications that help, among other things, mitigate risks, improve workflows, and increase systems' test effectiveness. The result is a system that helps meet expected objectives.

Finally, the IEE DMADV roadmap is also applicable to information technology (IT) projects. This system can complement existing IT development processes by providing, among other things, a system for capturing end-user customer needs and a system for testing the effectiveness of the newly developed product before going live.

Objectives of each DMADV step are:

- Define the goals of the project along with internal/external customer deliverables.
- Measure and determine customer needs and any specification requirements.
- Analyze the options for the process of meeting customer needs.
- Design the details needed to meet customer needs.
- Verify design performance and its ability to meet customer needs.

Davenport and Harris (2007) provide several case studies where companies have gained from the use of analytics. IEE offers the enterprise system framework for achieving these types of performance on an on-going basis:

- The value of Capital One's stock has grown two to four times faster than its largest competitors, increasing by 1000 percent over the past ten years. This performance outpaced the S&P 500 index by a factor of 10. Today, Capital One runs about three hundred experiments per business day to improve its ability to target individual customers. The company judges through these relative low-cost tests how successful products and programs would be before it engages in full-scale marketing; i.e., the verify step of DMADV. IEE offers the framework for not only this form of design verification but also putting in place the process for selecting the areas of the business to target improvement products and programs.

- Progressive Insurance hunts the insurance markets and business models markets that have been ignored using conventional data analysis. Progressive's innovation led to the first real-time on-line auto insurance offering and rate comparisons. The company uses analytics in price setting to such an extent that it believes when companies offer lower rates they are taking on unprofitable customers. The E-DMAIC system offers the structure for creating innovative products and conducting this form of analytics.

*Implementing Six Sigma* (Breyfogle 2003) provides more information about the tools used in these steps and some unique/ powerful applications for using DOE to improve the overall development process.

## 13.6   Process Improvement Projects

For simple improvements where there is no need for specific quantification of the amount of improvement from the project, a BPIE can be sufficient. However, for more complicated processes where the solution is not obvious, a formal roadmap system can be invaluable for describing the overall thought and data collection/analysis process.

How does a team determine whether an improvement idea could be a quick win, whether it is a BPIE or a P-DMAIC project? Use the following five criteria to determine its quick-win viability: easy to implement, fast to implement, cheap to implement, within the team's control, and reversible.

The P-DMAIC roadmap provides a work breakdown structure where a project can be subdivided into a plan that has easily digestible parts. This methodology systematically maps out the detail of paths and tasks needed to accomplish a project. This work breakdown structure flow can reveal the real level of complexity involved to achieve the project's goal. Potentially overwhelming projects can then become manageable, as well as uncovering unknown complexity. Planning teams move from theory to the real world relative to project scope and due dates. In addition, this project execution breakdown structure gives both participants and reviewers outside the team a presentation structure that can be checked for logical links and completeness at each level of the detailed plan.

> The P-DMAIC roadmap provides a work breakdown structure where a project can be subdivided into a plan that has easily digestible parts. This methodology systematically maps out the detail of paths and tasks needed to accomplish a project.

## 13.7 Enterprise Process Simplification

When improving the enterprise, it is important to start with the big picture and work downward. There can be fundamental issues with the overall enterprise process model that can be very difficult, if not impossible, to overcome when we simply focus on improving processes at lower levels of the organization.

For example, our enterprise process might have created a large number of SKUs (i.e., stock keeping unit) to address the wide variety of customer desires for product offering variations. For organizations that produce automobiles, this policy can lead to very large inventories. For insurance organizations that create and manage a completely new insurance policy for each of their client companies, this can lead to inefficiencies and to internal business process waste that can have a major bottom-line impact.

At the enterprise process level, we need to focus on what needs to be done to simplify the overall system. Direction to accomplish simplification of an existing process can be undertaken using the IEE process DFIEE roadmap.

## 13.8 Project Selection from the EIP Process

The E-DMAIC analyze phase included an EIP system for potential projects identification (see Figure 12.1). All these projects should be in alignment with the business goals and should be undertaken. However, organizations may not have the bandwidth to undertake all projects at once. When this occurs, organizations need a system where they can prioritize EIP created projects, if needed.

Table 13.1 illustrates a project prioritization selection matrix of identified EIP projects, which uses criteria that has different weighting. Projects with the largest total score have the highest perceived priority and would be assigned to the appropriate black belts or green belts.

**Table 13.1** EIP Project Selection Matrix

## EIP Project Selection Matrix

| | Potential impact to business strategy/goals | 30,000-foot-level metric data available | Smaller amount of resources needed for project | Available personnel for team | Time to complete < 6 months | Input (cause) data available | Champion has authority to implement changes | <<<Process Outputs | |
|---|---|---|---|---|---|---|---|---|---|
| | | | | | | | | <<<Importance - Training Project | |
| | | | | | | | | <<<Importance - Standard Project | |
| | | | | | | | | Training | Standard |
| | | | | | | | | ------ Total ------ | ------ Total ------ |
| Training* | 5 | 10 | 9 | 6 | 8 | 9 | 8 | 0 | 0 |
| Standard | 10 | 8 | 9 | 6 | 2 | 2 | 7 | 0 | 0 |
| | | ----------- Correlation of input to output ----------- | | | | | | | |
| Project 1 | | | | | | | | | |
| Project 2 | | | | | | | | | |

* Training -- First project assigned to coincide with a training course

A reader could make the point that this matrix can be used without conducting an E-DMAIC analysis and EIP drilldown. I will not disagree. Many Six Sigma and Lean Six Sigma deployments utilize a similar matrix. However, in IEE, we suggest focusing only on EIP listed projects that have alignment to business needs; i.e., as identified through an E-DMAIC analyze phase.

By doing this, we are prioritizing projects to execute that have been pulled for creation by metric improvement needs, which have alignment with business goals. This is different than simply listing projects that could be undertaken and then voting using a project selection matrix; i.e., a push for project creation. As noted earlier with a push for project creation system we can be spending much effort on suboptimizing processes that, when improved, do not truly impact the business metrics as a whole.

When using this prioritization matrix, care needs to be exercised. Users should not consider small project score separations to be important relative to establishing overall project priorities; i.e., similar scores in the right two matrix columns for two or more projects should be treated as equal scores. A project priority grouping can be identified if there is natural separation between ranked scores.

Often, people have difficulty establishing a criteria importance spread between categories. In an extreme situation, there are no between-categories spread when all categories are assigned an importance criterion of ten. Appendix Section D.10 describes the analytical hierarchy process (AHP), which is a methodology to get around this problem. AHP forces the creation of importance values that have larger separation.

A final note, the matrix does offer the option of setting up different criteria for training and standard projects. This option needs to be used with care. In a push for project creation deployment system, I have seen organizations spend a lot of time training where each person is to have a project during class. Often these projects are chosen to be easier or have a smaller scope than standard projects. When this overall system is examined as a whole, I have noted that often it is difficult getting these projects completed and often when these projects are completed the trainee never completes another project. Often a push for project creation deployment can loose focus and become a training system where emphasis is given to individual black belt or green belt certification and not the completion of projects by all trainees on an on-going basis, where projects have true business needs alignment.

# 13.9   P-DMAIC Define Phase Overview

The objective of the project define phase is to describe the CTQ/
business issue, the customer, and the involved core business process. During the define phase, a problem statement is formulated.
Customer requirements are gathered, and a project charter is created, where the project scope is determined by the team with the
support of management. Other activities during this phase include:
definition of the 30,000-foot-level metric; identification of both internal and external customers; identification and definition of what
is to be improved (e.g., defect or lead time); estimation of CODND;
development of high-level process map; initiation of a SIPOC.

The success of a project depends also on communication.
The project charter and periodic report-outs provide an effective
means for communication so that there is no misunderstanding
of the objectives and status of a project.

The following list describes focus areas for the define phase of
an IEE project:

- Projects should be aligned with the improvement needs of
  its high-level value chain and business goals. Constraints
  and assumptions should be included.
- A two-three sentence problem statement needs to focus on
  the symptoms and not the possible solution. Customer and
  business impact information should be included along with
  current DPMO or other baseline information, data sources
  for problem analysis, and a CODND estimate.

  Example: Companies are dissatisfied with the customer
  service call wait time in our XYZ office. Our service re-
  cords show an estimated median wait time of 80 seconds
  with 80% of wait times between 25 and 237 seconds.
  Note: This example illustrates how a 30,000-foot-level
  operational metric within an IEE enterprise pulls for
  project creation.
- Stakeholders (finance, managers, people who are working
  in the process, upstream/downstream departments, suppliers, and customers) need to agree to the usefulness of the
  project and its problem statement.
- The financial liaison person should work closely with the
  project leader and champion to create a cost benefit analysis for the project. This could include expense reduction,
  revenue enhancements, loss avoidance, reduced costs, or
  other CODND benefits.

- The project scope needs to be sized correctly and documented in a project charter format (see Table 13.2). All involved need to agree to the objectives, scope, boundaries, resources, project transition, and closure of the project charter. The details on this charter should be updated as the project proceeds through the overall IEE execution roadmap.
- Projects should be large enough to justify the investment of resources but small enough to ensure problem understanding and development of sustainable solutions. The scope should accurately define the bounds of the project so that project creep, a major cause for missed deadlines, is avoided.

   Example: Reduce the hold time of calls at the XYZ office with the intention of leveraging success to other call centers.
- Targeted improvement goals should be measurable. These goals should be tied to CODND benefits when appropriate.

   Example: Reduce the median call wait time to 40 seconds or less, yielding a $200,000 per year benefit at the XYZ office.
- Measurements should be described. If defects are the 30,000-foot-level metric, what constitutes a defect and how it will be tracked should be described. If lead time is the metric, the plans for lead time quantification and tracking should be described. Note: Some organizations may choose to report a sigma quality level metric; however, this is not recommended in an IEE implementation.
- The categories of a SIPOC should have been addressed, where the process portion of SIPOC is at high level, containing only 4–7 high-level steps (see Appendix Section D.1). How the SIPOC aligns with the high-level supply-chain map and its needs should be demonstrated along with the gap between voice of the process and voice of the customer.
- Team members should be selected by the champion and project leader (e.g., black belt) so that they provide different insights and skills (e.g., self-facilitation, technical/subject-matter expertise) needed for the successful completion of the project in a timely fashion. Names, roles, and amount of time for project dedication should be addressed for each team member.
- The Champion needs to work with the project leader so that the project status is sufficiently documented within a corporate database that can be conveniently accessed by others.

# 13.10   P-DMAIC Project Metrics

Each process improvement project has a problem statement. This statement needs to be written so that the business is compelled to support the problem resolution. An important aspect of the problem statement is project metric selection.

Since many organizational metrics are interdependent, it is not uncommon for a problem statement to identify more than one 30,000-foot-level metric as being impacted by the issue. Multiple metrics typically address differing problem aspects in cost, quality, and time. Even though this is okay, it does not mean that the project statement should target all listed 30,000-foot-level metrics.

Projects should be chartered with a single primary metric and have a goal to improve this measurement. This practice ensures that upcoming numerical analyses and decision-making steps will be relatively straight forward. Multiple metrics can make these steps confusing.

This strategy is consistent with the principles of Dr. Deming, who stated that cost savings will follow fixing the quality. A generalization of this position is that if you fix any aspect of a process, improvements in other areas will follow. For example, a reduction in lead time leads to a reduction in overall costs and possible improved quality.

To illustrate the creation of project metrics that have interdependencies, consider the following. The performance of a process is a function of three aspects: cost, quality, and time. Fix one of the three performance aspects and you should see improvements in the other two. In projects, we can track these other two measurement aspects as secondary project metrics. Secondary project metrics are chosen to ensure that a black belt does not improve a primary metric to the detriment of secondary metrics.

One final point is that project primary and/or project metrics can be an in-process metric such as defects per million opportunities (DPMO) or rolled throughput yield (RTY). These hidden factory metrics are described in Appendix Section B.3.

# 13.11   P-DMAIC Problem Statement

Each project has stakeholders. A project could have stakeholders from finance, managers, people who are working in the process, upstream/downstream departments, suppliers, and customers.

Upon completing the decision that a project will be undertaken, it is critical that the stakeholders agree to a project problem statement. The documentation of this agreement is part of the project define phase. In addition to containing a baseline statement with improvement goals, the problem statement should be compelling reason for the organization to assign time and resources to correct the problem.

A problem statement should reflect the current state of the problem. The problem statement needs to provide a complete, but concise, description of the problem relative to how often, when, and process location. The problem statement needs to include the data's source. A future state or solution should not be proposed. Impact estimate should address cost, customer satisfaction, and employee satisfaction. The problem statement is dynamic and can change over time.

Key parts of a problem statement are:

1. Current performance as a function of the 30,000-foot-level metric
2. Expected performance as a function of the 30,000-foot-level metric
3. Impact of the existing problem to the organization
   a. As stated in the 30,000-foot-level metric
   b. In dollars or other business metric
4. Time period that the baseline problem was determined
5. Objective of the project
   a. Usually a percentage gap between the current and expected performance; i.e., part 1 and 2 noted above
   b. An organizational benefit quantification in dollars or another metric, which is an improvement project staffing resource justification
   c. Target completion date

The following problem statement template and objective statement templates are not intended to be a recipe. The purpose of these templates is to aid in problem and objective statements' formulation.

Problem statement template:

In (<u>time period</u>) the (<u>process name</u>) produced (<u>performance level</u>), which was (\_\_\_) percent of the expected performance of (<u>target performance</u>), resulting in a (<u>value of the problem in dollars, man-hours, or other unit</u>) impact to the (<u>business metric</u>).

Objective statement template:

Improve (<u>process name</u>) performance gap of (<u>current – ex-</u><u>pected above</u>) by (__) percent to (<u>project goal</u>) by (<u>planned completion date</u>) resulting in a benefit of (<u>same units as problem statement</u>).

A problem statement:

- Is clearly aligned with the goals and strategic objectives of the business.
- Focuses on a core issue; e.g., TOC bottleneck system operation that can lead to more customers and cash.
- Addresses a chronic issue which is not well understood and has caused past difficulties.
- Is large enough to justify the investment of project resources.
- Is small enough to be completed in six months or less.
- Can be summarized in several short sentences that clearly communicate the problem and its estimated impact on the customer or the business.
- Is a mechanism that creates a laser sharp focus for the team effort and helps avoid going into tangential issues.
- Is a document acceptable to the champion, core team members, process owner(s), sponsors and other concerned executives.
- Is a living statement and captures the best understanding of the issue at the time.

A problem statement is not:

- An easily developed or quick statement that was developed by someone without team discussion.
- A plan to implement a pre-determined solution, i.e. a "just do it" project.
- A way to get the organization to address a pet peeve.
- A list of potential root causes of the problem or a summary of potential solution(s).
- A place to capture the background and/or past, recent, or future events about the issue.
- Set in concrete.

Problem statement creation steps are:

- Black belt or green belt creates a draft based on the best understanding of the project and conducts initial review with the champion and the process owner.

- Black belt/green belt shares the revised draft with the core team and invites full discussion on it. They incorporate their ideas and changes.
- Black belt/green belt again reviews the statement with the champion and process owner, not for semantics but for general concept.
- As better understanding is developed or the business needs change, black belt/green belt reflects the changes and starts the process again; i.e., there is flexibility.

Example problem statement:

- On-time deliveries of Product ABC ordered from our website are averaging 70%, as measured from shipping reports, where on-time shipment is defined as arriving on the date requested by the customer.
  - This resulted in increased customer complaints and shipping costs, along with lost sales.
  - Shipping penalties totaled $120,000 in the last six months; lost sales have not yet been quantified but are thought to exceed $1 million.
  - On-time shipment has dropped from 85% to 70% in the last nine months.

When needed, revisit and revise problem statement considering:

- Define—In the chartering process, identify the major pain.
- Measure—Clarify problem statement and create sharper focus.
- Analyze—As better insight is developed during data analysis, re-scope or re-direction as needed.
- Improve—During exploration of each improvement idea, consider its problem statement impact.
- Control—To close the loop, assess how well the project results addressed the original problem statement and project goal.

## 13.12  Example 13.1: Problem Statement

Let's evaluate the following problem statement: Our current customer financial reporting model is scattered across multiple business functions, is dependent upon several reporting applications, and requires manual intervention. These factors negatively impact our production capacity and create bottlenecks for lead time.

Reassessment of the statement was made relative to:

- What is the KPOV for this process?
- What are the customer requirements and business goals?
- Are potential causes included?
- Is background included?
- What is the real pain?
- Is the opportunity quantified?

This assessment led to the following:

- Revised Problem Statement: Currently, the lead time required to generate customer financial reports is $X_1$, resulting in decreased customer satisfaction and rework that costs the company $\$X_2$.
- Goal: Reduce lead time from request to customer receipt by $X_3$%, to a value of $X_4$ (i.e., goal).
- Baseline Metrics: Lead time to create customer financial reports, as measured from the customer request to delivery.

## 13.13   P-DMAIC Project Scope and Business Need Alignment

Project scope should be aligned with improvement needs of its high-level value chain. Project scope needs to be sized correctly and documented in a project charter. In the E-DMAIC analyze phase, Pareto charts (see Appendix D.13) can help prioritize drill-down opportunities, which often occur with project scoping. For example, a Pareto chart of identified failure categories in a 30,000-foot-level scorecard/dashboard value-chain metric could lead to focusing on reduction of the largest failure type that would be tracked at a 20,000-foot-level for the project (see Example 12.1.)

Theory of constraints (TOC) techniques in E-DMAIC analyze phase could also help identify constraint improvement opportunities, which can dramatically affect the overall system output.

As described earlier, IEE emphasizes the creation of projects that address true business needs at the entire system level.

A visual demonstration of a project's alignment to these needs is achieved through the identification of the impacted metric in the value chain along with the identification of the project in the EIP, which describes the organization's goals and strategy alignment.

## 13.14   Secondary Metrics

To reiterate, project focus should be given to improve one 30,000-foot-level metric; i.e., the primary KPOV metric.

Secondary metrics have been called an insurance policy that protects the company from the black belt. This statement is appropriate since secondary metrics can protect the degradation of other performance measurements when improving a 30,000-foot-level project primary metric.

The reason for this protection is that often seemingly positive process improvements result in a net organizational loss, caused by negative change effects in areas not targeted by the improvement project. The goal for all secondary metrics is to ensure that their performance does not degrade; however, in many, if not most, cases these performance metrics will also demonstrate improvements at project completion.

A simplistic view is that every improvement project targets one of three performance aspects; i.e., costs, quality, or time. This implies that the primary focus of a project is to improve quality, reduce cost, or shorten lead times. One of these three is to be molded into the problem statement. The other two performance metrics can become secondary metrics. For example, if a project focus is to reduce the time to process a customer order, one appropriate secondary metric would be a quality aspect such as delivery-error or incomplete-delivery rate. Another appropriate secondary metric would be costs such as staffing costs or customer credits. These metrics are selected to ensure that a demonstrated reduction in customer order processing time has not been achieved at the expense of an increase in errors from cutting corners to go faster or an increased business cost by adding people to solve the process problem. A secondary project charter metric inclusion demonstrates to the business leadership that the improvement leader is addressing the project from a big-picture point of view.

**Table 13.2** IEE Project Charter

| IEE Project Charter | | |
|---|---|---|
| **Project Title and Type (e.g. Black or Green Belt)** | | |
| **Project Description** | | |
| **Start Date** | | |
| **Completion Date** | | |
| **Primary KPOV Metric** | | |
| **Project Goal (in terms of the KPOV & $)** | | |
| **Secondary Metrics** | | |
| **Non-quantified Benefits** | **Customer** | |
| | **Financial** | |
| | **Internal Productivity** | |
| **Phase Milestones (Start and stop dates)** | **Define** | |
| | **Plan Projects & Metrics** | |
| | **Baseline Project** | |
| | **Consider Lean Tools** | |
| | **MSA** | |
| | **Wisdom of the Org.** | |
| | **Analyze Phase** | |
| | **Improve Phase** | |
| | **Control** | |
| **Team Support** | | |
| **Team Members** | | |

## 13.15   Project Charter and SIPOC

An example IEE DMAIC project charter format is shown in Table 13.2. All involved must agree to the objectives, scope, boundaries, resources, project transition, and closure. The details on this charter should be updated as the project proceeds within the overall project execution roadmap. The champion needs to work with the black belt so that the project status can be sufficiently documented within a corporate database that can be conveniently accessed by others.

At the beginning stages of an IEE project, the champion needs to work with the black belt and process owner so that the right people are on the team. Team selection should result in team members being able to provide different insights and skills (e.g., self-facilitation, technical/subject-matter expertise) needed to the completion of the project in a timely fashion.

In the project charter there is a section for non-quantified benefits. This section lists potential project organizational benefits less tangible than the primary and secondary metrics. For example, this section can include anticipated soft savings project benefits such as morale or lead time improvements. These statements will not impact any initial ROI estimate; however, these statements can provide compelling project execution support.

In the project execution roadmap, a SIPOC provides both project scope boundaries and direction for making process improvements. Appendix Section D.1 describes SIPOC creation.

## 13.16   Project Benefit Analysis

Chapter 9 discussed some basic enterprise process financial analysis concepts. This section will focus on assessing the business value of a project.

As discussed earlier, one way in which Six Sigma differs from many prior business improvement efforts is its focus on rigorous calculation and on tracking of financial benefits delivered by projects. To measure the benefits of IEE projects consistently, a uniform set of guidelines must be developed by each business, in alignment with internal finance policies. Procedures need to be established so that multiple projects do not claim the same savings. System credibility is lost when every project is reporting millions of dollars in savings, when as a company we know that it is not possible to have all of these savings.

Often, existing financial systems are not structured to quantify project value easily for its validation. It is important to establish a baseline measurement of the process before starting to improve the process and for the IEE Measurement and Improvement function to work closely with Finance to determine the validation strategy.

Traditional COPQ calculations look at costs across the entire company using the categories of prevention, appraisal, internal failure, and external failure, as described in Table 13.3. Organizations often do not disagree with these categories, but they typically do not expend the effort to determine this costing for their particular situations.

Organizations need to determine how they are going to determine the benefit of projects. The procedure that they use can affect how projects are selected and executed. I think that other categories need to be considered when making these assessments.

As noted earlier, I prefer the term cost of doing nothing differently (CODND) to the COPQ term. The reason I have included the term *differently* is that organizations often are doing something under the banner of process improvements. These activities could include lean manufacturing, TQM, ISO9000, and so on.

Let's use a days sales outstanding (DSO) project example to illustrate two options for conducting a project benefit analysis. For an individual invoice, its DSO would be from the time the invoice was created until payment was received. CODND considerations could include the monetary implications of not getting paid immediately; e.g., cost associated with interest charges on the money due to additional paperwork charges. COPQ calculations typically involve the monetary implications beyond a criterion. COPQ calculations typically would include costs associated with interest charges on the delinquent money after the due date for the invoice and additional paperwork/activity charges beyond the due date.

One might take the position that we should not consider incurred costs until the due date of an invoice since this is the cost of doing business. This could be done. However, consider that some computer companies actually get paid before products are built for their Internet on-line purchases and their suppliers are paid much later for the parts that are part of the product assembly process. If we examine the total CODND opportunity costs, this could lead to out-of-the-box thinking. For example, we might be able to change our sales and production process so that we too can receive payment at the time of an order.

Section 9.7 described various categories of hard and soft financial benefits. An organization could consider a further breakdown of hard and soft project benefits into the following categories that were used at IOMEGA (APQC 2001):

**Table 13.3** Traditional Quality Cost Categories and Examples

| PREVENTION |
| --- |
| Training |
| Capability Studies |
| Vendor Surveys |
| Quality Design |
| **APPRAISAL** |
| Inspection and Test |
| Test Equipment and Maintenance |
| Inspection and Test Reporting |
| Other Expense Reviews |
| **INTERNAL FAILURE** |
| Scrap and Rework |
| Design Changes |
| Retyping Letters |
| Late Time Cards |
| Excess Inventory Cost |
| **EXTERNAL FAILURE** |
| Warranty Costs |
| Customer Complaint Visits |
| Field Service Training Costs |
| Returns and Recalls |
| Liability Suits |

- Bottom-line hard dollar
  - Decreases existing business costs.
  - Example: defects, warranty, maintenance, labor, freight.
  - Takes cost off the books or adds revenue to the books.
- Cost avoidance
  - Avoids incremental costs that have not been incurred but would have occurred if project were not performed.
  - Example: enhanced material or changes that would affect warranty work.
- Lost profit avoidance
  - Avoids lost sales that have not been incurred, but would have occurred if project had not occurred.
  - Example: a project reduces frequency of line shutdowns.
- Productivity
  - Increases in productivity which improves utilization of existing resources.
  - Example: Redeployment of labor or assets to better use.
- Profit enhancement
  - Potential sales increase, which would increase gross profit.
  - Example: Change that was justifiable through a survey, pilots, or assumptions.
- Intangible
  - Improvements to operations of business which can be necessary to control, protect, and/or enhance company assets but are not quantifiable.
  - Example: Administrative control process that could result in high legal liability expense if not addressed.

Finally, it needs to be highlighted that if all product produced from a process can be sold and if the project improved the overall capacity of the process (i.e., improved the capacity of the process bottleneck), the project financial credit should be total additional revenue for the additional product sold less cost of goods sold. That is, all current fixed costs are already covered and should not be spread across the new production capacity resulting from the project.

## 13.17   Enterprise Process Improvement Demonstration

As part of the E-DMAIC improve phase, the creation of a repository and reporting system for the completion of all enterprise process improvement activities can prove to be very beneficial for future E-DMAIC analyze phase assessments. Efforts should be given to compile this information in a format that can be readily analyzed. Project completions should quantify their return on investment benefits and linkage to the enterprise's satellite-level metrics.

## 13.18 Applying IEE

The financial quantification of projects is very important within the IEE infrastructure of an organization. However, organizations should not overlook the value from soft savings and improved customer satisfaction. Also, organizations should consider TOC methodologies within the overall financial measurement strategy of an organization.

The financial liaison person should work closely with the project leader and champion to create a cost benefit analysis for the project. This could include expense reduction, revenue enhancements, loss avoidance, reduced costs, or other CODND benefits.

To reiterate:

- Projects should be large enough to justify the investment of resources but small enough to ensure problem understanding and development of sustainable solutions. The scope should accurately define the bounds of the project so that project creep, a major cause for missed deadlines, is avoided.
  - Example: Reduce the hold time of calls at the XYZ office with the intention of leveraging success to other call centers.
- Targeted improvement goals should be measurable. These goals should be tied to CODND benefits when appropriate.
  - Example: Reduce the median call wait time to 40 seconds or less, yielding a $200,000 per year benefit at the XYZ office.
- Measurements should be described. If defects are the 30,000-foot-level metric, what constitutes a defect and how it will be tracked should be described. If lead time is the metric, the plans for lead time quantification and tracking should be described. Note: Some organizations may chose to report a sigma quality level metric; however, as

noted in Section 1.19, this is not recommended in an IEE implementation.

Presentation effectiveness is essential to convey project status, analyses, and result to others.

## 13.19   Exercises

1. Describe the differences between an IEE DMADV project and a P-DMAIC project.
2. Describe a situation that you encountered as a customer where it would have been beneficial if the company had a BPIE system.
3. Describe the differences and similarities between your company's project selection process and the EIP process. State the benefits and detriments of each system. If desired, you may change the wording in the first sentence from "your company's project" to "a company's project."
4. After reading the following problem statement, answer the questions and create a new problem statement.
   The amount of money in accounts receivable is too high and customers pay too slowly. A new computer system which tracks payments will increase our ability to track payment performance by customer and cut working capital by 50%, resulting in $2 MM in savings for the business.
   - Describe the KPOV for this process.
   - Describe the customer requirements and business goals.
   - Note whether potential causes are included.
   - Note whether the business already has a solution.
   - Note whether background is included.
   - Describe the real pain.
   - Note whether the opportunity is quantified, including any investment cost.
5. Create a project charter for the problem statement created in exercise.
6. Demonstrate a possible alignment of the project described in Exercise 5 to the value chain and EIP.
7. Create the SIPOC for the project described in Exercise 5.

8. Brainstorm potential CODND categories for the project described in Exercise 5. Estimate the percentage of the revenue lost from problem categories identified within your project.
9. Develop a list of next steps project action items.
10. Repeat exercises 5–9 for a project in your organization.

# 14

# E-DMAIC—Control Phase and Summary

## 14.1 E-DMAIC Roadmap Component

In the P-DMAIC execution roadmap, the final step is "C" for control. For satisfactory project completion, there needs to be a control mechanism that prevents degradation. Similarly, within an overall implementation, there needs to be some form of control mechanism at the enterprise level. The preceding chapters described the first four organizational enterprise phases of E-DMAIC. This chapter describes what items to consider in the E-DMAIC control phase.

The next section includes a checklist for this phase. I am providing this list up front in the roadmap phase so that the reader can view the big picture objectives of this phase. The reader can reference this checklist as needed when progressing through the phase.

## 14.2 Checklist: Enterprise Process Control Phase

Organizations have established control systems that involve audits, regulatory compliance assessments, personnel performance

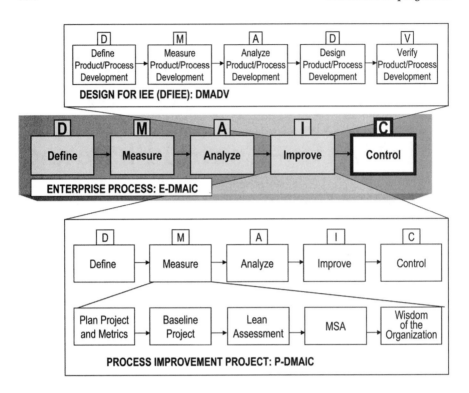

appraisals, codes of conduct, SOX assessments, and so forth. However, organizations often view these activities as independent, non-related entitites and they are often not questioned relative to improvement opportunities.

These seemingly independent control systems can be connected at the enterprise level. One advantage of doing this is that it is easier to assess whether all these E-DMAIC control phase measures are conducted efficiently and effectively. Ownership of this big picture composition and feedback system can reside with the EPM function (see Figure 7.6).

E-DMAIC control-phase activities include:

- Deploy enterprise standardization so that important process elements are performed consistently in the best possible way.
- Ensure effective business process audits and business process management with their documented procedures in the value chain.

- Coordinate and improve, as needed, customer-relationship management and SOX systems.
- Ensure that operational and design process control plans are in place and followed.
- Institutionalize process error-proofing wherever possible.
- Ensure that 30,000-foot-level scorecard/dashboard metrics with improvement objectives are tracked/reported correctly/effectively and incorporated into performance plans.
- Work with the conducting of regular monthly management meetings, giving inputs, when appropriate, to how data are presented and analyzed.
- Create a sensei (i.e., teacher or mentor) system for team members.
- Ensure the timely completion of projects. Ensure the establishment and execution of a system that assesses project selection quality and completion duration, with focus on continuous improvement.
- Ensure that project report-outs are complete and accurate.
- Ensure an effective delivery of presented report-outs to executives and others.
- Ensure that P-DMAIC executions have a control plan and the control plan is executed.
- Ensure that completed project results are effectively leveraged.
- Ensure timely and effective project coaching.
- Ensure creation and execution of company-specific reward and recognition plan.
- Coordinate and manage the business metric and improvement system.
- Coordinate the project management system, which includes general awareness of project status.
- Ensure that systems are created for conducting appropriate audits both efficiently and effectively.
- Coordinate management project report-outs.
- Institute and manage project tracking system.
- Ensure effective control plan initiation.
- Coordinate IEE DNA general awareness throughout the organization. (see Section 14.8)

The following chapter sections highlight the specifics of some of these activities.

## 14.3   Support Systems and Organizations

Organizations need a system to control IEE execution as described in Figure 4.2. Corporate strategy needs to address how the business intends to engage in its environment. Compensation policies, information systems, or training policies are critically important and should reinforce/support strategy (Hambrick and Fredrickson 2001). However, these internal organizational arrangement choices are not a part of strategy.

In IEE, these systems are to be described and executed as part of the organization's value chain (see Figure 7.1). The controls that ensure key processes' execution are to be described in control plan (see Section 14.7).

## 14.4   Management Project Reviews

The success of E-DMAIC improve phase initiated projects is very dependent upon management's project reviews. These regular review meetings and their effectiveness are a part of the E-DMAIC control phase.

Regular reviews are essential to keep focus and direction toward the successful completion of individual projects and the collection of EIP projects that benefit the enterprise as a whole. A targeted report-out frequency is:

- Weekly: To champion from black belts/green belts
- Monthly: To business/function leadership from champions
- Quarterly: To executives from business/function leadership

Meetings with example agendas and topics are:

- Weekly thirty-minute champion-black belt meeting agenda: Activities, recent accomplishments, issues/needs, and next-week plan. The project master black belt can also attend this meeting, along with other separate black belt meetings to resolve technical or other issues.
- Monthly Business/function leadership meeting agenda: Description of projects with anticipated financial gains, 30,000-foot-level scorecard/dashboard metrics report-out progression with goal, recent accomplishments, issues/needs, and next-month plans. All current projects need

regular review for the purpose of maintaining schedules, results, and the resolution of problems/road blocks.

- Quarterly executive meeting agenda: Satellite-level metrics with improvement goals, value chain with key 30,000-foot-level scorecard/dashboard metrics, EIP, summary of projects, recent accomplishments, issues/needs, and next-month plan.

During weekly project reviews, management's use of P-DMAIC roadmap checklists described in Volume III can expedite meetings and help build a consistent thought process between management and black belts/green belts. As a communication tool, this roadmap helps ensure that nothing gets overlooked. During the meeting, management needs to ask open-ended questions so that insight is gained to the methodologies, logic, and data used in the decision-making process.

In addition to process improvement and design project report-outs, BPIE activity should also be reported in status meetings.

## 14.5  Project Tracking System and 30,000-Foot-Level Metrics

Organizations need to have a system for project tracking. Initially, when there are not many projects, this system could be a simple Excel™ spreadsheet. In time, organizations need to migrate to a computer system that can roll up project status and report-outs across functions and business units.

This system needs to be able to drill down to project specifics and offer a repository for leveraging project success to other business areas, in addition to providing lessons learned. Instantis Enterprise Track is a system that provides this form of repository and communication flexibility. This system is a fully featured, web-based solution for companies to initiate, track and manage Six Sigma and other performance initiatives across their entire organization. This system can be part of a company becoming a learning organization (Senge 1990).

In this system, a decision support system (DSS) could be the database repository for the process and/or system solutions. When someone's problem is similar to a previously solved problem, he/she can gain access to a potential solution through a DSS keyword or problem description search entry. This system could also provide a financial project repository tracking system.

The EPM (see Figure 7.6) functional assessment of 30,000-foot-level scorecard/dashboard metrics can provide a system of control for the effectiveness of project selection and execution in the E-DMAIC improve phase. In addition, these metrics can provide insight to what should be done to the overall project implementation process.

## 14.6   Control Plan: Is and Is Nots

A control plan offers a systematic approach for process control and identifying/resolving issues. It offers a troubleshooting guide for process owners through its documented response plan. A good control plan strategy is a means to:

- Reduce process tampering.
- Provide a vehicle for the initiation/implementation of process improvement activities.
- Describe the training needs for standard operating procedures.
- Document maintenance schedule requirements.

> A control plan offers a systematic approach for process control and identifying/resolving issues. It offers a troubleshooting guide for process owners through its documented response plan.

Control plans should reduce the amount of firefighting and save money through fire preventive actions; however, often control plans are not set to the optimum conditions, as illustrated in Figure 14.1. Excessive controls cause unnecessary expense, and a lack of controls can lead to expensive problems.

A control plan is *not a*:

- way to establish excessive and unnecessary controls.
- plan to add inspection or audits.
- list of next steps of a project.
- way to create more documents or a bureaucracy.
- way get the organization to address a pet peeve.
- way to create more cost, additional lead time, or customer issues.

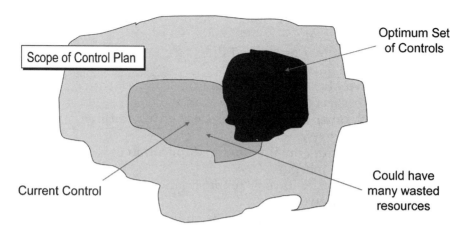

**Figure 14.1:** Scope of control plan.

- set of ambiguous or vague instructions with no owners.
- firefighting tool.

## 14.7   Enterprise Control Plan

In the final P-DMAIC roadmap step, a control plan documents how project gains are to be maintained. Volume III describes a traditional APQP control plan for this documentation. Similarly, an E-DMAIC control plan can address enterprise controls.

The value chain as shown in Figure 7.1 can link all internal documents and procedures. A control plan can be used to document key required activities to maintain the gains for both manufacturing and transactional processes. Control plan entries can be linked so that they become a part of the value chain. This control plan can become the single repository for the documentation of existing controls such as financial audits and equipment calibrations.

The AIAG control plan format described in Volume III is most conducive to manufacturing and process-level control scenarios. The following generic control plan creation system is applicable to both transactional and manufacturing situations.

Table 14.1 illustrates the collection of the following steps for nine examples (Ex. a–Ex. i) as part of an enterprise control plan. Individual entries can be linked to a high-level value-chain step, a sub-process step, an attached document, internet web page linkage, referenced document, etc.

1. Identify a value-chain process output or input to monitor/ control.
   - Ex. a: Customer order lead time
   - Ex. b: Part flatness
   - Ex. c: Telephone response time
   - Ex. d: Process temperature
   - Ex. e: Number of people in grocery check-out line
   - Ex. f: Defective rate
   - Ex. g: Internet domain name reapplication
   - Ex. h: Profit margins
   - Ex. i: Number of days to report financials
2. Assign ownership
   - Ex. a (lead time): Operations manager
   - Ex. b (part flatness): Process owner
   - Ex. c (tel. resp. time): Call center manager
   - Ex. d (proc. temp.): Operator
   - Ex. e (no. in check-out line): Check-out supervisor
   - Ex. f (defective rate): Operations manager
   - Ex. g (domain reapplication): Internet manager
   - Ex. h (profit margins): President
   - Ex. i (days to report financials): CFO
3. Describe input or output measurement
   - Ex. a (lead time): Hours from order initiation to fulfillment
   - Ex. b (part flatness): Inches in thousandths
   - Ex. c (tel. resp. time): Seconds
   - Ex. d (proc. temp.): Degrees Centigrade
   - Ex. e (no. in check-out line): Number of people
   - Ex. f (defective rate): Percent non-conformance
   - Ex. g (domain reapplication): Currently need to apply or not
   - Ex. h (profit margins): Corporate profit margins
   - Ex. i (days to report financials): Days
4. Describe response tracking; i.e., with engineering process control, if applicable
   - Ex. a (lead time): 30,000-foot-level; i.e., high-level output tracking
   - Ex. b (part flatness): 30,000-foot-level; i.e., high-level output tracking
   - Ex. c (tel. resp. time): 30,000-foot-level; i.e., high-level output tracking
   - Ex. d (proc. temp.): 50-foot-level pre-control chart
   - Ex. e (no. in check-out line): 50-foot-level pre-control chart

- Ex. f (defective rate): 30,000-foot-level; i.e., high-level output tracking
- Ex. g (domain reapplication): 50-foot-level signal within 90 days of due date; on Jan. 1, check to ensure signal is properly set for activation during the year
- Ex. h (profit margins): Satellite-level; i.e., business-level output tracking
- Ex. i (days to report financials): 30,000-foot-level; i.e., high-level output tracking

5. Select subgrouping/sampling period, if appropriate
- Ex. a (lead time): Weekly
- Ex. b (part flatness): Daily
- Ex. c (tel. resp. time): Weekly
- Ex. d (proc. temp.): About 30 minutes, per pre-control chart rules
- Ex. e (no. in check-out line): About 5 minutes, per pre-control chart rules
- Ex. f (defective rate): Weekly
- Ex. g (domain reapplication): N/A, examine yearly
- Ex. h (profit margins): Monthly
- Ex. i (days to report financials): Monthly

6. Determine sample size
- Ex. a (lead time): All
- Ex. b (part flatness): Five
- Ex. c (tel. resp. time): All
- Ex. d (proc. temp.): One
- Ex. e (no. in check-out line): All
- Ex. f (defective rate): All
- Ex. g (domain reapplication): N/A
- Ex. h (profit margins): One
- Ex. i (days to report financials): One

7. Describing tracking process to assess whether predictable process or not
- Ex. a (lead time): Mean and standard deviation
- Ex. b (part flatness): Mean and log standard deviation
- Ex. c (tel. resp. time): Mean and standard deviation
- Ex. d (proc. temp.): Individual value
- Ex. e (no. in check-out line): Mean
- Ex. f (defective rate): Mean
- Ex. g (domain reapplication): N/A
- Ex. h (profit margins): Individual value
- Ex. i (days to report financials): Individual value

8. Determine prediction methodology, if applicable
   - Ex. a (lead time): Normal probability plot of all data in stable/predictable region
   - Ex. b (part flatness): Lognormal probability plot of all data in stable/predictable region
   - Ex. c (tel. resp. time): Normal probability plot of all data in stable/predictable region
   - Ex. d (proc. temp.): N/A
   - Ex. e (no. in check-out line): N/A
   - Ex. f (defective rate): Total non-conformances divided by units produced in stable/predictable region
   - Ex. g (domain reapplication): N/A
   - Ex. h (profit margins): Normal probability plot of all data in stable/predictable region
   - Ex. i (days to report financials): Normal probability plot of all data in stable/predictable region
9. Established measurement criterion or objective
   - Ex. a (lead time): 80% frequency of occurrence
   - Ex. b (part flatness): ± 0.001 inch
   - Ex. c (tel. resp. time): One minute or less
   - Ex. d (proc. temp.): 50°C ± 2°C
   - Ex. e (no. in check-out line): Between 2 and 4 people
   - Ex. f (defective rate): 1.5%
   - Ex. g (domain reapplication): Loss of service is less than 90 days
   - Ex. h (profit margins): 80% frequency of occurrence
   - Ex. i (days to report financials): 10 days is upper specification limit
10. Describe device or individual making measurement
    - Ex. a (lead time): Computer
    - Ex. b (part flatness): Dial indicator
    - Ex. c (tel. resp. time): Computer
    - Ex. d (proc. temp.): Thermocouple
    - Ex. e (no. in check-out line): Visual computer sensor
    - Ex. f (defective rate): Visual inspection
    - Ex. g (domain reapplication): Manual assessment
    - Ex. h (profit margins): Financial system
    - Ex. i (days to report financials): Manual time stamp
11. Describe metric report-out destination
    - Ex. a (lead time): Value chain and monthly executive meeting
    - Ex. b (part flatness): Customer
    - Ex. c (tel. resp. time): Value chain and monthly executive meeting

- Ex. d (proc. temp.): Operator
- Ex. e (no. in check-out line): Store check-out supervisor
- Ex. f (defective rate): Value chain and monthly executive meeting
- Ex. g (domain reapplication): Internet manager
- Ex. h (profit margins): Value chain and monthly executive meeting
- Ex. i (days to report financials): Value chain and monthly executive meeting

12. Assess measurement response
    - Ex. a (lead time): Determine if process is predictable. If process is predictable, determine process capability/performance metric.
    - Ex. b (part flatness): Determine if process is predictable. If process is predictable, determine process capability/performance metric.
    - Ex. c (tel. resp. time): Determine if process is predictable. If process is predictable, determine process capability/performance metric.
    - Ex. d (proc. temp.): Determine if an adjustment is needed, per pre-control chart rules.
    - Ex. e (no. in check-out line): Determine if an adjustment is needed, per pre-control chart rules.
    - Ex. f (defective rate): Determine if process is predictable. If process is predictable, determine process capability/performance metric.
    - Ex. g (domain reapplication): Determine if it is time for re-application.
    - Ex. h (profit margins): Determine if process is predictable. If process is predictable, determine process capability/performance metric.
    - Ex. i (days to report financials): Determine if process is predictable. If process is predictable, determine process capability/performance metric.

13. Create action reaction plan
    - Ex. a (lead time): If process is predictable and the response is not satisfactory, pull for project creation or continue/expedite existing project's completion. Investigate special cause conditions and take necessary actions.
    - Ex. b (part flatness): If process is predictable and the response is not satisfactory, pull for project creation or continue/expedite existing project's completion. Investigate special cause conditions and take necessary actions.

- Ex. c (tel. resp. time): If process is predictable and the response is not satisfactory, pull for project creation or continue/expedite existing project's completion. Investigate special-cause conditions and take necessary actions.
- Ex. d (proc. temp.): Adjust temperature per pre-control chart rules.
- Ex. e (no. in check-out line): Add or reassign checkers per pre-control chart rules.
- Ex. f (defective rate): If process is predictable and the response is not satisfactory, pull for project creation or continue/expedite existing project's completion. Investigate special-cause conditions and take necessary actions.
- Ex. g (domain reapplication): Domain reapplication is initiated when signal is presented.
- Ex. h (profit margins): If processes are predictable and the response is not satisfactory relative to meeting business goals, reassess EIP work, project selection, and project execution. Investigate special-cause conditions and take necessary actions.
- Ex. i (days to report financials): If process is predictable and the response is not satisfactory, pull for project creation or continue/expedite existing project's completion. Investigate special-cause conditions and take necessary actions.

When projects experience a pull for creation in the IEE system, any resulting project control metrics should be placed in the enterprise control plan. To illustrate this, let's consider that an improvement is to be made in order lead time. Upon project completion, management needs to require a scorecard format that includes a control chart and process capability/performance statement rather than a traditional scorecard format.

These metrics exemplify an enterprise scorecard or dashboard system creation through the value chain and customer needs. I suggest that the reader now re-read Chapter 3 to compare the E-DMAIC scorecard/dashboard system to traditional scorecard methodologies. Differences between the E-DMAIC scorecard/dashboard system and traditional scorecard systems include:

- Wrong behavior can occur when there is tabled number reporting against goals.
- Wasted effort, misdirected activities, and playing games with the numbers can be the result of reporting measurements

# Table 14.1 E-DMAIC Control Plan Illustration

| | 1 | 2 | 3 | 4 | 5 | 6 | 7 | 8 | 9 | 10 | 11 | 12 | 13 |
|---|---|---|---|---|---|---|---|---|---|---|---|---|---|
| | Location and ownership | | | | Metric description | | Tracking process to determine whether predictable process or not | Prediction methodology, if applicable | Process capability/ performance measurement spec. or report-out statement | Metric evaluation and reactions | | | |
| | Value chain process output or input to monitor/control | Owner | IEE Tracking methodology | Input or output measurement description | Select subgrouping/ sampling period | Sample size | | | | Device or individual making measurement | Metric report-out destination | Metric assessment | Reaction plan |
| a | Customer order lead time | Operations manager | 30,000-foot-level | Hours from order init. To fulfillment | Weekly | All | Mean and standard deviation | Normal prob. Plot of all data from stable region | Median and 80% freq. of occurrence | Computer | Value chain and monthly exec. Meeting | 1 | 2 |
| b | Part flatness | Process owner | 30,000-foot-level | Inches in thousandsths | Daily | Five | Mean and log standard deviation | Log-normal probability plot of all data from stable region | ± 0.001 in. | Dial indicator | Customer | 1 | 2 |
| c | Telephone response time | Call center manager | 30,000-foot-level | Seconds | Weekly | All | Mean and standard deviation | Normal prob. Plot of all data in stable region | 60 sec. or less | Computer | Value chain and monthly exec. Meeting | 1 | 2 |
| d | Process temperature | Operator | 50-foot-level pre-control chart | Degrees Centigrade | About 30 min., pre per-control rules | One | Individual value | N/A | 50 °C ± 2 °C | Thermocouple | Operator | Determine if an adjustment is needed, per pre-control chart rules. | Adjust temperature per pre-control chart rules. |
| e | No. of people in grocery check-out line | Check-out supervisor | 50-foot-level pre-control chart | Number of people | About 5 min., per pre-control rules | All | Mean | N/A | Between 2 and 4 | Visual computer sensor | Store check-out supervisor | Determine if an adjustment is needed, per pre-control chart rules. | Add or reassign checkers per pre-control chart rules. |
| f | Defective rate | Oeprations manager | 30,000-foot-level | Percent non-conformance | Weekly | All | Mean | Total non-conformances divided by units produced in stable region | 1.50% | Visual inspection | Value chain and monthly exec. Meeting | 1 | 2 |
| g | Internet domain name reapplication | Internet maanager | 50-foot-level signal within 90 days of due date, Jan 1 checkout | Currently need to apply or not | N/A examine yearly | N/A | N/A | N/A | Loss of service is less than 90 days | Manual assessment | Internet manager | Determine if it is time for reapplication. | Domain reapplication is initiated when signal is presented. |
| h | Profit margins | President | Satellite-level | Corporate profit margins | Monthly | One | Individual value | Normal prob. Plot of all data in stable region | Median and 80% freq. of occurrence | Financial system | Value chain and monthly exec. Meeting | 1 | 3 |
| i | Number of days to report financials | CFO | 30,000-foot-level | Days | Monthly | One | Individual value | Normal prob. Plot of all data in stable region | 10 days is upper spec. limit | Manual time stamp | Value chain and monthly exec. Meeting | 1 | 2 |

1. Determine if process is predictable. If process is predictable, determine process capability/performance metric.

2. If process is predictable and the response is not satisfactory, pull for project creation or continue/expedite existing project's completion. Investigate special cause conditions and take necessary actions.

3. If processes are predictable and the response is not satisfactory relative to meeting business goals, reassess EIP work, project selection, and project execution. Investigate special cause conditions and take necessary actions.

that do not have the characteristic of a good metrics (see Section 3.2).

- Traditional scorecard systems do not highlight the need for improving the $X$s and/or process to get improvements in the $Y$; i.e., $Y=f(x)$. For a metric to improve, typically a focused project effort is needed, which requires a commitment of people resource. This resource commitment is often lacking when sole focus is given to meeting next period's numbers; e.g., arbitrarily set goals.

- Sub-optimization and no true benefit for the enterprise as a whole can be the result when a traditional scorecard system disseminates measurement goals through the organizational chart with a red-yellow-green tracking and no underlying system for making improvements.

The IEE measurement and improvement system can transition an organization from a firefighting mode to a system where organizational improvements impact the business as a whole.

Improved behaviors can result when owned metrics have a 30,000-foot-level reporting style during periodic (e.g., monthly) management status meetings. Cascading metric report-outs in this format from CEO/president/board room downward throughout the organization can lead to a reduction in firefighting and wasted efforts for the whole enterprise. During this status meeting, some metrics would be reported to demonstrate continued stability/predictability, while other metrics that were to be improved toward a SMART goal would lead to process improvement project status reporting. This form of metric reporting can lead to more constructive status meeting discussions and less need for micromanagement, which some managers have a tendency to do.

## 14.8   E-DMAIC Summary

Spear and Bowen (1999) articulated four Lean DNA rules and their view of the Toyota reasoning process. Jackson (2006) added a fifth rule with some rewording of the original rules. To expand the DNA definition to an IEE system, I added four additional rules with some rewording of previous rules. The IEE DNA rules are:

**Rule 1:** *Standardize processes and work*; i.e., create efficient and effective processes that have reduced variability and improved quality.

**Rule 2:** *Zero ambiguity*; i.e., internal and external customer requirements are perfectly clear.

**Rule 3:** *Flow the process*; i.e., material and information flow directly with minimal waste and variation.

**Rule 4:** *Speak with data*; i.e., compile and present the most appropriate data so that the right question is answered, and both statistical and visualization tools are used effectively.

**Rule 5:** *Develop leaders who are teachers*; i.e., leaders need to truly understand and then coach employees in E-DMAIC and P-DMAIC execution.

**Rule 6:** *Align work to the value chain*; i.e., align and document processes in the value chain so that information is readily accessible to fulfill employee and supplier needs.

**Rule 7:** *Report metrics at the 30,000-foot-level*; i.e., avoid scorecard systems that track against goals or calendar point performance metric reporting, which often leads to wasted resources through firefighting. Metrics need to be created so that there are no playing games with the numbers.

**Rule 8:** *Build strategies after analyzing the value chain, its metrics, and goals*; i.e., avoid creating strategies in isolation and aligning work activities to these strategies. Execution possibilities for strategy statements such as those in Section 3.4 are very team dependent and can lead to detrimental activities for the enterprise as a whole.

**Rule 9:** *Let metric improvement needs pull for project creation*; i.e., a push for project creation system can lead to the suboptimization of processes that don't favorably impact the business as a whole.

From the describe E-DMAIC roadmap, the reader will see how his/her organization can benefit from KCA in an IEE system. The EPM function (see Figure 7.6) can become the repository for this long-lasting organizational governance system that contains meaningful enterprise scorecards/dashboard metrics and an improvement system that helps organizations get out of the firefighting mode. Additional articles/information about IEE and the creation of a level five system are at www.SmarterSolutions.com.

Volume III provides the P-DMAIC details to execute an improvement project, which in IEE would initiate from the improve phase of the E-DMAIC roadmap.

## 14.9   Exercises

1.  Compare the scorecard/dashboard measurement system described in Chapter 3 to the E-DMAIC system. List the advantages and disadvantages of each.
2.  Consider that a company's governance model defines the composition of cross-organizational and cross-functional teams which will monitor the processes, the metrics, the meeting frequency, etc. This organization has governance models for many key strategic areas like total customer experience, warranty, etc. List the advantages and disadvantages of this governance when compared to the IEE governance model using the E-DMAIC roadmap.

# PART III
Appendix

# Appendix A: Infrastructure

## A.1  Provider Selection

All Six Sigma and Lean Six Sigma training and deployments are not equal. Breyfogle (2003a) provides basic provider selection considerations.

Organizations need to select a provider who identifies and best fulfills their true needs. Table A.1 is a selection matrix that can be used to help facilitate the selection process.

## A.2  Roles and Responsibilities

IEE roles and responsibilities build upon the structure of traditional Six Sigma. This organizational structure includes:

- Executive
  - Motivates others towards a common vision
  - Sets the standard, demonstrate the behaviors
  - Uses satellite-level and 30,000-foot-level scorecard/dashboard metrics
  - Asks the right questions
  - Uses IEE tools in day-to-day operations
  - Is visible
  - Gives a short presentation for each IEE training wave
  - Attends project completion presentations conducted by IEE team
  - Stays involved

415

# Table A.1  Provider Selection Matrix

**Provider Selection Matrix**

| Characteristic → Weighting ↓ / Provider | Experienced Provider (long term company) | Provides a sustainable business system, not just an organization to run projects | Has a system that provides for operational firefighting reduction | Book-training/usage that compliments workshop material | Provides a sytem for the integration of the enterprise scorecard, strategy, goals, and projects that supports analytics, innovation and governance. | Project execution roadmap with true integration of Lean, Six Sigma, and other tools | Technical expertise | An Industry Leader not a follower | Has a single system that is efficient with manufacturing and Transactional processes | Ranking |
|---|---|---|---|---|---|---|---|---|---|---|
| | 3 | 10 | 7 | 2 | 9 | 8 | 6 | 4 | 5 | |
| A | | | | | | | | | | 0 |
| B | | | | | | | | | | 0 |
| C | | | | | | | | | | 0 |
| D | | | | | | | | | | 0 |

Note 1:  Sort on the ranking columns and choose from the highest scores to charter projects
Note 2: Recommended that weights not be duplicated in order to force better rankings.

| Matrix header | Description |
|---|---|
| Experienced Provider (long term company) | Company has been in existence and applying Six Sigma and Lean tools for many years.  Many providers ability to support a full deployment is difficult to verify Age of the company is one good indicator of the ability to be there in the future. |
| Provides a sustainable business system, not just an organization to run projects | Six Sigma and Lean Six Sigma deployments typically stall out after a few years with a push for project creation system. This is because the deployment hunts for project and pound their chest in Tarzen like fashion boasting how much was saved. However, this financialy-validated savings is often localized and not felt by the enterprise as a whole.  The most common issue with project based deployment is when resources are committed to improve the capacity of one facet of the work where it is not the throughput constraint.  At a newspaper, that would be like increasing the printing capacity, when there is no ability to deliver any more or to sell any more.  The increased capacity improved the printing area performance metric, but ended up being an expense to the enterprise with no ability to benefit the revenue. |
| Has a system that provides for operational firefighting reduction | Provides a system of measurement that separate at the enterprise level common-cause variability from special-cause variabily.  Through this system organization can transition from fire-fighting to fire prevention.  This is key, because it is the reduction in the resources assigned to crisis management or firefighting that may be one of the biggest improvements realized.  Although this does not occur on its own, it usually needs to be part of the overall enterprise system and the deployement to truly take hold. |
| Book-training/usage that compliments workshop material | Workshop training material aligns with their books that address various user needs; e.g., technical book for black belts and novel book for high-level view of the system.  An organization could go into a deployment with the goal to become self sufficient.  Some of it is related to training the right people to manage the improvement system, but the training materials must be usable after the class completes.  This includes a text book that provides a deeper explanation that the course notes.  The course notes should be references to a text as backup material.  Any hand outs or Improvement systemroadmaps should be referenced to the class notes and the text.  In this way, the practitioners are able to find what they need to do their job without wasting a lot of time.  Doing their improvements independently leads to better practitioners and a better chance of self sufficiency. |
| Provides a sytem for the integration of the enterprise scorecard, strategy, goals, and projects that supports analytics, innovation and governance. | Provides enterprise system that integrates scorecards, strategies, and goals so that the best improvement and design projects for the business as a whole are created.  It includes a system-view scorecard improvement that pulls for the creation of the most beneficial project for the enterprise.  The enterprise effort should identify the key constraints to organization success and target projects to remove the constraint.  Articles about Dell's financial reporting problems (e.g., Richtel 2007) highlights this need; i.e., you need to have scorecards that lead to the most appropriate activity.  A Business Week article (Hindo 2007) about 3M's reduction in Six Sigma activities because innovation was stifled highlights the importance of integrating innovation at the enterprise level.  Each case could be assignable to the workforce working to performance metrics that did not support the overall enterprise. |
| Project execution roadmap with true integration of Lean, Six Sigma, and other tools | Often organizations that deploy Lean or Six Sigma do not truly integrate Lean and Six Sigma concept.  People who are strong in Lean push lean, while people strong in Six Sigma push Six Sigma.  Many have gone further and realized many other improvement genre used excellent tools and have also added them to their program.  Best in class organizations no longer have a lean or a six sigma program, they have an enterprise improvement strategy that uses the best tools at the right time.  A provider should have a system or roadmap to help the practitioners to use the right tools.  A single system that includes all the methods if superior to incrementally introducing the different systems since no un-learning is then required.  Right now fully transactional companies are realizing that all of the manufacturing improvement tools are applicable in their world too.  These tools should be integrated. |
| Technical expertise | Have the expertise to provide coaching and rent a master black belt to solve tough technical problems and enterprise deployment/metric reporting structure.  No provider will teach everything that is possible.  Most organizations develop this resource over time. For a deployment, you want a provider that can use the higher end tools to support the practitioners and the business before the internal worforce is ready. |
| An Industry Leader not a follower | This is about choosing a provider that is active in keeping the material content not just up-to date but being in the lead.  Is recognized industry thought leader that regularly provides articles and books, which have how-to substance. Publications describe both the norm and how to go Beyond Lean Six Sigma.  Although the source of the training material is difficult to discern, many providers either license other providers material or wrote there own based on what their black belts thought was important.  With this approach the quality of the material can degrade with each |
| Has a single system that is efficient with manufacturing and transactional processes | All organizations have a mixture of business models.  Manufacturing firms have transactional processes in HR, Procurement, Compliance and other areas.  Transactional organizations have processes equivalent to manufacturing, in that they produce documents, issue claim payments, provide customer solutions and other actions that the manufacturing paradigm can lead to clear insight and improvements.  Why have a provider that only teaches one or the other flavor of process improvement, when you risk not recognizing all improvement opportunities? |

- Steering team (measurements and improvements function)
    - Same as executive roles and responsibilities, plus
    - Develops project selection criteria
    - Sets policies for accountability for project results
    - Develops policies for financial evaluation of project benefits
    - Establishes internal and external communication plan
    - Identifies effective training and qualified trainers
    - Develops human resource policies for IEE roles
    - Determines computer hardware and software standards
    - Sets policies for team reward and recognition
    - Identifies high potential candidates for IEE roles
- Champion
    - Removes barriers to success
    - Develops incentive programs with executive team
    - Communicates and executes the IEE vision
    - Determines project selection criteria with executive team
    - Identifies and prioritize projects
    - Question methodology and project improvement recommendations
    - Verifies completion of phase deliverables
    - Drives and communicates results
    - Approves completed projects
    - Leverages project results
    - Rewards and recognizes team members
- Master black belt
    - Functions as change agents
    - Conducts and oversees IEE training
    - Coaches black belts/green belts
    - Leverages projects and resources
    - Formulates project selection strategies with steering team
    - Communicates the IEE vision
    - Motivates others towards a common vision
    - Approves completed projects
- Black belt
    - Leads change
    - Communicates the IEE vision
    - Leads the team in the effective utilization of the IEE Methodology
    - Selects, teaches, and uses the most effective tools
    - Develops a detailed project plan
    - Schedules and leads team meetings

- Oversees data collection and analysis
- Sustains team motivation and stability
- Delivers project results
- Tracks and reports milestones and tasks
- Calculates project savings
- Interfaces between Finance and Information Management (IM)
- Monitors critical success factors and prepare risk abatement plans
- Prepares and presents executive level presentations
- Completes 4–6 projects per year
- Communicates the benefit of the project to all associated with the process
- Green belt: Similar to black belt except that the green belt typically
  - Addresses projects that are confined to their functional area
  - Has less training than black belts
  - Leads improvement projects as a part-time job function
- Yellow belt
  - Supports black belt and green belt project execution as a team member
  - Offers suggestions for improving day-to-day work and measurement systems
- Sponsor (maybe also be a champion role)
  - Functions as change agents
  - Removes barriers to success
  - Ensures that process improvements are implemented and sustained
  - Obtains necessary approval for any process changes
  - Communicates the IEE vision
  - Aids in selecting team members
  - Maintains team motivation and accountability

## A.3   Reward and Recognition

When building an IEE infrastructure, reward and recognition need to be addressed. Lessons learned from past Six Sigma deployments can be very beneficial.

Successful implementations of Six Sigma have developed special reward and recognition systems. The following list summarizes the black belt recognition program for one company. Note that this plan does not mention rewarding others in the Six Sigma work (Snee and Hoerl 2003):

- Base pay
  - Potential increase at time of selection
  - Retain current salary grade
  - Normal group performance review and merit pay
- Incentive compensation
  - Special plan for black belts
  - Target award at 15% of base pay
  - Performance rating on 0–150% scale
  - Measured against key project objectives
  - Participation ends at end of black belt assignment

Another company's plan is more complete in that it includes the recognition of green belts, master black belts, champions and other team members.

- Black belt selection—Receive Six Sigma pin
- Black belt certification—$5,000 certification bonus plus plaque
- Black belt project completion
  - $500 to $5,000 in cash or stock options for first project
  - Plaque with project name engraved for first and subsequent projects
- Black belt Six Sigma activity awards
  - Recognize efforts and achievements during projects with individual and team awards—cash, tickets, dinners, shirts, etc.
- Green belt recognition
  - Similar to black belt recognition
  - No certification bonus
- Project team member recognition
  - Similar to black belt and green belt recognitions
  - No certification awards
- Annual Six Sigma celebration event
  - Presentation of key projects
  - Dinner reception with senior leadership

It should be noted that all rewards need not be monetary. Peer and management recognition such as opportunity for project presentation is a greater reward than money. The most appropriate plan is company dependent; i.e., what will work for one company or individual will not necessarily work for another.

# Appendix B: Six Sigma Metrics

## B.1   Sigma Quality Level

The purpose of this section is to provide a basic understanding of sigma quality level so that the reader can understand the methodology. IEE discourages use of sigma quality level metric at both the enterprise and project execution level; however, the reader needs a basic understanding since the term can arise in conversations with other Six Sigma practitioners. I will reference a failure rate unit of parts per million (ppm); however, DPMO could be used instead of ppm.

The sigma level, i.e., sigma quality level, sometimes used as a measurement within a Six Sigma program, includes a $\pm 1.5\sigma$ value to account for "typical" shifts and drifts of the mean that can occur over time. This sigma quality level relationship is not linear. In other words, a percentage unit improvement in parts-per-million (ppm) defect rate does not equate to the same percentage improvement in the sigma quality level.

Figure B.1 shows the sigma quality level associated with various services, considering the $1.5\sigma$ shift of the mean. From this figure, we note that the sigma quality level of most services is about four sigma, while world class is considered six. A goal of IEE implementation is continually to improve processes and become world class.

Figures B.2–B.4 illustrate various aspects of a normal distribution as it applies to Six Sigma program measures and the implication of the $1.5\sigma$ shift. Figure B.2 illustrates the basic measurement concept of Six Sigma according to which parts are to be manufactured consistently and well within their specification range. Figure B.3 shows the number of parts per

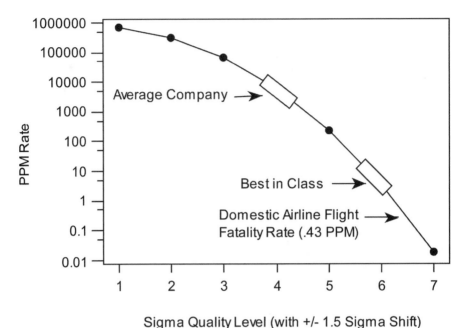

**Figure B.1:**  Implication of the sigma quality level. Parts per million
(ppm) rate for part or process step.

million that would be outside the specification limits if the data
were centered within these limits and had various standard deviations. Figure B.4 extends Figure B.3 to non-central data
relative to specification limits, in which the mean of the data is
shifted by 1.5σ. Figure B.5 shows the relationship of ppm defect
rates versus sigma quality level for a centered and 1.5σ shifted process, along with a quantification for the amount of improvement needed to change a sigma quality level. Volume III,
Table L has a finer conversion of ppm rates to sigma quality level
values.

A metric that describes how well a process meets requirements
is process capability. A Six Sigma quality level process is said
to translate to process capability index values for $C_p$ and $C_{pk}$ requirement of 2.0 and 1.5, respectively (see Breyfogle 2003). To
achieve this basic goal of a Six Sigma program might then be
to produce at least 99.99966% quality at the process step and
part level within an assembly; i.e., no more than 3.4 defects per
million parts or process steps if the process mean were to shift
by as much as 1.5σ. If, for example, there was on the average one
defect for an assembly that contained forty parts and four process

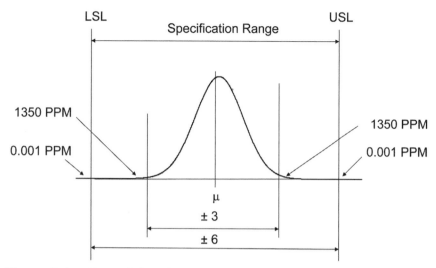

**Figure B.2:** Normal distribution curve illustrates the three sigma and six sigma parametric conformance. LSL = lower specification limit and USL = upper specification limit.

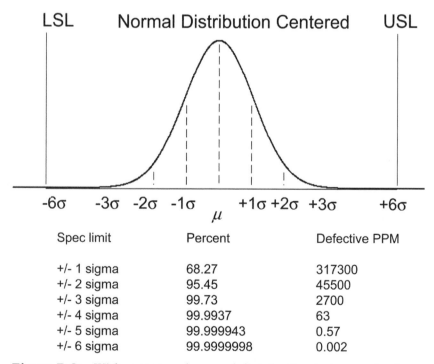

| Spec limit | Percent | Defective PPM |
|---|---|---|
| +/- 1 sigma | 68.27 | 317300 |
| +/- 2 sigma | 95.45 | 45500 |
| +/- 3 sigma | 99.73 | 2700 |
| +/- 4 sigma | 99.9937 | 63 |
| +/- 5 sigma | 99.999943 | 0.57 |
| +/- 6 sigma | 99.9999998 | 0.002 |

**Figure B.3:** With a centered normal distribution between six sigma limits, only two devices per billion fail to meet the specification target.

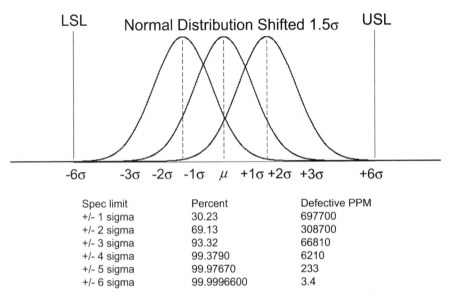

**Figure B.4:**  Effects of a 1.5σ shift where only 3.4 ppm fail to meet specifications.

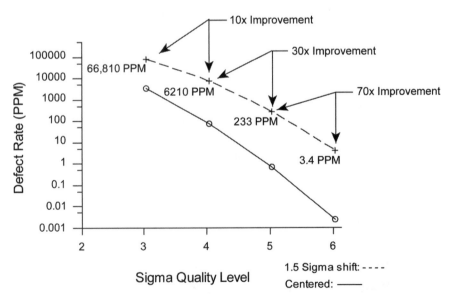

**Figure B.5:**  Defect rates (ppm) vs. sigma quality level.

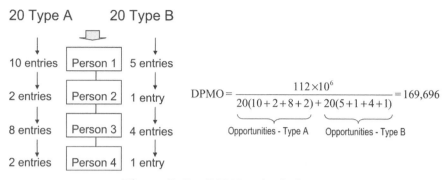

**Figure B.6:** DPMO calculations.

steps, practitioners might consider that the assembly would be at a four sigma quality level from Figure B.5, because the number of defects in parts per million is: $(1/160)(1 \times 10^6) \approx 6250$.

## B.2   Defects per Million Opportunities (DPMO)

I will use the example shown in Figure B.6 to illustrate the calculation of DPMO. In this illustration, a sales contract is completed in four process steps, where defects may or may not be reworked. A total of 40 random contracts were recorded over a stable/predictable period of time in the 30,000-foot-level control chart. From these 40 samples, 20 contracts were type A and another 20 were type B. The number of defects in these contracts was 112, which yielded an estimate for the process DPMO rate of 169,696. Some organizations might then convert this DPMO rate to a sigma quality level of 2.4 to 2.5 using Volume III, Table L.

## B.3   Rolled Throughput Yield (RTY)

Reworks within an organization that have no value and are often not considered within the metrics of a factory are often referred to as the hidden factory. The Six Sigma metric rolled throughput yield (RTY) is a metric that includes the hidden factory impact. RTY measures the percent of product that goes through the process without being scrapped or reworked. Reworks within an operation have no value and comprise what is termed the hidden factory. Process yield is not the same as rolled throughput yield since this scrapped product yield metric ignores rework. Process yield is the percentage of units that are not scrapped. RTY measures how well products or services are processed by organizations.

Figure B.7 compares the two metrics, where $Y$ is the yield at each of the three process steps. In this illustration:

- 64.3% (0.90×0.84×0.85 = 0.643) of the units completed the process without being reworked or scrapped.
- Rework expenses = 21.5% (215 units)
- Scrap expenses = 14.3% (143 units)

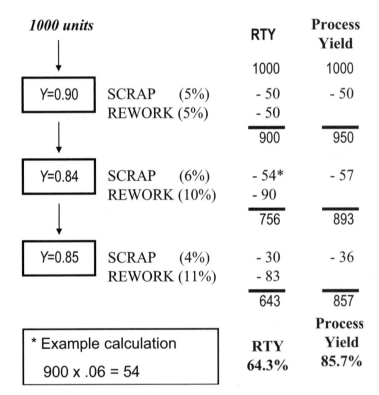

**Figure B.7:**   RTY and process yield illustration.

# Appendix C: Articles

## C.1 Sarbanes-Oxley (SOX) Act of 2002

The Sarbanes-Oxley (SOX) legislation act was created in 2002 partly in response to the Enron and WorldCom financial scandals. SOX protects shareholders and the public from enterprise process accounting errors and from fraudulent practices. In addition, it also ensures a degree of consistency in access to and reporting of information that could impact the value of a company's stock.

The following SOX Sections 302, 304, and 409 have the most applicability in an IEE environment.

### Sec. 302 Corporate Responsibility for Financial Reports

a) Regulations Required—The Commission, shall, by rule, require, for each company filing periodic reports under section 13(a) or 15(d) of the Securities Exchange Act of 1934 (15 U.S.C. 78m, 78o(d)), that the principal executive officer or officers and the principal financial officer or officers, or persons performing similar functions certify in each annual or quarterly report filed or submitted under either such section of such Act that—

1) the signing officer has reviewed the report;
2) based on the officer's knowledge, the report does not contain any untrue statement of a material fact or omit to state a material fact necessary in order to make the statements made, in light of the circumstances under which such statements were made, not misleading;

3) based on such officer's knowledge, the financial statements, and other financial information included in the report, fairly present in all material respects the financial condition and results of operations of the issuer as of, and for, the periods presented in the report;

4) the signing officers—

   A) are responsible for establishing and maintaining internal controls;

   B) have designed such internal controls to ensure that material information relating to the issuer and its consolidated subsidiaries is made known to such officers by others within those entities, particularly during the period in which the periodic reports are being prepared;

   C) have evaluated the effectiveness of the issuer's internal controls as of a date within 90 days prior to the report; and

   D) have presented in the report their conclusions about the effectiveness of their internal controls based on their evaluation as of that date;

   E) the signing officers have disclosed to the issuer's auditors and the audit committee of the board of directors (or persons fulfilling the equivalent function) —

5) the signing officers have disclosed to the issuer's auditors and the audit committee of the board of directors (or persons fulfilling the equivalent function) —

   A) all significant deficiencies in the design or operation of internal controls which could adversely affect the issuer's ability to record, process, summarize, and report financial data and have identified for the issuer's auditors any material weaknesses in internal controls; and

   B) any fraud, whether or not material, that involves management or other employees who have a significant role in the issuer's internal controls; and

6) the signing officers have indicated in the report whether or not there were significant changes in internal controls or in other factors that could significantly affect internal controls subsequent to the date of their evaluation, including any corrective actions to the date of their evaluation, including any corrective actions with regard to significant deficiencies and material weaknesses.

b) Foreign Reincorporations have no effect—Nothing in this section 302 shall be interpreted or applied in any way to allow any issuer to lessen the legal force of the statement required under this section 302, by an issuer having reincorporated or having engaged in any other transaction that resulted in the transfer of the corporate domicile or offices of the issuer from inside the United States to outside of the United States.

c) Deadline—The rules required by subsection (a) shall be effective not later than 30 days after the date of enactment of this Act.

## Sec 404 Management Assessment of Internal Controls

a) Rules Required—The commission shall prescribe rules requiring each annual report required by section 13(a) or 15(d) of the Securities Exchange Act of 1934 (15 U.S.C 78m or 78o(d)) to contain an internal report, which shall—

   1) state the responsibility of management for establishing and maintaining an adequate internal control structure and procedures for financial reporting; and

   2) contain an assessment, as of the end of the most recent fiscal year of the issuer, of the effectiveness of the internal control structure and procedure of the issuer for financial reporting.

b) Internal Control Evaluation and Reporting—With respect to the internal control assessment required by subsection (a), each registered public accounting firm that prepares or issues the audit report for the issuer shall attest to, and report on, the assessment made by the management of the issuer. An attestation made under this subsection shall be made in accordance with standards for attestation engagements issued or adopted by the Board. Any such attestation shall not be the subject of a separate engagement.

## Sec 409 Real Time Issuer Disclosures

Section 13 of the Securities Exchange Act of 1934 (15 U.S.C. 78m), as amended by this Act, is amended by adding at the end the following:

"(1) Real Time Issuer Disclosures—Each issuer reporting under section 13(a) or 15(d) shall disclose to the public on a rapid and current basis such additional information concerning material changes in the financial condition or operations of the issuer, in plain English, which may include trend and qualitative information and graphic presentations, as the Commission determines, by rule, is necessary or useful for the protection of investors and in the public interest."

## C.2    Control Charting at the 30,000-Foot-Level: Continuous Response

The following article was a published article in ASQ Quality Progress' 3.4 Part per Million series (Breyfogle 2003b) with some updates.

### Control Charting at the 30,000-foot-level

*Separating special-cause events from common-cause variability*

By Forrest W. Breyfogle III

For a given process, do you think everyone would create a similar looking control chart and make a similar statement relative to process control and predictability? What about their statement about its process capability for given specification limits? Not necessarily. Process statements are not only a function of process characteristics and sampling chance differences but can also be dependent upon sampling approach.

This can have dramatic implications:

- One person could describe a process as out of control, which would lead to activities that immediately address process perturbations as abnormalities, while another person could describe the process as being in control/predictable. For this second interpretation, the perturbations are perceived as fluctuations typically expected within the process, where any long-lasting improvement effort involves looking at the whole process.
- One person could describe a process as not predictable, and another person could describe it as predictable.

To illustrate how different interpretations can occur, let's analyze the following process time series data to determine its state of control and predictability and then its capability relative to customer specifications of 95 to 105 (see Table C.1). This type of data traditionally leads to an $\bar{x}$ and $R$ control chart, as shown in Figure C.1.

Whenever a measurement on a control chart is beyond the upper control limit (UCL) or lower control limit (LCL), the process is said to be out of control. Out of control conditions are called special cause conditions, and out of control conditions can trigger a causal problem investigation. Since so many out of control conditions are apparent in Figure C.1, many causal investigations

**Table C.1** Process Time Series Continuous-Response Data

| Subgroup | Sample One | Sample Two | Sample Three | Sample Four | Sample Five |
|----------|------------|------------|--------------|-------------|-------------|
| 1 | 102.7 | 102.2 | 102.7 | 103.3 | 103.6 |
| 2 | 108.2 | 108.8 | 106.7 | 106.6 | 109.1 |
| 3 | 101.9 | 103.0 | 100.6 | 101.4 | 101.3 |
| 4 | 103.9 | 105.5 | 104.3 | 104.5 | 104.5 |
| 5 | 97.2 | 99.0 | 96.5 | 94.9 | 96.5 |
| 6 | 94.4 | 93.0 | 93.0 | 95.2 | 93.6 |
| 7 | 104.7 | 103.6 | 103.7 | 104.7 | 104.5 |
| 8 | 102.5 | 102.7 | 101.2 | 100.6 | 103.1 |
| 9 | 101.9 | 103.1 | 101.0 | 101.2 | 101.4 |
| 10 | 95.0 | 95.3 | 95.3 | 94.4 | 94.2 |

could have been initiated. But out of control processes are not predictable, and no process capability statement should be made about how the process is expected to perform in the future relative to its specification limits.

When creating a sampling plan, we may select only one sample instead of several samples for each subgroup. Let's say this is what happened and only the first measurement was observed for each of the 10 subgroups. For this situation we would create an individuals control chart like the one shown in Figure C.2.

This control chart is very different from the $\bar{x}$ and $R$ charts shown in Figure C.1. Since the plotted values are within the control limits, we can conclude only common cause variability exists and the process should be considered to be in control or predictable.

The dramatic difference between the limits of these two control charts is caused by the differing approaches to determining sampling standard deviation, which is a control limit calculation term. To illustrate this, let's examine how these two control chart limit calculations are made.

For $\bar{x}$ charts, the UCL and LCL are calculated from the relationships

$$\text{LCL} = \bar{\bar{x}} - A_2 \bar{R} \qquad \text{UCL} = \bar{\bar{x}} + A_2 \bar{R}$$

where $\bar{\bar{x}}$ is the overall average of the subgroups, $A_2$ is a constant depending upon subgroup size and $\bar{R}$ is the average range within subgroups.

For individuals control charts the UCL and LCL are calculated from the relationships

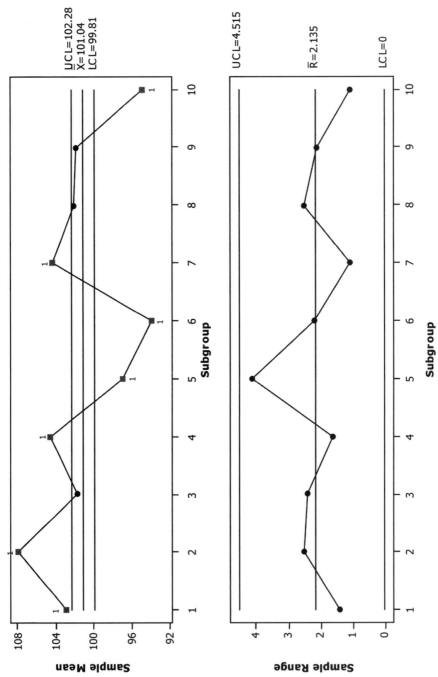

**Figure C.1:** $\bar{x}$ and R chart of five samples from each subgrouping.

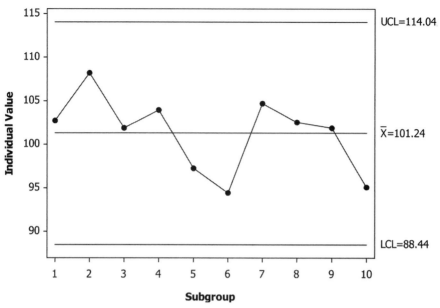

**Figure C.2:** Individuals control chart of sample one from each subgrouping.

$$UCL = \bar{x} + 2.66(\overline{MR}) \qquad\qquad LCL = \bar{x} - 2.66(\overline{MR})$$

where $\overline{MR}$ is the average moving range between subgroups.

The limits for the $\bar{x}$ chart are derived from within-subgroup variability ($\bar{R}$), while sampling standard deviations for individuals control charts are calculated from between-subgroup variability ($\overline{MR}$).

## The 30,000-Foot-Level View

Which control charting technique is most appropriate? It depends on how you categorize the source of variability relative to common and special causes. To explain, I will use a manufacturing situation, though the same applies in transactional environments.

Let's say new supplier shipments are received daily and there is a difference between the shipments, which unknowingly affects the output of the process. To answer our original common vs. special cause question, we need to decide if the impact of day-to-day differences on our process should be considered a component of common or special cause variability. If these day-to-day differences are a noise variable to our process that we cannot control, we will probably use a control charting procedure that considers the day-to-day variability a common cause.

For this to occur, we need a sampling plan where the impact from this type of noise variable occurs between subgroupings; I call the plan that

> **How to Achieve *MC²***
>
> 1. Create an IEE enterprise system, where measurements are aligned with the business's needs.
> 2. Observe measures using 30,000-foot-level control charts.
> 3. Report process capability and performance metrics for predictable processes at the 30,000-foot-level.
> 4. If the process COPQ/CODND relative to hard or soft measures needs improvement, consider this area as an opportunity for one or more Six Sigma projects.
> 5. Follow the detailed project execution define-measure-analyze-improve-control roadmap for making improvements.
> 6. Observe and report success on the 30,000-foot-level control chart, showing the before and after project response level.
> 7. Report the project's financial and customer benefits.
> 8. Leverage the project findings to other areas of the business.

accomplishes this *infrequent sampling/subgrouping* sampling and the view of the process at this level, the 30,000-foot-level view. When creating control charts at the 30,000-foot-level, we need to include between-subgroup variability within our control chart limit calculations, as was achieved in the earlier individuals control charting procedure.

## Building Upon Six Sigma's Strengths

Keith Moe, past executive vice president of 3M, says a business must create more customers and cash ($MC^2$). Business existence (E) depends on this. In other words, $E=MC^2$, where "How to Achieve $MC^2$" is described in the sidebar.

When we select projects we should have a system that focuses on $MC^2$, as opposed to creating projects that may not be in direct alignment to business needs. Let's call this approach Integrated Enterprise Excellence (IEE). The IEE methodology takes some unique paths, including creating a system where operational metrics and strategic plans pull (used here as a lean term) for the creation of meaningful projects aligned with business needs.

Operational and Six Sigma project responses should be tracked so the right activities occur. We need to create a system of metrics that pull for project creation when a process will not produce a consistent desirable response. By selecting the right measurement approach, we can get out of the fire-fighting mode where we're working to fix common cause, non-compliant occurrences as though they were special cause conditions.

To illustrate this approach, let's say we have a 30,000-foot-level response that is aligned to the needs of the business ($MC^2$). In some situations, we will have many responses for each sub-grouping—we'll use the wait time for all daily incoming calls to a call center for this example. We would like to use a methodology that has infrequent subgrouping/sampling with multiple samples for each subgroup but still addresses between-subgroup variability when calculating the control limits.

In this situation, we can track the subgroup mean and log standard deviation using two individuals control charts to assess whether the process is in control or predictable. When the process is in control or predictable processes, the data can later be used to determine the overall process capability and performance metric.

For the data in Table C.1, this approach would lead to the individuals control charts shown in Figure C.3 for the mean and Figure C.4 for the log of the standard deviation.

Our data analysis conclusion using this approach is that the process is in control or predictable, which is quite different from the conclusion we made from Figure C.1. A process capability analysis of all the data collectively yields Figure C.5.

Rather than report process capability in $C_p$, $C_{pk}$, $P_p$, and $P_{pk}$ units, which are often associated with Six Sigma (see Volume III), it is more meaningful to report a process capability and

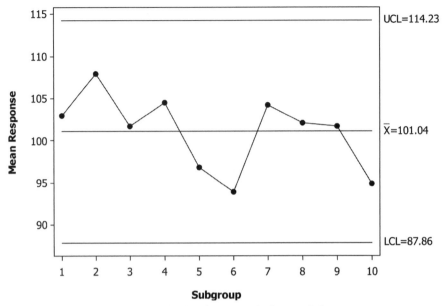

**Figure C.3:** Individuals control chart of the mean.

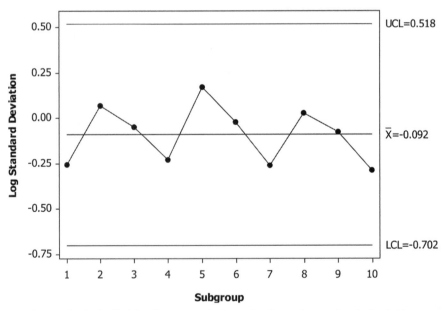

**Figure C.4:** Individuals control chart for log of standard deviation.

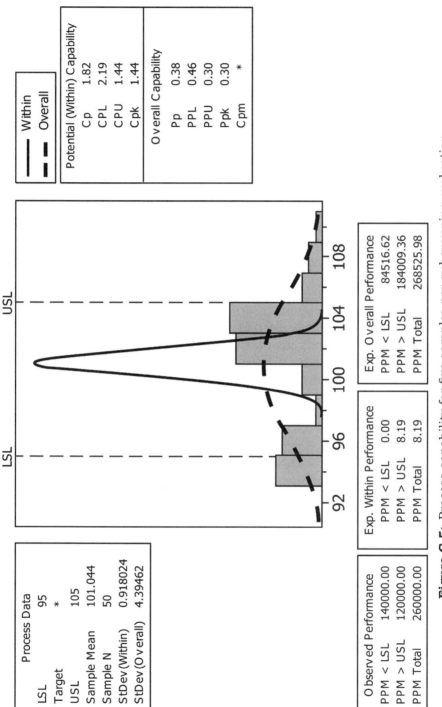

**Figure C.5:** Process capability for five samples per subgrouping evaluation.

performance metric of expected overall performance parts per million. In this case, it's 268,525.98 or 27% nonconformance.

Figures C.3 and C.4 indicate the process is predictable. Our best estimate is that, in the future, the process would have a nonconformance rate of about 27%. This prediction is based on the assumption there will be no overall change in future process response levels. This assumption will be continually assessed as we monitor the 30,000-foot-level control chart.

We then need to calculate the cost of poor quality (COPQ) or the cost of doing nothing differently (CODND) for this process. If the COPQ/CODND amounts are unsatisfactory, we should pull (used as a lean term) for creating a Six Sigma project. With this overall approach, the entire system is assessed when process improvements are addressed. This differs from the use of Figure C.1, which could lead you to create unstructured activity that is unproductive if you're trying to understand the cause of isolated events, which are really common cause.

Metrics drive behavior; however, you need to be sure to use the most appropriate sampling and control charting techniques. The 30,000-foot-level control and corresponding capability and performance metrics give a high-level view of what the customer is feeling. My intent in looking at the big picture is not to get you to use these metrics to fix problems, it is to get you to separate common cause process variability from special cause conditions, which may require immediate attention because something changed, perhaps dramatically.

## C.3   Control Charting at the 30,000-Foot-Level: Pass/ Fail Response

The following article was a published article in ASQ Quality Progress' 3.4 Part per Million series (Breyfogle 2004b) with some updates.

### Control Charting at the 30,000-Foot-Level, Part 2

*Use the right approach to determine special cause variability.*

by Forrest Breyfogle III

In my November 2003 "3.4 per Million" column (see Section C2), I described a traditional and a 30,000-foot-level procedure for creating control charts and making process capability/performance metric assessments for a continuous response. In this column, I will extend this methodology to an attribute response.

## Separating Special Cause From Common Cause Events

The control charting terms "common cause" and "special cause" variability can lead to different interpretations and action plans. To address this, I will present what I call a Shewhart approach and then a Deming approach. I will elaborate on my preferred methodology and explain how it can be integrated with a lean Six Sigma project-by-project improvement strategy.

In the 1920s, Walter Shewhart of Bell Laboratories developed a theory that there are two components to variation: a steady component from random variation and intermittent variation due to assignable causes (Shewhart 1980). Shewhart's improvement approach was that assignable causes could be removed with an effective diagnostic program, while random causes could not be removed without making basic process changes.

From this work, Shewhart developed the standard control chart. This control chart used three standard deviation limits of the sampling distribution to separate steady component from assignable causes. Shewhart's control charts came into wide use in the 1940s because of war production efforts. Western Electric was later credited with adding sequence and runs tests to control charts (Western Electric 1956).

Dr. Deming later gained fame for his work with Japan in its process improvement efforts after World War II. Later in his career, he made significant headway helping American industries become more competitive. Within his work, Deming (1986) noted:

- "A fault in the interpretation of observations, seen everywhere, is to suppose that every event (defect, mistake, accident) is attributable to someone (usually the one nearest at hand), or is related to some special event.
- "We shall speak of faults of the system as common causes of trouble, and faults from fleeting events as special causes.
- "Confusion between common causes and special causes leads to frustration of everyone, and leads to greater variability and higher costs, exactly contrary to what is needed.
- "I should estimate that in my experience most troubles and most possibilities for improvement add up to proportions something like this: 94% belong to the system (responsibility of management), 6% [are] special."

From these authoritative descriptions, we could paraphrase their conclusions as:

- Shewhart: A special cause is an assignable cause that could be internal or external to the system.
- Deming: A special cause is an unusual event external to the system.

This basic philosophic difference between Shewhart and Deming impacts process tracking. Consider, for example, that a key process input variable (KPIV) affects a process output. You might not know how this KPIV affects your process or even whether it adversely impacts the output of the process relative to customer needs. This type of KPIV could be created from differences between daily raw material batches or the number of daily phone calls received by a call center, which differ by day of the week.

The question is: Should these KPIVs (raw material batches or day of the week) be considered special cause? A Dr. Deming approach would view normal output levels from these KPIVs as common cause; however, since these variables are assignable, a Shewhart approach would consider their impact to the process as special cause.

The distinction between the two approaches is not trivial; a business would approach the solution differently depending on which approach was indicated. Therefore, it is important to understand the implications of the two alternatives before making a procedure selection.

I would like to suggest an approach that builds upon the strengths of Six Sigma and is in alignment with Dr. Deming's approach. I will refer to it as Integrated Enterprise Excellence (IEE). With this approach, I will track the organization using high level metrics so typical response levels from inputs within the system (even though they are assignable) will be reported as common cause variability.

For this to occur, I need an infrequent subgrouping/sampling plan so potential input variables, which can affect the response, occur between these subgrouping intervals. I then need to create a control chart so the magnitude of the between-subgroup variability affects the lower control limit (LCL) and upper control limit (UCL) calculations.

With this approach, high level business metrics such as revenue and profit would typically be tracked using a monthly infrequent subgrouping/sampling plan. High level operational metrics such as cycle time, inventory, a critical part dimension and defective rates might have a daily or weekly infrequent subgrouping/sampling plan (see Glossary). Within the IEE approach, high level business metrics, which are not bounded by typical annual or quarterly boundaries, are referred to as satellite level metrics. High level operational or key process output variable (KPOV) metrics are referred to as 30,000-foot-level metrics.

### Attribute Process Capability/Performance Metrics

To illustrate how different actions can result from these interpretations of special cause variability, let's analyze the following process time-series data to determine whether the process is in control/predictable and then describe its process capability/performance metric.

Consider the daily transactions shown in Table C.2, which include the noted non-conformances and calculated non-conformance rate for each period. Traditionally proportion (*p*) non-conformance rates are tracked over time using a *p* chart to detect special cause occurrences. This approach would be appropriate with a Shewhart strategy.

Whenever a measurement is beyond the LCL or UCL on a control chart, the process is said to be out of control. Out of control conditions are special cause conditions, which can trigger causal problem investigations.

For the *p* chart of this data, which is shown in Figure C.6, many causal investigations could have been initiated because there are many out of control signals. Out of control processes are not predictable; hence, no process capability claim should be made.

For *p* charts, the LCL and UCL are:

$$ \text{LCL} = \bar{p} - 3\sqrt{\frac{\bar{p}(1-\bar{p})}{n}} \qquad \text{UCL} = \bar{p} + 3\sqrt{\frac{\bar{p}(1-\bar{p})}{n}} $$

From these equations, the LCL and UCL are determined using the average non-conformance rate ($\bar{p}$) and subgroup size (*n*). When the subgroup size is large, as it can be in many business situations, the distance between the LCL and UCL can become quite small. Variability from day-to-day material lot differences or day-to-day transaction differences can create the type of out of control signals shown in Figure C.6.

An individuals (*X*) chart is a control chart that captures between-subgroup variability. When adjacent subgroups are used to determine average moving range ($\overline{MR}$), the individuals control chart has a LCL and UCL of:

**Table C.2** Process Time-Series Non-conformance Data

| Day | Non-conformances | Subgroup size | Non-conformance rate |
|-----|------------------|---------------|----------------------|
| 1   | 287              | 10,000        | 0.0287               |
| 2   | 311              | 10,000        | 0.0311               |
| 3   | 222              | 10,000        | 0.0222               |
| 4   | 135              | 10,000        | 0.0135               |
| 5   | 188              | 10,000        | 0.0188               |
| 6   | 175              | 10,000        | 0.0175               |
| 7   | 142              | 10,000        | 0.0142               |
| 8   | 215              | 10,000        | 0.0215               |
| 9   | 272              | 10,000        | 0.0272               |
| 10  | 165              | 10,000        | 0.0165               |
| 11  | 155              | 10,000        | 0.0155               |
| 12  | 160              | 10,000        | 0.016                |
| 13  | 224              | 10,000        | 0.0224               |
| 14  | 245              | 10,000        | 0.0245               |
| 15  | 103              | 10,000        | 0.0103               |
| 16  | 273              | 10,000        | 0.0273               |
| 17  | 294              | 10,000        | 0.0294               |
| 18  | 217              | 10,000        | 0.0217               |
| 19  | 210              | 10,000        | 0.021                |
| 20  | 241              | 10,000        | 0.0241               |

$$\text{LCL} = \bar{x} - 2.66(\overline{\text{MR}}) \qquad \text{UCL} = \bar{x} + 2.66(\overline{\text{MR}})$$

The control limits are a function of the average moving range between adjacent subgroups. The individuals control chart is not robust to non-normal data; therefore, for some situations, data need to be transformed when creating the control chart (see Volume III).

When attribute control chart subgroup sizes are similar, an individuals control chart can often be used in lieu of a *p* chart. The advantage of this approach is that between-subgroup variability will impact control chart limit calculations. An individuals control chart of the non-conformance rate in Table 1 is shown in Figure C.7.

This individuals control chart indicates the process is in control and is quite different from the conclusion drawn from the control chart in Figure C.6. When a process is in control, it can also be said to be predictable. When a process is in control/predictable, we can not only make a statement about the past but also use historical data to make a statement about what we might expect in the future, assuming things stay the same.

The process capability/performance metric for this process can then be said to have a non-compliance rate about 0.021. That is, since the process is in control/predictable, I estimate the future non-conformance rate will be about 0.021, unless a significant

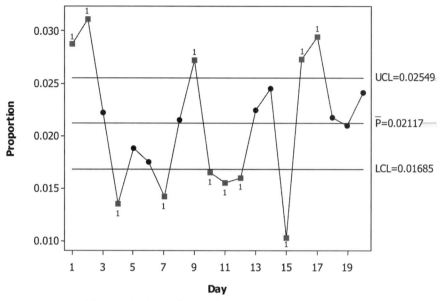

**Figure C.6:** p chart of non-conformance rate.

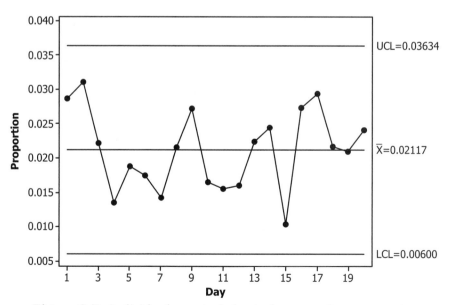

**Figure C.7:** Individuals control chart of non-conformance rate.

change is made to the process or something else happens that either positively or negatively affects the overall response. This situation also implies that Band-Aid or firefighting efforts can waste resources when fundamental business process improvements are really what's needed.

If improvement is needed for this 30,000-foot-level metric, a Pareto chart of defect reasons can give insight to where improvement efforts should focus. The most frequent defect type could be the focus of a new Six Sigma project. For this Six Sigma implementation strategy, I could say common cause measurement improvement needs create a pull for project creation.

A subtle, but important, distinction between the two approaches is the customer view of the process. In the example above, the Shewhart approach (*p* chart) encourages a firefighting response for each instance outside the control limits, while the IEE approach encourages looking at the issue as an organic whole—an issue of capability rather than stability. If the problem is an ongoing one, the IEE view is more aligned with the customer view (whether internal or external) of process performance. The process is stable/predictable, though perhaps not satisfactory, from the customer perspective.

## Pulling for Project Creation

The selection of projects within Six Sigma is critical. However, organizations often work on projects that may not be important to the overall business. With this procedure, organizations could even be suboptimizing processes to the detriment of the overall enterprise.

Business existence and excellence (*E*) depends on more customers and cash ($MC^2$). The previously described IEE system focuses on $E = MC^2$ for project selection.

Within IEE, operational high level metrics at the enterprise level pull (used as a lean term) for project creation. These projects can then follow a refined define-measure-analyze-improve-control (DMAIC) roadmap that includes lean tools for process improvement or a define-measure-analyze-design-verify (DMADV) roadmap for product or process design needs.

# Appendix D: Basic Lean and Quality Tools

## D.1 Supplier-Input-Process-Output-Customer (SIPOC)

Most performed work involves a process. The output of a process is the product or service produced. As described earlier, important process variables that describe the output lead time or defective rates level are called key process output variables or KPOVs ($Ys$). Key process input variables or KPIVs ($Xs$) are the inputs that affect the process KPOVs. IEE and Six Sigma provide a methodology for identifying and then controlling KPIVs, that affect the KPOVs, or change the process so that the KPOVs improve.

Project scope should be aligned with improvement needs of its high-level value chain. A SIPOC (suppliers-inputs-process-outputs-customer) diagram adds supplier and customer to the IPO described earlier. SIPOC can be useful as a communication tool that helps team members view the project the same way and helps management know where the team is focusing its efforts.

The purpose of the SIPOC is to show all the components of the work process flow and to show how these components are related to one another. The SIPOC is a high-level flow diagram used to delineate:

- Suppliers (providers of resources required)
- Inputs (resources required by the process)
- Activities or process steps
- Outputs (deliverables from the process, including know defects)
- Customers (anyone who receives an output)

445

For each SIPOC category, the team creates a list. For example, the input portion of SIPOC would have a list of inputs to the process, while the process steps portion of SIPOC should be high-level, containing only 4–7 high-level steps. In a SIPOC

- Inputs don't need to line up in rows
- Inputs and outputs should be nouns
- Process steps should be verbs
- Little Ys could be outputs of interim steps

An example SIPOC for a project that is to improve service and reduce inventory is illustrated in Figure D.1.

A SIPOC is important to the project, in that it is the first concrete description of the project scope. A project scope will include only improvements in the "P" process columns steps and the quality of the "I" input column inputs. If there are other areas being considered in the project, the SIPOC is not properly defined, and should be adjusted.

The SIPOC should be revisited at each phase of the project. Doing so ensures that the project remains focused on the scope as originally defined or that scope changes are deliberate. The SIPOC also reveals hidden partners in the process as KPIVs, KPOVs, and their sources are identified. Finally, the SIPOC is a useful check for the adequacy and completeness of the control plan.

| Suppliers | Inputs | Process | Outputs | Customers |
|---|---|---|---|---|
| AOM system | Flat data files | Receive flat files from system. | Reports | PPMs |
| QAD system | Orders/invoices | Execute programs to create reports. | Report files | Site Managers |
| | Inventory | Transmit reports to their destinations. | Data files | Executives |
| | | Process report data to create finshed service reports. | | |
| | | Publish the final reports. | | |

**Figure D.1:** SIPOC diagram illustration.

## D.2   Flowcharting

In both the E-DMAIC analyze phase and the measure phase of the project execution roadmap, it is advantageous to represent system structure and relationships using flowcharts. A flowchart provides a picture of the steps that are needed to create a deliverable. The process flowchart document can maintain consistency of application, identify opportunities for improvement, and identify key process input variables. It can also be very useful to train new personnel and to describe activities expediently during audits.

A flowchart provides a complete pictorial sequence of a procedure to show what happens from start to finish. Applications include procedure documentation, manufacturing processes, work instructions, and product-development steps. Flowcharting can minimize the volume of documentation, including ISO 9000 documentation.

Figure D.2 exemplifies the form of a process flowchart and includes frequently used symbols to describe the activities associated with a process chart.

An arrowhead on the line segment that connects symbols shows the direction of flow. The conventional direction of a flowchart is top to bottom or left to right. Usually the return-loop flow is left and up. When a loop feeds into a box, the arrowhead may terminate at the top of the box, at the side of the symbol, or at the line connecting the previous box. The use of on-page connectors can simplify a flowchart by reducing the number of interconnection lines.

An illustration of a process can proceed down the left side of a page, have a line or on-page connector that connects the last box of the left column with the first box of the right column and continue down the right side of a page. Boxes should be large enough

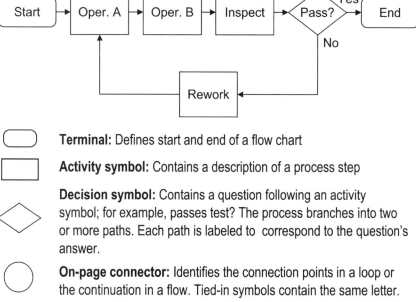

**Figure D.2:** Process flowchart and frequently used symbols.

to contain all necessary information to describe who does what. Notes can contain nondirective information.

When creating a flowchart, consider and describe the purpose and the process to be evaluated. Define all steps to create a product or service deliverable. This can be done in several different ways. One common approach is to conduct a meeting for those familiar with a process. The team then describes the sequence of steps on a wall or poster chart using one self-stick removable note for each process step. With this approach, the team can easily add or rearrange process steps. After the meeting, one person typically documents and distributes the results.

I prefer to use another approach when documenting and defining new processes. While conducting a team meeting to either define or review a process, I use a process-flowcharting computer program in conjunction with a projector that displays an image on a screen. This approach can significantly reduce time, greatly improve accuracy, and dramatically diminish the reworking of process description. Process-flowcharting programs offer the additional benefit of easy creation and access to subprocesses. These highlighted subprocesses can be shown by double-clicking with a mouse.

Flowchart creation using software offers flexibility, as illustrated in Figures 7.1–7.6. A value-stream map, as illustrated in Figure 7.4, can be integrated with the flowcharting of process steps. A value-stream map is useful to show both physical product flow and information flow.

## D.3 Logic Flow Diagram

Figure D.3 illustrates a logic flow diagram. This tool is sometimes combined with a process flow chart. The methodology can be used in both the E-DMAIC analyze phase and the P-DMAIC measure phase. When lead time or WIP is a 30,000-foot-level scorecard/dashboard enterprise value chain or project metric, the logic flow map can provide insight to the identification of waste in overproduction, waiting, transportation, and inventory. This insight can help direct improvement efforts.

The logic flow map provides a snapshot of process activities in terms of value added, non-value added but necessary, and waste (non-value added). Symbols describe activities such as work delay, inspection, operation activity, transportation, and storage. These tools, along with a cause-and-effect diagram and the value stream mapping method described in a later section, can help a black belt gain insight to the process and to opportunities for improvement.

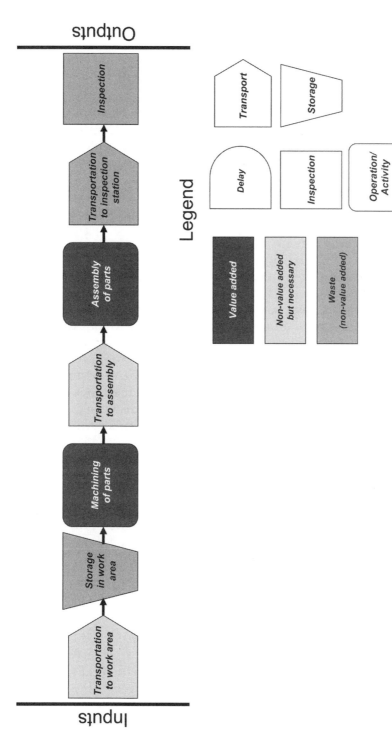

**Figure D.3:** Logic flow map.

# D.4   Spaghetti Diagram

Figure D.4 illustrates a spaghetti diagram. This tool can be used in both the E-DMAIC analyze phase and the P-DMAIC measure phase. When lead time is a 30,000-foot-level scorecard/dashboard enterprise value chain or project metric, the spaghetti diagram provides a picture of activities that can identify waste in transportation and motion. This picture can help identify where targeted improvement efforts should focus. This tool can be a part of the standardized work chart (see Table D.3).

# D.5   Observation Worksheet

Before suggesting or implementing changes, existing processes need to be understood. This is accomplished by walking and observing the current process in action. This activity to improve current-conditions understanding applies not only to manufacturing but also transactional processes, where, for example, we might walk through user application sequences in a computer menu.

When walking the process, a form should be used to summarize all observations. An example worksheet template is shown in Table D.1. This step-by-step documentation describes activities, distance from last step, estimated task time, observations, and return rate.

This tool can be used in both the E-DMAIC analyze phase and the P-DMAIC measure phase. When lead time, defective/defective rates, or WIP is a 30,000-foot-level scorecard/dashboard enterprise value chain or project metric, the observation worksheet provides information that can identify waste in overproduction, waiting, transportation, inventory, overprocessing, motion, and defects. This description can help identify where targeted improvement efforts should focus.

# D.6   Lean Assessment Matrix

Table D.2 illustrates a lean assessment matrix. This tool can be used in both the E-DMAIC analyze phase and the P-DMAIC measure phase. When lead time, defective/defective rates, or WIP is a 30,000-foot-level scorecard/dashboard enterprise value chain or project metric, the lean assessment matrix provides a picture

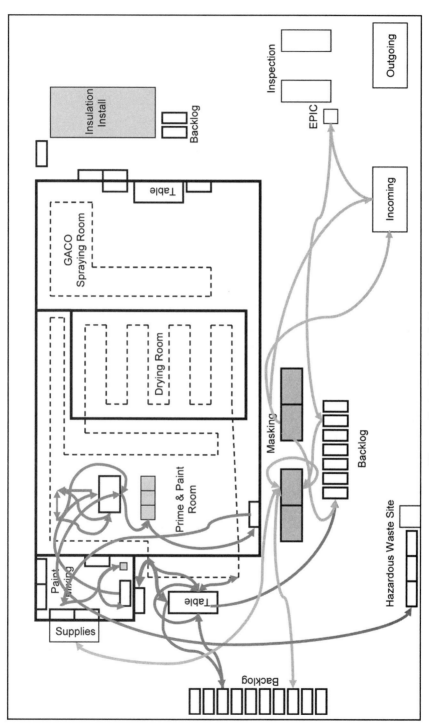

**Figure D.4:** Spaghetti diagram.

**Table D.1** Observation Worksheet

Value Stream Observation Worksheet

| Process # | Description | Inventory | Estimated Cycle Time for Task | Observations | Return Rate |
|---|---|---|---|---|---|
| | | | | | |
| | | | | | |
| | | | | | |
| | | | | | |
| | | | | | |
| | | | | | |
| | | | | | |
| | | | | | |
| | | | | | |
| | | | | | |
| | | | | | |
| | | | | | |
| | | | | | |
| | | | | | |

**Table D.2** Lean Assessment Matrix Example

| Lean Area | | Project Importance | | |
|---|---|---|---|---|
| Category | Principle | None | Some | Major |
| | | | | |
| Workplace | Organization | x | | |
| Workplace | Standardized work | | x | |
| Workplace | Visual controls | | x | |
| | | | | |
| People | Effectiveness | | | x |
| People | Quality at source | | x | |
| | | | | |
| System | Tool reliability | x | | |
| System | Cellular flow | | x | |
| System | Batch reduction or elimination | | | x |
| System | Pull vs. push system | | | x |
| System | Point of use systems | x | | |

Instructions: Describe the level of project importance for each Lean principle by entering an "X" in the appropriate box

of activities that can identify waste in overproduction, waiting, transportation, inventory, overprocessing, motion, and defects. The lean assessment matrix helps prioritize the importance of areas in the workplace, people, and system for targeted improvement efforts.

# D.7 Standardized Work Chart

The posting of a standardized work chart or standard work sheet at each work station becomes a means of visual control. Table D.3 illustrates an example layout, which includes a spaghetti diagram (See Figure D.4). A link in the overall enterprise value chain (see Figure 7.1) is a potential repository for these charts.

As part of TPS, the standard work sheet includes lead time, work sequence, and standard inventory (Ohno 1988). Ohno states, "A proper work procedure, however, cannot be written from a desk. It must be tried and revisited many times in the production plan. Furthermore, it must be a procedure that anybody can understand on sight."

As a tool, the standardized work chart can be used in both the E-DMAIC analyze phase and the P-DMAIC measure phase. When lead time or defective/defect rates is a 30,000-foot-level scorecard/ dashboard enterprise value chain or project metric, the standard sheet provides a picture of activities that can identify waste in waiting, transportation, overprocessing, and motion. This picture can help identify where targeted improvement efforts should focus.

# D.8 Combination Work Table

Table D.4 illustrates the layout of a combination work table. This tool can be used in both the E-DMAIC and the P-DMAIC measure phase. When lead time or defective/defect rates are a 30,000-foot-level scorecard/dashboard enterprise value chain or project metric, the combination work table provides a picture of activities that can identify waste in waiting, transportation, overprocessing, and motion. This picture can help identify where targeted improvement efforts should focus.

# D.9 Cause-and-Effect Diagram

An effective tool as part of a problem-solving process is the cause-and-effect diagram, also known as an Ishikawa diagram, after its originator Karoru Ishikawa, or fishbone diagram. This technique is useful to trigger ideas and promote a balanced approach in group brainstorming sessions in which individuals list the perceived sources or causes of a problem, i.e., effect. The technique

**Table D.3** Standardized Work Chart (or Standard Work Sheet) Example

## Standardized Work Chart

Part No:

Process Name:

Part Name:

Revision & Date:

Takt Time =

Cycle time =

Other:

Work Layout

| Seq | Work Element | Observation |
|-----|--------------|-------------|
| 1 | Issue Material | Issues faster than usage |
| 2 | Step 1 | |
| 3 | Step 2 | Seems to take longer than others |
| 4 | Step 3 | Other room makes travel difficult |
| 5 | Step 4 | |
| 5 | Deliver | Long walk to Shipping |
| 6 | | |
| 7 | | |
| 8 | | |
| 9 | | |
| 10 | | |

Work Layout labels: Supplier, Step 1, Step 2, Step 3, Step 4, Shipping

## Table D.4 Combination Work Table Example

### Combination Work Table

| | | Hand Work ▬▬ | Machine time ▬▬ | ······· Walking | Wait |
|---|---|---|---|---|---|

Department/Operation:

Qty per shift:   Takt time:

Revision/date:

| Seq-uence | Work Element | Element Time | | | | Time (seconds) |
|---|---|---|---|---|---|---|
| | | Wait | Hand Wk. | Walking | Machine | 2  4  6  8 10 12 14 16 18 20 22 24 26 28 30 32 34 36 38 40 42 44 46 48 50 52 54 |
| 1 | Issue Material | | | | 0 | |
| 2 | Draw 1 | | 6.04 | 1 | 0 | |
| 3 | Draw 2 | 1.00 | 9.14 | 1 | 0 | |
| 4 | Draw 3 | | 3.88 | 1 | 0 | |
| 5 | Draw 4 | | 6.86 | 1 | 0 | |
| 6 | Deliver | | | | 0 | |

Consider a cellular work layout where there are multiple cells which are staffed based on work load. Each has two operators and they all share a shipping clerk.

can be useful, for example, to determine the factors to consider within a regression analysis or DOE.

A cause-and-effect diagram provides a means for teams to focus on the creation of a list of process input variables that could affect key process output variables. With this strategy, we can address strata issues based on key characteristics: e.g., who, what, where, and when. The analysis of this stratification later through both graphical and analytical techniques can provide needed insight for pattern detection, providing an opportunity for focused improvement efforts.

When constructing a cause-and-effect diagram, it is often appropriate to consider six areas or causes that can contribute to a characteristic response or effect: materials, machine, method, personnel, measurement, and environment. Each one of these characteristics is then investigated for sub-causes. Sub-causes are specific items or difficulties that are identified as factual or potential causes to the problem, i.e., effect.

There are variations to creating a cause-and-effect diagram. A team may choose to emphasize the most likely causes by circling them. These causes could, for example, be used as initial factor considerations within a DOE. Besides the identification of experimental factors within the cause-and-effect diagram, it can also be beneficial to identify noise factors ($n$), e.g., ambient room temperature and a raw material characteristic that cannot be controlled, and factors that can be controlled ($c$), e.g., process temperature or speed, by placing the letter $n$ or $c$ next to the named effect. Figure D.5 shows another option where focus was given to targeted categories for the effect, and an importance and ease-of-resolution matrix were included.

## D.10    Cause-and-Effect Matrix and Analytical Hierarchy Process (AHP)

A matrix diagram is useful to discover relationships between two groups of ideas. The typical layout is a two-dimensional matrix. A cause-and-effect matrix is sometimes called a prioritization matrix or characteristic selection matrix. This matrix prioritizes items within a matrix diagram, as illustrated in Table D.5.

Cause-and-effect matrices are used to help decide upon the order of importance of a list of items. This list could be activities, goals, or characteristics that were compiled through a cause-and-effect

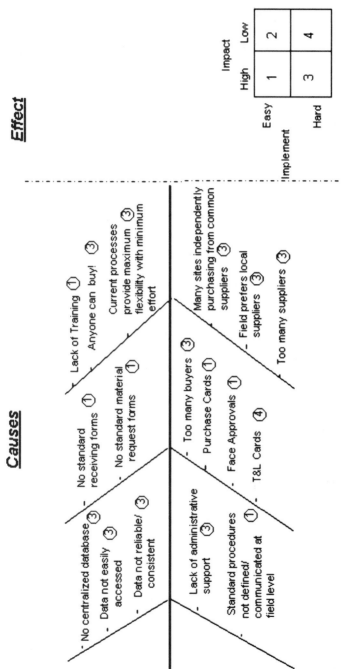

**Figure D.5:** Completed cause-and-effect diagram.

**Table D.5** Cause-and-Effect Matrix Example

| | | Key process output variables (with prioritization) | | | | | | Results | Percentage |
|---|---|---|---|---|---|---|---|---|---|
| | | A | B | C | D | E | F | | |
| | | 5 | 3 | 10 | 8 | 7 | 6 | | |
| Key process input variables | 1 | 4 | 3 | | 3 | | | 53 | 5.56% |
| | 2 | 10 | | 4 | 6 | | 6 | 174 | 18.24% |
| | 3 | | 4 | | | | | 0 | 0.00% |
| | 4 | | | 9 | 5 | 9 | 8 | 241 | 25.26% |
| | 5 | 4 | | | | 6 | | 62 | 6.50% |
| | 6 | | 6 | | 5 | | 2 | 52 | 5.45% |
| | 7 | 5 | | 4 | | 5 | | 100 | 10.48% |
| | 8 | | 3 | | 4 | | 5 | 62 | 6.50% |
| | 9 | 6 | | 3 | | 2 | | 74 | 7.76% |
| | 10 | | 2 | 4 | | | | 40 | 4.19% |
| | 11 | 4 | | | 4 | 2 | 5 | 96 | 10.06% |

diagram, tree diagram, or other means. Through prioritization, matrices teams have a structured procedure to narrow focus to key issues and opinions that are most important to the organization. The prioritization matrix provides the means to make relative comparisons, presenting information in an organized manner. A quality function deployment (QFD) matrix is an example application of a characteristic selection matrix format (see Breyfogle 2003).

Within a cause-and-effect matrix, we can assign relative importance to weights responses. Sometimes these weights are simply assigned by the organization or team. However, there are several techniques for more objectively establishing these prioritization criteria. The analytical hierarchy process (AHP) is one of these techniques (Canada and Sullivan 1989). Within the AHP approach, a number of decision-makers can integrate their priorities into a single priority matrix using a pair-wise fashion. This result of this matrix is a prioritization of the factors.

Figure D.6 shows the result of a paired comparison of all characteristics that are being considered within the selection of black belts. Within this AHP, for example, the cell response of B2 when comparing factor "A: Fire in the belly" with factor "B: Soft skills" would indicate that the team thought factor B was more important than factor A at a medium level. After completing the matrix, the team sums values for all factors and then normalizes these values to a scale, for example 100. An AHP could be used to quantify the importance category used in the creation of a cause-and-effect matrix; i.e., the top numeric row shown in Table D.5.

The cause-and-effect matrix, or characteristic selection matrix, is a tool that can aid in the prioritization of importance of process input variables. This relational matrix prioritization by a team

| | B: Soft skills | C: Project management | D: Analytic skills | E: Statistical knowledge |
|---|---|---|---|---|
| A: Fire in the belly | B2 | A2 | A2 | A3 |
| | B: Soft skills | B1 | B2 | B3 |
| | | C: Project management | C1 | C3 |
| | | | D: Analytic skills | D2 |

| | | |
|---|---|---|
| 1 | Low | Low |
| 2 | Medium | Medium |
| 3 | High | High |

| Description | Score | Percent |
|---|---|---|
| B: Soft skills | 8 | 38 |
| A: Fire in the belly | 7 | 33 |
| C: Project management | 4 | 19 |
| D: Analytic skills | 2 | 10 |
| E: Statistical knowledge | 0 | 0 |

For example: Tabled B values are B2, B1, B2, and B3, which yields a score of: 2 + 1 + 2 + 3 = 8

**Figure D.6:** Illustration of analytical hierarchy process (AHP) for categories within prioritization matrix: black belt selection process.

can help with the selection of what will be monitored to determine if there is a cause-and-effect relationship and whether key process input controls are necessary. The results of a cause-and-effect matrix can lead to other activities such as FMEA, multi-vari charts, correlation analysis, and DOE.

To construct a cause-and-effect matrix, do the following:

1. List horizontally the key process output variables that were identified when documenting the process. These variables are to represent what the customer of the process considers important and essential.
2. Assign a prioritization number for each key process output variable, where higher numbers have a larger priority; e.g., using values from 1 to 10. These values do not need to be sequential as noted earlier. Figure D.6 shows the result of a paired comparison of all characteristics that are being considered in the selection of black belts. This procedure could be used to quantify the importance category used in the creation of a cause-and-effect matrix.
3. List vertically on the left side of the cause-and-effect matrix all key process input variables that may cause variability or nonconformance to one or more of the key process output variables.
4. Reach by consensus the amount of effect each key process input variable has on each key process output variable. Rather than use values from 1 to 10, where 10 indicates the largest effect, consider a scale using levels "0, 1, 3, and 5" or "0, 1, 3, and 9."

5. Determine the result for each process input variable by first multiplying the key process output priority (step 2) by the consensus of the effect for the key process input variable (step 4) and then summing up these products.
6. The key process input variables can then be prioritized by the results from step 5 and/or a percentage of total calculation.

Additional cause-and-effect matrix considerations are:

1. Do not duplicate weight values. Try to spread them from 10 to 1.
2. Try to limit the columns from 2 to 5. More than five causes too much averaging and the tool loses some power in discrimination.
3. All columns must be independent; e.g., you should not use overall defect rate with another column being a specific defect rate because an improvement to the specific defect will create gains in both columns identically.
4. Two methods in selecting the column measures:
   a) The primary process metric is first and weighted 10. Secondary metrics are then included with weights <5.
   b) If the primary metric has segments (as overall cycle time (CT) can be broken into the CT for each major process step, where all step times = total time), then you would use the segment of the primary metric by step on the top of the matrix. In this case, you might weight them based on relative fraction of the primary metric in each category.
5. Considering the Kano model for customer needs, all the column categories should be in the same Kano type. Mixing Kano types is a common problem which causes weighting issues. This could happen if a defect rate column is used (performance metric) along with safety (basic metric) since who could not rate safety as a 10, which would make it equal in weight to the primary project metric. You should just assume all the basic issues are to be considered, but not in the matrix.
6. Keep the number of causes (rows) from 5 to 15. If you get much greater than 15, the tool loses some power of discrimination.
7. Always state the direction of goodness for the column characteristics, such as reduces cost or improves yields. Stating

the column title with a direction of goodness reduces the confusion when scoring the relationship between the columns and rows, where a strong negative relationship and a strong positive relationship may both be scored equally.

Table D.5 cause-and-effect selection matrix example indicates a consensus that focus should be given to key process input variables numbered 2 and 4.

The results from a cause-and effect matrix can give direction for:

- The listing and evaluation of KPIVs in a control plan summary
- The listing and exploration of KPIVs in an FMEA.

## D.11 Affinity Diagram

Using an affinity diagram, a team can organize and summarize the natural grouping from a large number of ideas and issues that could have been created during a brainstorming session. From this summary, teams can better understand the essence of problems and breakthrough solution alternatives.

To create an affinity diagram, record each brainstorming idea individually on a self-stick removable note, using at a minimum a noun and verb to describe each item. An affinity diagram often addresses 40–60 items but can assess 100–200 ideas. Next, place the self-stick removable note on a wall and ask everyone, without talking, to move the notes to the place where they think the issue best fits. Upon completion of this sorting, create a summary or header sentence for each grouping. Create subgroups for large groupings as needed with a subhead description. Connect all finalized headers with their groupings by drawing lines around the groupings, as illustrated in Figure D.7.

## D.12 Nominal Group Technique (NGT)

Nominal group technique expedites team consensus on relative importance of problems, issues, or solutions. A basic procedure for conducting an NGT session is described below; however, vot-

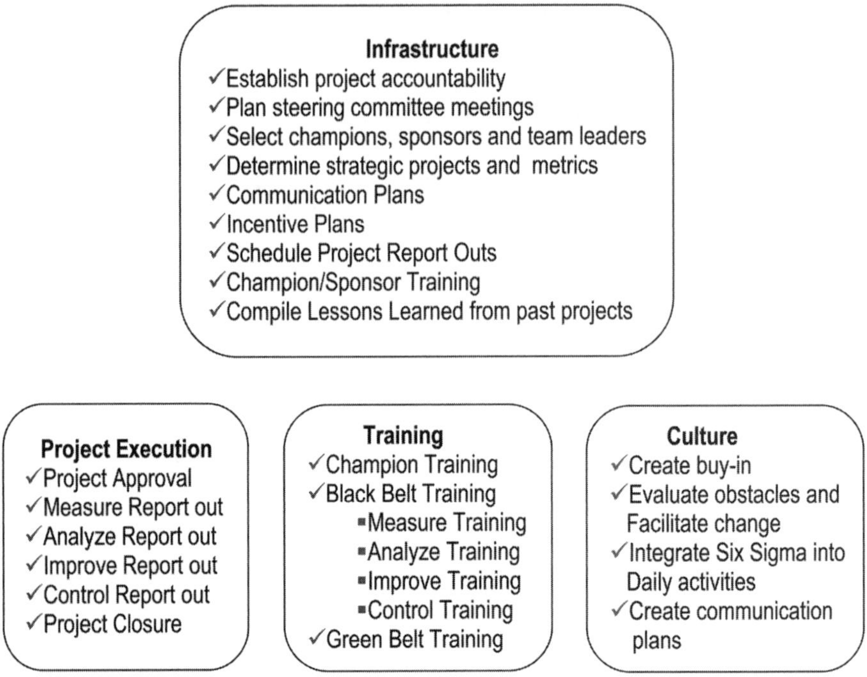

**Infrastructure**
✓Establish project accountability
✓Plan steering committee meetings
✓Select champions, sponsors and team leaders
✓Determine strategic projects and metrics
✓Communication Plans
✓Incentive Plans
✓Schedule Project Report Outs
✓Champion/Sponsor Training
✓Compile Lessons Learned from past projects

**Project Execution**
✓Project Approval
✓Measure Report out
✓Analyze Report out
✓Improve Report out
✓Control Report out
✓Project Closure

**Training**
✓Champion Training
✓Black Belt Training
  ▪Measure Training
  ▪Analyze Training
  ▪Improve Training
  ▪Control Training
✓Green Belt Training

**Culture**
✓Create buy-in
✓Evaluate obstacles and
  Facilitate change
✓Integrate Six Sigma into
  Daily activities
✓Create communication
  plans

**Figure D.7:** Affinity diagram: essential elements of a Six Sigma implementation.

ing procedures can differ depending upon team preferences and the situation.

An NGT is conducted by displaying a generated list of items, perhaps from a brainstorming session, on a flipchart or board. A final list is then created by eliminating duplications and making clarifications. The new final list of statements is then prominently displayed, and each item is assigned a letter, A, B, ..., Z. On a sheet of paper, each person ranks the statements, assigning the most important a number equal to the number of statements with the least important assigned the value of one. Results from the individual sheets are combined to create a total overall prioritization number for each statement.

## D.13  Pareto Charts

The Pareto principle states that 80 percent of the trouble comes from twenty percent of the problems, i.e., the vital few problems. A Pareto chart is a graphical technique used to quantify problems so that effort can be expended in fixing the "vital few" causes, as opposed to the "trivial many." The chart is named after Vilfredo Pareto (born 1848), an Italian economist.

A procedure to construct a Pareto chart is as follows:

1. Define the problem and process characteristics to use in the diagram.
2. Define the period of time for the diagram. This time period can be a region of predictability in an attribute 30,000-foot-level control chart, which can be much better than creating a stacked Pareto bar chart that tracks over time defect types by week or day. A stacked Pareto bar chart often leads to firefighting the current problems without getting to a root cause correction so that the defect type is less likely to occur in the future.
3. Total the number of times each characteristic occurred.
4. Rank the characteristics according to the totals from step 3.
5. Plot the number of occurrences of each characteristic in descending order in a bar graph form along with a cumulative plot of the magnitudes from the bars. Sometimes, however, Pareto charts do not have a cumulative percentage overlay.
6. Trivial columns can be lumped under one column designation; however, care must be exercised not to forget a small but important item.

Much insight can often be gained for process improvement opportunities by displaying a Pareto chart of the total number of each defect-category occurrence in the latest predictability region of an attribute 30,000-foot-level control chart. From this categorization, much benefit can be gained through quality improvements efforts by creating and executing a project that targets the defect type that provides the most opportunity for overall process improvement; i.e., a pull for project creation.

Pareto chart can consider data from different perspectives. For example, a Pareto chart of defects by machine may not be informative, while a Pareto chart of defects by manufacturing shifts could illustrate a problem source. Figures 9.5 and 12.5 illustrate Pareto chart usage.

Pareto charts are also useful in other situations such as time pacing, which is the undertaking of events such as new product introduction, factory re-layout, or regular interval staff training (Bicheno 2004). In timing pacing, a product quantity analysis would have the following two Pareto charts: value of products sold by product type and number of products manufactured by product type. In timing pacing, a contribution analysis would have the following two Pareto charts: total TOC throughput by product type and unit TOC throughput per bottleneck minute by product type.

Care must be exercised when using a Pareto chart to identify where focus efforts should target. A Pareto bar might appear taller than other bars simply by chance. A statistical significance test is useful in conjunction with a Pareto chart to determine if bar-height differences are statistically significant.

## D.14   Force Field Analysis

Force field analysis can be used to analyze what forces in an organization are supporting and driving toward a solution and which are restraining progress. The technique forces people to think together about the positives and negatives of a situation and the various aspects of making a change permanent.

After an issue or problem is identified, a brainstorming session can be conducted to create a list of driving forces and then a list of restraining forces. A prioritization is then conducted of the driving forces that could be strengthened. There is then a prioritization of the restraining forces that could be reduced to better achieve the desired result. An example presentation format for this information is shown in Figure D.8, where the weight of the line could be used to indicate the importance of a force. Table D.6 shows example action plans that could be

| Driving Forces | | Restraining Forces |
|---|---|---|
| Financial objectives are not being met. → | ← | Executive management is not aware of how to find a better system to fulfill their needs. |
| Strategic plans are too generic and not getting implemented. → | ← | Little time to consider alternative approaches. |
| Too many customer complaints. → | | Executive management is fearful that implementing a new system would make them look bad if the system fails. |
| The balanced scorecard is not beneficial and leads to the wrong activities. → | ← | |
| Too much firefighting. → | ← | Resources are stretched since people are working current problems. |
| Financially validated Lean Six Sigma projects sound good but don't seem to translate to the bottom-line. → | ← | If a new system is instituted, not sure how awareness can quickly be built. |

**Figure D.8:** Force field analysis for identifying and executing an enhanced system for measurements and improvements.

**Table D.6** Action Items for Restraining Forces for Identifying and Executing an Enhanced System for Measurements and Improvements

| Restraining Forces | Action Items |
|---|---|
| Executive management is not aware of how to find a better system to fulfill their needs. | Dedicate someone to search the Internet for articles and books about improved business systems that aligns business metrics, strategies, and improvement; i.e., more than a just-do-project system. This system is to have a metric reporting system that gets the organization out of the firefighting mode. This information is to be analyzed by a steering committee, which is to provide recommendations for further investigation. |
| Little time to consider alternative approaches. | Allocate 50% of a leading thinking, influencer person's time to conduct a search for alternative business-system approaches. This person is to investigate opportunities and attend public one-day overview sessions from various providers to see which offering best fits their needs. |
| Executive management is fearful that implementing a new system would make them look bad if the system fails. | Train a couple Black Belts and then conduct an on-site workout that creates the structure for a business measurement, analysis, and improvement system. With this start small and grow large implementation the downside risks are minimal, while the upside potential is huge. |
| Resources are stretched since people are working current problems. | Identify a business system that truly gets people out of the firefighting mode, not just do projects that may or may not be truly aligned to business needs. |
| If a new system is instituted, not sure how awareness can quickly be built. | Identify a business system that has easy-to-read books that can be disseminated to not only employees but suppliers and customers as well. These books and articles need to enhance an understanding of the techniques at various reader's needs and level of understanding. |

created for addressing the restraining forces identified in a force field analysis.

# D.15  Why-Why Diagram or Five Whys

A simple problem-solving tool is the five whys. Insight can be gained into why a particular procedure is followed or why a problem exists by asking "why" repeatedly, where five is a good rule of thumb. An example why-why diagram or five whys fault tree analysis is shown in Figure D.9. A why-why diagram is similar to a fault tree diagram.

**Figure D.9:** Why-why diagram modified from Higgins (1994).

# Appendix E: Basic Statistical Considerations

## E.1　Continuous versus Attribute Response

Continuous or variables data can assume a range of numerical responses on a continuous scale, as opposed to data that can assume only discrete levels. Data are said to be continuous when there are no boundaries between adjacent values. For example, a process response might be 2.0, 2.0001, or 3.00005.

Attribute, or discrete, data have the presence or absence of some characteristic in each transaction; e.g., proportion nonconforming in a pass/fail test. Binary attribute data can take a pass/fail or on-time/not-on-time syntax. For example, 1 out of 1000 transactions is *defective*. This situation is often modeled by the binomial distribution.

Another attribute situation occurs when a transaction can have multiple failures, or *defects*. For example, on the average there may be 3 *defects* out of 1000 transactions. For this situation, we would count the total number of defects for the 1000 transactions. This situation can often be modeled by the Poisson distribution.

Percentage can be either continuous or attribute based on the type of data used in the calculation. If attributes are used in the calculation, the response is attribute, while if a continuous response is used in the calculation, the response is considered continuous. An illustration of each is:

- Attribute response: Last week 10,000 transactions were executed and there were 100 defective transactions. This 1% [(100/10,000)×100] would be an attribute since the numerator and denominator are attribute data.

- Continuous response: A batch contained 500 pounds before processing. After processing 475 pounds remained. The process yield of 95% [(475/500) × (100)] could be considered a continuous response output.

If data can be presented in either continuous or attribute format, the continuous format is preferred.

## E.2   Transformations and Individuals Control Chart

A population is considered normally distributed when plotted data plot follow the characteristic bell-shaped curve as illustrated in Figure B.2. In this figure, we note that the tails of a normal distribution approach plus and minus infinity. When data fit a normal distribution, percentage of population statements can be made for various $x$-values using the analytical techniques described in Volume III.

However, for many situations data do not follow a normal distribution. Consider the company that is tracking the difference between the time payment was received and the invoice's due date. A normal distribution in general does not fit this situation well since there is a lower boundary. To illustrate this natural boundary, consider how we would not expect to pay for a product before we decided to purchase it; that is, there is a natural lower boundary and the distribution curve would tend to be skewed to the right.

The individual control chart can give false special cause signals when data are not inherently from a normal distribution. Because of this, certain type of data may need a normalizing transformation before the creation of an individuals chart (Breyfogle 2004c). In addition, this inherent distribution needs to be addressed in the formulation of a process capability/performance metric; e.g., probability plot.

It should be noted that a normal distribution might still a data set even though we would expect that the underlying characteristic of the population to be from another distribution. This occurs, for example, when the data are distantly removed from the lowest naturally boundary.

A general approach for transforming data to a normal distribution is a Box-Cox transformation (Box et al. 1978), where values

$(Y)$ are transformed to the power of $\lambda$; i.e., $Y^\lambda$. This relationship has the following characteristics:

$$\lambda = -2 \quad Y \text{ transformed} = 1/Y^2$$
$$\lambda = -0.5 \quad Y \text{ transformed} = 1/\sqrt{Y}$$
$$\lambda = 0 \quad Y \text{ transformed} = \ln(Y)$$
$$\lambda = 0.5 \quad Y \text{ transformed} = \sqrt{Y}$$
$$\lambda = 2 \quad Y \text{ transformed} = Y^2$$

Care needs to be exercised when transforming data since an unnatural transformation can cause special cause data to appear as common-cause occurrence in an individuals control chart and provide an erroneous process capability/performance metric statement.

The most frequent encountered transformations in IEE are:

- Logarithm transformation (Box-Cox: $\lambda = 0$); e.g., cycle time or lead time
- Square root transformation (Box-Cox: $\lambda = 0.5$); e.g., defect counts and defective rates

Satellite-level and 30,000-foot-level chart reporting that utilize transformations should note this transformation in the control chart and probability plot header. Data transformations should be transparent to the readers of the report-out.

# List of Acronyms and Symbols

Some symbols used locally in the volume are not shown.

| | |
|---|---|
| ABC | activity-based costing |
| AFR | average failure rate |
| AHP | analytical hierarchy process |
| AIAG | Automotive Industry Action Group |
| ANOM | analysis of means |
| ANOVA | analysis of variance |
| APQP | advanced product quality planning |
| AQL | accept quality level |
| AQP | advanced quality planning |
| ARL | average run length |
| ASQ | American Society for Quality (Previously ASQC, American Society for Quality Control) |
| ASTM | American Society for Testing and Materials |
| BB | black belt |
| $b$ | Weibull distribution shape parameter (slope of a Weibull probability plot); a parameter used in the NHPP with Weibull intensity model |
| BOK | body of knowledge |
| BPIEs | business process improvement events |
| °C | Celsius temperature |
| CI | confidence interval |
| CL | centerline of a control chart |
| CDF | cumulative distribution function |
| CFM | continuous flow manufacturing |
| CAP | change acceleration process |
| CEO | chief executive officer |
| CFO | chief financial officer |

| | |
|---|---|
| $C_p$ | capability index (AIAG 1995)—does not address process centering within specification limits |
| $C_{pk}$ | Capability index (AIAG 1995)—addresses process centering within specification limits |
| CPM | critical path method |
| CRM | customer relationship management |
| C&E | cause-and-effect (diagram) |
| C/O | changeover |
| CODND | cost of doing nothing differently |
| COPQ | cost of poor quality |
| C/T (CT) | cycle time |
| CTC | critical to cost |
| CTD | critical to delivery |
| CTP | critical to process |
| CTQ | critical to quality |
| $df$ | degrees of freedom |
| DFA | design for assembly (Example of DFX) |
| DFIEE | design for integrated enterprise excellence |
| DFM | design for manufacturability (Example of DFX) |
| DFMEA | design failure mode and effects analysis |
| DFLSS | design for Lean Six Sigma |
| DFSS | design for Six Sigma |
| DFX | design for X or a characteristic; e.g., DFA or DFM |
| DMAIC | define-measure-analyze-improve-control |
| DMADV | define-measure-analyze-design-verify |
| DOE | design of experiments |
| DPMO | defects per million opportunities |
| DPU | defects per unit |
| DSO | days sales outstanding |
| DSS | decision support system |
| $e$ | 2.71828 |
| EBIDA | earnings before interest, depreciation, and amortization |
| ECMM | enterprise cascading measurement methodology |
| EDA | exploratory data analysis |
| E-DMAIC | enterprise process DMAIC (roadmap) |
| EIP | enterprise improvement plan |
| EPE | every part every (batch size); e.g., EPE day |
| EPM | enterprise process management |
| ERP | enterprise process resource planning |
| EVOP | evolutionary operation |
| ERP | enterprise process resource planning |
| EWMA | exponentially weighted moving average |

| | |
|---|---|
| $\exp(x)$ | $= e^x = (2.71828...)^x$ |
| °F | Fahrenheit temperature |
| $F_0$ | test criterion value from the $F$ distribution |
| FIFO | first-in-first-out |
| FG | finished goods |
| FMEA | failure mode and effects analysis |
| FR | functional requirement |
| FT | fault tree |
| FV | future value |
| $F(x)$ | describes the CDF where the independent variable is $x$ |
| $f(x)$ | describes the PDF where the independent variable is $x$ |
| GAAP | generally accepted accounting principles |
| Gage R&R | gage repeatability and reproducibility |
| GB | green belt |
| $H_0$ | null hypothesis |
| $H_a$ | alternative hypothesis |
| HPP | homogeneous Poisson process |
| HR | human resources |
| ICA | interim containment action |
| ICP | innovation creation process |
| IEE | integrated enterprise (process) excellence |
| in. | inches |
| I-MR chart | individuals control chart and moving range (Same as $XmR$ chart) |
| IPO | input-process-output |
| JIT | just-in-time |
| K | temperature in degrees Kelvin (273.16 + °C); Boltzmann's constant |
| KCA | knowledge-centered activity |
| KTS | knowledge-transfer sessions |
| KPIV | key process input variable |
| KPOV | key process output variable |
| LCL | lower control limit |
| LDL | lower decision level (in ANOM) |
| L/T | lead time |
| ln | $\log_e = \log_{2.718}$ |
| log | $\log_{10}$ |
| min | minutes, minimum |
| MBA | master of business administration |
| MBB | master black belt |
| MP | maintenance prevention |

| | |
|---|---|
| mph | miles per hour |
| MR | moving range |
| MRP | material requirements planning |
| MS | mean square |
| MSA | measurement systems analysis |
| msec | milliseconds |
| MTBF | mean time between failures |
| Mu | greek letter μ, which often symbolizes the mean of a population |
| N/A | not applicable |
| $n$ | sample size |
| NGT | nominal group technique |
| NHPP | non-homogeneous Poisson process |
| NIST | National Institute of Standards and Technology |
| NPV | natural process variation, net present value |
| NTF | no trouble found |
| OEM | original equipment manufacturer (customers) |
| ORT | ongoing reliability test |
| $P$ | probability |
| PCA | permanent corrective actions |
| PDCA | plan-do-check-act |
| PDF | probability density function |
| P-DMAIC | project DMAIC (roadmap) |
| PDSA | plan-do-study-act |
| PE ratio | (or P/E ratio) price-earnings ratio |
| PERT | program evaluation and review technique |
| PFMEA | process failure mode and effects analysis |
| PI | prediction interval |
| P&L | profit and loss |
| PP&E | plant property and equipment |
| PPAP | production part approval process |
| ppm | parts per million (defect rate) |
| PM | preventive maintenance, productive mainte-nance, performance measurement |
| $P_p$ | performance index (AIAG 1995); calculated using long-term standard deviation |
| $P_{pk}$ | performance index (AIAG 1995); calculated using long-term standard deviation |
| PV | part variation, present value |
| QFD | quality function deployment |
| RFQ | request for quotation |
| ROCE | return on capital employed |

| | |
|---|---|
| ROI | return on investment |
| RQL | reject quality level |
| $R$ | range |
| RM | raw material |
| RMR | rejected material review |
| RPN | risk priority number (in FMEA) |
| RO | results orchestration |
| ROI | return on investment |
| ROIC | return on invested capital |
| ROCE | return on capital employed |
| RTY | rolled throughput yield |
| $r$ | number of failures, correlation coefficient |
| $s$ | standard deviation of a sample |
| S&A | sales and administration |
| SBU | strategic business unit |
| SIPOC | supplier-input-process-output-customer |
| SMART | *see* Glossary |
| SME | subject matter expert |
| SMED | single-minute exchange of die |
| SOD | severity, occurrence, and detection (used in FMEA) |
| SOP | standard operating procedure |
| SPC | statistical process control |
| $SS$ | sum of squares |
| Std. dev. | standard deviation |
| SWOT | strengths, weaknesses, opportunities, and threats |
| $S^4$ | Smarter Six Sigma Solutions |
| $t$ | time |
| TOC | theory of constraints |
| TPM | total productive maintenance |
| TPS | Toyota production system |
| TQC | total quality control |
| TQM | total quality management |
| $T_q$ | $q$% of the population is expected to be below this value for a population |
| TRIZ | Teoriya Resheniya Izobretatelskikh Zadatch (theory of problem solving) |
| UCL | upper control limit |
| UDL | upper decision level (ANOM) |
| VA time | value-added time |
| VOC | voice of the customer |

| | |
|---|---|
| VOP | voice of the process |
| WIP | work in progress, Work in process |
| *XmR* (chart) | control chart of individual and moving range measurements |
| $\bar{x}$ | mean of a variable $x$ |
| YB | yellow belt |
| α | alpha, risk of rejecting the null hypothesis erroneously |
| β | beta, risk of not rejecting the null hypothesis erroneously |
| μ | mu, population true mean |
| ν | nu, degrees of freedom |
| ρ | rho, actual failure rate of population, correlation coefficient between two variables |
| Σ | mathematical summation |
| σ | sigma, population standard deviation |

# Glossary

**Abscissa:** The coordinate representing the distance from the $y$ axis in a two-dimensional plot.

**Active experimentation:** Experiments are conducted where variable levels are changed to assess their impact on responses.

**Activity-based Costing (ABC):** Technique for businesses to understand the components and drivers of overhead costs. Through ABC, organizations can more realistically assign indirect overhead costs to products or services.

**Advanced quality planning (AQP) or Advanced product quality planning (APQP):** The act of ensuring that a new product or service will meet customer expectations.

**Affinity diagram:** A methodology by which a team can organize and summarize the natural grouping from a large number of ideas and issues.

**Alpha (α) risk:** Risk of rejecting the null hypothesis erroneously. Also called type I error or producer's risk.

**Alternative hypothesis ($H_a$):** *See* Hypothesis testing.

**Analysis of means (ANOM):** A statistical procedure to compare the means of individual groups to the grand mean.

**Analysis of variance (ANOVA):** A statistical procedure for analyzing the differences in the means of two or more groups.

**Attribute data (Discrete data):** The presence or absence of some characteristic in each device under test, e.g., proportion nonconforming in a pass/fail test.

**Autocorrelation:** In time series analyses, correlation between values and previous values of the same series.

**Average:** A location parameter; frequently the arithmetic mean.

**Balanced scorecard (the):** The balanced scorecard (Kaplan and Norton 1992) tracks business organizational functions in the areas of financial, customer, and internal business process and learning & growth. In this system, an organization's vision and strategy is also to lead to the cascading of objectives, measures, targets, and initiatives throughout the organization. This volume describes issues with this system and an alternative IEE system that overcomes these shortcomings.

**Bar charts:** Horizontal or vertical bars that graphically illustrate the magnitude of multiple situations.

**Baseline:** Beginning information from which a response change is assessed.

**Benchmarking:** A discovery process for determining what is the best practice or performance within your company, a competitor, or another industry.

**Beta ($\beta$) risk:** Chance of not rejecting the false null hypothesis; also called type II error or consumer's risk.

**Bias:** The difference between the observed average of measurements (trials under repeatability conditions) and a reference value; historically referred to as accuracy. Bias is evaluated and expressed at a single point with the operating range of the measurement system (AIAG 2002).

**Bimodal distribution:** A distribution that is a combination of two different distributions resulting in two distinct peaks.

**Binomial distribution:** A distribution that is useful to describe discrete variables or attributes that have two possible outcomes: e.g., a pass/fail proportion test, heads/tails outcome from flipping a coin, defect/no defect present.

**Black belts (BBs):** Process improvement Six Sigma and IEE practitioners who typically receive four weeks of training over four months. It is most desirable that Black Belts are dedicated resources; however, many organizations utilize part-time resources. During training, Black Belt trainees lead the execution of a project that has in-class report-outs and critiques. Between training sessions Black Belt trainees should receive project coaching, which is a very important for their success. They are expected to deliver high quality report-outs to peers, champions, and executives. Upon course completion, black belts are expected to continue delivering financial beneficial projects; e.g., 4–6 projects per year with financial benefits of $500,000–$1,000,000. Black belts can mentor green belts.

**Black box:** Describes a system where the interior operations are not known.

**Bottleneck:** The slowest operation in a chain of operations; it will pace the output of the entire line.

**Bottom line:** The final profit or loss that a company experiences at the end of a given period of time.

**Box-Cox transformation:** A general approach for transforming data to a normal distribution, where values ($Y$) are transformed to the power of $\lambda$; i.e., $Y^\lambda$.

**BPIE:** *See* Business process improvement event system.

**Brainstorming:** Consensus-building among experts about a problem or issue using group discussion.

**Burning platform:** Term used to describe a sense of urgency; e.g., the organization had a burning platform to improve their on time delivery or they would loose their major customer's business.

**Business process improvement event (BPIE) system:** A system for identifying and timely resolving reoccurring problems. The resolution for these issues could involve a simple agree-to procedure change, a DMADV design project, or P-DMAIC process improvement project.

**Capability/performance metric:** *See* Process capability/performance metric.

**Capability, Process**: See Process capability.

**Categorical variables:** Represent types of data which may be divided into groups. Examples of categorical variables are race, sex, age group, and educational level. While the latter two variables may also be considered in a numerical manner by using exact values for age and highest grade completed, it is often more informative to categorize such variables into a relatively small number of groups.

**Cause-and-effect diagram (C&E diagram):** This technique, sometimes called an Ishikawa diagram or fishbone diagram, is useful in problem solving using brainstorming sessions. With this technique, possible causes from such sources as materials, equipment, methods, and personnel are typically identified as a starting point to begin discussion.

**Cell:** A grouping of data that, for example, comprises a bar in a histogram.

**Champions**: Executive-level managers who are responsible for managing and guiding the Lean Six Sigma or IEE deployment and its projects.

**Changeover:** The time from the last piece of one batch to the first piece of the next batch.

**Checks sheets**: Sheets that are use do systematically record and compile data from historical or current observations.

**Chi-square test:** The proper statistical name is the chi-square test of independence. This is different from the chi-square goodness of fit test, which has a different purpose. The only similarity is that the chi-square statistic is used for estimating significance. The term chi-square test is used to describe a chi-square test of independence.

**Collins three circles:** (1) What can you be the best in the world? (2) What drives your economic engine? (3) What are you deeply passionate about? (Collins 2001)

**Common cause:** Natural or random variation that is inherent in a process over time, affecting every outcome of the process. If a process is in-control, it has only common-cause variation and can be said to be predictable. When a process experiences common-cause variability but does not meet customer needs it can be said that the process is not capable. Process or input variable change is needed to improve this situation; i.e., this is metric is creating a pull for project creation.

**Concurrent engineering:** An approach to the development of new products where the product and its associated processes, such as manufacturing, distribution, and service, are all developed in parallel.

**Confidence interval:** The region containing the limits or band of a parameter with an associated confidence level that the bounds are large enough to contain the true parameter value.

The bands can be single-sided to describe an upper/lower limit or double-sided to describe both upper and lower limits.

**Consumer's risk:** *See* Beta *(β)* risk.

**Continuous data** (Variables data): Data that can assume a range of numerical responses on a continuous scale, as opposed to data that can assume only discrete levels.

**Continuous distribution:** A distribution used in describing the probability of a response when the output is continuous (*see* Response).

**Continuous data response:** *See* Response.

**Continuous flow manufacturing (CFM):** Within CFM, operations and machines are efficiently used to build parts. Non-value added activities in the operation are eliminated. Flexibility is a substitute for work-in-process inventory. A product focus is established in all areas of operation.

**Control chart:** A procedure used to track a process with time for the purpose of determining if common or special causes exist.

**Control:** The term *in control* or predictable is used in process control charting to describe when the process indicates that there are no special causes. *Out of control* indicates that there is a special cause or that the process is unpredictable.

**Corrective action:** Process of resolving problems.

**Cost of doing nothing differently (CODND):** To keep IEE from appearing as a quality initiative, I prefer to reference the Six Sigma metric COPQ as the cost of doing nothing differently (CODND), which has even broader costing implications than COPQ. I make reference to the CODND.

**Cost of poor quality (COPQ):** Traditionally, cost of quality issues have been given the broad categories of internal failure costs, external failure costs, appraisal costs, and prevention costs. See Glossary description for cost of doing nothing differently. Within Six Sigma, COPQ addresses the cost of not performing work correctly the first time or not meeting customer's expectations.

**Customer:** Someone for whom work or a service is performed. The end user of a product is a customer of the employees within a company that manufactures the product. There are also internal customers in a company. When an employee does work or performs a service for someone else in the company, the person who receives this work is a customer of this employee.

**Cycle time:** Frequency that a part/product is completed by process. Also, time it takes for operator to go through work activities before repeating the activities. In addition, cycle time can be used to quantify customer order to delivery time.

**Dashboard:** *See* Scorecard.

**Days sales outstanding (DSO):** In general, the average number of days it takes to collect revenue after a sale has been made. In this volume, DSO is considered to be the number of days beyond the due date that a payment is to be received; i.e., for an invoice 3 indicates that payment was received three days late, while −2 indicates receipt was two days early.

**Discrete data:** Discrete data are based on counts. Only a finite number of values are possible, and the values cannot be subdivided meaningfully; e.g., the number of parts damaged in shipment.

**Defect:** A nonconformity or departure of a quality characteristic from its intended level or state.

**Defective:** A nonconforming item that contains at least one defect or having a combination of several imperfections, causing the unit not to satisfy intended requirements.

**Deming, Dr. W, Edwards:** As an American statistician, Dr. Deming is known for his top management teachings in Japan after World War II. Dr. Deming made a significant contribution to Japan becoming renown for its high-quality, innovative products.

**Descriptive statistics:** Descriptive statistics help pull useful information from data, whereas probability provides among other things a basis for inferential statistics and sampling plans.

**Design for Integrated Enterprise Excellence (DFIEE):** A process used when developing new products/services, processes, or information technology (IT) projects. This development is to be efficient and effective with a focus on up front understanding of customer requirements. IEE uses a DMADV process for DFIEE execution.

**Design for X (DFX):** Examples of DFX (Dodd 1992) are design for assembly, design for performance, design for ergonomics, design for manufacturability, design for quality, design for recyclability, design for redesign, design for reliability, design for maintainability, design for serviceability, and design for test. Example nomenclature is DFA for design for assembly.

**Design of experiments (DOE):** A structured experiment where the response effects of several factors are studied at one time.

**DFSS:** *See* Design for Six Sigma.

**Degrees of freedom (*df* or *v*):** Number of measurements that are independently available for estimating a population parameter. For a random sample from a population, the number of degrees of freedom is equal to the sample size minus one.

**Delphi technique:** A method of *predicting* the future by surveying experts in the area of concern.

**Design of experiments (DOE):** Experiment methodology according to which factor levels are assessed in a fractional factorial experiment or full factorial experiment structure.

**Discrete data (Attribute data):** The presence or absence of some characteristic in each device under test; e.g., proportion nonconforming in a pass/fail test.

**Discrete distribution:** A distribution function that describes the probability for a random discrete variable.

**Discrete random variable**: A random variable that can only assume discrete values.

**Distinct data categories:** The number of data classifications (ndc) or categories that can be reliably distinguished, determined by the effective resolution of the measurement system and part variation from the observed process for a given application (AIAG 2002).

**Distribution:** A pattern that is followed from a random sample from a population. Described normal, Weibull, Poisson, binomial, and lognormal distributions are applicable to the modeling of various industrial situations.

**DMAIC:** Define-measure-analyze-improve-control Six Sigma roadmap.

**DMADV:** Define-measure-analyze-design-verify DFSS roadmap.

**DNA rules:** DNA is the material, inside the nucleus of cells, which carries genetic information. The scientific name for DNA is deoxyribonucleic acid. DNA rules describe the basic building blocks of a system; e.g., IEE DNA rules.

**Dot plot:** A plot of symbols that represent individual observations from a batch of data. Volume III describes the creation of this plot.

**DPMO:** When using the non-conformance rate calculation of defects per million opportunities (DPMO), one needs first to describe what the opportunities for defects are in the process; e.g., the number of components and solder joints when manufacturing printed circuit boards. Next, the number of defects is periodically divided by the number of opportunities to determine the DMPO rate.

**Drill down**: To drill down is to transition from general category information to more specific details by moving through a hierarchy.

**Early-life failures:** *See* Bathtub curve.

**E-DMAIC (Roadmap):** An IEE enterprise define-measure-analyze-improve-control roadmap, which contains among other things a value-chain measurement and analysis system where metric improvement needs can pull for project creation.

**Enron effect:** At the beginning of the 21st century, the executive management style in Enron and other companies led to the downfall of these companies and to executives' spending time behind bars. In Enron, executive management had to do whatever it took to meet prescribed numbers. Enron lacked metrics that gave a true picture of what was happening. This resulted in a smoke-and-mirror system which had integrity issues relative to the handling of business challenges. In addition, this system encouraged executive management to have no respect for either the financial or the general well-being of others inside and outside the company. I make reference to the result of this management style as the Enron effect.

**Enterprise cascading measurement methodology (ECMM):** A system where meaningful measurements are statistically tracked over time at various functional levels of the business. This leads to a cascading and alignment of important metrics throughout the organization.

**Enterprise improvement plan (EIP):** A project drill-down strategy that follows: goal—strategies—high potential area—projects.

**Enterprise process management (EPM):** Rather than having a governance model that addresses initiatives as separate entities, in IEE a value-chain EPM function can be created that orchestrates this system. The EPM function is responsible for integrating, overseeing, and improving the execution of these processes, utilizing an E-DMAIC roadmap.

**EPM:** *See* Enterprise process management.

**Error (experimental):** Ambiguities during data analysis caused from such sources as measurement bias, random measurement error, and mistake.

**Error proofing:** *See* Mistake proofing.

**Experimental error:** Variations in the experimental response under identical test conditions; also called *residual error.*

**Exploratory data analysis (EDA):** The examination of the appearance of data for the purpose of gaining insight to the development of a theory of cause-and-effect.

**Failure:** A device is said to fail when it no longer performs its intended function satisfactorily.

**Failure mode and effects analysis (FMEA):** Analytical approach directed toward problem prevention through the prioritization of potential problems and their resolution. Opposite of fault tree analysis.

**Failure rate:** Failures/unit time or failures/units of usage, i.e., 1/MTBF. Sample failure rates are: 0.002 failures/hour, 0.0003 failures/auto miles traveled, 0.01 failures/1000 parts manufactured. Failure rate criterion $(\rho_a)$ is a failure rate value that is not to be exceeded in a product. Tests to determine if a failure rate criterion is met can be fixed or sequential in duration. With fixed-length test plans, the test design failure rate $(\rho_t)$ is the sample failure rate that cannot be exceeded in order to certify the criterion $(\rho_a)$ at the boundary of the desired confidence level. With sequential test plans, failure rates $\rho_1$ and $\rho_0$ are used to determine the test plans.

**Fault tree analysis**: A schematic picture of possible failure modes and associated probabilities. A fault tree analysis is the opposite of failure mode and effects analysis.

**50-foot-level:** Low-level tracking of a key process input variable; e.g., process temperature when manufacturing plastic parts or daily sales person activity. This type of chart can involve frequent sampling to make sure that the desired input level is maintained over time. Tracking at the 50-foot-level can lead to the timely detection and resolution of problems or undesirable drifts in input levels so that the 30,000-foot-level metric for product/service quality, timeliness, and other metrics is not jeopardized.

**Firefighting**: The practice of giving much focus to fixing the problems of the day/week. The usual corrective actions taken in firefighting, such as tweaking a stable/predictable process, do not create any long-term fixes and may actually cause process degradation.

**Force field analysis:** Representation of the conflicting forces in an organization which are supporting and driving toward a solution and those which are restraining progress.

**Gantt chart:** A bar chart that shows activities as blocks over time. A block's beginning and end correspond to the beginning and end date of the activity.

**Gemba:** The workplace, where value is added. A manager's office is not considered to be gemba.

**Governance, corporate:** The system by which business corporations are directed and controlled. The corporate governance structure specifies the distribution of rights and responsibilities among different participants in the corporation, such as, the board, managers, shareholders and other stakeholders, and spells out the rules and procedures for making decisions on corporate affairs. By doing this, it also provides the structure through which the company objectives are set, and the means of attaining those objectives and monitoring performance. Organization for Economic Cooperation and Development (OECD) April 1999.

**Green belts (GBs)**: Part-time practitioners who typically receive two weeks of training over two months. Their primary focus is on projects that are in their functional area. The inference that someone becomes a green belt before a black belt should not be made. Business and personal needs/requirements should influence the decision whether someone becomes a black belt or green belt. If someone's job requires a more in-depth skill set, such as the use of design of experiments (DOE), then the person should be trained as a black belt. Also, at deployment initiation black belt training should be conducted first so that this additional skill set can be used when coaching others.

**Groupthink:** The tendency where highly cohesive groups can lose their critical evaluative capabilities (Janis 1971).

**Hard savings:** Savings that directly impact the bottom line.

**Hidden factory:** Reworks within an organization that have no value and are often not considered within the metrics of a factory.

**Histogram:** A frequency diagram in which bars proportionally in area to the class frequencies are erected on the horizontal axis. The width of each section corresponds to the class interval of the variate.

**Hoshin kanri:** Japanese name for policy deployment. Used by some Lean companies to guide their operations strategy.

**Hypothesis:** A tentative statement, which has a possible explanation to some event or phenomenon. Hypotheses are not a theoretical statement. Instead, hypotheses are to have a testable statement, which might include a prediction.

**Hypothesis testing:** Consists of a null hypothesis ($H_0$) and alternative hypothesis ($H_a$) where, for example, a null hypothesis indicates equality between two process outputs and an alternative hypothesis indicates non-equality. Through a hypothesis test, a decision is made whether to reject a null hypothesis or not reject a null hypothesis. When a null hypothesis is rejected, there is $\alpha$ risk of error. Most typically, there is no risk assignment when we fail to reject the null hypothesis. However, an appropriate sample size could be determined so that failure to reject the null hypothesis is made with $\beta$ risk of error.

**IEE:** *See* Integrated enterprise excellence.

**IEE scorecard/dashboard metric reporting process:**

1. Assess process predictability.
2. When the process is considered predictable, formulate a prediction statement for the latest region of stability. The usual reporting format for this statement is:
   a. When there is a specification requirement: nonconformance percentage or defects per million opportunities (DPMO)
   b. When there are no specification requirements: median response and 80% frequency of occurrence rate

**IEE Workout:** *See* Workout (IEE).

**In control:** The description of a process where variation is consistent over time; i.e., only common causes exist. The process is predictable.

**Individuals control chart:** A control chart of individual values where between-subgroup variability affects the calculated upper and lower control limits; i.e., the width between the upper and lower control limits increases when there is more between subgroup variability. When plotted individuals chart data is within the upper and lower control limits and there are no patterns, the process is said to be stable/predictable and typically referenced as an in control process. In IEE, this common cause state is referenced as a predictable process. Control limits are independent of specification limits or targets. Volume III describes the creation of this chart.

**Inferential statistics:** From the analysis of samples, we can make statements about the population's using inferential statistics. That is, properties of the population are inferred from the analysis of samples.

**Information technology:** Computer systems and applications, which involves development, installation, and/or implementation.

**Infrequent subgrouping/sampling:** Traditionally, rational subgrouping issues involve the selection of samples that yield relatively homogeneous conditions within the subgroup for a small region of time or space, perhaps five in a row. For an $\bar{x}$ and $R$ chart, the within-subgroup variation defines the limits of the control chart on how much variation should exist between the subgroups. For a given situation, a differing subgrouping/sampling methodology can dramatically affect the measured variation within subgroups, which in turn affects the width of the control limits. For the high-level metrics of IEE, we want infrequent subgrouping/sampling so that short-term variations caused by KPIV perturbations are viewed as common cause variability; i.e., typical process variability is to occur between subgroups in an individuals control chart. This type of control chart can reduce the amount of firefighting in an organization. However, this does not mean that a problem does not exist within the process. When process capability/performance metric improvements are needed for these metrics, we can initiate an IEE project; i.e., IEE projects are pulled into the system, as they are needed by the metrics.

**Innovation:** Act of introducing something new, which can involve both radical and incremental change to products, services, or processes.

**Integrated Enterprise (process) Excellence (IEE, I double E):** A roadmap for the creation of an enterprise process system in which organizations can significantly improve both customer satisfaction and their bottom line. IEE is a structured approach that guides organizations through the tracking and attainment of organizational goals. IEE goes well beyond traditional Lean Six Sigma and the balanced scorecard methods. IEE integrates enterprise process measures and improvement methodologies with tools such as Lean and theory of constraints (TOC) in a never-ending pursuit of excellence. IEE becomes an enabling framework, which integrates, improves, and aligns with other initiatives such as Total Quality Management (TQM), ISO 9000, Malcolm Baldrige Assessments, and the Shingo Prize. IEE is the organizational orchestration that moves toward the achievement goal of the three *R*s of Business; i.e., everyone is doing the Right things and doing them Right at the Right time.

**Inventory turns:** The number of times that a company's inventory cycles or turns over per year.

**ISO 9000**: The International Organization for Standardization (ISO) series of developed and published standards. The intent of these standards is to define, establish, and maintain an effective quality assurance system in both manufacturing and service industries.

**IT:** *See* Information technology.

**Inventory turns:** Quantifies the number of times in a year invested in goods that are to be sold turns over.

**Jidoka (autonomation):** A term used in Lean meaning automation with a human touch. This approach applies the following four principles: detect the abnormality, stop, fix or correct the immediate condition, and investigate the root cause and install a countermeasure.

**Jim Collin's three circles:** See Collin's three circles.

**Just-in-time (JIT):** An inventory management strategy where manufacturing material and component needs are immediately fulfilled by the supplier.

**Kaikaku:** Radical improvement.

**Kaizen:** Continuous incremental improvement.

**Kaizen event or blitz:** An intense short-term project that gives focus to improve a process. Substantial resources are committed during this event; e.g., Operators, Engineering, Maintenance, and others are available for immediate action. A facilitator directs the event, which usually includes training followed by analysis, design, and area rearrangement.

**KPIV (key process input variable):** Factors within a process correlated to an output characteristic(s) important to the internal or external customer. Optimizing and controlling these is vital to the improvement of the KPOV.

**KPOV (key process output variable):** Characteristic(s) of the output of a process that are important to the customer. Understanding what is important to the internal and external customer is essential to identifying KPOVs.

**Knowledge-centered activity (KCA):** A term used that means striving to obtain knowledge wisely and utilize it wisely.

**Law of physics**: A physical law or a law of nature that is considered true.

**Lean:** Improving operations and the supply chain with an emphasis on the reduction of wasteful activities such as waiting, transportation, material hand-offs, inventory, and overproduction.

**Lead time:** Time for one piece to move through a process or a value stream. Lean time can also describe the setup time to start a process.

**Level Five System:** Collins (2001) describes in *Good to Great* a level five leader as someone who is not only great when he is leading an organization but also the organization remains great after the person is no longer affiliated with it. I describe the level-five-leader-created legacy as being a *Level Five System*.

**Malcolm Baldrige Award:** An award that recognizes yearly up to five companies that demonstrate outstanding quality management systems. The award, started in 1988, would later become known as the Malcolm Baldrige National Quality Improvement Act which was created under the direction of ASQ and the National Institute of Standards and Technology. The Act established a national award that recognizes total quality management in American industry.

**Master black belts (MBBs):** Black belts who have undertaken two weeks of advanced training and have a proven track record delivering results through various projects and project teams. They should be a dedicated resource to the deployment. Before they train, master black belts need to be certified in the material that they are to deliver. Their responsibilities include coaching black belts, monitoring team progress, and assisting teams when needed.

**Mean:** The mean of a sample ($\bar{x}$) is the sum of all the responses divided by the sample size. The mean of a population *(µ)* is the sum of all responses of the population divided by the population size. In a random sample of a population, $\bar{x}$ is an estimate of the *µ* of the population.

**Mean square:** Sum of squares divided by degrees of freedom.

**Mean time between failures (MTBF):** A term that can be used to describe the frequency of failures in a reparable system with a constant failure rate. MTBF is the average time that is expected between failures MTBF = 1/failure rate.

**Measurement systems:** The complete process of obtaining measurements. This includes the collection of equipment, operations, procedures, software, and personnel that affects the assignment of a number to a measurement characteristic.

**Median:** For a sample, the number that is in the middle when all observations are ranked in magnitude. For population, the value at which the cumulative distribution function is 0.5.

**Metric:** A measurement that quantifies a particular characteristic.

**Milkrounds:** An application illustration is when a vehicle collects parts from several suppliers during an established route that starts and ends at the plant.

**Mini kaizen:** Recognizes that the best expert for a job is the person who does the job. Everyone is encouraged to make small improvements that are within their power to implement. The collection of thousands of small improvements have can have a major impact. Its implementation requires both conscious and sub-conscious day-to-day and minute-by-minute thinking about improvements by all employees. Required also is that these employees possess this type of thinking skills.

**Mistake-proofing:** A structured approach for process or design creation so that specific mistakes will not occur or which makes a mistake obvious at a glance; i.e., error-proofing or poke-yoke.

**Multi-vari chart:** A chart that is constructed to display the variance within units, between units, between samples, and between lots.

**Nominal group technique (NGT):** A voting procedure to expedite team consensus on relative importance of problems, issues, or solutions.

**Nonconformance:** Failure to meet specification requirement.

**Non-stationary process:** A process with a level and variance that can grow without limit.

**Normal distribution:** A bell-shaped distribution that is often useful to describe various physical, mechanical, electrical, and chemical properties.

**Null hypothesis ($H_0$):** *See* Hypothesis testing.

**One-at-a-time experiment:** An individual tries to fix a problem by making a change and then executing a test. Depending on the findings, something else may need to be tried. This cycle is repeated indefinitely.

**One piece flow:** The production or procurement of one unit at a time, as opposed to large lots.

**Ordinal**: Possesses natural ordering.

**Ordinate:** The coordinate representing the distance from the $x$ axis in a two-dimensional plot.

**Orming model**: Tuckman (1965) described the four stages of team development as forming, storming, norming, and performing. These stages are often referenced as the orming model.

**Outlier:** A data point that does not fit a model because of an erroneous reading or some other abnormal situation.

**Out of control**: Control charts exhibit special-cause(s) conditions. The process is not predictable.

**Pacemaker:** The point in the overall process where Lean production is scheduled.

**Pareto chart:** A graphical technique used to quantify problems so that effort can be expended in fixing the "vital few" causes, as opposed to the "trivial many." Named after Vilfredo Pareto, an Italian economist.

**Pareto principle:** Eighty percent of the trouble comes from 20% of the problems, i.e., the vital few problems.

**Passive analysis:** In IEE and a traditional DMAIC, most Six Sigma tools are applied in the same phase. However, the term "passive analysis" is often used in IEE to describe the analyze phase more descriptively, where process data are observed passively, i.e., with no process adjustments, in an attempt to find a causal relationship between input and output variables. It should be noted that *improvements* can be made in any of the phases. If there is low-hanging fruit identified during a brainstorming session in the measure phase, this improvement can be made immediately, yielding a dramatic improvement to the 30,000-foot-level output metric.

**P-DMAIC (Roadmap):** An IEE project define-measure-analyze-improve-control roadmap for improvement project execution, which contains a true integration of Six Sigma and Lean tools.

**Performance, Process:** *See* Process performance.

**Plan-do-check-act (PDCA):** Frequently referred to as the Deming cycle or Shewhart cycle. Sometimes the check step is replaced with a study step; i.e., PDSA. PDCA has the following components: Plan—Recognize a need for change then establish objectives and process for delivering desired results; Do—Implement change that is to be assessed; Check—study results and identify lessons learned; Act—Use lessons learned to take appropriate action. If change was not satisfactory repeat the process.

**Point estimate:** An estimate calculated from sample data without a confidence interval.

**Poisson distribution:** A discrete probability distribution where the probability of a number of events occurring in a fixed period of time has an average rate and is independent of the time since the last event. A distribution that is useful, for example, to design reliability tests, where the failure rate is considered to remain constant as a function of usage.

**Population:** Statistically a population is a group of data from a single distribution. In a practical sense, a population could also be considered to be a segment or a group of data from a single source or category. In the process of explaining tools and techniques, multiple populations may be discussed as originating from different sources, locations, or machines.

**Predictable:** The control limits in a control chart are calculated from the data. Specifications in no way affect the control limits. This chart is a statement of the voice of the process (VOP) relative to whether the process is considered in statistical control or not; i.e., stable/predictable or not. Since people often have difficulty in understanding what *in control* means, I prefer to use the term *predictable* instead of *in control.*

**Predictable process:** A stable, controlled process where variation in outputs is only caused by natural or random variation in the inputs or in the process itself.

**Preventive action:** An action that is taken to eliminate from reoccurrence a potential nonconformity cause or other undesirable situation.

**Price-earnings ratio (PE ratio or P/E ratio):** A company's evaluation ratio of its current share price compared to its earning per share. PE ratio = market value per share/ earnings per share.

**Proactive testing:** In IEE and a traditional DMAIC, most Six Sigma tools are applied in the same phase. The descriptive term proactive testing is often used within IEE to describe the improve phase. The reason for this is that within the improve DMAIC phase design of experiments (DOE), tools are typically used. In DOE you can make many adjustments to a process in a structured fashion, observing/analyzing the results collectively; i.e., proactively testing to make a judgment. It should be noted that improvements can be made in any of the phases. If there is low-hanging fruit identified during a brainstorming session in the measure phase, this improvement can be made immediately, yielding a dramatic improvement to the 30,000-foot-level output metric.

**Probability ($P$):** A numerical expression for the likelihood of an occurrence.

**Probability density function (PDF) [$f(x)$]:** A mathematical function that can model the probability density reflected in a histogram.

**Probability plot:** Data are plotted on a selected probability paper coordinate system to determine if a particular distribution is appropriate (i.e., the data plot as a straight line) and to make statements about percentiles of the population. The plot can be used to make prediction statements about stable/predictable processes. Volume III describes the creation of this plot.

**Problem solving:** The process of determining the cause from a symptom and then choosing an action to improve a process or product.

**Process:** A method to make or do something that involves a number of steps; a mathematical model such as the HPP (homogeneous Poisson process).

**Process capability indices ($C_p$ and $C_{pk}$):** $C_p$ is a measurement of the allowable tolerance spread divided by the actual $6\sigma$ data spread. $C_{pk}$ has a similar ratio to that of $C_p$, except that this ratio considers the shift of the mean relative to the central specification target.

**Process capability:** AIAG (1995b) definition for the variables data case is $6\sigma$ range of a process's inherent variation; for statistically stable processes, where $\sigma$ is usually estimated by $\bar{R}/d_2$. For the attribute data case, it is usually defined as the average proportion or rate of defects or defectives; e.g., center of an attribute control chart. Bothe (1997) definition is: "Process capability is broadly defined as the ability of a process to satisfy consumer expectations."

**Process capability/performance metric:** IEE uses the term process capability/performance metric to describe a process's predictive output in terms that everyone can understand. The process to determine this metric is: (1) An infrequent subgrouping/sampling plan is determined so that the typical variability from process input factors occurs between subgroups, e.g., subgroup by day, week, or month. (2) The process is analyzed for predictability using control charts. (3) For the region of predictability, the non-compliant proportion or parts per million (ppm) are estimated and reported. If there are no specifications, the estimated median response and 80% frequency of occurrence are reported.

**Process cycle efficiency:** the amount of value-added process time divided by total lead time.

**Process performance:** The AIAG (1995b) definition is the 6σ range of a process's total variation, where σ is usually estimated by *s*, the sample standard deviation.

**Process flow diagram (chart):** Path of steps of work used to produce or do something.

**Producer's risk:** *See* Alpha (α) risk.

**Pull**: A Lean term that results in an activity when a customer or down-stream process step requests the activity. A homebuilder that builds houses only when an agreement is reached on the sale of the house is using a pull system. *See also* Push.

**Pull for project creation:** This term is derived from the Lean term, pull. An IEE deployment objective is that performance metric ownership is assigned through the business value chain, where metric tracking is at the 30,000-foot-level. In the E-DMAIC process, the enterprise is analyzed as a whole to determine what performance metrics need improvement and by how much so that whole-organizational goals can be met. These metric improvement needs would then create a pull for project creation. *See also* Push for project creation.

**Push:** A Lean term that results in an activity that a customer or down-stream process step has not specifically requested. This activity can create excessive waste and/or inventory. A homebuilder that builds houses on the speculation of sale is using a push system. If the house does not sell promptly upon completion, the homebuilder has created excess inventory for his company, which can be very costly. *See also* Pull.

**Push for project creation:** This term is derived from the Lean term, push. Lean Six Sigma deployments are to create and execute projects that are to be beneficial to the business. However, when assessing the typical Lean Six Sigma project selection process we note that either a deployment steering committee or some level of management selects projects from a list that they and others think are important. For this type of deployment, for example, there is often a scurry to determine a project to work on during training. I refer this system as a push for project creation; i.e., people are hunting for projects because they need to get certified or whatever. With this deployment system, there can be initial successes since agree-to low hanging fruit projects can often be readily identified and provide significant benefits; however, it has been my experience that this system of project determination is not typically long lasting. After some period of time, people have a hard time defining and/or agreeing to what projects should be undertaken. In addition, this project creation system does not typically look at the system as a whole when defining projects to undertake. This system of project selection can lead to suboptimization, which could be detrimental enterprise as a whole. Finally, this Lean Six Sigma deployment system typically creates a separate function entity that manages the deployment, which is separate from operational scorecards and functional units. In time, people in these functions can be very visible on the corporate radar screen when downsizing forces occur or their in a change in executive management, even thought the function has been claiming much past success. *See also* Pull for project creation.

***p*-value or *p*:** The significance level for a term in a model.

**Qualitative factor:** A factor that has categorical levels. For example, product origination where the factor levels are supplier A, supplier B, and supplier C.

**Quantitative factor:** A factor that is continuous. For example, a product can be manufactured with a process temperature factor between 50°C and 80°C.

**Quality function deployment (QFD):** A technique that is used, for example, to get the voice of the customer in the design of a product.

**Radar chart:** A chart that is sometimes called a spider chart. The chart is a two-dimensional chart of three or more quantitative variables represented on axes originating from the same point.

**Randomizing:** A statistical procedure used to avoid bias possibilities as the result of influence of systematic disturbances, which are either known or unknown.

**Random:** Having no specific pattern.

**Range:** For a set of numbers, the absolute difference between the largest and smallest value.

**Ranked sample values:** Sample data that are listed in order relative to magnitudes.

**Reference value:** A measured value that is recognized and serves as an agreed-upon reference or master value for comparisons. This can be: a theoretical or established value based on scientific principles; an assigned value based on some national or international organization; a consensus value based on collaborative experimental work under the auspices of a scientific or engineering group; or, for a specific application, an agreed-upon value obtained using an accepted reference method. A reference value is consistent with the definition of a specific quantity and is accepted, sometimes by convention, as appropriate for a given purpose. Other terms used synonymously with reference value are accepted reference value, accepted value, conventional value, conventional true value, assigned value, best estimate of the value, master value, and master measurement (AIAG 2002).

**Regression analysis:** Data collected from an experiment are used to quantify empirically through a mathematical model the relationship that exists between the response variable and influencing factors. In a simple linear regression model, $y = b_0 + b_1 x + \varepsilon$, $x$ is the regressor, $y$ is the expected response, $b_0$ and $b_1$ are coefficients, and $\varepsilon$ is random error.

**Reliability:** The proportion surviving at some point in time during the life of a device. Can also be a generic description of tests which are conducted to evaluate failure rates.

**Response**: Three described outputs are continuous (variables), attribute (discrete), and logic pass/fail. A response is said to be continuous if any value can be taken between limits (e.g., 2, 2.0001, and 3.00005). A response is said to be attribute if the evaluation takes on a pass/fail proportion output; e.g., 999 out of 1000 sheets of paper on the average can be fed through a copier without a jam. In this series of volumes, a response is considered to be logic pass/fail if combinational considerations are involved that are said always to cause an event either to pass or fail; e.g., a computer display design will not work in combination with a particular keyboard design and software package (see Breyfogle 2003a).

**Return on capital employed (ROCE):** A ratio for the assessing the efficiency and profitability of a company's capital investments. ROCE = (EBIT)/(total assets – current liabilities), where EBIT = earnings before interest and taxes.

**Return on equity (ROE):** A corporate profitability measure that shows company profit generation with the money shareholders have invested. ROE = net income/shareholder's equity.

**Return on invested capital (ROIC):** A calculation used to assess how well a company's management is able to allocate capital into its operations for profitability. ROIC = (net income – dividends)/(total capital), where total capital is company shares and long term debt.

**Return on investment (ROI):** An investment performance measure for evaluating the investment efficiency. ROI = (gain from investment – cost of investment)/(cost of investment).

**Risk priority number (RPN):** Product of severity, occurrence, and detection rankings within an FMEA. The ranking of RPN prioritizes design concerns; however, issues with a low RPN still deserve special attention if the severity ranking is high.

**Rolled throughput yield (RTY):** For a process that has a series of steps, RTY is the product of yields for each step.

**Root cause analysis:** A study to determine the reason for a process nonconformance. Removal or correction of the root cause eliminates future nonconformance from this source.

**Run chart:** A time series plot permits the study of observed data for trends or patterns over time, where the $x$-axis is time and the $y$ axis is the measured variable.

**Sample:** A selection of items from a population.

**Sampling distribution:** A distribution derived from a parent distribution by random sampling.

**Sample size:** The number of observations made or the number of items taken from a population.

**Sarbanes-Oxley (SOX):** This legislation act was created in 2002 partly in response to the Enron and WorldCom financial scandals. SOX protects shareholders and the public from enterprise process accounting errors and from fraudulent practices. In addition, it also ensures a degree of consistency in access to and reporting of information that could impact the value of a company's stock.

**Satellite-level:** Used to describe a high-level IEE business metric that has infrequent subgrouping/sampling so that short-term variations, which are caused by typical variation from key process input variables, will result in control charts that view these perturbations as common cause variability. This metric has no calendar boundaries and the latest region of stability can be used to provide a predictive statement for the future.

**Scorecard:** A scorecard helps manage an organization's performance through the optimization and alignment of organizational units, business processes, and individuals. A scorecard can also provide goals and targets, which is to help individuals understand their organizational contribution. Scorecards span the operational, tactical and strategic business aspects and decisions. A dashboard displays information so that an enterprise can be run effectively. A dashboard organizes and presents information in a format that is easy to read and to interpret. In this series of volumes, I make reference to the IEE performance measurement as either a scorecard or scorecard/dashboard.

**Sensei:** Teacher or mentor.

**Shewhart control chart:** Dr. Shewhart is credited with developing the standard control chart test based on $3\sigma$ limits to separate the steady component of variation from assignable causes.

**Shingo prize:** Established in 1988, the prize promotes awareness of Lean manufacturing concepts and recognizes companies in the United States, Canada, and Mexico that achieve world-class manufacturing status. The philosophy is that world-class business performance may be achieved through focused core manufacturing and business process improvements.

**Sigma:** The Greek letter ($\sigma$) that is often used to describe the standard deviation of a population.

**Sigma level or sigma quality level:** A quality that is calculated by some to describe the capability of a process to meet specification. A six sigma quality level is said to have a 3.4 ppm rate. Pat Spagon from Motorola University prefers to distinguish between sigma as a measure of spread and sigma used in sigma quality level (Spagon 1998).

**Significance:** A statistical statement indicating that the level of a factor causes a difference in a response with a certain degree of risk of being in error.

**SIPOC (supplier-input-process-output-customer):** A tool that describes the events from trigger to delivery at the targeted process. Provides a snapshot of workflows, where the process aspect of the diagram consists of only four to seven blocks.

**Six Sigma:** A term coined by Motorola that emphasizes the improvement of processes for the purpose of reducing variability and making general improvements.

**SMART goals:** Not everyone uses the same letter descriptors for SMART. My preferred descriptors are italicized in the following list: S—*specific*, significant, stretching; M—*measurable*, meaningful, motivational; A—agreed upon, attainable, achievable, acceptable, action-oriented, *actionable*; R—realistic, *relevant*, reasonable, rewarding, results-oriented; T—*time-based*, timely, tangible, trackable.

**Smarter Six Sigma Solutions (S⁴):** Term used in this series of volumes to describe the *wise* and often unique application of statistical techniques to create meaningful measurements and effective improvements.

**Smarter Six Sigma Solutions assessment (S⁴ assessment):** A term introduced in *Implementing Six Sigma* (Breyfogle 2003). The methodology uses statistically based concepts while determining the *best* question to answer from the point of view of the customer. Assessment is made to determine if the right measurements and the right actions are being conducted. This includes noting that there are usually better questions to ask to protect the customer than "What sample do I need?" or "What one thing should I do next to fix this problem?"; i.e., a one-at-a-time approach. IEE resolution may involve putting together what often traditionally are considered separated statistical techniques in a smart fashion to address various problems.

**Socratic method:** A method that uses dialect for philosophical inquiry. Typically, at any point in time, it involves two speakers where the discussion is led by one person and the other agrees to certain assumptions put forward for his/her acceptance or rejection. Socratic dialog happens when two people seek to answer a question through reflecting and thinking. This dialog starts from the concrete, asking all sorts of questions until details are uncovered, which serves as a platform for making more general judgments.

**Soft savings:** Savings that do not directly impact the financial statement as do hard savings. Possible soft savings' categories are cost avoidance, lost profit avoidance, productivity improvements, profit enhancement, and other intangibles.

**Soft skills:** A person who effectively facilitates meetings and works well with other people has good soft skills.

**Span time:** Cycle time for specific task.

**Special causes:** Variation in a process from a cause that is not an inherent part of that process. That is, it's not a common cause.

**Specification:** A criterion that is to be met by a part or product.

**Stability:** Refers to both statistical stability of measurement process and measurement stability over time. Both are vital for a measurement system to be adequate for its intended purpose. Statistical stability implies a predictable, underlying measurement process operating within common-cause variation.

**Stakeholders:** Those people or organizations who is not directly involved with project work but are affected its success or can influence its results. Example stakeholders are process owners, managers affected by the project, and people who work in the studied process. Stakeholders also include internal departments, which support the process, finance, suppliers, and customers.

**Standard deviation $(\sigma, s)$:** A mathematical quantity that describes the variability of a response. It equals the square root of variance. The standard deviation of a sample ($s$) is used to estimate the standard deviation of a population ($\sigma$).

**Stationary process:** A process with an ultimate constant variance.

**Statistical process control (SPC):** The application of statistical techniques in the control of processes. SPC is often considered a subset of SQC, where the emphasis in SPC is on the tools associated with the process but not on product acceptance techniques.

**Statistical quality control (SQC):** The application of statistical techniques in the control of quality. SQC includes the use of regression analysis, tests of significance, acceptance sampling, control charts, distributions, and so on.

**Stock options:** A stock option is a specific type of option with a stock as the underlying instrument; i.e., the security that the value of the option is based on. A contract to buy is known as a call contract, while a contract to sell is known as a put contract.

**Stories:** An explanation for the up-and-down from previous quarter or yearly scorecard/dashboard metrics. This is not dissimilar to a nightly stock market report of the previous day's activity, where the television or radio reporter gives a specific reason for even small market movements. This form of reporting provides little, if any, value when it comes to making business decisions for a data-driven company.

**Supermarket:** An inventory of parts that are controlled for the production scheduling of an upstream process.

**Subcause:** In a cause-and-effect diagram, the specific items or difficulties that are identified as factual or potential causes of the problem.

**Subgrouping:** Traditionally, rational subgrouping issues involve the selection of samples that yield relatively homogeneous conditions within the subgroup for a small region of time or space, perhaps five in a row. Hence, the within-subgroup variation defines the limits of the control chart on how much variation should exist between the subgroups. For a given situation, differing subgrouping methodologies can dramatically affect the measured variation within subgroups, which in turn affects the width of the control limits. For the high-level metrics of IEE, we want infrequent subgrouping/sampling so that short-term typical KPIV perturbations are viewed as common-cause variability. A 30,000-foot-level individuals control chart, which is created with infrequent subgrouping/sampling, can reduce the amount of firefighting in an organization. However, this does not mean that a problem does not exist within the process. IEE describes approaches to view the process capability/performance metric, or how well the process meets customer specifications or overall business needs. When improvements are needed to a process capability/performance metric, we can create an IEE project that focuses on this need; i.e., IEE projects are pulled for creation when metric improvements are needed.

**Takt time:** Customer demand rate; e.g., available work time per shift divided by customer demand rate per shift.

**Test:** Assessment of whether an item meets specified requirements by subjecting the item to a set of physical, environmental, chemical, or operating actions/conditions.

**The balanced scorecard:** *See* Balanced scorecard (the).

**Theory of constraints (TOC):** Constraints can be broadly classified as being internal resource, market, or policy. The outputs of a system are a function of the whole system, not just individual processes. System performance is a function of how well constraints are identified and managed. When we view our system as a whole, we realize that the output is a function of the weakest link. The weakest link of the system is the constraint. If care is not exercised, we can be focusing on a subsystem that, even though improved, does not impact the overall system output. We need to focus on the orchestration of efforts so that we optimize the overall system, not individual pieces. Unfortunately, organization charts lead to workflow by function, which can result in competing forces within the organization. With TOC, systems are viewed as a whole and work activities are directed so that the whole system performance measures are improved.

**Three *Rs* of business:** Everyone doing the Right things and doing them Right at the Right time.

**30,000-foot-level:** A Six Sigma KPOV, CTQ, or *Y* variable response that is used in IEE to describe a high-level project or operation metric that has infrequent subgrouping/sampling so that short-term variations, which might be caused by KPIV perturbations, will result in charts that view this variability as common cause. It is not the intent of the 30,000-foot-level control chart to provide timely feedback for process intervention and correction, as traditional control charts do. Example 30,000-foot-level metrics are lead time, inventory, defective rates, and a critical part dimension. There can be a drill down to a 20,000-foot-level metric if there is an alignment; e.g., the largest product defect type. A 30,000-foot-level individuals control chart can reduce the amount of firefighting in an organization when used to report operational metrics. As a business metric, 30,000-foot-level reporting can lead to more efficient resource utilization and less playing games with the numbers.

**Throughput, TOC:** The rate of generating money in an organization. This is a financial value-added metric which equates to revenues minus variable costs.

**Time-line chart:** Identification of the specific start, finish, and amount of time required to complete an activity.

**Time-value diagram:** A Lean tool that can describe a process or series of process steps from concept to launch to production, order to delivery to disposition, or raw materials to customer receipt to disposal. It consists of steps that add value to a product. Within Lean, steps are eliminated that do not add value, where a product can be tangible or intangible.

**TOC:** *See* Theory of constraints.

**TOC throughput:** *See* Throughput, TOC

**Total quality management (TQM):** A management program, which worked on continuous product/service improvements through workforce involvement.

**Toyota production system (TPS):** Toyota developed techniques that focus on adding value and reducing waste through setup, lead time, and lot size reduction. The term has become synonymous with Lean manufacturing.

**TQM:** *See* Total quality management.

**Treatment:** *See* Levels.

**Trend chart:** Shows data trends over time. A trend chart is sometimes called a run chart.

**t test:** A statistical test that utilizes tabular values from the *t* distribution to assess, for example, whether two population means are different.

**Type I error:** *See* Alpha ($\alpha$) risk.

**Type II error:** *See* Beta ($\beta$) risk.

**Type III error:** Answering the wrong question.

**Unimodal:** A distribution that has one peak.

**Usage:** During a life test, the measure of time on test. This measurement could, for example, be in units of power-on hours, test days, or system operations.

**Value-added (VA) time:** The execution time for the work elements for which a customer is willing to pay.

**Value chain:** Describes in flowchart fashion both primary and support organizational activities and their accompanying 30,000-foot-level or satellite-level metrics. Example primary activity flow is develop product—market product—sell product—produce product—invoice/collect payments—report satellite-level metrics. Example support activities include IT, finance, HR, labor relations, safety & environment, and legal.

**Value stream mapping:** At Toyota, value stream mapping is known as "material and information flow mapping." In the Toyota production system, current and future states/ideal states are depicted by practitioners when they are developing plans to install Lean systems. Infinite attention is given to establishing flow, eliminating waste, and adding value. Toyota views manufacturing flows as material, information, and people/process. The described value stream mapping covers the first two of these three items (Rother and Shook 1999).

**Variables data (Continuous data):** Data that can assume a range of numerical responses on a continuous scale, as opposed to data that can assume only discrete levels.

**Variables:** Factors within a fractional factorial designed experiment or response surface experiment.

**Variance (Finance):** Difference between actual and budget.

**Variance (Statistical) [$\sigma^2$, $s^2$]:** A measure of dispersion of observations based upon the mean of the squared deviations from the arithmetic mean.

**Variance inflation factor (VIF):** A calculated quantity for each term in a regression model that measures the combined effect of the dependencies among the regressors on the variance of that term. One or more large VIFs can indicate multicollinearity.

**Validation** is proof after implementation of an action over time and that the action does what is intended. *See also* Verification.

**Verification:** The act of establishing and documenting whether processes, items, services, or documents conform to a specified requirement. Verification is proof before implementation that an action does what is intended. *See also* Validation.

**Visual factory:** Management by sight. Visual factory involves the collection and display of real-time information to the entire workforce at all times. Work cell bulletin boards and other easily-seen media might report information about orders, production schedules, quality, delivery performance, and financial health of business.

**Voice of the customer (VOC):** The identification and prioritization of true customer needs and requirements, which can be accomplished through focus groups, interviews, data analyses, and other methods.

**Voice of the process (VOP):** A quantification of what the process delivers. A voice of the process to voice of the customer needs assessment can identify process improvement focus areas; e.g., a 30,000-foot-level assessment indicates an 11% delivery-time non-conformance rate.

**Waste:** Seven elements to consider for the elimination of muda, a Japanese term for waste, are correction, overproduction, processing, conveyance, inventory, motion, and waiting.

**WIP:** A general description for inventory that is being processed within an operation or is awaiting another operation.

**Work in process (WIP):** *See* WIP.

**Work in progress (WIP):** *See* WIP.

**Workout (IEE):** An IEE workout is a week-long concentrated effort to build the E-DMAIC framework; i.e., a kaizen event to create the E-DMAIC framework. Typically on Monday there is a one-day executive workshop, which among other things describes IEE and its structure. On Tuesday through Wednesday the facilitator works with an IEE in-house technical team and others to build the E-DMAIC framework with its process drill-downs. On Friday, a two-hour report-out of the customization of the E-DMAIC system, as described on Monday, is presented to the executive team that attended the Monday session. This presentation will include, among other things, a comparison of a sample of their 30,000-foot-level metric report-outs with their current reporting methods. After the week-long session, the workout facilitator will continue work with the IEE in-house technical team to continually refine their E-DMAIC system.

**Yellow belts (YBs):** Process improvement team members who typically receive three-days of training, which helps them in the effectiveness of their participation in project execution such as data collection, identifying voice of the customer, and team meetings.

# References

AIAG 1995. *Statistical Process Control (SPC) Reference Manual*. 3d ed. Chrysler Corporation, Ford Motor Company, General Motors Corporation.

AIAG 2002, Automotive Industry Action Group, *Measurement Systems Analysis (MSA) Reference Manual*, Third Edition, Chrysler Corporation, Ford Motor Company, General Motors Corporation.

APQC 2001. *Benchmarking Study: Deploying Six Sigma to Bolster Business Processes and the Bottom Line*. Houston, TX: APQC.

Austin 2004. http://www.ci.austin.tx.us/budget/eperf/index.cfm

Babich, P. 2005. *Hoshin Handbook*. 3d ed. Poway, CA: Total Quality Engineering.

Berger, R. W., W. B. Donald, A. K. Elshennawy, and H. F. Walker. 2002. *The Certified Quality Engineer Handbook*. Milwaukee, WI: ASQ,

Bicheno, J. 2004. *The New Lean Tool Box: Towards Fast, Flexible Flow*. Buckingham, England: Production and Inventory Control, Systems and Industrial Engineering Books.

Bierman, H. Jr. 1993. Capital budgeting in 1992. *Financial Management* 22(3): 24.

Bissell, B. 1992. *Facing the Challenge of Change*, Distributed by W. R. Shirah, Richmond, VA.

Bothe, D. R. 1997. *Measuring Process Capability*. New York: McGraw-Hill.

Box, G. E. P., W. G. Hunter, and S. J. Hunter. 1978. *Statistics for Experimenters.* New York: Wiley.

Brassard, M., and D. Ritter. 1994. *The Memory Jogger II.* Methuen, MA: GOAL/QPC

Breyfogle, F. W. 1992. *Statistical Methods for Testing, Development, and Manufacturing,* Hoboken, NJ: Wiley.

Breyfogle, F. W. 2003a. *Implementing Six Sigma: Smarter Solutions® using Statistical Methods.* 2d ed. Hoboken, NJ: Wiley.

Breyfogle. F. W. 2003b. Control Charting at the 30,000-foot-level: Separating special-cause events from common-cause variability. *Quality Progress* (November): 67–70.

Breyfogle, F. W. 2004a. Starting a Six Sigma Initiative. *ISixSigma, Ask the Expert.* http://www.isixsigma.com/library/content/ask-05.asp

Breyfogle, F. W. 2004b. Control charting at the 30,000-foot-level, Part 2. *Quality Progress* (November): 85–7.

Breyfogle, F. W. 2004c. *XMR* control charts and data normality. February 15, 2004. www.smartersolutions.com/pdfs/XmRControlChartDataNormality.pdf

Breyfogle, F. W. 2005a. 21 common problems (and what to do about them). *Six Sigma Forum Magazine,* (August): 35–7.

Breyfogle, F. W. 2005b. Control charting at the 30,000-foot-level, Part 3. *Quality Progress, 3.4 per Million Series* (November): 66–70.

Breyfogle, F. W. 2006. Control charting at the 30,000-foot-level, Part 4. *Quality Progress, 3.4 per Million Series* (November): 59–62.

Breyfogle, F. W. 2008a. *Integrated Enterprise Excellence, Volume I— The Basics: Golfing Buddies Go Beyond Lean Six Sigma and the Balanced Scorecard.* Austin, TX: Bridgeway Books.

Breyfogle, F. W. 2008b. *Integrated Enterprise Excellence, Volume II— Business Deployment: A Leaders' Guide for Going Beyond Lean Six Sigma and the Balanced Scorecard,* Austin, TX: Bridgeway Books.

Breyfogle, F. W. 2008c. *Integrated Enterprise Excellence, Volume III— Improvement Project Execution: A Management and Black Belt*

*Guide for Going Beyond Lean Six Sigma and the Balanced Score-card.* Austin, TX: Bridgeway Books.

Breyfogle, F. W. 2008d. *The Integrated Enterprise Excellence System: An Enhanced, Unified Approach to Balanced Score-cards, Strategic Planning, and Business Improvement,* Austin, TX: Bridgeway Books.

BusinessWeek. 2007. Six Sigma: so yesterday? In an innovation economy, it's no longer a cure-all. *BusinessWeek* McGraw Hill, June 11, 2007.

Callandra, A. 1968. A modern parable. *Saturday Review* (December 21).

Canada. J. R., and W. G. Sullivan. 1989. *Economic and Multi-attribute Evaluation of Advanced Manufacturing Systems.* Englewood Cliffs, NJ: Prentice-Hall.

Collins, J. 2001. *Good to Great: Why Some Companies Make the Leap ... and Others Don't.* New York: HarperCollins Publishers Inc.

Cunningham, J. E., and O. J. Fiume. 2003. *Real Numbers: Management Accounting in a Lean Organization.* Durham, NC: Managing Times Press.

Davenport, T. H., and J. G. Harris. 2007. *Competing on Analytics: The New Science of Winning.* Boston, MA: Harvard Business School Publishing Corp.

De Bono, E. 1999. *Six Thinking Hats.* New York: Little, Brown and Company.

Deming, W. E. 1982. *Quality, Productivity and Competitive Position.* Cambridge, MA: MIT Center for Advanced Engineering Study,

Deming, W. E. 1986. *Out of the Crisis.* Cambridge, MA: Massachusetts Institute of Technology,

Dodd, C. W. 1992. Design for 'X'. *IEEE Potentials.* (October):, 44–46.

Drucker, P. F. 1954. *The Practice of Management,* HarperCollins, New York, NY.

Fiume, O. J. 2006. Management accounting for lean businesses. *Connecticut Quality Council Presentation* (October 4).

Foxconn. 2006. Foxconn Strategy. http://www.foxconn.com/about/strategy.asp

Goldratt, E. M. 1992. *The Goal.* 2d ed. New York: North River Press.

Goodman, J. A. 1991, Measuring and quantifying the market impact of consumer problems. Presentation on February 18 at the St. Petersburg-Tampa Section of the ASQ.

Grove, A. S. 1999. *Only the Paranoid Survive.* Currency, New York, NY.

Hall, R. W. 1998. Standard work: holding the gains. *Target* (Forth Quarter): 13–9.

Hambrick, D. C., and J. W. Fredrickson. 2001. Are you sure you have a strategy? *Academy of Management Executive* 15(4).

Hamel, G., and C. K. Prahalad. 1994. Competing for the future. *Harvard Business Review* (July–August).

Harry, M. J. 1994. *The Vision of Six Sigma: Tools and Methods for Breakthrough.* Phoenix, AZ: Sigma Publishing Company.

Higgins, J. M. 1994. *101 Creative Problem Solving Techniques.* Winter Park, FL: New Management Publishing Company.

Hindo, B. 2007. At 3M, A struggle between efficiency and creativity: how CEO George Buckley is managing the yin and yang of discipline and imagination. *BusinessWeek*, McGraw Hill (June 11, 2007).

Jackson, T. L. 2006. *Hoshin Kanri for the Lean Enterprise.* New York: Productivity Press.

Janis, I. 1971. Groupthink. *Psychology Today* (June).

Jones, D. 1999. *Everyday Creativity.* St. Paul, MN: Star Thrower Distribution Corp.

Johnson, R. B., and R. W. Melicher. 1982. *Financial Management.* 5th ed. Boston, MA: Allyn and Bacon, Inc.

Juran, J. M., and A. B. Godfrey. 1999. *Juran's Quality Control Handbook,* 5th ed. New York: McGraw-Hill,

Kaplan, R. S., and D. P. Norton. 1992. The balanced scorecard – measures that drive performance. *Harvard Business Review* (January–February).

Kaplan, R. S., and D. P. Norton. 1996. *The Balanced Scorecard.* Boston, MA: Harvard Business School Press.

Kelly, J. 2006. CEO firings at a record pace so far this year: leaders are getting pushed aside as boards, wary of Enron-type problems, become more vigilant. *Bloomberg News, Austin American Statesman* (October 1, 2006).

Kotter, J. P. 1995. Leading change: why transformation efforts fail. *Harvard Business Review* (Product number 4231).

Lloyd, M. E. 2005. Krispy Kreme knew early of slowing sales, suit says. *Austin American Statesman, Business Briefing, Dow Jones Newswire* (January 4, 2005).

MacInnes, R. L. 2002. *The Lean Enterprise Process Memory Jogger.* Salem, NH: GOAL/QPC

McIntosh, R. I., S. J. Culley, A. R. Mileham, G. W. Owen. 2001. *Improving Changeover Performance.* London: Butterworth Heinemann.

Minitab. 2007. *Minitab Statistical Software.* Release 15. State College, PA.

Moe, K. 2006. Excerpts from a retired 3M VP executive presentation at Smarter Solutions, Inc. training.

Nelson, L. S. 1983. Exact critical values for use with the analysis of means. *Journal of Quality Technology* 15(1): 40–42.

Ohno, T. 1988. *Toyota Production System: Beyond Large-Scale Production.* Portland, OR: Productivity Press.

Petruno, T. 2006. Options inquiries smell of scandal. *Austin American Statesman, Business & Personal Finance, Los Angeles Times Article* (July 16, 2006).

Quickbase. 2006. https://www.quickbase.com/help/chart

Richtel, M, 2007, Dell, Admitting Managers Inflated Sales Reports, Will Restate Income, *New York Times* (August 17, 2007).

Rother, M., and J. Shook. 1999. *Learning to See: Value Stream Mapping to Create Value and Eliminate Muda.* Brookline, M.A.: The Lean Enterprise Institute, www.lean.org, 617-871-2900.

Scholtes, P. R. 1988. *The Team Handbook: How to Use Teams to Improve Quality.* Madison, WI: Joiner Associates.

Schonberger, R. 1987. Frugal Manufacturing. *Harvard Business Review*. Sep. p. 95

Senge, P. M. 1990. *The Fifth Discipline: The Art and Practice of the Learning Organization*. New York: Doubleday/Current.

Shewhart, W. A. 1980. *Economic Control of Quality of Manufactured Product*. ASQ Quality Press, 1931 article reprinted.

Sickafus, E. 1997. *Unified Structured Inventive Thinking*. Grosse Ile, MI: Ntelleck.

Snee, R. D., and R. W. Hoerl. 2003. *Leading Six Sigma: A Step-by-Step Guide Based on Experience with GE and other Six Sigma Companies*. Prentice Hall, Englewood Cliffs, NJ.

Spagon, P. 1998. Personal communications.

Spear, S. J., and H. K. Bowen. 1999. Decoding the DNA of the Toyota Production System. *Harvard Business Review* (September).

Strategosinc. (2006. http://www.strategosinc.com/just_in_time.htm

Teamwork. 2002. A project of the Team Engineering Collaboratory. Dr. Barbara O'Keefe, University of Illinois-Urbana/Champaign, http://www.vta.spcomm.uiuc.edu/.

Thurm, S. 2007. Now, it's business by data, but numbers still can't tell future. *Wall Street Journal* (July 23): B1.

Toastmasters International. 1990. *Communication and Leadership Program*, Mission Viejo, CA.

Treacy, M., and F. Wiersema, F. 1997. *The Discipline of Market Leaders: Choose Your Customers Narrow Your Focus, Dominate Your Market*. Reading, MA: Addison-Wesley.

Tuckman, B. W. 1965. Developmental sequence in small groups. *Psychological Bulletin* 63(6): 384–99.

US Dept of Interior. 2003. *OMB and Bureau Scorecard Actions: Getting to Green*. http://www.doi.gov/ppp/scorecard.html

Vitalentusa. 2006. http://www.vitalentusa.com/learn/6-sigma_vs_kaizen_1.php

Western Electric. 1956. *Statistical Quality Control Handbook*. Newark, NJ: Western Electric Co.

Womack, J. P., and D. T. Jones. 1996. *Lean Thinking*. New York: Simon & Schuster.

Womack, J. P., D. T. Jones, D. Roos. 1990. *The Machine that Changed the World*. New York: Harper Perennial.

# Index